D1256173

William Taylor and the Mapping of the Methodist Missionary Tradition

William Taylor and the Mapping of the Methodist Missionary Tradition

The World His Parish

Douglas D. Tzan

LEXINGTON BOOKS
Lanham • Boulder • New York • London

Published by Lexington Books
An imprint of The Rowman & Littlefield Publishing Group, Inc.
4501 Forbes Boulevard, Suite 200, Lanham, Maryland 20706
www.rowman.com

6 Tinworth Street, London SE11 5AL, United Kingdom

Copyright © 2019 by The Rowman & Littlefield Publishing Group, Inc.

Excerpts from *In These Houses* © 1988 by Brenda Marie Osbey. Published by Wesleyan University Press and reprinted by permission.

All rights reserved. No part of this book may be reproduced in any form or by any electronic or mechanical means, including information storage and retrieval systems, without written permission from the publisher, except by a reviewer who may quote passages in a review.

British Library Cataloguing in Publication Information Available

Library of Congress Cataloging-in-Publication Data Available

ISBN: 978-1-4985-5908-9 (cloth)
ISBN: 978-1-4985-5909-6 (electronic)

Contents

Introduction

Methodist founder John Wesley once claimed the world was his parish. Ninety years after his death, in 1881, leaders of twenty-eight Methodist churches representing some 20 million Methodists met in London. At this Œcumenical Methodist Conference, over a dozen speakers referenced Wesley's words to describe the mission and scope of their religious movement. In the opening sermon, the American bishop of the Methodist Episcopal Church Matthew Simpson used the phrase to reference both Wesley's commitment to seize every opportunity to share the gospel and the contexts around the world to which attendees would return at the close of the conference. Other speakers used the phrase to assert that Methodists should evangelize the entire world, live holy lives, employ useful methods such as publishing to communicate their message, minister to the poor and marginalized, and be unrestrained by ecclesiastical limits.[1]

William Taylor, an American Methodist preacher, missionary, evangelist, author, occasional layman, and bishop, was not present at that conference. More than any attendee, however—more even than John Wesley—Taylor made the whole world his field of work. At the time of the conference, he was leading revivals in Colorado and recruiting people to serve missions he had started on visits to India and South America. Taylor's participation in the South African revival of the 1860s had made him an evangelical celebrity. Prior to that, Taylor had been an itinerant revivalist in Australasia, the British Isles, and the eastern United States, and a missionary in gold rush-era California. A few years after the conference, in 1884, Taylor would be elected the Methodist Episcopal Church's Bishop of Africa. At the time of his death in 1902, Methodism on six continents bore Taylor's mark.

1

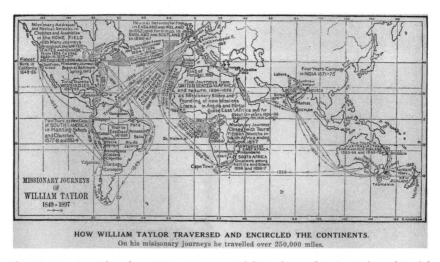

HOW WILLIAM TAYLOR TRAVERSED AND ENCIRCLED THE CONTINENTS.
On his missionary journeys he travelled over 250,000 miles.

Figure 0.1   Map Taken from Centenary Memorial Service and Presentation of Burial Lot to Methodist Episcopal Church. [Oakland?]: William Taylor Memorial Association, 1921. *Source:* Used with the permission of the Archives of the California-Nevada Annual Conference of The United Methodist Church.

This book is the first comprehensive and critical reconstruction of the whole life and career of this noteworthy Methodist mission leader. It explores how Taylor's approach to mission developed and changed over time as he responded to events in his life and how his theological priorities affected his choices. Through much of Taylor's career, he sought out apostolic models for different facets of missionary work and attempted to replicate them in his own day. Most of these models elevated Paul, the early Christian apostle and author of most of the New Testament, as the paradigmatic Christian missionary. In the most enduring aspect of Taylor's Pauline model, he argued that just as Paul supported himself as a "tentmaker"—and he supported himself by selling books—Christian missionaries should be self-supporting (cf. Acts 18:3).

Protestants had long made the formation of self-supporting indigenous churches a primary goal of the missionary enterprise. The American Congregationalist Rufus Anderson and the Anglican Henry Venn had each promoted the creation of self-governing, self-replicating, and self-supporting churches as the objective of missionary work.[2] But Taylor proposed meeting that goal at the start of the missionary encounter. He thought missionaries themselves should be self-supporting. In Taylor's vision, missionaries would seek employment in the secular economy of the missionary context until they could be sustained by the voluntary contributions of converts. Still today, some Christians use this concept of "tentmaking" missions as a way of supporting missionary outreach.[3]

Inspired by his intercontinental exploits and Pauline vision, Taylor was a popular missionary hero to nineteenth-century Methodists and to others who were a part of emerging holiness movements in America and around the world. As a result, Taylor has been the subject of popular and scholarly interest for over a century. Past historiography, however, has either been hagiographic and self-serving or scholarly but limited in scope. Relentlessly self-promoting, most of Taylor's sixteen books (plus two written in his name) were first-person accounts of his ministry or contained extensive autobiographical content. During his life and in the generation after his death, others followed Taylor's lead and offered biographies that followed closely to Taylor's own accounts of his labors.[4]

More recently, different portions of Taylor's career have been the subject of scholarly articles, chapters, or book sections treating single periods or aspects of his life.[5] Four recent historians merit special mention, as they highlight the significance of and illustrate ongoing interest in Taylor's life and career. First, historian David Bundy's landmark articles and papers draw attention to select aspects of Taylor's "Pauline" mission theory, his position in the late nineteenth-century holiness movement, and the role of his missionaries in the emergence of world Pentecostalism. Bundy also lays important historiographic groundwork by identifying some important sources and most of Taylor's published books. Bundy's work is foundational, and he is to be credited with establishing Taylor as an important figure to scholars of Christian mission. Unfortunately, Bundy's work also glosses over Taylor's early life, uncritically relies on Taylor's own interpretation of significant events, and is marked by some factual errors.[6] More recently, Jay Riley Case devotes two chapters of his book *An Unpredictable Gospel: American Evangelicals and World Christianity, 1812–1920* to Taylor's time in South Africa and his relationship with American Methodist leadership to illustrate ways evangelical foreign missions impacted American Christianity.[7] Robert F. Lay's annotated edition of Taylor's California journal offers a valuable and insightful exploration of Taylor's ministry in gold rush-era California. Lay demonstrates the importance of Taylor's early career but does not trace those developments further.[8] Finally, historian David Hempton's study of Methodism as a religious movement names Taylor as an archetypal example of a Methodist approach to mission that was "entrepreneurial and pragmatic, opportunistic and optimistic, flexible and adaptable."[9]

Taylor was, indeed, representative of a Methodist approach to foreign missions that differed in key aspects of theology and practice from other evangelicals. In addition to offering a synoptic view of Taylor's story, this book considers the nineteenth-century Protestant missionary enterprise from a Methodist angle of view. During Taylor's life, his own denomination, the Methodist Episcopal Church, was the largest church in the United States.

Unfortunately, historian Nathan Hatch's call to move Methodism toward the center of the study of American Christianity has not been picked up by historians of Christian mission.[10] Indeed, the study of nineteenth-century American foreign missions has often focused on the work of northern Congregationalists and Presbyterians. In his study of the American foreign mission thought, for example, William Hutchison gave only scant notice to Methodist foreign missions.[11]

It is a contention of this book that Taylor was representative of the Methodist missionary tradition and that his life offers a close study of ways Methodists approached their missionary task. A word on that assertion is warranted since some of the recent scholarship mentioned earlier casts Taylor as "maverick" out of sync with his church and a forerunner of holiness and, eventually, Pentecostal Christians who left established Methodist churches.[12] While an influence on such movements is part of his legacy, Taylor always believed himself to be a faithful Methodist. Moreover, those alternate interpretations do not match evidence in the sources available, including Taylor's own writing. They view Taylor's entire career through the lens of a screed he wrote in the 1880s in the midst of a conflict with church leaders over the independence of missions he started. In that book, Taylor—by his own admission—reinterpreted his story to describe a long-running conflict with church leaders where previously there had been none.[13] That clash is a part of Taylor's story, but it is not his whole story, nor is it the key to the whole. Taylor's global career was only possible because Methodists of both the American and British traditions accepted and claimed him as one of their own. Both before that conflict and when tempers cooled at the end of the 1880s, Taylor was claimed and celebrated by Methodists as their missionary hero and the man who truly made the world his parish.

The account that follows uses Taylor's career to map several contours of the Methodist missionary tradition. Some of these themes were mentioned by speakers at the 1881 conference. Methodists were eager to seize openings for missionary expansion, seeing them as providential works of God. They held a commitment to reach all peoples with their message, and believed God desired the salvation of all. They expected that those saved by God's grace would lead morally rigorous and holy lives and pursue entire sanctification—a work of God's salvation believed to remove in the faithful the inclination to sin. Marginalized persons could be particularly receptive to the Methodist message of salvation for all and the empowerment of sanctification it offered. They often relied on practical means, such as print media, as a way to communicate their message. In addition, Methodists believed the church to be a connectional network transcending any local congregation of believers; for Methodists, the church was an evolving and growing system of relationships. These relationships were structured in local, regional, and, eventually, international conferences, unofficial gatherings, societies and agencies, and relationships among preachers, laity, missionaries, and in Taylor's own Methodist Episcopal Church, bishops. Taylor's story shows that Methodists held a high view of human freedom and potential, found that the experience of sanctification propelled missionary outreach, and used revivalism both as a method of evangelistic outreach and leadership development. Finally, Methodists were a pragmatic people; missionary outreach that could be deemed successful was understood to be blessed by God. Endeavors that did not "work"—for some this included Taylor's vision of missionary self-support—were not.

Methodists were not the only evangelical Protestants to embrace some or all of these emphases. Certainly a belief in God's providence was widely held by other Christians. Other evangelicals wanted to evangelize the world and were willing to use whatever means were available to do so. For example, the modern missionary movement was launched when William Carey convinced Baptists to adopt the pragmatic posture of using "Means for the Conversion of the Heathens" to cite the title of his famous *Enquiry*.[14] As the nineteenth century progressed, new theologies of sanctification influenced Christian missionaries from a variety of traditions. Examples of such emphases in a non-Methodist sources abound.[15] It is my hope that by focusing attention on these features in a specific missionary tradition this book will provide a point of reference that other researchers may triangulate against as they consider the impact of such beliefs elsewhere in the missionary movement.

In many respects, what made these emphases Methodist was not their presence but their combination. As such, this narrative not only illustrates those themes, but connections and tensions between them. Marginalized persons might respond positively to the Methodist message of salvation for all, only to find racism within the structures that governed church life and restricted participation in church leadership. Methodist missions often lived in the tension between a desire to regularize religious practices and resistance to such ecclesiastical limitations. A belief that the Holy Spirit might inspire individual entrepreneurial initiatives was not easily reconciled with a desire to order and organize the work of the church. The belief that entire sanctification was available to all the faithful, and that doctrine's role as an engine propelling missionary outreach, could empower people to action. Such initiatives were valued but sometimes failed without organizational support. Sometimes that belief inspired persons ill-suited to missionary work. A desire to seize every opportunity and reach every person with the gospel often strained against pragmatic concerns to prevent depletion of resources by overexpansion. As much as they aspired to it, Methodists found it challenging to manage a worldwide parish.

Taylor's global odyssey also offers a grassroots view of some nineteenth-century American missionary seeds of early twenty-first-century world

Christianity. Historian Mark A. Noll argues that nineteenth-century American Christianity offers a template for understanding contemporary world Christianity, because in both contexts a "conversionistic and voluntaristic Christianity" has thrived.[16] In addition, historian Dana L. Robert has located the origins of world Christianity in the Christian concept and practice of mission.[17] What follows is a story of a nineteenth-century American missionary of the kind Noll describes who understood and lived out his missionary calling in several different contexts around the world.

The first chapter of this book introduces Taylor and the social context, and theological and ecclesiastical concerns of antebellum American Methodism. It provides an outline of Taylor's early life and family of origin, the entry of Taylor's family into the Methodist Episcopal Church, his early career in the Methodist ministry, and call to missionary service. Chapter 2 explores Taylor's work as one of the first Protestant missionaries in gold rush-era California. In that context, Taylor worked to organize church institutions and reach diverse immigrants with his message of salvation and holiness. Taylor's work in California, however, came to an abrupt end when a fire destroyed part of his ministry. Chapter 3 follows Taylor's career as an itinerant evangelist and author. He used Methodist connectional networks to cross and bridge the continents, and his revivalism was welcomed by Methodists in the United States, Canada, the British Isles, and Australasia as way of meeting their missionary commitment within "Christian" lands and developing new church leadership. Chapter 4 traces Taylor's work in identifiably cross-cultural settings and the gradual development of his Pauline vision for mission. It explores the challenges faced in these missions by language and religion and Taylor's search for theological solutions to these challenges. The final chapter recounts Taylor's reengagement with American Methodism, beginning with his work in missionary recruitment, his start of new missions in South America, conflicts that arose out of his work, and Taylor's tenure as a missionary Bishop of Africa.

The primary aim of this work is to tell Taylor's story to illustrate the texture of the Methodist missionary tradition. This focus means that some worthy subjects are not discussed or are mentioned only briefly. During the final decades of Taylor's career, for example, Methodist women emerged as a missionary force. I have tried to illustrate that development through the lives of some women missionaries who crossed paths with Taylor, but these descriptions are in no way proportional to the scale of woman's missions within the Methodist tradition. In addition, because Taylor never visited East Asia, Methodist missions there are barely mentioned. Also, since Taylor largely interacted with the two largest branches of the nineteenth-century Methodist family—the Methodist Episcopal Church in the United States and the Wesleyan Methodists of Great Britain and its overseas dominions—some other Methodist traditions are noted only in passing. My weak defense for these gaps is that while Methodists believed the whole world was their field of work, the whole world is too much to cover in one book.

Finally, although I have gleaned many sources on Taylor's life for this account, information about Taylor's wife and family is scarce. The little that is known about them is shared when appropriate. For much of Taylor's life, he lived as if he were a single man. The silence about his family that follows is a function of the available source material, and in no way represents an opinion that their experience as a missionary wife and family is unimportant. No doubt, Taylor's story would look quite different from their perspective.

Many people have been a very present support to me through the process of research and writing of this book and the dissertation on which it is based. First, I want to thank Dana Robert for her sage advice, insightful observations, and feedback on drafts of my work in the dissertation stage, and the encouragement to "craunch" down on Taylor.

My research allowed me the opportunity to interact with several wonderful librarians, archivists, and researchers around the world who were always very helpful and hospitable to me. At Boston University, I would like to thank Rhoda Bilansky and the Interlibrary Loan staff at Mugar Library, Kara Jackman, archivist and special collections librarian of B.U. School of Theology, and Jennifer Duperon, legal information librarian of Boston University School of Law. I also would like to thank Patrick Kerwin and Jennifer Brathovde at the Library of Congress, Rebekah Hughes, Laura Mummert, Ashley Chu, and Emily MaGee at the Taylor University Archives, Stephen Yale at the California-Nevada Conference Archives of The United Methodist Church, Kathleen Correia of the California State Library California History Section, Martha Smalley and Joan R. Duffy of Yale Divinity School Library, Deborah Shapiro of the Smithsonian Institution Archives, and Dori Gottschalk-Fielding of the Seymour Library of Auburn, New York. Thank you to Wanda Hall at the Lovely Lane Museum and Archives in Baltimore, Jason Bruner who searched the archives at Princeton, Vaughan Stanley at Washington and Lee University, Nan Card at the Rutherford B. Hayes Presidential Center, An Cardoen of the Royal Museum for Central Africa in Belgium, Katrina Denman of the Huntington Library, Elizabeth Ratigan of the Historical Society of Washington, D.C., Jo Smith of the Methodist Church of New Zealand, Betty Bolden and Matthew Baker at Union Theological Seminary, Jennifer Hardin of the Cincinnati Art Museum, Joanne Houmard of the University of Mount Union, Philip Stone of Wofford College, Sara De Weever at Claflin University, Frances LaTorre of the Alameda County Superior Court, Kate Dannals and Tara Olivero of Goucher College.

Special thanks are due to the staff of the Methodist Library at Drew University and the General Commission on Archives and History (GCAH) of The United Methodist Church, Christopher J. Anderson, Mark Shenise,

Frances Lyons, Dorothy Meaney, and Corey Fick. The GCAH awarded this manuscript the 2015 Jesse Lee Prize in Methodist History. I am both honored by that award and will be forever grateful for the encouragement that award represented at just the right moment.

In this project, I spoke and corresponded with several other scholars whose work and interests intersected with my own. For your scholarly collegiality and recommendation of sources, I would like to express my appreciation to my friends from the doctoral programs at B.U., Eric Baldwin, Anneke Stasson, Kevin Taylor, Sarah Mount Elewononi, Erika Hirsh, Daryl Ireland, Bruce Yoder, David Scott, Hye Jin Lee, and Ben Hartley. Thanks also to scholars further afield such as Bruce Birch, Robert Evans, David Durham, Bruce Evensen, Randy Maddox, Marilyn Warshawsky, Linda T. Grimm, and Jane Donovan. Thank you to Rick Buckingham for your help in proofreading my text along the way. I am also grateful to Robert Lay for sharing with me an early proof of Taylor's journal and graciously sharing sources he found in his own research.

The transformation of this work from dissertation to book took place in Sykesville, Maryland. Thank you to my colleagues, friends, and the good people at St. Paul's and Gaither United Methodist Churches in Sykesville, Maryland, for your support through this process, especially Terri Rae Chattin, Colleen Goodman, Kim Donnelley, and EunJoung Joo. I am also grateful to Piper Wallis for her contacts and her cover and my editor, Mike Gibson, for bringing this book to print.

Finally, but most importantly, I want to give thanks to God and to my family. To my parents, thank you for your love, support, and occasional "scholarships." To my daughter Maya, although I disagree with your historical interpretation of Taylor, thank you for the motivation you provided me. To my daughter Lucy—C. S. Lewis was right; girls do grow faster than books. You are much bigger now than when this project started! To Mandy, it feels cliché and insufficient just to thank you for your love and support, so thank you for spending your rainy days with me.

NOTES

1. *Proceedings of the Ecumenical Methodist Conference, Held in City Road Chapel, London, September, 1881* (Cincinnati: Walden and Stowe, 1882), 11, 19, 48, 80, 88, 100, 236, 381, 444, 473, 537, 546, 564, 587. For other uses of the phrase, see Dana L. Robert and Douglas D. Tzan, "Traditions and Transitions in Mission Thought," in *The Oxford Handbook of Methodist Studies*, ed. William J. Abraham and James E. Kirby (New York: Oxford University Press, 2009), 431–4.

2. Paul William Harris, *Nothing But Christ: Rufus Anderson and the Ideology of Protestant Foreign Missions* (New York: Oxford University Press, 1999), 112–32;

Wilbert R. Shenk, *Henry Venn—Missionary Statesman* (Maryknoll: Orbis Books, 1983), 44–46.

3. "GoLiveServe," accessed June 27, 2018, goliveserve.org; "Worldwide Tentmakers," accessed June 27, 2018, worldwidetentmakers.com.

4. See B. S. Taylor, "The World's Missionary Evangelist," *Christian Standard*, April 7, 1883ff.; E. Davies, *The Bishop of Africa; or, the Life of William Taylor, D.D. With an Account of the Congo Country, and Mission* (Reading: Holiness Book Concern, 1885); John Paul, *The Soul Digger; or, Life and Times of William Taylor* (Upland: Taylor University Press, 1928).

5. Daryl M. Balia, "Bridge Over Troubled Waters: Charles Pamla and the Taylor Revival in South Africa," *Methodist History* 30, no. 2 (1992): 78–90; Daryl M. Balia, "Reaping Where Others Have Sown: William Taylor's Impact on Methodism," in *Perspectives in Theology and Mission from South Africa*, ed. Daryl M. Balia (Lewiston: Snow Lion Publications, 1993), 119–27; Eric G. Clancy, "William ('California') Taylor: First Overseas Evangelist to Australia," *Church Heritage* 6, no. 3 (1990): 41–62; Peter Feinman, "William Taylor in Chile: A Methodist Missionary Case Study," *Methodist History* 47, no. 2 (2009): 84–100; Sampath Kumar, "The Impact of William Taylor's Urban Mission on the Methodist Church in India During the 19th Century," in *Doing Contextual Theology: A Festschrift in Honour of Bruce John Nicholls*, ed. Bruce Nicholls and Sunand Sumithra (Bangalore: Theological Book Trust, 1992), 139–52; Wallace G. Mills, "The Taylor Revival of 1866 and the Roots of African Nationalism in the Cape Colony," *Journal of Religion in Africa* 8, no. 2 (1976): 105–22; Charles W. Turner, "'California' Taylor of Rockbridge: Bishop to the World," *Southern California Quarterly* 62, no. 3 (1980): 229–38.

6. David Bundy, "Bishop William Taylor and Methodist Mission: A Study in Nineteenth Century Social History (Part 1)," *Methodist History* 27, no. 4 (July 1989): 197–210; David Bundy, "Bishop William Taylor and Methodist Mission: A Study in Nineteenth Century Social History (Part 2)," *Methodist History* 28, no. 1 (October 1989): 3–21; David Bundy, "The Legacy of William Taylor," *International Bulletin of Missionary Research* 18, no. 4 (1994): 172–6; David Bundy, "The Development of Models of Missions in Methodism During the Early American Republic: With Attention to the Antecedents of the Holiness Movement," Paper presented at the Currents in World Christianity incorporating North Atlantic Missiology Project, Cambridge, 1997; David Bundy, "William Taylor as an Interpreter of African Culture: The Foundation for a Theory of Mission," Paper presented at the Currents in World Christianity Project incorporating North American Missiology Project, Cambridge, 1998; David Bundy, "Unintended Consequences: The Methodist Episcopal Missionary Society and the Beginnings of Pentecostalism in Norway and Chile," *Missiology: An International Review* 27, no. 2 (1999): 211–29; David Bundy, "Pauline Missions: The Wesleyan Holiness Vision," in *The Global Impact of the Wesleyan Traditions and Their Related Movements*, ed. Charles Yrigoyen, Jr. (Lanham: Scarecrow Press, 2002), 13–26.

7. Jay Riley Case, *An Unpredictable Gospel: American Evangelicals and World Christianity, 1812–1920* (New York: Oxford University Press, 2012), 103–55.

8. Robert F. Lay, ed., *Lessons of Infinite Advantage: William Taylor's California Experiences. With Isabelle Anne Kimberlin Taylor's Travel Diary, 1866–67, Written*

During a Voyage with Her Family En Route from the Cape of Good Hope, South Africa, to London and Subsequent Travels Throughout Europe (Lanham: Scarecrow Press and The Center for the Study of World Christian Revitalization Movements, 2010).

   9. David Hempton, *Methodism: Empire of the Spirit* (New Haven: Yale University Press, 2005), 168.

   10. Nathan O. Hatch, "The Puzzle of American Methodism," *Church History* 63, no. 2 (1994): 189.

   11. William R. Hutchison, *Errand to the World: American Protestant Thought and Foreign Missions* (Chicago: University of Chicago Press, 1987).

   12. See in particular the work of Bundy and Case cited above.

   13. William Taylor, *Ten Years of Self-Supporting Missions in India* (New York: Phillips & Hunt, 1882), 448–9.

   14. Andrew F. Walls, "Missionary Societies and the Fortunate Subversion of the Church," in *The Missionary Movement in Christian History: Studies in the Transmission of Faith* (Maryknoll: Orbis Books, 1996), 243–4.

   15. Andrew Porter, "Cambridge, Keswick and Late Nineteenth Century Attitudes to Africa," *Journal of Imperial and Commonwealth History* 5, no. 1 (1976): 5–34; Andrew Porter, "Evangelical Enthusiasm, Missionary Motivation and West Africa in the Late Nineteenth Century: The Career of G. W. Brooke," *Journal of Imperial and Commonwealth History* 6, no. 1 (1977): 23–46; Jay Riley Case, *An Unpredictable Gospel: American Evangelicals and World Christianity, 1812–1920* (New York: Oxford University Press, 2012).

   16. Mark A. Noll, *The New Shape of World Christianity: How American Experience Reflects Global Faith* (Downers Grove: IVP Academic, 2009), 116.

   17. Dana L. Robert, *Christian Mission: How Christianity Became a World Religion* (Malden: Wiley-Blackwell, 2009).

Chapter 1

Birth and New Birth

In 1888, as a man of sixty-seven years, and after an already full career on six continents, William Taylor thought back over his life. His memories of the past, the needs of the present, and his future legacy mingled together in his mind. As the Bishop of Africa for the Methodist Episcopal Church, Taylor spent many days sailing between North America, Europe, and Africa. He often filled monotonous days at sea writing, and his most recent project was a monthly magazine, *The African News*, launched to promote and support his African missions. He had promised the editor he would provide copy for a children's column. To pass the time, Taylor decided to sketch out his memories of his own childhood and early ministry. The exercise would be, he thought, "a recreation and pleasure."[1]

More than nostalgia for the past and present entertainment was at work in that moment, however, for Taylor also wondered how he would be remembered. Opinions of him in America were sharply divided. Taylor certainly had his fans. His surprising election to the episcopacy four years earlier and the missionary volunteers that followed him to Africa, South America, or India were testimony of that. For them he was the Methodist Livingstone, a missionary hero who had won souls and started Methodist missions all over the world and who had now turned his attention to newly opened parts of Africa. These supporters followed Taylor's work, travels, and example. They would remember him a generation after his death as a spiritual giant for whom traversing the wide expanses of the world was an easy task, as if he possessed the "seven-league boots" of legend.[2]

Taylor also knew that others believed he was at best an embarrassment and at worst a threat to his church. Other church leaders had sought to distance the Methodist Episcopal Church from his actions and to find ways to circumscribe his authority to protect their church from the disaster they were certain Taylor would bring. Speaking for Taylor's critics both inside and out of his church, an 1885 *New York Times* editorial predicted the certain death of the bishop and his missionaries in Africa. It did so on the racist and sexist assumption that it was impossible for women, children, and most men to live in Africa. For thinking otherwise, the *Times* lambasted Taylor as "an alleged Bishop and an undoubted crank" and proclaimed he was "a lunatic of a very dangerous kind."[3]

While Taylor's ego assured him he was a hero, and no lunatic, such criticism bothered him. He often felt the need to defend his honor against attacks such as these. Such responses could escalate simple misunderstandings into major conflicts; Taylor could be his own worst enemy in this regard. The conflict over Taylor's role and place in his church that burned in 1888 was ignited in 1881 by several public critiques of his work. Taylor did his part to pour gasoline on the fire by rushing a book to print meant to vindicate himself and his missionary methods. *Ten Years of Self-Supporting Missions in India* (1882) did little to resolve the crisis, and even Taylor's supporters lamented its argumentative tone. Then in the fall of 1882, at a meeting called to resolve questions over the status of Taylor and his missionaries in the Methodist Episcopal Church, Taylor rashly resigned his ministerial credentials and went to South America. Just two years later, Taylor was, to his and everyone else's surprise, elected to the episcopacy of his church. It was in that capacity as Missionary Bishop of Africa that Taylor traversed the Atlantic in 1888.

Tempers had not cooled by 1888, when Taylor set pen to paper to write about his childhood and early life. Details of those critiques, Taylor's perception of them, and the fallout from that conflict will be explored in future chapters. But this conflict between Taylor and leaders of his church is mentioned here because when Taylor set pen to paper to tell the story of his early life and ministry, he did so as a more subtle means of engaging his critics and defending his name. If *Ten Years* was Taylor at his most fiery, defensive, and polemic, these autobiographical reflections showed he could sound other notes as well. He could also be engaging, charismatic, and winsome. He could tell a good story. There was a reason Taylor had his fans.

By telling the story of his childhood, entry into Methodism, and early years of his ministry as a Methodist preacher, Taylor sought to set the record straight and to represent himself to the Methodist world as the person he saw himself, and his fans saw him, to be: he was a loyal, old-school Methodist, of the kind that had grown and flourished on the frontiers of antebellum America and would around the world, he believed, if allowed to spread. His Methodism was one of free grace for all people, emotional exuberance, and moral rigor. It was characterized by camp meetings and itinerant preachers who lived lives of heroic sacrifice. It celebrated the power of God to sanctify believers through faith and empower them to take their message to the ends of the earth.

Taylor's shipboard recollections first published in *The African News* would eventually be compiled with other previously published material and released as his autobiography, *The Story of My Life, an Account of What I Have Thought and Said and Done in My Ministry of More Than Fifty-Three Years in Christian Lands and among the Heathen. Written by Myself (1895)*. These writings were not Taylor's first attempt at autobiography but they would be his last. They were his thoughts of the past sketched with an eye to the future and seeking to meet the needs of the present.

They are worth exploring at the outset of this biography, because although Taylor rarely referred to the early years of his life, they had a lasting impact on the shape of his ministry. He grew up in the Virginia backcountry surrounded by a family of pioneer settlers who valued independence and self-sufficiency. With his parents, he adopted the Methodist faith brought to him by circuit-riding preachers. As a young man, he was inducted into that fraternity of preachers, embraced its ethos, and began his family life. Taylor was quickly identified as a promising, if potentially disruptive, force in his church. Perhaps for both of those reasons, he was dispatched by the Methodist Episcopal Church to be one of its first missionaries in California.

EARLY LIFE

Unlike their son and their own parents, William Taylor's parents, Stuart Taylor (born 1796) and Martha Hickman (born 1800), never ventured far from home. The couple married in 1819 and settled on a farm near Stuart's family on Hogback Mountain near Rockbridge Baths in Rockbridge County, Virginia. In this mountainous region, Stuart and Martha lived, worked, raised their family, worshipped first in a Presbyterian church and later among the Methodists, and were buried. In this region too, William came of age, was called and began his career in the Methodist ministry.[4]

Born May 2, 1821, William was the oldest of his parents' eleven children—five sons and six daughters—but the Taylor family was not limited to this single household. William's grandparents had been among the pioneer European settlers in the area, and a large clan of grandparents, aunts, uncles, and cousins called the region home. His paternal grandfather, James Taylor, immigrated to Rockbridge County in the mid-eighteenth century with four brothers from County Armagh, Ireland. James Taylor had married Ann Paul, the daughter of another Scotch-Irish family. William's mother was of English backcountry stock, from neighboring Bath County, Virginia.[5] These were a part of the great Scotch-Irish migration in which over a quarter of a million emigrants from northern Britain and Ireland settled in a large swath of the Appalachian backcountry.[6]

This network of relatives played an important role in William's growth and development. He recalled living for prolonged periods of his childhood with different branches of his family. These visits probably coincided with the births of siblings and the needs of the larger family for the extra labor a boy could provide. In one of his earliest recorded memories, William recalled living with his grandmother for several months at about the age of four. He credited her with teaching him the beginnings of literacy and spelling, the Lord's Prayer, and the bedtime prayer, "Now I lay me down to sleep."[7]

From the time of his grandparents' settlement to the years William came of age, western Virginia developed from a pioneer, subsistence existence to an increasingly diversified market economy. The family lived in a small, cabin-style home of three rooms and probably grew crops common to the region such as corn, tobacco, beans, squash, and gourds. They supplemented their farming income with trade work. Stuart was a tanner and currier, and William later remembered him as a "mechanical genius" who used iron, wood, or leather to meet the needs on his own farm and the demands of the market. Martha made cloth, a major trade commodity produced locally, weaving both linen from flax and wool spun from sheep. Children were expected to contribute their work to the household economy. William learned his father's trade, and he recalled helping to graze the cattle.[8]

Throughout William's childhood, many neighbors left the region to seek new opportunities elsewhere. From 1830 to 1840 the population in Rockbridge County declined as white settlers and their black slaves moved west.[9] Particularly attractive for Virginians were the rich farmlands in Alabama and Georgia opened by Andrew Jackson's 1813–1814 brutal and genocidal campaign against the Muskogee (Creek) Indians.[10] The parents of William's future wife were a part of that migration.[11] For William, growing up with pioneer grandparents in a region where neighbors constantly left for new opportunities in the west probably made him more willing than others might have been to embrace a pioneer life for himself and his family when the opportunity arose.

Values of independence, self-reliance, pride, and courage were cultivated in boys of the southern backcountry like William at an early age.[12] In one early memory, dated by the older William to about his fifth year, he went with his grandmother to visit another home and spent the day hunting for water snakes with a boy his age. William's grandmother allowed him to spend the night with the friend provided he would walk the two miles back to his grandmother's alone the next day.[13] William's father was long remembered in the community for his courage. In the early twentieth century, local historian Oren F. Morton recorded several reminiscences of Stuart Taylor. Most celebrated Stuart's hunting skill, such as the time Stuart intentionally entered a bear's den and fought with the animal before killing it by hand with a knife.[14]

Figure 1.1 "Birthplace of Bishop William Taylor." Undated photos of the Taylor home in Virginia in the Bishop Taylor Collection Box 1, file 10. *Source:* Reproduced with permission of the Ringenberg Archives & Special Collections, Taylor University, Upland, IN.

One expression of those values that Taylor later used to describe his vision of Christian mission was the aphorism: "root hog or die." This bit of back-country, southern folk wisdom was first recorded in print by the frontiersman known as Davy Crockett.[15] It became the chorus of a popular nineteenth-century American folk song and referred to the practice of allowing pigs to forage since they were highly self-sufficient animals.[16] There was no standard form of this saying. "Pig" could be substituted for "hog," "or" could be replaced by "and," and the punctuation could vary but the import was the same. The hog was commanded to be self-reliant or starve: "root hog or die." As an adult, Taylor imparted this home-spun advice to "self-supporting" missionaries he recruited.[17]

Despite celebrating virtues such as self-sufficiency, like many white, southern farming families, the Taylors were dependent on and benefited from slave labor. In his autobiography, William wrote about his family's slaveholding many years after emancipation, and he sought to cast his family's actions in a positive light. He claimed that while his Taylor ancestors had bought slaves when they settled in Virginia, his Paul ancestors were opposed to slavery. The Pauls convinced later generations of Taylors to emancipate individuals "as fast as they came into possession of slaves by inheritance," and William wrote that his father freed the last of the Taylor slaves.[18]

In practice, the process was much slower than Taylor implied. Manumissions in southwestern Virginia were often legally and logistically difficult to arrange.[19] In 1830, when William was nine, there were two slaves enumerated

Figure 1.2 "Taylor Farm." Undated photos of the Taylor home in Virginia in the Bishop Taylor Collection Box 1, file 10. *Source:* Reproduced with permission of the Ringenberg Archives & Special Collections, Taylor University, Upland, IN.

at the property, a male aged between ten and twenty-four and girl under the age of ten.[20] Ten years later, the family continued to hold a man aged twenty-five to thirty-four.[21] In 1850, a thirteen-year-old slave girl was counted with the family, and as late as 1860, a twenty-year-old slave woman still resided in a separate house on the property.[22] A pattern of inheritance and eventual manumission after the slave had worked for his or her freedom, or the freedom of family members, rather than immediate manumission, would better account for these slaves' enumeration and turnover.

Nevertheless, there is evidence that Stuart and Martha sought to negotiate a way between the idea of opposition to slavery and their existence in an economic and legal system that brought them into possession of human beings and profit from their labor. In 1834, Martha freed a fifty-year-old man named Cyrus Taylor.[23] In addition, Rockbridge County was home to a vigorous antislavery tradition that persisted even as antislavery sentiment faded elsewhere in Virginia. Stuart and Martha seemed to identify themselves with that tradition. The Presbyterian minister who founded the church they joined had previously been forced to resign a pastorate for his antislavery sentiments, and in the 1820s he operated a school for both blacks and whites.[24] The Taylors eventually became Methodist, but when the Methodist Episcopal Church divided over slavery in 1844, unlike other Methodists in the community,

William's parents refused to affiliate with the southern church. At the outbreak of the Civil War, Stuart identified himself as a Union loyalist.[25]

BECOMING A METHODIST

Whatever the nature of these slaves' status and relationship to the Taylor family, as an adult William credited one of them with provoking his first evangelical awakening. The experience took place in William's seventh year following a conversation with the family's servant girl—possibly the child enumerated with the family in 1830. She told William the story of the conversion of a black collier. This secondhand testimony of two African Americans pushed the young boy to feel anguish over his own sin and seek salvation as they had. As related by the adult Taylor, "I said to myself, 'If this black man has found Jesus and got his sins forgiven, then, somehow, Jesus isn't so far away after all. If this poor sinner has found him why can't I find him?'"[26] The boy confessed his sins to God and placed his trust in Jesus, finding himself overcome by a sense of peace. Not long after, however, he relapsed into doubt and sin when Satan tempted him to believe that God expected him to sell his childhood possessions.[27]

Taylor related this story as an adult to illustrate theological beliefs that had become important to him. Among evangelicals, conversion narratives served as theological statements about their understandings of identity and God's saving work in the world.[28] Methodists shared with other evangelicals a conviction that a conversion experience was at the heart of a vital Christian life. Such a life-changing experience was to accompany faith in Jesus Christ. Through faith, believers were justified by God and had their sins forgiven. Their sinful human nature was given a "new birth," and believers were told to expect a peaceful assurance confirming their new status with God.[29]

Unlike other evangelicals, Methodists believed this new relationship with God might not persevere. While Taylor would claim this conversion to be his first, it would not be his last. This belief was informed by a theological framework known as Arminianism, after the seventeenth-century theologian Jacob Arminius. Arminianism was adopted by John Wesley and his Methodist followers. Unlike the Calvinist orthodoxy that emerged after the Reformation in which only certain people were predestined for salvation, in the Arminian line of thought God desired the salvation of all people. God's freely imparted grace empowered individuals to work out their salvation in cooperation with God. Accordingly, people were believed to possess a great deal of spiritual freedom, and it was possible for a convert to return to a life of sin.[30]

Taylor told his story of redemption and relapse as a cautionary tale that one must be on alert to guard one's salvation. It also served to convey his belief in the importance of wise spiritual counsel and that anyone properly empowered by God could be a spiritual agent and authority. God could overturn social hierarchies; even slave girls in the antebellum south could be evangelists.[31] In this respect, the adult Taylor embraced the egalitarian potential of evangelicalism more than many of his era. As will be seen, in his missions socially marginalized persons often found a measure of inclusion and leadership denied them elsewhere.[32]

As a young boy, however, such considerations lay in the distant future. At the moment, that encounter was also significant because it represented Taylor's first encounter with a form of Christianity other than the Presbyterian faith of his family—African American evangelicalism. The appeal of the Methodist message of God's free grace for all was most evident in its reception by slaves and free people of African descent in North America and the Caribbean. The first Methodist societies to emerge outside the British Isles—in Antigua, Maryland, and New York—developed as biracial fellowships and provided formal and informal opportunities for black leadership. In addition to presenting a message of theological agency in which slaves could assert control over their spiritual lives, if not their physical bodies, Methodists emphasized oral communication and presented a form of Christianity in which literacy was not a requirement for participation. Moreover, for a time, following the leadership of John Wesley, Methodists became known for their opposition to slavery and the slave trade.[33]

In 1784, the founders of the Methodist Episcopal Church followed Wesley's lead by prohibiting slaveholding among its membership. By the early 1800s, however, American Methodist leaders had made the decision to prioritize evangelism over an antislavery commitment. The church retreated from its antislavery stance.[34] By the time of Taylor's birth, black Methodists in the United States were frustrated with the church's racism and, in some communities, began the process of creating separate institutions and leadership. Most notably, in 1816 black Methodists in Philadelphia, under the leadership of Richard Allen, formed the African Methodist Episcopal Church.[35]

Outside of those northern, urban, institutional expressions of black Methodism, evidence exists that some African Americans in the rural south identified themselves as Methodists and spread their faith at their own initiative. Historian Will Gravely found fugitive slave notices describing runaways as Methodist preachers or suggesting that runaways would be found in Methodist meetings.[36] There is evidence that Methodism had been adopted by some slaves in Rockbridge County, including those owned by the Taylor family. In 1832, Rockbridge Methodists licensed a former slave named Isaac Liggins as an exhorter, a layperson who gave testimony to his experience of faith and encouraged others to live with greater devotion and holiness.[37] In 1848, a woman of Rockbridge County named Susan Taylor, presumably a relative of William, freed a man named Othello Richards.[38] Richards proceeded to buy the freedom of his wife, Mary, and children, Caroline, Nancy, Eugenia, Wesley M., Francis Asbury, and Samuel.[39] The youngest three children were given names favored by Methodists, and in 1850, when the family immigrated to Liberia, Richards was identified as a Methodist preacher. In Liberia, the Richards family became important leaders in Liberian Methodism.[40]

Taylor was primed to hear the slave girl's story and to be moved to this first conversion because of his religious upbringing among the Presbyterians. Among the Scotch-Irish, allegiance to the Presbyterian church was strong, particularly in Taylor's native region. The Lexington Presbytery, based in the Rockbridge County seat, was founded in 1786, and nine of the thirteen churches in Rockbridge County in 1835 were Presbyterian.[41] All of William's grandparents were Presbyterian, and about the time of their marriage and William's birth, Stuart and Martha joined Bethesda church, a newly formed Presbyterian congregation near their home in Rockbridge Baths.[42] Presbyterians shared with Methodists a belief in the importance of a conversion experience. The minister responsible for organizing that congregation, Andrew B. Davidson, was remembered by others as a "very earnest preacher, shedding tears at times, when he plead with the unconverted to come to Christ."[43] William remembered him approvingly as "an earnest, impressive speaker, often causing his congregation to weep aloud on account of their shortcomings, and all the people of that region held the preacher in affectionate reference."[44]

Despite such positive statements about his childhood pastor, the Taylors became Methodist in 1833. William's account of those events do not mention or allude to theological differences between Methodists and Presbyterians as contributing to the decision. While it is unlikely a twelve-year-old boy would have been sensitive to such issues, as an adult, William would decry some Reformed doctrines such as that of election—the belief that God designated certain people, and not others, for salvation—as a threat to true Christianity, far more dangerous than higher criticism of the Bible or the theory of evolution.[45] Rather, the events that led Stuart and Martha to leave the Presbyterian church for the Methodists, and William's own entry into the Methodist church at the age of twelve, illustrate the importance of large-scale camp meeting revivalism to the American Methodist tradition, as well as the power revivalism exercised to bring about conversions through social pressure and family networks.

The Taylors became Methodists at the tail end of a period of spectacular growth for that denomination. In less than a century, Methodists had grown from a handful of members in 1760 to become the largest Christian denomination in the United States.[46] Historian John Wigger noted that the importance of camp meetings to American Methodists to this growth has been overemphasized. Camp meetings were, nonetheless, an important and well-established element in the Methodist evangelistic system, and by the 1830s, had been so for over a generation.[47]

With possible antecedents in gatherings of pietistic Protestants of central Europe and Scottish communion seasons, camp meetings became an American phenomenon at Cane Ridge, Kentucky, in 1801.[48] Methodists quickly made camp meetings their own by building on existing Methodist practices such as outdoor preaching and quarterly meetings—gatherings where several Methodist societies came together to handle business and worship. For organizers of camp meetings, the main goal was to provide a means for the conversion and salvation of those in attendance, which often took place through emotional and physical displays. The meetings also provided opportunities for social activity in sparsely populated regions as participants left homes for several days to attend the gatherings. These events were major religious and social events for small farmers of rural America.[49]

In William's retelling of his family's conversion, his father happened upon a Methodist preacher at the meeting house where their Presbyterian congregation met. Surprised to find a crowd gathered on a weekday, Stuart heard a message that provoked in him a period of spiritual turmoil. Two weeks later, on the pretext of taking cattle into the mountains to graze, Stuart took twelve-year-old William and a farmhand to a Methodist camp meeting at Cold Sulphur Springs, about 10 miles from the family home. There, William watched his father weep and confess his sins. On the way home, the following day, Stuart laughed and cried and witnessed to his son, "William I am converted to God; converted among the Methodists. God bless the Methodists! I hated and dreaded them, but God has wonderfully saved me at a Methodist camp meeting."[50]

These events clearly made a deep impression on William. Of note in his memory was the negative association of Methodism, both in Stuart's words and in the response of his family. On arriving home, Martha wept in grief at the news. Even years later, William remembered a social stigma attached to his family as a result of his father's actions. Martha's side of the family, in particular, was unhappy with the change, and William remembered that his maternal grandfather was cool to his religion and profession.[51] In 1833, when the family made their break with the Presbyterians, there were few Methodists in Rockbridge County.[52] In early America, Methodism spread principally among persons of English and African descent, never flourished in areas of Presbyterian strength, and frequently found growth difficult in places where existing religious institutions limited social space for a new religious movement.[53] Moreover, in colonial and early Republican America, Methodism was often considered an antisocial threat to social order, family stability, gender, and racial conventions.[54]

Soon, however, Martha and William followed Stuart into the Methodist fold. At another camp meeting a week later, they both joined the church.

William never recorded the story of his mother's conversion. Indeed, Taylor wrote very little about his mother at all. While it is tempting to extrapolate from silence into speculation about the nature of their relationship, it's not clear what conclusions could be drawn absent any evidence. Three things, however, are notable. First, Taylor's silence over the nature of his relationship with his mother would be replicated in his relationship with his wife. Second, there were women whose piety Taylor admired, and he would rely on them greatly in his work and ministry. If Taylor's mother (or wife) had demonstrated the piety he admired, he probably would have mentioned it. Finally, in following Stuart into Methodism, the Taylors were somewhat unusual. White women, not men, tended to lead their families into Methodism, were often among the initial converts, foundational leaders, and numerically dominant in the membership.[55]

Whatever the nature of Taylor's relationship with his mother or his parents' relationship with each other, the headstone placed at their grave memorialized both their marriage and their conversions. After Stuart and Martha died in 1874 and 1875, respectively, the couple were given a joint headstone, at the base of which was written, "They labored together, Together they rest. 'And their words do follow them.' Rev. 14:13."[56] In addition to their dates of birth, marriage, and death, was inscribed for Stuart, "Born again John iii. 7 August 25th 1833." Martha's conversion a week and a day later is marked with the words, "Born again John iii 7, September 2nd, 1833."[57] For his part, Stuart became a leader in a new Methodist society in Rockbridge Baths. In time, he became a Methodist local preacher and was remembered in the community for his singing voice, a trait he seems to have passed to his son.[58]

William also became a member of the church at the same time as his mother following a somewhat comical series of events. Preachers told William to expect a sense of peace confirming that he had been saved, an experience Methodists called assurance. No doubt wishing to share what his parents had, William was distressed by his failure to feel anything. He was counseled that he would feel the desired sense of assurance if he shouted, "Glory to God for salvation in Jesus!"[59] The boy did so, and the exhorter counseling him responded with the shout, "Hallelujah! William is saved."[60] Quickly embraced by his father, William was swept up in the confusion of the moment and the joy of his parents. Narrating this story as an old man, Taylor claimed that he kept silent about the lack of spiritual peace he felt for fear of being seen as a hypocrite.[61] Perhaps so, but sharing an experience with and being accepted by one's parents brings its own kind of peace.

The conversion Taylor claimed made a lasting change in his life took place several years later at a camp meeting in Panther Gap, Virginia. Taylor recorded the most detailed account of this experience in his autobiography. Written many years after the fact, it was probably a well-rehearsed narrative told, like his earlier stories, with a message in mind. This story was told not only to celebrate what God had done for him but also that through his conversion, he had been empowered to serve God. Taylor was twenty years old at the time, and he noted that even though he lacked confidence in his own salvation, his leadership potential had been marked by church leaders—both Presbyterian and Methodist—who asked him to pray for the salvation of others. At camp meetings, however, these duties prevented him from going forward as a "seeker" who could receive prayers himself.[62] At Panther Gap, however, after the meeting closed for the night, he remained behind to pray. Two men encouraged him with song and words:

> And as I lay there in silence I realized the presence of an invisible person, seemingly but a few feet distant from me, and it came to my mind, "Jesus has come;" and in a moment I received him, and trusted him to take me in hand and do the best he could for one utterly abandoned and lost; and I sweetly realized in my soul, "O, he loves me; he saves me! I do love God, I do love the brethren, I have indeed passed from death unto life. Glory to God!"[63]

Though Satan tempted him to doubt, Taylor "rested on the bosom of Jesus, and he lifted up a standard against the enemy of my soul and kept me in safety."[64] From that moment on, Taylor claimed he "was as keen on the scent for souls as a setter after the game," seeking out other people for conversion.[65]

A different account of Taylor's conversion was recorded after Taylor had been elected bishop. James Gamble, the Methodist preacher in charge at the Panther Gap meeting, was asked to provide his memory of the new bishop's conversion. Gamble's story differs from Taylor's in several details, and is probably less reliable as a description of the events than Taylor's own. After over four decades, Gamble would probably not remember with specificity the conversion of one young man from countless camp meetings. Nevertheless, his story is worth noting because it presents another description of what such experiences might look like. Gamble recalled that when the camp broke for lunch, Taylor went with some others into a grove of trees. Before long the diners "heard the shout of glory up in the woods, and down came Wm. Taylor shouting glory into the Camp and through the Camp praising God."[66]

BECOMING A METHODIST PREACHER

On two accounts, Gamble's story rings true. First, such ecstatic demonstrations were often evident at camp meetings. Second, Gamble claimed he recommended that his successor as presiding elder on the district, N. J. Brown Morgan, keep watch on Taylor as a young man who might be of use in church leadership.[67] To feed and sustain growth of the church, Methodist preachers were proactive in identifying new leaders to fill positions and moving them into positions of greater responsibility.[68]

Historians have long credited the organizational structure of the Methodist Episcopal Church as a contributing factor to the church's rapid growth in early nineteenth-century America. The structure was easily replicable in new regions, and Methodist itinerants were eager organizers. The foundational body of American Methodist organization was the annual conference. In Taylor's time, this was a yearly gathering of preachers responsible for the church's work in a designated region. Preachers in an annual conference met to worship, examine the character of existing preachers, approve new ones, and handle other church business. An authoritative bishop presided over that meeting and dispatched those preachers to new preaching appointments within that conference. For administrative oversight, conferences were subdivided into districts supervised by preachers called presiding elders. Local fellowships of Methodists, or societies, relied on strong lay leadership to sustain Methodist piety between the visits of a preacher and to maintain continuity as preachers came and went. Each Methodist society was subdivided into classes.[69] Class leaders were laity who exercised pastoral care over their class. Laity could also be licensed as exhorters who gave public testimony to their faith and encouraged others. New itinerants were recruited from among those lay leaders.[70]

Descriptions of this structure, however, are only the skeleton of antebellum Methodism. Human relationships gave that skeleton muscle and brought it to life. As with his childhood memories, Taylor's reminiscences of the first years of his career were recorded when he was an old man. While time may have dimmed some recollections, Taylor's writing recalls with affection the names of his mentors, earliest colleagues, and laity he served. Some of that warmth was the glow of nostalgia. But it was also a mark of the intensity of his relationships with people who nurtured him as a young adult and became his friends and role models.

Shortly after his conversion, Taylor was licensed as an exhorter following the recommendation of the preacher in charge of the circuit and the approval of his local Methodist society. From the fall of 1841 until the following October, Taylor served in this capacity at meetings led by visiting preachers. In the absence of a preacher, he led prayer meetings twice a week. In this way, Taylor began to learn the skills that were deemed essential to being an effective Methodist preacher.[71] The remainder of Taylor's time was spent in school. He completed his formal education at a normal school in Lexington, and taught for three months at Rapp's School House in South Buffalo, Virginia.[72]

In the summer of 1842, Taylor and some friends, including the snake-hunting companion of his childhood, attended a camp meeting in neighboring

Botetourt County. Morgan, then the presiding elder of the Rockingham District, informed Taylor that he wanted to send him out as a preacher. Taylor hesitantly agreed.[73] In many ways, Taylor fit the template for Methodist preachers that had been established in the early days of American Methodism. He came from the middling artisan class, had experienced a dramatic mystical conversion, and began his preaching career as a young adult.[74]

Befitting a clergy that came from tradespeople, early American Methodism spurned formal education for its clergy and instead trained preachers using an apprenticeship model. New preachers were matched with more experienced ones, and in that way they were taught the skills of their evangelistic trade.[75] Morgan initially proposed sending Taylor to work with Francis A. Harding, who would later become known for his role in the debate that split the Methodist Episcopal Church over slavery. For reasons unknown, Morgan reconsidered and instead sent Taylor to serve as the junior preacher on the Franklin circuit, directing him first to complete a round on his home circuit.[76]

On October 1, 1842, at the age of twenty-one, with a horse, reins, and saddlebag given him by his father, Taylor began his career as a Methodist preacher. Over the next several years, Taylor served as the junior preacher on various circuits of the Rockingham District. Although paired with several different senior preachers, it was Morgan who became Taylor's first mentor and advocate in the church. Taylor wrote little about what the relationship meant to him but the bond was clearly important. He described Morgan as his "nursing father," and Taylor would name his first child Stuart Morgan to honor both his father and mentor.[77]

From that October day until his death, Taylor rarely stopped traveling. While the global scope of his travels was unusual, the idea that a preacher would constantly itinerate was a characteristic Methodist practice. Because preachers regularly moved to new appointments within the conference and often traveled within their appointments on a circuit, they described their ministry as itinerancy. When an itinerant left the ministry, he was said to have located. In rural areas, such as those where Taylor began his career, itinerancy meant that preachers could expect to travel and minister on a regular tour through a large portion of the countryside entrusted to them. These regions were known as circuits, and Methodist preachers were also known as circuit riders. When Taylor entered the Methodist ministry, a preacher could expect to be appointed to a new circuit every year or two.[78]

The life of an itinerant was a difficult one, requiring sacrifice. But it was a sacrifice that those committed to it found filled with meaning and purpose. They saw themselves as members of a select fraternity of heroic men called to share their gospel with the world.[79] One of those itinerants, James Watts, served as a Methodist itinerant in western Virginia and Rockingham County for over a decade.[80] Reflecting on the sacrifices of his calling, Watts prayed in his journal,

> I have in some time forsaken father and mother, brothers and sisters for thy sake, and for the sake of preaching the gospel as a traveling preacher; And now for a number of years I have left my wife & children, more than half of my time and sometimes more than seven eights [*sic*] of my time to proclaim salvation in the name of Jesus, to a lost world. And shall I do no good. Shall my labors be all in vain. Shall I undergo so many privations, and trials and all for nothing. O my GOD, let me feel for the souls of the people. May I feel tenderly and labor earnestly for the good of souls. O for grace to help me.[81]

Such men became Taylor's role models as he entered into that fraternity himself.

Taylor's first foray into the life of a Methodist preacher was well received. At a quarterly meeting held for church business on his circuit, Taylor was recommended to be admitted into the itinerancy. Members of the Franklin circuit also petitioned the bishop to reappoint Taylor to them. The request was denied, but the petition no doubt boosted the young man's self-confidence. The following two years, Taylor itinerated on the Deerfield and then the Fincastle circuit, all in familiar regions of western Virginia. The Deerfield circuit came within 10 miles of his home, and Fincastle was in neighboring Botetourt County.[82]

Taylor was preceded on the Deerfield circuit by another early friend, Charles A. Reid. Although Taylor wrote little about Reid, Taylor would bequeath his name to another son. It is easy to see why the two were friends. Both young men were from Rockbridge Baths, came from Presbyterian families, and entered the Methodist ministry months apart. While their regular duties as preachers prevented them from spending much time together as young adults, Taylor recalled that in those early years they traveled to and roomed together at annual conference. Unlike Taylor, Reid would spend his career in the Baltimore Conference, serving mostly in Maryland, until his death in 1890.[83]

Although Methodists did not consider formal schooling to be necessary for their clergy, learning was not rejected. By 1816, the practice of apprenticeship was supplemented by an educational curriculum known as the Course of Study. In this program, preachers were expected to become versed in a curriculum of books on subjects ranging from the Bible to church history, theology, philosophy, English grammar, and composition. Before a young man would be approved and admitted into full connection as a Methodist preacher, he would be examined on those subjects.[84] It is worth noting that this educational program was considered the capstone of the training process of Methodist preachers, and not its foundation. Taylor was not examined on his competence in these fields until after he had been preaching regularly for two and a half years and demonstrated his abilities as an itinerant preacher. In preparation for his examination, Taylor read the books in this course of study while traveling on horseback to his appointments and early each morning, taking notes on each book.[85]

Despite this study, Methodists emphasized holy living over doctrinal orthodoxy and effective preaching over theological precision. Preachers were also expected to demonstrate their commitment to the itinerant system and the sacrifices it demanded. In the early years of American Methodism, marriage and family life had been the greatest challenge to the Methodist system. Preachers who chose to marry were generally required to locate. By the mid-nineteenth century, marriage had become less of an obstacle to the ministry.[86] Nevertheless, in Taylor's conference, it was prohibited until after two years of service, and a preacher who married before his fourth year could be censured. Accordingly, the only question Taylor remembered being asked in his examination was one asked of all candidates: were they engaged to be married? Many candidates simply admitted they were. Taylor, however, provoked a discussion when he stated that he had no "confirmed" engagement and would "not consummate any such till I have served four years as a single man."[87]

Taylor's ambiguous and suggestive reply was due to the fact that he had recently begun to court his future wife, Isabelle Anne Kimberlin. The oldest child of Jacob Kimberlin and Harriet Richey, Anne, as she called herself, was born in Virginia in February 1825. The Kimberlins migrated to Alabama, where Anne spent her early years. By 1843, the family had returned to Botetourt County, Virginia. Her mother had died some time previously, and in that year her father died. Anne appeared in court records at the age of eighteen when she and her younger siblings were listed as orphans.[88] William and Anne met during his time on the Fincastle circuit when she, her three sisters, and brother joined the Methodist church. Sometime after February 1845, the two became engaged.[89]

Unfortunately, the historical record both at this stage of life and later rarely provides access to Anne's voice and actions, interests, and motivations. The few exceptions to this silence in the sources will be noted. Most contemporary mentions of Anne celebrated her as a wife who sacrificed herself for the sake of her husband's global ministry. This was certainly the case and a common role for minister's wives in nineteenth-century America.[90] Several instances indicate, however, that Anne was less than willing in her sacrifices. She would be forced into a sacrificial role because over the course of his life, William prioritized the demands of his ministry over family life and her wishes.

For the appointment year of 1845–1846, Taylor was sent to be the preacher on a new circuit in Virginia, known as Sweet Springs. Straddling present-day Virginia and West Virginia, it was formed from parts of two preexisting circuits and some new territory that Methodist itinerants had not yet entered.[91] As such, Sweet Springs offered a professional challenge. Taylor was responsible for regularizing the Methodist presence in the region. As he later wrote, organizing the circuit was "the thing I was sent to do."[92] To that end, he visited scattered farms and settlements to find if any Methodists lived in the area, determined a schedule of preaching appointments at private homes or public buildings, and assigned lay leaders to conduct class meetings.[93] Much of the growth of the Methodist church in the early nineteenth century was the result of this kind of organizing effort on the rural frontier.[94]

In this first solo venture, Taylor proved himself quite successful. To the preexisting Methodists in the region, Taylor added about 100 new converts, so that by the end of his tenure the membership of the circuit totaled 308.[95] Membership growth was only one measure of success. One of the principal challenges that a Methodist preacher faced in an unorganized region such as Sweet Springs was that no reliable mechanism for financial support existed. Methodist itinerants lived Spartan lifestyles but still needed money. As a single man, Taylor was entitled to a salary of $100, to be collected as voluntary contributions on the circuit with the conference covering any shortfall.[96] It was no small task to convince rural settlers with little disposable cash to support a preacher.[97] By the end of his year, however, Taylor had collected more salary than he was entitled. The surplus was given to the conference to cover deficits on other circuits. In recognition of the firm financial foundation of the circuit, the following year a married preacher, entitled to $200, was appointed to Sweet Springs.[98]

Taylor's success was noted by his church's superiors who moved this promising young minster to increasingly prominent positions. Here both Taylor's prioritization of his ministry over family life and Morgan's patronage were evident. In early 1846, while William's four-year period to serve as a single man was not yet completed, and Morgan's tenure as Presiding Elder in the Rockingham District was ending, Morgan encouraged him to marry Anne and accept the conference's censure. He promised to arrange for William to be appointed to a station church in Christiansburg, Virginia. In this way, the couple would be given some stability and live relatively close to home as they began their life together. William refused the offer and insisted on fulfilling his four-year obligation before marrying. Next, Morgan attempted to arrange for Taylor to be appointed with him as a junior preacher at Foundry church in the District of Columbia. In this, Morgan was unsuccessful, but Taylor was appointed as the junior preacher in nearby Georgetown, to congregations known today as Dumbarton and Mt. Zion United Methodist Church, under Henry Taring. Nevertheless, Morgan insisted that the two dine together weekly.[99]

Georgetown, at the time, was an independent town within the federal District of Columbia. A port on the Potomac River predating the national capital, it attracted commerce and a cosmopolitan and fashionable mix of people who lived there and commuted to Washington.[100] Coming from the country, Taylor probably experienced some sense of dislocation adjusting to town living. He alluded to such in his autobiography. He certainly experienced new interactions with the different social classes that made up Methodism in the capital city and the wider nation. The tension that emerged could be particularly acute in places like Georgetown where different people lived and worshipped close at hand. Taylor's recollections of those years noted his discomfort with the social ways of the upper class but also his pleasure at finding himself moving in centers of national power.[101]

Based on patterns he demonstrated later in life, Taylor likely took advantage of opportunities Georgetown afforded him to satisfy his curiosity about other ways of life. On one occasion, Taylor and other Methodists toured Georgetown College (now University), the first Roman Catholic institution of higher learning in the United States.[102] Like other Protestants, American Methodists of the era were concerned that Roman Catholicism represented a threat to the nation. Nativist sentiment was on the rise in the 1840s.[103] An article in the Methodist press detailing the tour expressed alarm that some Methodist youth studied at this Catholic school and indignation at what the correspondent saw as Jesuit trickery to inculcate their faith in their pupils.[104] Such accusations were staples of Methodist, anti-Catholic literature.[105] In time, Taylor would articulate a more nuanced perspective on immigration and Catholicism. He argued immigration offered an opportunity for evangelism, rather than a threat to the American republic, and sought ways to engage with, rather than simply oppose, Roman Catholic beliefs.

In Taylor's second year in Georgetown, Thomas Sewell replaced Tarring. Sewell became ill, however, and most of the work of the charge fell to Taylor. To help with the extra responsibilities, Taylor sought out the help of Methodists who had come to the city to work in the government.[106] Notable among these was Henry W. Hilliard, a Whig member of the House of Representatives from Alabama. Hilliard had been a Methodist preacher in South Carolina and Alabama, and an educator, before turning to a career in law and politics. He believed in the legality of slavery but was pro-Union. During the Civil War, Hilliard briefly commanded a Confederate regiment, and in Reconstruction, he cast himself as a scalawag Republican. Hilliard would be appointed Minister to Brazil, where he authored an important letter supporting emancipation in that country.[107] Taylor also befriended Henry Slicer, a Methodist preacher and Senate chaplain.[108] These visits to the Capitol also allowed Taylor the opportunity to hear the oratory of Henry Clay and Daniel Webster as they debated war with Mexico, and on one occasion, Taylor met and preached to President James K. Polk.[109]

Despite these brushes with power, as the junior preacher in Georgetown, part of Taylor's responsibility was to minister to black Methodists in town. In 1814, they had built a separate church, known as Mount Zion, becoming the first African American congregation in the District of Columbia. Taylor's service there was a mark both of enduring racism and increasing segregation in the Methodist Episcopal Church and the unwillingness of the Methodist Episcopal Church to fully ordain black preachers. Throughout 1846, Taylor preached and taught that congregation's Sunday school. Such schools were the only options for education open to blacks in Georgetown, and Taylor later recalled with some pride that one of his pupils was scolded by her owners as being "saucy" and "spoiled" for what Taylor had taught her.[110]

In the 1840s, the future of slavery was a hotly contested issue in America. In contrast to most historiography that has portrayed Taylor as a maverick and rebel, all available evidence suggests that on this issue he sought to avoid controversy. But to play the moderate in a conflicted time was not easy, and as the debate over slavery took shape among American Methodists, Taylor's own Baltimore Conference was a battleground. Straddling the free state of Pennsylvania, the slave states of Maryland and Virginia, and the federally controlled District of Columbia, moderation on the slavery issue was valued by conference leaders as the best way to reach the most people. If a preacher owned slaves in Virginia, he could not minister in Pennsylvania, and a preacher with strong antislavery convictions could not serve Virginia slave owners. The Baltimore Conference consistently prevented its preachers from maintaining any connection with slavery, but strong antislavery opinions were also viewed with suspicion. Tarring and Taylor's predecessors at Georgetown may have been moved from this appointment because their antislavery stance offended the congregation.[111]

In 1844, this debate reached a boiling point both in the Baltimore Conference and in the Methodist Episcopal Church as a whole when Francis Harding came into possession of five slaves by marriage. Rather than follow the direction of the conference to manumit these slaves in order to maintain his status as a Methodist preacher, Harding appealed the decision to the General Conference—the legislative body governing the church. Every four years, annual conferences sent delegates to this national—and eventually international—assembly to deal with issues facing the whole denomination. The 1844 General Conference refused to overturn Baltimore's decision. Moreover, it required Bishop James Andrew who had also come into possession of slaves by marriage to refrain from acting as bishop while he owned slaves. White southern Methodists, who had campaigned for the election of a slaveholding bishop, announced they would leave the church. Plans were formulated that resulted in division along sectional lines. In 1846, the Methodist Episcopal Church, South, was formed.[112]

Reaction to the Harding and Andrew decisions and the formation of the southern church varied in the Baltimore Conference. In 1846, the preachers of that conference voted unanimously to remain in the (northern) Methodist Episcopal Church. At the same time, a resolution was overwhelmingly passed rejecting abolitionism and refusing to make non-slaveholding a requirement for church membership. For the next several years, rumors often circulated that individual preachers or churches would transfer to the southern church, and several did so. For the next decade and a half, up to and after the start of the American Civil War, Methodist societies in the region split over the issue.[113]

Taylor tried to avoid controversy and to keep quiet about slavery as much as possible. Silence became impossible, however, after William and Anne were married on October 21, 1846.[114] Anne was the joint heir, with her young sisters and brother, to two families of fourteen slaves—Samuel and Lucy Kimberlain, their seven children (Calvin, Albert, Paralee, Samuel, Aminda, Anderson, and John), and Maria White and her four children (George W., John, Jane, and James). With his marriage, Taylor suddenly found himself in a position almost identical to that of Harding and Andrew two years earlier.[115]

Taylor was called to address this problem at the 1847 meeting of the Baltimore Conference. He stated his desire to free the slaves he had inherited but explained that immediate divestment of his new connection to slavery was not an option without creating other moral problems. Anne shared the title to these persons with her minor siblings. Until her siblings reached their majorities, the only way that inheritance could be divided would be to sell the slaves or separate their families. Taylor expressed the hope that when the time came, his sisters-in-law and brother-in-law would consent to manumission. In the meantime, Taylor asked that the conference accept his pledge to free everyone who came to him through his wife. This pledge was accepted, and Taylor passed his examination to be ordained Elder in the church and complete the ordination process in his church.[116]

In 1852 the Kimberlains and Whites, who remained in Virginia when the Taylors went to California, were freed and given a thousand dollars and passage to Liberia with the American Colonization Society.[117] In 1847, however, that outcome was not guaranteed. Slaves often learned that a pledge of freedom was not the same as freedom. If Taylor had died, or if one of Anne's siblings refused to cooperate, the plan would have unraveled. In addition, the fact that these slaves were freed should not obscure that this was a moment of choice for Taylor. Without much difficulty, he could have affiliated with the Methodist Episcopal Church, South, and kept his wife's inheritance. It is also notable that manumission of these slaves was another example of William prioritizing his own career over the desires of his wife. In a letter written many years later, Anne intimated that she may have been an unwilling participant in this plan. The slaves were her inheritance, after all. She called them "my slave patrimony."[118] Certainly at the time, Taylor's moderate stance that avoided discussion of the morality of slavery, and focused on legal issues and a desire for family unity—both his own and that of the slaves—was well received by church leaders. It both avoided conflict and maintained loyalty to the church. In the following year, Taylor's moderation was rewarded, and he was appointed to Baltimore.

Taylor's move to Baltimore in early 1848 meant that he narrowly missed becoming involved in an event that illustrated how problematic the issue of slavery continued to be for Methodists. In part because the church claimed constituents on all sides and social locations of the issue, it wasn't always possible to avoid controversy. On April 15, 1848, just under eighty slaves, including some parishioners at Mt. Zion and other Methodist churches in the District, attempted to escape to freedom on board a schooner. The captain of the *Pearl*, a Methodist from New Jersey, was a party to this plan. Adverse tides and a storm delayed the escape, and the fugitives were caught and sold south. Slicer, who followed Sewall and Taylor at Georgetown, became embroiled in the episode when he appeared to sanction, or at least be indifferent to, the plight of those who were being transported and whose families were being broken up. Slicer was seen cordially greeting the slave driver, a man who had given money to a Methodist church in Baltimore where his wife and daughter were members.[119]

All this transpired shortly after Taylor left Georgetown. In March 1848, Taylor was appointed to North Baltimore. Although he was still the junior preacher on this circuit, this appointment was a clear sign that church leaders had marked Taylor as a preacher with potential. An appointment in that city carried with it a measure of prestige among Methodists. From the arrival of the first Methodist migrants to Maryland in the 1760s, Methodism had flourished around the shores of the Chesapeake Bay, and Baltimore was its first, unofficial "capital." Historian Russell E. Richey eulogized Baltimore as "the heart and soul of early Methodism, its center, its capital, its place of greatest strength, its site of its holiest memories, its Jerusalem."[120] By 1848, other Methodist urban centers, such as New York and Cincinnati, had emerged, but Baltimore remained important to American Methodists. Thus, in the span of only a few years, Taylor had drawn the favorable attention of his church's leaders and had been brought from the backcountry of Virginia to one of the principal urban centers of American Methodism. Taylor was clearly a young man going places. Those places would not ultimately be, however, in Baltimore.

BECOMING A METHODIST MISSIONARY

In January 1848, James Marshall discovered gold in a mill race being constructed by Mormon laborers for his business partner, John Sutter, on the American River in California. As news of the discovery spread, residents of the Pacific coast of North America, then peoples around the Pacific in Chile, the Pacific Islands, Australia, China, and finally, individuals from the eastern United States and Europe began to make their way to California in search of gold. It took almost a full year for news of the discovery to reach the eastern United States, where the start of the gold rush was marked by President Polk's December 1848 address confirming the discovery. Wherever the news reached, it put into motion a mass migration that historians have resorted to hyperbole to describe. Whether "the world rushed in" or the California gold rush represented "the most astonishing mass movement of peoples since the Crusades," the speed and global scope of it was unprecedented.[121]

Taylor would join this migration as a Methodist missionary. Most of his time in Baltimore would be spent preparing for his mission. But before he was recruited for that task and while news of gold slowly made its way east, Taylor faithfully began his ministry in North Baltimore by participating in various aspects of church and public life. Baltimore at the time was enjoying a period of prewar prosperity fueled by the city's emergence as a regional commercial center and steam-powered industries. This growth contributed to a rapid expansion of churches and church buildings in the city. Between 1843 and 1861 more new churches were formed than had previously existed in the city; nearly half of those new churches were Methodist.[122]

At his charge, Taylor was tasked with pastoral oversight at a Methodist chapel on Harford Avenue, and he shared preaching duties with the other preachers on his circuit at Exeter Street and Monument Street chapels. In the fall, these colleagues, with help from other area ministers, held a revival at Monument Street that the local press noted saw "a large number of persons . . . at the altar, uniting themselves with this branch of the Christian church."[123] In Georgetown, Taylor preached in city markets, and he continued that practice in the outdoor markets of Belair, near Baltimore.[124] Taylor found that these outdoor sermons served to publicize and attract people to revival services. When the Maryland governor declared November 23, 1848, a day of Thanksgiving, businesses closed and military companies paraded through the city. On the occasion, Colonel Pickell's Baltimore National Blues marched to Exeter Street to hear Taylor preach.[125] In addition, in August, at a camp meeting north of the city near the Pennsylvania line, Taylor preached on the doctrine of entire sanctification and first met Phoebe Palmer, a leading voice in the growing Wesleyan holiness movement, and a theologian who would influence Taylor's views on the doctrine.[126]

This theological doctrine was one that set Methodists apart from other Protestants and would be central to Taylor's own sense of missionary call. For Wesley, entire sanctification was an act of salvation beyond justification, or forgiveness of sins, that could be experienced in this life. In this view, the sanctified person was believed to have been delivered from the inclination to sin, defined as a voluntary transgression of God's law. Also referred to as full salvation, Christian perfection or holiness, entire sanctification was at once a gradual and an instantaneous experience, and like justification, sanctification could be lost and regained. The doctrine was carried to America by Methodist immigrants, but early American Methodists tended to emphasize primary evangelism over exhortations to Christian perfection and holiness.[127]

The 1830s saw a revival of interest in the doctrine, both in American Methodism and in American Christianity as a whole. In 1835 in New York, Palmer and her sister, Sarah Lankford, claimed experiences of sanctification and began holding meetings to promote the experience among other Christians. At Oberlin College, Ohio, Presbyterians Charles G. Finney and Asa Mahan experienced and began to proclaim the possibility of a second spiritual crisis like conversion that resulted in sanctification. In 1839, Timothy Merritt published *The Guide to Christian Perfection*, calling for special efforts to revive the doctrine among Methodists.[128]

Taylor had begun to seek entire sanctification in his early years as a preacher in Virginia. A schoolteacher on the Sweet Springs circuit gave Taylor copies of Merritt's *Guide*, and he read other classic Methodist texts on the subject. At camp meetings, he heard preachers expound on sanctification but found that the experience eluded him.[129] As he wrote, "I always responded to such calls and went forward for entire sanctification, but without success."[130]

In 1845, Taylor finally entered the desired state. His experience was precipitated by his worry that he had committed to preach in two different places the same day. He was concerned that failure to fulfill his commitments would damage his reputation and future ministry. While considering his conflicting commitments late one night, Taylor was struck by the power of God's promises. He wrote,

> In a moment the oft-repeated fact went through me like an electric shock, "With God all things are possible." I nestled on the bosom of Jesus and rested my weary head and heart near to the throbbing heart of infinite love and sympathy. I laughed and cried, and said, "Yes, all things are possible with God. He can arrange for two appointments at the same hour twenty miles apart. I don't know how. He may have a dozen ways of doing it, and I will let him to do it in any way he may choose. Yes, and I will let him do anything else he had engaged for me."[131]

In the end, a lay person offered to cover one of the appointments and removed the conflict. Although he was not praying for holiness, Taylor claimed that in this experience he "was fully united to [God] in the bonds of mutual fidelity, confidence, and love."[132]

Although occasioned by conflict and experienced in an instant, Taylor understood holiness to be an ongoing state that shaped all of life's decisions. Taylor's commitment to his sanctification would become a defining aspect of his life. His desire to maintain that spiritual state would drive many of his life choices, including his decision to become a missionary to California in late 1848.

In May of that year, as a treaty ending the US war with Mexico moved toward ratification, but before word of gold reached the east, the Methodist Episcopal General Conference voted to send two missionaries to newly conquered California. Tasked with selecting these men, Bishop Beverly Waugh considered many applicants. In October, he made his first selection, an Indiana minister named Isaac Owen.[133] Taylor would be the second. Unlike Owen or others who volunteered for the job, however, Taylor did not seek appointment as a missionary. While Methodist preachers were appointed to their charges by a bishop, those sent as missionaries were traditionally selected from volunteers.[134] It is not readily apparent, therefore, why Waugh approached Taylor or why Taylor agreed to become a missionary. Indeed, other than a membership in the Missionary Society of his church, Taylor had demonstrated no special interest in missions.[135] Nevertheless, at some point late in 1848, Waugh summoned Taylor to make the offer.[136]

Waugh certainly weighed practical considerations. Having selected in Owen a missionary who would travel overland, a missionary sent by ship from the east coast could transport books and other resources to supply the new mission. Taylor's character and health were also elements in Waugh's decision. Dependability, good health, and a measure of experience were certainly important qualities that would serve the mission well. He would describe Taylor to Owen as "a most reliable man" with "a robust Constitution—is pious, zealous—steady & uniform," a "Tried man," and "all that you could reasonably expect in a Colleague."[137]

Beyond these qualities, one tantalizing possibility behind Taylor's selection rests in an encounter Taylor had with an unnamed bishop of his church at a love feast in Baltimore. This incident illustrates some potentially empowering and disrupting effects of the doctrine of entire sanctification, and its impact on Taylor's choices. At love feasts, Methodists gave testimonies to the ways they believed God had been at work in their lives. According to Taylor, the bishop in question testified that although he believed that entire sanctification was available to all believers, he himself had not yet attained it. Taylor found this message disturbing. He worried the bishop's words would put new converts off the pursuit of full salvation, if even a bishop of the church could not claim it after decades of faith. At the same time, Taylor worried that, as a young preacher, it would be arrogant for him to claim publically for himself a spiritual blessing that his superior in the church could not. As the love feast proceeded, Taylor struggled in prayer and felt Satan tempting him to keep silent. In the end, Taylor believed he emerged victorious from his spiritual struggle by rising to give testimony to his sanctification to the congregation.[138]

Taylor never named the unsanctified bishop of his story but it was likely Waugh. Taylor was only in Baltimore for a few months before Waugh consulted him about the California mission, and Waugh lived and was based in the city. If so, it is tempting to speculate that Taylor may have been sent to California as a punishment to a young upstart who needed to learn his place. Punitive appointments were not unheard of for rebellious preachers. For his part, Taylor claimed he had no reason to think he had offended the bishop in question. He saw his missionary appointment as a statement of Waugh's confidence, not repudiation.[139]

Whatever the case, this episode clearly illustrates the influence of Palmer's theology on Taylor's sense of missionary call and the potential of the doctrine of entire sanctification, particularly as articulated by Palmer, both to uncouple spiritual authority from ecclesiastical or social hierarchy and to be an important impetus to Methodist missionary work. In Palmer's theology, sanctification was readily available to all believers. It began with the Christian consecrating himself or herself to Christ and surrendering everything to God. She described Christ as the "altar" that made the believer holy. In faith, he or she was then to trust in God's will. Finally, the believer was to give testimony to his or her sanctification. This last stage—testimony—was a critical stage in the process, because the refusal to testify would result in the loss of one's sanctification. To remain silent when given an opportunity to testify was to jeopardize one's own salvation.[140] Within a generation, Methodist women inspired and empowered by their own experiences of entire sanctification would organize the Woman's Foreign Missionary Society of the Methodist Episcopal Church as a missionary organization separate from the official mission board of their denomination.[141]

Taylor certainly believed his sanctification was his chief missionary qualification, and references to it and to Palmer's themes of sacrifice of self, trust in God's will, and the obligation to testify infused both contemporary and later accounts of his missionary call. Newspaper descriptions of a farewell worship service for the missionary family in April 1849 noted that Taylor spoke to the congregation about his motives for being a missionary.[142] These were described as being "fully sacrificed to California. His whole heart was there," and he offered everything—"home, country, friends, life"—to God.[143]

As Taylor wrote his friend, James Sewell, from California two years later, "We are all well and still walking in 'the way of Holiness.' I still, as firmly as ever, believe in the doctrine of entire sanctification to God, Tis that alone that will enable us as a church to fulfill the great end for which God raised us up."[144] Just after Taylor's appointment was official, Palmer wrote the Taylors to give them her advice as they started their missionary career. She related an anecdote of "a plain man of ordinary talents" who, empowered only by his sanctification, was able to provoke a revival in his town.[145] About his interview with Waugh, Taylor wrote of going to California:

> I had not thought of such a possibility, and had no thought of offering myself for that or any other specific work, but I was called to preach the Gospel by the Holy Spirit, under the old commission, "Go yet into all the world and preach the Gospel to every creature," and I suppose that includes California.[146]

Taylor went on to say that he placed himself at the bishop's disposal, and trusted that his choices would express God's will.

Also telling in Taylor's memory of this pivotal moment in his life was that the impact of this offer on Anne and his family came as an afterthought. Taylor agreed to the bishop's offer, but Waugh advised him to consult his wife first. William went home and told Anne what he and the bishop had discussed. According to the story, Anne retired to pray over the matter and soon returned with her consent. According to William, she said,

> Lord, Bishop Waugh wants to send us to California. Thou knowest, Lord, that I don't want to go, and can see no possible way of getting there; but all things are possible with thee, and if it is thy will to send us to California, give me the desire to go.[147]

William's account of this missionary call ends with Anne's experience of peace presented as a confirmation that a mission to California was God's will for them.

But Anne's initial reluctance should be noted. She had already given birth to the couple's first child, Morgan Stuart, and was expecting their second. The Taylors were also caring for Anne's two sisters, the oldest a widow in poor health, the youngest still a minor.[148] Relocation to the other side of the continent would not be easy.

Marital negotiations aside, Taylor's appointment to California as a Methodist missionary was finalized by Waugh on January 1, 1849, not long after news of gold in California had been confirmed in the east.[149] As a result, the Methodist mission to California took on a new urgency and excitement. The discovery of gold captivated Americans. For Baltimore's Methodists,

Taylor's mission provided an avenue to participate in the event vicariously. At church gatherings around Baltimore in early 1849, Taylor spoke about his plans for the mission and raised money and gifts. Contributions were directed toward the framing of a wooden chapel in Baltimore that would be disassembled and sent with Taylor to California. William was given a copy of Harper's *Illuminated Bible* to take with him.[150] In addition to paying the cost of transport, the Methodist Missionary Society in New York authorized Taylor to spend $200 to outfit himself for the mission.[151] Baltimore's Methodists offered other gifts to help the family build a nice and comfortable home once in California. Anne was presented with a counterpane to decorate their bed, and a Baltimore hardware merchant offered the Taylors the free gift of anything in his store.[152] By April 1849, preparations were complete. William, Anne, Morgan Stuart, and Anne's sisters departed Baltimore for California on a clipper ship, the *Andalucia*.[153] William began his life as a Methodist missionary.

This chapter has traced Taylor's early life and religious influences and illustrated some motivations that compelled Methodists like him to become missionaries. Taylor came of age in a social context that celebrated self-reliance as a virtue and considered pioneering a life in a new place a viable option. Such factors probably predisposed Taylor to accepting the sacrifices missionary life would require, but they did not make him a missionary. Taylor became a missionary because of what he understood it meant to be a Methodist. For Taylor, that religious identity was shaped in the early years of his life as he entered the membership of the Methodist Episcopal Church, joined its ministry, and adopted its theology and practices. Methodist beliefs such as God's free and saving grace for all people, the necessity for all to accept that grace with an emotional conversion and new birth, the imperative of living a life consecrated to God and in submission to God's will, and the duty of testifying to God's gracious work in one's life were the foundations of a Methodist missionary call. As an old man, Taylor knew he could tell this story of his early life and ministry to defend himself against his critics because he knew his story embodied a religious and theological identity shared by other Methodists. Those who embraced it, like Taylor, also embraced the missionary identity that came with it.

The next chapter will follow Taylor's work in California to illustrate the practices of the Methodist missionary tradition in America as American Methodists sought to bring their faith to Europeans who moved westward across the continent. San Francisco, however, would be a context unlike anything he—or anyone else—had ever experienced. Taylor's experience there would make him into a passionate and entrepreneurial supporter of cross-cultural missions. An unexpected catastrophe, however, would bring both an abrupt end to Taylor's time in California and launch him into the wider world.

NOTES

1. Wm. Taylor, "My Autobiography," *African News*, January 1889.
2. Benjamin Caulfield, "The Giant with Seven-League Boots," *Christian Advocate* 96 (April 28, 1921): 551; Elmer Riley Dille, "William Taylor, The Greatest Modern World-Herald of the Cross," *Methodist Review* 104 (September 1921): 680; Wade Crawford Barclay, *The Methodist Episcopal Church, 1845–1939: Widening Horizons, 1845–95*, vol. 3, History of Methodist Missions (New York: Board of Missions and Church Extension of the Methodist Church, 1957), 894; Ralph E. Diffendorfer, ed., *The World Service of the Methodist Episcopal Church* (Chicago: Methodist Episcopal Church, Council of Boards of Benevolence, Committee on Conservation and Advance, 1923), 109; Robert F. Lay, ed., *Lessons of Infinite Advantage: William Taylor's California Experiences: With Isabelle Anne Kimberlin Taylor's Travel Diary, 1866–67, Written During a Voyage with Her Family En Route from the Cape of Good Hope, South Africa, to London and Subsequent Travels Throughout Europe* (Lanham: Scarecrow Press and The Center for the Study of World Christian Revitalization Movements, 2010), 9; Halford E. Luccock, Paul Hutchinson, and Robert W. Goodloe, *The Story of Methodism* (New York: Abingdon, 1949).
3. "A Dangerous Crank," *New York Times*, April 10, 1885.
4. J. E. Abrams, "Bishop Taylor's Boyhood Home," *Christian Advocate*, July 24, 1902; Jonathan Bryan, Photo of Rev Stuart Taylor and Martha E. Taylor Headstone, Shaw Cemetery, Rockbridge County, VA, accessed May 5, 2018, www.findagrave.com/memorial/57481920/stuart-taylor.com; William Taylor, *Story of My Life; an Account of What I Have Thought and Said and Done in My Ministry of More Than Fifty-Three Years in Christian Lands and among the Heathen. Written by Myself*, ed. John Clark Ridpath (New York: Hunt & Eaton, 1896), 26.
5. Rockbridge County (Va.) Chancery Cases, 1781–1958. Admr. of Stuart Taylor v. Heir(s) of Stuart Taylor, 1899–005, Local Government Records Collection, Rockbridge Court Records, Library of Virginia; Wm. Taylor Membership Document, Daniel Steele Collection, 1824–1914, Manuscript History Collection, Boston University School of Theology; Taylor, *Story of My Life,* 25–26, 32.
6. David Hackett Fischer, *Albion's Seed: Four British Folkways in America* (New York: Oxford University Press, 1989), 606–18.
7. Taylor, *Story of My Life,* 32–33.
8. Abrams, "Bishop Taylor's Boyhood Home"; Photographs and Their Copies of William Taylor's Birthplace near Rockbridge Baths, Va, Bishop William Taylor Collection, Taylor University Archives; E. Estyn Evans, "The Scotch-Irish: Their Cultural Adaptation and Heritage in the American Old West," in *Essays in Scotch-Irish History*, ed. E. R. R. Green (London: Routledge & Kegan Paul, 1969), 84; Oren F. Morton, *A History of Rockbridge County, Virginia* (Staunton: McClure, 1920), 106; William Taylor, *Seven Years' Street Preaching in San Francisco, California Embracing Incidents, Triumphant Death Scenes, Etc*, ed. W. P. Strickland (New York: Published for the author by Carlton & Porter, 1856), 140; Taylor, *Story of My Life*, 26–27.

9. *Abstract of the Returns of the Fifth Census* . . . . (Washington, DC: Duff Green, 1832), 18; *Compendium . . . from the Returns of the Sixth Census,* . . . . (Washington, DC: Thomas Allen, 1841), 38.

10. Daniel Walker Howe, *What Hath God Wrought: The Transformation of America, 1815–1848* (New York: Oxford University Press, 2007), 125–32.

11. William Taylor, *Cause and Probable Results of the Civil War in America. Facts for the People of Great Britain* (London: Simpkin, Marshall, 1862).

12. Fischer, *Albion's Seed*, 687–90.

13. Taylor, *Story of My Life*, 33.

14. Morton, *History*, 275.

15. David Crockett, *A Narrative of the Life of David Crockett, of the State of Tennessee* (Philadelphia: E. L. Carey & A. Hart, 1834), 117–18; "Root, Hog, or Die," in *Dictionary of American Regional English*, ed. Joan Houston Hall (Cambridge: Belknap Press of Harvard University Press, 1985), 638.

16. Charles H. Faulkner, "'Here Are Frame Houses and Brick Chimneys': Knoxville, Tennessee, in the Late Eighteenth Century," in *The Southern Colonial Backcountry: Interdisciplinary Perspectives on Frontier Communities*, ed. David Colin Crass et al. (Knoxville: University of Tennessee Press, 1998), 154; For some examples of the folk song, see "Root Hog or Die, or, The Yankee Boys," Box 193, Item 209, "Root, Hog, or Die," Box 015, Item 114b, "Root Hog, or Die, or, Do Jog Along," Box 022, Item 024, Lester S. Levy Collection of Sheet Music, Special Collections at the Sheridan Libraries of the Johns Hopkins University, accessed March 29, 2012, http://levysheetmusic.mse.jhu.edu.

17. "Mr. Walker's Statement, with Comments," *Christian Advocate*, January 19, 1888; Mrs. C. B. Ward to Bishop W. J. Oldham, December 10, 1912, Missionary Files: Methodist Episcopal Church, 1912–1949 (misfiles), United Methodist Church Archives—GCAH; Goodsil F. Arms, *History of the William Taylor Self-Supporting Missions in South America* (New York: Methodist Book Concern, 1921), 49.

18. Taylor, *Story of My Life*, 26.

19. Eric Burin, "A Manumission in the Mountains: Slavery and the African Colonization Movement in Southwestern Virginia," *Appalachian Journal* 33, no. 2 (2006): 164–86.

20. 1830 Census, Rockbridge Co., Virginia (Series: M19; Roll: 199; Page: 339), accessed June 25, 2018, Ancestry.com.

21. 1840 Census, Rockbridge Co., Virginia (page 161), accessed June 25, 2018, Ibid.

22. 1850 Slave Schedules, Rockbridge Co., Virginia (Northeast District, page 167), accessed June 25, 2018, Ibid.; 1860 Slave Schedule, Rockbridge Co., Virginia (District 6, page 52), accessed June 25, 2018, Ibid.

23. Registration of Cyrus Taylor, October 8, 1834, Rockbridge County (Va.) Register of Free Negroes, 1831–1860, Library of Virginia.

24. Neely Young, *Ripe for Emancipation: Rockbridge and Southern Antislavery from Revolution to Civil War* (Buena Vista: Mariner Publishing, 2011), 1–8, 49–50, 63.

25. Taylor, *Story of My Life*, 31.

26. Ibid., 34.

27. Ibid.; William Taylor, *Ten Years of Self-Supporting Missions in India* (New York: Phillips & Hunt, 1882), 92–96.

28. D. Bruce Hindmarsh, *The Evangelical Conversion Narrative: Spiritual Auto-biography in Early Modern England* (New York: Oxford University Press, 2005), 8–15.

29. David Bebbington, *Evangelicalism in Modern Britain: A History from the 1730s to the 1980s* (London: Routledge, 1993), 5–10.

30. Richard P. Heitzenrater, *Wesley and the People Called Methodists* (Nashville: Abingdon Press, 2013), 11–13.

31. Taylor, *Ten Years*, 92–96, 225–6.

32. Jay Riley Case, *An Unpredictable Gospel: American Evangelicals and World Christianity, 1812–1920* (New York: Oxford University Press, 2012), 136–44.

33. Sylvia R. Frey and Betty Wood, *Come Shouting to Zion: African American Protestantism in the American South and British Caribbean to 1830* (Chapel Hill: University of North Carolina Press, 1998), 82–84; William Gravely, "'…Many of the Poor Affricans Are Obedient to the Faith': Reassessing the African American Presence in Early Methodism," in *Methodism and the Shaping of American Culture*, ed. Nathan O. Hatch and John H. Wigger (Nashville: Kingswood Books, 2001), 175–95; Heitzenrater, *Wesley and the People*, 343; Cynthia Lynn Lyerly, *Methodism and the Southern Mind, 1770–1810* (New York: Oxford University Press, 1998), 64–65.

34. Russell E. Richey, Kenneth E. Rowe, and Jean Miller Schmidt, *The Methodist Experience in America: A History* (Nashville: Abingdon Press, 2010), 143–6.

35. Richard S. Newman, *Freedom's Prophet: Bishop Richard Allen, the AME Church, and the Black Founding Fathers* (New York: New York University Press, 2008), 158–82.

36. Gravely, "…Many of the Poor," 187.

37. Albert M. Cupp, *A History of Methodism in Rockbridge County, Virginia* (n.p., n.d.), 12.

38. Registration of Othello Richards, October 2, 1848, Rockbridge County (VA) Register of Free Negroes, 1831–1860, Library of Virginia.

39. "List of Emigrants," *African Repository and Colonial Journal* 26, no. 8 (August 1850): 248.

40. Tom W. Shick, *Behold the Promised Land: A History of Afro-American Settler Society in Nineteenth-Century Liberia* (Baltimore: Johns Hopkins University Press, 1980), 77–82.

41. Morton, *History*, 106; Howard McKnight Wilson, *The Lexington Presbytery Heritage: The Presbytery of Lexington and Its Churches in the Synod of Virginia, Presbyterian Church in the United States* (Verona: McClure Press, 1971), 73, 84.

42. Henry Miller, *Sketch of Bethesda Church, Lexington Presbytery, Virginia* (Richmond: Whittet & Shepperson, 1910), 26.

43. Ibid., 14–15.

44. Taylor, *Story of My Life*, 26.

45. William Taylor, *How to Be Saved and How to Save the World. Vol. 1* (Adelaide: Alfred Waddy, 1866), Chapters 6–7.

46. Roger Finke and Rodney Stark, "How the Upstart Sects Won America: 1776–1850," *Journal for the Scientific Study of Religion* 28, no. 1 (1989): 31.

47. John H. Wigger, *Taking Heaven by Storm: Methodism and the Rise of Popular Christianity in America* (Urbana: University of Illinois Press, 2001), 96.

48. Leigh Eric Schmidt, *Holy Fairs: Scottish Communions and American Revivals in the Early Modern Period* (Princeton: Princeton University Press, 1989); W. R. Ward, *The Protestant Evangelical Awakening* (Cambridge: Cambridge University Press, 1992), 71–77; Paul K. Conkin, *Cane Ridge: America's Pentecost* (Madison: University of Wisconsin Press, 1990), 64–114.

49. Russell E. Richey, *Early American Methodism* (Bloomington: Indiana University Press, 1991), 21–32; Richey, Rowe, and Schmidt, *Methodist Experience*, 83–84; Karen B. Westerfield Tucker, *American Methodist Worship* (New York: Oxford University Press, 2011), 74–78.

50. Taylor, *Story of My Life*, 26–28.

51. Ibid., 28, 49.

52. Cupp, *History*, 11–13.

53. David Hempton, "Methodist Growth in Transatlantic Perspective, ca. 1770–1850," in *Methodism and the Shaping of American Culture*, ed. Nathan O. Hatch and John H. Wigger (Nashville: Kingswood Books, 2001), 41–85; David Hempton, *Methodism: Empire of the Spirit* (New Haven: Yale University Press, 2005), 19–20.

54. Lyerly, *Methodism*, 146–75.

55. Ibid., 100–1.

56. Bryan, Photo of Taylor Headstone.

57. Ibid.

58. 1870 Census, Rockbridge Co., Virginia (Roll: M593_1675; Page: 451B), accessed June 25, 2018, Ancestry.com; Cupp, *History*, 28–30.

59. Taylor, *Story of My Life*, 36.

60. Ibid.

61. Ibid.

62. Ibid., 39–40.

63. Ibid.

64. Ibid., 40.

65. Ibid.

66. James Gamble to Bro. Widerman, November 16, 1885, William Taylor Collection, Lovely Lane Museum and Archives.

67. Ibid.

68. Donald G. Mathews, "The Second Great Awakening as an Organizing Process: 1780–1830: An Hypothesis," *American Quarterly* 21, no. 1 (1969): 36.

69. Ibid.; William Warren Sweet, *Religion on the American Frontier: Vol. IV The Methodists: A Collection of Source Material* (Chicago: University of Chicago Press, 1946), 31–50.

70. Jennifer L. Woodruff Tait, "Laity," in *The Cambridge Companion to American Methodism*, ed. Jason E. Vickers (New York: Cambridge University Press, 2013), 191–5.

71. Wm. Taylor Membership Document; Taylor, *Story of My Life*, 42–43.

72. Cupp, *History*, 70.

73. Taylor, *Story of My Life*, 43.

74. Wigger, *Taking Heaven by Storm*, 48–55.

75. Ibid., 71.

76. Taylor, *Story of My Life*, 45–46.

77. *Minutes of the Annual Conferences of the Methodist Episcopal Church . . . 1873* (New York: Nelson & Phillips, 1873), 28–30; Taylor, *Story of My Life*, 43–46.

78. Wigger, *Taking Heaven by Storm*, 56–62.

79. Ibid., 62–64.

80. John W. Hedges, *Crowned Victors: The Memoirs of Over Four Hundred Methodist Preachers, Including the First Two Hundred and Fifty Who Died on This Continent* (Baltimore: Methodist Episcopal Book Depository, 1878), 384.

81. Diary of James Watts, Bessie McNear O'Neal Papers, 1805–ca. 1877 and n.d., Accession #4452, Special Collections, University of Virginia Library.

82. *Minutes of the Annual Conference of the Methodist Episcopal Church, . . . 1839–45* (New York: T. Mason and G. Lane, 1840), 331, 438; Taylor, *Story of My Life*, 46–51.

83. *Minutes of the Annual Conferences of the Methodist Episcopal Church: Spring Conferences of 1890* (New York: Hunt & Eaton, 1890), 112–13; Cupp, *History*, 30.

84. *The Doctrines and Discipline of the Methodist Episcopal Church, 1848* (New York: Lane & Scott, 1848), 215–18; Stan Ingersol, "Education," in *The Cambridge Companion to American Methodism*, ed. Jason E. Vickers (New York: Cambridge University Press, 2013), 256–66; Gerald O. McCulloh, *Ministerial Education in the American Methodist Movement* (Nashville: United Methodist Board of Higher Education and Ministry, Division of Ordained Ministry, 1980), 12.

85. Taylor, *Story of My Life*, 58, 63.

86. Wigger, *Taking Heaven by Storm*, 64–67.

87. Taylor, *Story of My Life*, 63.

88. Charles T. Burton, *Botetourt County, Virginia Children*, vol. 1 (Troutville, VA: n.p., n.d.); Taylor, *Cause and Probable Results*, 22; Anne Lowry Worrell, *Early Marriages, Wills, and Some Revolutionary War Records, Botetourt County, Virginia* (Baltimore: Genealogical Publishing, 1975), 58.

89. Taylor, *Story of My Life*, 60, 90.

90. Leonard I. Sweet, *The Minister's Wife: Her Role in Nineteenth-Century American Evangelicalism* (Philadelphia: Temple University Press, 1983), 44–75.

91. *Minutes . . . 1839–45*, 566.

92. Taylor, *Story of My Life*, 83.

93. Ibid., 64–84.

94. Mathews, "The Second Great Awakening," 35–38.

95. *Minutes of the Annual Conferences of the Methodist Episcopal Church, . . . 1846–1851* (New York: Carlton & Phillips, 1854), 4.

96. *The Doctrines and Discipline of the Methodist Episcopal Church, 1844* (New York: G. Lane & C. B. Tippett, 1844), 182.

97. Wigger, *Taking Heaven by Storm*, 56–62.

98. Transcribed Minutes of the Baltimore Conference, 1846, Lovely Lane Museum and Archives; Taylor, *Story of My Life*, 83.

99. *Minutes . . . 1846–1851*, 6; Taylor, *Story of My Life*, 84, 87.

100. National Capital Planning Commission and Frederick Albert Gutheim, *Worthy of the Nation: The History of Planning for the National Capital* (Washington, DC: Smithsonian Institution Press, 1977), 21–22, 41–43. 51.

101. Taylor, *Story of My Life*, 88–89.

102. F. A. Crafts, "Visit to a Jesuit College," *Zion's Herald and Wesleyan Journal*, June 30, 1847; Robert Emmett Curran, *The Bicentennial History of Georgetown University: From Academy to University*, vol. 1 (Washington, DC: Georgetown University Press, 1993), 124–30.

103. Charles Yrigoyen Jr., "Methodists and Roman Catholics in 19th Century America," *Methodist History* 28, no. 3 (April 1990): 172–3.

104. Crafts, "Visit to a Jesuit College."

105. Yrigoyen Jr., "Methodists and Roman Catholics."

106. Texts and Topics of Sermons Heard in Washington, DC, 1844–57, William R. Woodward Collection, Lovely Lane Museum and Archives; *Minutes . . . 1846–1851*, 98; Taylor, *Story of My Life*, 92.

107. David I. Durham, *A Southern Moderate in Radical Times: Henry Washington Hilliard, 1808–1892* (Baton Rouge: Louisiana State University Press, 2008).

108. Hy. Slicer to Bp. Simpson, December 29, 1853, Container 5, Matthew Simpson Papers, Manuscript Division, Library of Congress.

109. Taylor, *Story of My Life*, 92.

110. Texts and Topics of Sermons; Graeme Donovan, "Behold! A Sower," in *Many Witnesses: A History of Dumbarton United Methodist Church, 1772–1990*, ed. Jane Donovan (Georgetown: Dumbarton United Methodist Church, 1998), 253–4; Jane Donovan, "Let the Oppressed Go Free," in *Many Witnesses: A History of Dumbarton United Methodist Church, 1772–1990*, ed. Jane Donovan (Georgetown: Dumbarton United Methodist Church, 1998), 104; Kathleen M. Lesko, Valerie Melissa Babb, and Carroll R. Gibbs, *Black Georgetown Remembered: A History of Its Black Community from the Founding Of "The Town of George" In 1751 to the Present Day* (Washington: Georgetown University Press, 1991), 6–10; Pauline Gaskins Mitchell, "The History of Mt. Zion United Methodist Church and Mt. Zion Cemetery," *Records of the Columbia Historical Society of Washington, D.C.* 51 (1984): 103–4; Richey, Rowe, and Schmidt, *Methodist Experience*, 145; Taylor, *Story of My Life*, 92.

111. Graeme Donovan, "Will the Border Hold?," in *Many Witnesses: A History of Dumbarton United Methodist Church, 1772–1990*, ed. Jane Donovan (Georgetown: Dumbarton United Methodist Church, 1998), 173–4.

112. Homer L. Calkin, "The Slavery Struggle, 1780–1865," in *Those Incredible Methodists: A History of the Baltimore Conference of the United Methodist Church*, ed. Gordon Pratt Baker (Baltimore: Commission on Archives and History, The Baltimore Conference, 1972), 206–14; Donald G. Mathews, *Slavery and Methodism: A Chapter in American Morality, 1780–1845* (Princeton: Princeton University Press, 1965), 242, 65–68; Richey, Rowe, and Schmidt, *Methodist Experience*, 182–9.

113. Calkin, "The Slavery Struggle," 212–14.

114. Taylor, *Story of My Life*, 90–91.

115. "Taylor and Bland,—The Slave-holding Ministers," *California Christian Advocate*, June 10, 1852; "List of Emigrants," *The African Repository* 30, no. 7 (July 1854): 214.

116. Taylor, *Story of My Life*, 90–91.

117. "Taylor and Bland."

118. [Anne Taylor] to Bro. Leonard, January 27, 1892, Taylor, W. (Bishop) 1886–1890, Missionary Files (Microfilm Edition), United Methodist Church Archives—GCAH.

119. Josephine F. Pacheco, *The Pearl: A Failed Slave Escape on the Potomac* (Chapel Hill: University of North Carolina Press, 2005), 92–111; Mary K. Ricks, "The 1848 *Pearl* Escape from Washington, D.C.: A Convergence of Opportunity, Motivation, and Political Action in the Nation's Capital," in *In the Shadow of Freedom: The Politics of Slavery in the National Captial*, ed. Paul Finkelman and Donald R. Kennon (Athens: Ohio University Press, 2011), 195–219.

120. Russell E. Richey, "The Formation of American Methodism: The Chesapeake Refraction of Wesleyanism," in *Methodism and the Shaping of American Culture*, ed. Nathan O. Hatch and John H. Wigger (Nashville: Kingswood Books, 2001), 199.

121. H. W. Brands, *The Age of Gold: The California Gold Rush and the New American Dream* (New York: Doubleday, 2002), 24; J. S. Holliday, *The World Rushed In: The California Gold Rush Experience* (New York: Simon and Schuster, 1981).

122. Gary Lawson Browne, *Baltimore in the Nation, 1789–1861* (Chapel Hill: University of North Carolina Press, 1980).

123. "Local Matters: Revivals," *The Sun*, November 1, 1848.

124. Taylor, *Seven Years'*, 26–27.

125. "Local Matters: Thanksgiving Day," *The Sun*, November 25, 1849.

126. Taylor, *Story of My Life*, 100.

127. John Leland Peters, *Christian Perfection and American Methodism* (Grand Rapids: Francis Asbury Press of Zondervan Publishing House, 1985), 32–60; 90–101.

128. Melvin E. Dieter, *The Holiness Revival of the Nineteenth Century*, Second ed. (Lanham: Scarecrow Press, 1996), 16–23.

129. Taylor, *Story of My Life*, 69–73.

130. Ibid., 73.

131. Ibid., 76.

132. Ibid., 77.

133. B. Waugh to Rev. Isaac Owens, October 16, 1848, Isaac Owen Papers, 1830–1866, Bancroft Library, University of California, Berkeley.

134. Wade Crawford Barclay, *Early American Methodism, 1769–1844: Missionary Motivation and Expansion*, vol. 1, History of Methodist Missions (New York: Board of Missions and Church Extension of the Methodist Church, 1949), 100–1.

135. "Report of the Baltimore Conference Missionary Society," *Christian Advocate*, April 19, 1848.

136. Taylor later claimed the interview took place in September 1848, but that chronology does not match other evidence. Lay, ed., *Lessons of Infinite Advantage*, 143; Taylor, *Story of My Life*, 100–2.

137. B. Waugh to Rev. Isaac Owen, January 1, 1849, Isaac Owen Papers, 1830–1866, Bancroft Library, University of California, Berkeley.

138. Taylor, *How to Be Saved*, 356–8.

139. Ibid., 357; Taylor, *Story of My Life*, 100–2.

140. Charles Edward White, *The Beauty of Holiness: Phoebe Palmer as Theologian, Revivalist, Feminist, and Humanitarian* (Grand Rapids: Francis Asbury Press, 1986), 136–40.

141. Dana L. Robert, "Holiness and the Missionary Vision of the Woman's Foreign Missionary Society of the Methodist Episcopal Church," *Methodist History* 39, no. 1 (October 2000).

142. "Local Matters: Meeting in the Aid of the California Mission," *The Sun*, April 12, 1849.

143. Junius, "Letter from Baltimore," *Christian Advocate*, April 19, 1849.

144. William Taylor to James Sewell, January 30, 1851, William Taylor Collection, Lovely Lane Museum and Archives.

145. "Fruits of Holiness," *Christian Standard*, June 23, 1892.

146. Taylor, *Story of My Life*, 101.

147. Ibid., 102.

148. Ibid.

149. Waugh to Owen, January 1, 1849.

150. "Local Matters: The California Mission," *The Sun*, January 13, 1849; "Local Matters: Interesting Occasion," Ibid., February 1849.

151. Missonary Society of the Methodist Episcopal Church, Missions Minutes 1819–1916, [1979], Scholarly Resources, Wilmington, DE, January 17, 1849.

152. William Taylor, *California Life Illustrated* (New York: Published for the author by Carlton & Porter, 1858), 33, 47.

153. Taylor, *Story of My Life*, 105.

Chapter 2

California and Bust

There were three ways for an American to get to California in 1849. Most traveled overland following the Oregon Trail for much of the journey. Americans along the Atlantic seaboard like Taylor, however, were more likely to travel by sea. The quickest and most dangerous route was to sail to Panama, cross the isthmus by boat and mule, and sail on to San Francisco. Rampant disease and irregular shipping on the Pacific coast made this route risky. The last and longest path was to go around the horn of South America. Whichever path they followed, most Americans went to California in search of quick and easy wealth. They hoped to find gold and return home with newfound riches.

Taylor went to California with other priorities. Like other Methodist missionaries sent west in North America to regions of American settlement and colonization, he sought to establish the basic institutions of his religion in a place where it did not fully exist. Such regions were a significant arena of Methodist missionary work in this era. As historian Andrew Walls noted, "The main missionary achievement of the nineteenth century was the Christianizing of the United States."[1] Church authorities and lay migrants began that work, but there was much more to be done by missionaries such as Taylor. This chapter will focus on Taylor's time in California to highlight several features of the Methodist missionary tradition in America, but he did not work alone. Many others traveled to California to join in the effort. Some were missionaries sent, like Taylor, by the various Methodist denominations in America; others went on their own accord.

Taylor and others went because they believed God desired the salvation of all people. This theological idea was a key factor motivating Methodist missions, and Taylor's encounter with the diverse collection of humanity that gathered in California made that concept real to him in new ways. He became inspired to imagine how the whole world might be reached with his message. While Methodists were clear that God's salvation was for to all people, they also recognized that not all received or welcomed that message. Not everyone embraced the Methodist invitation to live a life of holiness and moral serious- ness. Other, more practical challenges also presented themselves to Methodist missionaries. Money and personnel were always in short supply, for example. In all Taylor's work, he believed such challenges could be overcome with personal initiative and by trusting God to provide. Although he accomplished a lot in his time in California, a surprising disaster would bring a premature end to Taylor's ministry there, and after seven years, the Taylors would return east penniless.

Taylor's mission, however, began with a spirit of promise. The missionary family initially planned to travel by way of Panama, but reports of disease prompted the secretaries of the Methodist mission board in New York, the body paying for the Taylors' transport, to reconsider. They worried that route was too dangerous. The demand of gold-seekers for passage, however, meant that all tickets around South America were booked for months in advance. Their departure was put on hold until, in early April, space unexpectedly opened on the *Andalusia*, a clipper ship sailing from Baltimore carrying ten first class and 100 steerage passengers.[2] Taylor later wrote that he believed the tickets to be a providential act of "the God of the seas."[3] Clear sailing seemed to be ahead.

AROUND THE HORN

For most passengers, after an initial wave of nausea, the journey to California was a monotony to be endured before reaching their anticipated fortunes. For Taylor, when the *Andalucia* set sail on April 18, his mission began.[4] Several sources exist to illumine this launch of Taylor's missionary career. They demonstrate that his priority was to impart the ascetic values of his faith to his floating congregation. He believed activities such as gambling, swearing, dancing, and the failure to keep the Sabbath were sins that could both jeopar- dize an individual's salvation and physical well-being.[5]

Taylor set to work on his first Sunday at sea offering Bibles to passengers. Many already carried their own, but others made fun of Taylor's efforts, ostentatiously pretending to read. Scattered irreverence aside, most passen- gers were willing to accept Taylor's shipboard ministrations. His sermon on the deck that morning was well attended, and most joined the hymn singing. The captain endorsed Taylor's work, and sat next to him as he preached, an arrangement that prompted the captain's niece to quip that her uncle had probably never been "so near a pulpit before."[6]

For his part, Taylor had never been confined so near to people who did not share his piety. He became concerned with moral life onboard and believed that he was "surrounded by a miserable set of sinners," many of whom were "a disgrace to humanity."[7] On the second Sunday at sea, Taylor preached on Matthew 22:42—"What think ye of Christ?" Despite the apparent Christological theme of this text, his focus was on the "folly & wickedness of profane swearing & gambling."[8] Gambling drew most of his ire. Taylor granted it was unlikely that any passengers were "confirmed gamblers." Rather, he suspected people played cards to pass the time. But, he argued, this activity rested at the top of a slippery slope. A young man might come to enjoy cards so much he would forget to eat. Over time his skill would improve, and he would wonder "what a pity there was not a prize at stake."[9] Thus primed, he would be ready to fall into the destruction that awaited him in California. While Taylor admitted that not all would succumb, some would. To the rest, he asked them to consider the judgment of God against them for contributing to the eternal ruin of this young man by gambling with him.[10]

What the passengers thought of Taylor's jeremiad is not known. His willingness to back up moral concern with action, however, soon sparked a conflict on the ship. Some passengers spent fair nights at sea with music and dancing on the deck. One evening in mid-May, William and a very pregnant Anne paraded through the middle of one of these dances, bringing the festivities to a halt. Tempers flared and the dancers threatened Taylor with violence. The offended parties cooled down, but the following Sunday, many voted with their feet and shunned Taylor's sermon.[11]

With the mediation of another passenger, Taylor addressed the issue before his message. He expressed his regret that he had caused offense but defended his duty to the ship's welfare. He believed toleration of such sin both put those individuals in moral danger and jeopardized the ship's safety. Taylor thought that God would, at times, allow tragedies to discipline sinners and bring them to repentance and greater faith. To flagrantly sin in such a way was to tempt disaster. Many passengers seemed to accept this explanation and resumed attending Taylor's sermons. Not all were disposed to give him a hearing, however. The next week, several men loudly contributed drunken "Amens" to his message.[12]

In San Francisco, Taylor would learn to parry and even adroitly incorporate interruptions of this sort into his sermons in creative and humorous ways. He would also develop a more inviting manner of preaching. His change in this respect shows that the populist preaching style that contributed to Methodist growth in America was a learned skill.[13] At this stage of life, however, Taylor was more inclined to assert his authority and demand a hearing. As the ship neared Rio de Janeiro, Taylor's sermon was interrupted by the sight of sails in the distance. Though Taylor protested that "he was talking of something more important" than passing vessels, his congregation took a different view and rushed to the rails as soon as he was done.[14]

Despite such conflicts, the Taylors participated in shipboard life. William was as interested as others in passing ships. He tracked the *Andalucia*'s progress and reported that his son Morgan was "the pet of the ship."[15] The biggest addition the Taylors made to life onboard, however, was another passenger. On June 21 about 400 miles west of the Rio de la Plata, Anne gave birth to a baby girl. The birth caused great excitement on board, and passengers discussed potential names, such as Andalusia or Atlanta. Eventually, the parents settled on the name Oceana Wilson, in honor of her birth at sea and, possibly, the ship's captain.[16]

Unfortunately, Oceana's birth was not without complications. Anne suffered from diarrhea, probably caused by cholera. Worried that she or the baby would die in childbirth, William spent her labor in prayer. Mother and child survived but neither were well. Dehydration caused by Anne's illness and limited fresh water restricted her milk, and alternate sources were unavailable at sea. To supplement the baby's intake and serve as a pacifier, Anne placed grated crackers, sugar, and medicines in a rag for the infant to suck. By the end of the trip, Oceana suffered from a combination of malnutrition and effects of the medicines.[17]

Winter weather in the southern hemisphere prevented Taylor from preaching on the deck for a time. It was, nevertheless, a relatively easy passage around the Horn, and on July 27, the ship stopped for a few days in Valparaiso, Chile. A few days out of port, Taylor made one last attempt to enforce moral discipline on the ship. On the night of August 3, a sudden squall broke two masts and their yards. Passengers were awakened by a crash and a call for "all hands." Sails hung in disorder and lines lay scattered. There were no injuries, and the ship was in no immediate peril, but another storm would put them at risk. The ship made for Callao, Peru, for repairs. The following day, however, the captain proposed repairing the ship at sea with timber in the hold. Many passengers enthusiastically offered to help the crew with the work, and plans were made to start early the next day.[18]

That day, however, was Sunday. The needs of the ship conflicted with Taylor's Sabbatarian sensibilities. He reproached the captain for his proposal to repair the ship on a Sunday. The captain not only refused to take the reprimand but dressed down Taylor in turn. Chastened, Taylor retreated with his family below decks to avoid the impression that he sanctioned the work while others made the needed repairs.[19] As Taylor's sermon on gambling and attempt to stop the dance illustrated, Methodists of the mid-nineteenth century often viewed moral questions as matters of personal holiness that could impact the lives of others, positively or negatively. They were less interested than other American evangelicals in establishing elements of a Christian social order, but had, however, embraced the Puritan idea that Sundays were a day to refrain from labor and a marker of Christian society.[20]

Taylor's Sabbatarian stand was not extraordinary. Among overland migrants, for example, women often insisted on the need to rest from travel on Sundays. Like Taylor, they often lost that argument to men who insisted on pressing on.[21] Isaac Owen, Taylor's first coworker in the California mission, traveled to California overland and also sought to enforce Sabbath observance and moral life in his party of emigrants. Unlike Taylor, Owen was accompanied by others who shared his concerns and collectively enforced them. His group of 134 men, and an unknown number of women and children, included four other ministers. That company adopted bylaws forbidding Sabbath-breaking, gambling, swearing, and drunkenness. Nicknamed "the Missionary Train," the company halted travel every Sunday to rest and hold morning and evening preaching services.[22]

Laymen were often more lax in their Sabbath observance. Even those who regularly rested on Sundays made accommodations for contingencies that arose.[23] For many on the *Andalucia*, Taylor's actions contrasted unfavorably with those of Robert Kellan, a Methodist layman and local preacher. Kellan came aboard in Valparaiso and was an experienced sailmaker. He helped supervise repairs and circulated among the workers. The following Sunday the passengers asked Kellan, instead of Taylor, to preach.[24]

The *Andalucia* entered the Golden Gate on September 21. On the five-month sea voyage, Taylor learned lessons that would serve him well as an evangelist. Most significantly, Taylor took the rebukes of the captain and passengers to heart. Years later, he offered only praise for the captain's response to the storm and made no mention of his own principled opposition.[25] Indeed, after that incident and for the remainder of the trip, Taylor made new efforts to interact with other passengers. When he next preached, he changed his style and preached a more inviting message. By the final Sunday on board ship, Taylor once again gathered a substantial portion of the passengers into a congregation.[26]

ORGANIZING METHODISM

As the first Methodist missionaries to California, the initial work of organizing Methodism in that region fell to Taylor and Owen. The foundations of their work, however, were laid by others. As antebellum Methodism spread in North America, multiple levels of the church operated at once, sometimes in concert and sometimes independently. At the grassroots, lay Methodists migrated to new regions and started class meetings or Sunday schools. The church's Missionary Society provided some funding for new initiatives, but, unlike other denominations, it left strategic and administrative decisions to annual conferences, bishops, and presiding elders. Preachers and missionaries sent to new regions sought out lay settlers, regularized their practices, and connected them with the larger denomination.

The first Methodist missions to the Pacific coast were initiated in 1832 when rumors of potential Indian converts in the west and American interest in Oregon prompted the church to mobilize. The Missionary Society funded several parties of missionaries selected by the church's bishops. That mission grew, cresting in 1839 when a group of fifty-one Methodists set sail for Oregon, the largest single American missionary endeavor to that date. Soon thereafter, however, support for the effort dwindled. The Missionary Board overextended itself financially and believed that the potential for Indian converts had been exaggerated. Indian deaths from disease, the challenges of working cross-culturally, and increased American settlement in Oregon meant that the missionaries worked more with whites than Indians. In addition, since most of the missionaries were farmers, tradesmen, and families, the Board judged the mission had become like a colony.[27]

The Mexican-American War, however, revived Methodist interest in the Pacific coast. Although politically controversial, Methodists saw the war as a providential opportunity to spread the gospel to areas previously under Mexican control.[28] The General Conference of the Methodist Episcopal Church met in 1848 while a treaty with Mexico ceding California to the United States moved toward ratification but before news of gold at Sutter's Mill reached the east. Oregon Methodists also had requested that body establish them as an annual conference. The General Conference obliged, in part, by calling for the dispatch of two missionaries to California (Owen and Taylor) and by creating the Oregon and California Mission Conference.[29]

The designation as a mission conference was significant. For whites in the Methodist Episcopal Church, annual conferences were the institutional building blocks of midcentury expansion and the basic body of ecclesiology. The church spread by subdividing or replicating these judicatory bodies responsible for outreach within their bounds. Unlike annual conferences, however, mission conferences were given no representation at the church's governing General Conference and were prohibited from drawing dividends from book sales to supplement preacher's salaries, pay retired or disabled preachers, their widows, and children. Mission conferences did receive some funding from the Missionary Society.[30] For example, the society paid Taylor's transportation costs to California and gave him $750 to cover his expenses and those of the mission for a year.[31]

Mission conferences also marginalized people of color and those outside the United States in the church, denying them access to the church's governance and funding structures. Although their theology pushed Methodists to share their message with all people, racism and xenophobia could be equally compelling forces. Although it was quickly dominated by white American emigrants, Oregon and California was created as a mission conference to serve Pacific coast Indians and territory formerly part of Mexico. It was the third mission conference of the church. The first, Liberia, was established in 1836. The church would use this model elsewhere as it expanded around the world, and Taylor and others would chafe against these limitations.[32]

William Roberts, appointed to be superintendent of the Oregon and California mission, was the first Methodist to visit California in an official capacity. He stopped there on his way to Oregon in 1847. As superintendent, he was the executive responsible for oversight of the mission in the first years of Taylor's tenure. Roberts's primary concern was the Methodist mission in Oregon, but on his brief visit to San Francisco, he organized a Methodist class meeting and Sunday school, and returned again early in 1849 to check on their status. On both visits, Roberts had found it nearly impossible to find shelter or a place to preach in San Francisco, so he arranged for a church to be framed in Oregon and shipped there.[33]

Roberts could make these initial efforts because lay Methodist migrants preceded him to California. Historian David Hempton's observation that Methodist expansion was "carried primarily by a mobile laity" holds true in California as elsewhere.[34] When Taylor disembarked from the *Andalucia*, his first task was to find those settlers. John Troubody, the first Methodist Taylor met, was English-born but had lived in Pennsylvania and Missouri before arriving in California. Fortunate to find gold, Troubody and his wife bought and donated a lot on Powell Street in San Francisco on which they were constructing the church Roberts had sent. Troubody introduced Taylor to Asa White, the patriarch of a large family of adult children and grandchildren from Illinois who had migrated first to Oregon. White had been a local preacher before his move west, and most of his adult children, sons-in-law, and grandchildren were Methodists. Every Sunday afternoon they hosted a class meeting in the blue tent they called home. In time, the whites would move on from the city and their tent became the founding "structure" for three additional Methodist congregations in California. In all, Taylor found about twenty people forming a preexisting nucleus of Methodism in San Francisco.[35]

White held a letter for Taylor from Roberts welcoming him to California and informing him that he was to work in San Francisco. Owen, traveling overland, was appointed to Sacramento.[36] Taylor began his first Sunday in California, preaching in the Baptist church in the morning and attending the class meeting in the White's tent that afternoon. He recalled that many of the testimonies of those present gave thanks to God for their safe arrival, as Taylor most likely did himself.[37]

Practical concerns dominated Taylor's first months in California. Poor health continued to plague both Anne and Oceana. They hoped to improve once settled in a home, but the lack of housing remained a problem and was further hindered by hyperinflationary prices. The flood of gold into the economy and the demand of countless emigrants for goods and services inflated costs.[38] For example, Taylor learned that the Baptist minister rented his home for $500 a month. At that rate, Taylor's $750 from the Missionary Society would not last long. According to the Methodist *Discipline*, Taylor was entitled to a home provided by the Methodists he served, but they had already contributed all they could toward the construction of their church.[39]

Taylor's solution to this problem was good illustration of both his impulsiveness and sense of providential self-sufficiency informed by his social origins and theology of entire sanctification. He would act and trust for God to provide. Taylor resolved to find lumber from a nearby redwood forest. Several laymen accompanied him on the expedition. Together they assaulted the giant trees with hand tools and gunpowder. But after almost a week, they had not retrieved any useable wood. Taylor returned to the forest alone the next week and tried a different approach. He used his axe to chip shingles from trees that he traded for joists. He bought rough cut timber in the forest at a discount that he finished himself and shipped back to San Francisco. With a combination of paid, volunteer, and his own labor a cabin was soon completed.[40] The family fenced a garden, and Anne bought some chickens make the house "look more homelike."[41] In the end, Taylor believed his housing problem was resolved by the combination of faith and his own initiative. The only difficulty Taylor confessed at the time that the needs of his family had taken time away from his pastoral work. Through it all he trusted in God's care. He testified, "I have increasing evidence that all my interests are safe in the hands of the Lord."[42]

Despite Taylor's concerns about inactivity, his ministry continued apace. The church he brought from Baltimore was shipped to Sacramento for use there. The chapel from Oregon was completed by October 7. Taylor preached the dedicatory sermon with Baptist, Presbyterian, and Congregationalist clergy assisting. A Methodist preacher from New England who had left the ministry to come to California as the chaplain of a mining company baptized Oceana. Although the content of Taylor's sermon is not known, he chose as his text Isaiah 40:3-5, possibly to indicate that he saw the chapel to be a part of God's transformation of the California "wilderness."[43]

Building a parsonage and a chapel were not just necessities for a preacher and his congregation. They were also small and practical pieces of the missionary strategy adopted by American Methodists in the United States. In the mid-nineteenth century, Methodists sought to establish their presence in towns and cities of the expanding nation. A departure from the mobile preachers of Asbury's day, this strategy required resident clergy to live in their communities rather than to itinerate over a large region. Methodists hoped a consistent pastoral presence would allow the church to build and maintain the institutions that structured religious life—regular Sunday worship, class meetings, mission society meetings, Sunday schools, publications, and schools.[44]

Taylor and Owen adopted this strategy for their work in California when the two men first met in Sacramento in January 1850. Over several days, they shared their impressions of California, endorsed this missionary approach, and developed a plan for its implementation.[45] As Taylor later wrote,

> A book depository was to be established, and the country supplied with a pure religious literature; academies and a university were to be founded for the education of the rising generation; but at present we had to explore, and organize societies, so far as possible, without neglecting the charges to which we had been appointed.[46]

In other words, Methodist institutions would be created throughout California, but the first step was to organize Methodist societies to be served by missionaries who would join them. To this end, Taylor took responsibility for San Francisco and communities to the south while Owen served Sacramento and points north. In the early years of the mission, both men traveled through their regions to accomplish this goal.[47]

It would be some time before additional missionaries arrived to serve those communities, however. The first arrived in the fall of 1850, over a year after Taylor and Owen. More followed, but their numbers never matched the need Taylor perceived, and he quickly became frustrated by what he believed was the inaction of the Mission Board. For Taylor, that slow pace contrasted unfavorably with the initiative taken by others. Like the preacher who baptized Oceana, a few went to California at their own expense rather than wait to be sent by church officials. Some of these served Methodist societies informally until the church's structure caught up to them. James Corwin, for example, asked to be transferred to California with Owen. When his request was denied, he resigned his credentials and accompanied the Owen family across the plains. He served Methodists in Stockton until 1853 when he was returned to the regular ministry. Taylor noted and approved of this kind of initiative, and would later encourage others to follow this pattern in missions he started elsewhere.[48]

The dispatch of formal missionaries to California was delayed by the expense involved. Like other Protestants, Methodists found California's inflation limited the number of missionaries that could be sent. It cost eight times more to support a missionary in California than elsewhere in North America. This economic differential created tensions between missionaries in need of support and eastern mission boards who imagined California as a land of easy and abundant wealth.[49] Southern Methodists attempted to address that challenge and fund their California missions by spreading out the financial burden. They called on each annual conference to send a preacher to California and commit $1,000 for his support.[50]

The question of Taylor's salary came before San Francisco's Methodists in late November 1849 when they held their first quarterly conference. Taylor hoped they would pay his salary and commit to becoming a "self-sustaining station."[51] In other words, he hoped they would support him fully without appealing to the Missionary Society to cover any deficit. Going into the meeting, Taylor had some doubt about this outcome since when the problem of housing had been raised earlier, some insisted that the Missionary Society was obliged to support him.[52]

Taylor was fortunate that San Francisco Methodists were both generous and willing to adjust his salary to the local economy so that no additional appeal was necessary. They committed to pay him $2,000 for the year, to include the $750 already given by the Missionary Society. This decision was a clear accommodation to California prices since the Methodist *Discipline* only entitled Taylor to a salary of $232.[53]

Later in life, Taylor would advocate what he called "self-supporting missions" and posit a theological rationale for this mission theory. He would argue that a missionary could support himself or herself through secular employment until such time as he or she would be supported by the voluntary contributions of the new church. Before it became anything else to Taylor, however, and before any theological rationale was attached to it, for Taylor the concept of self-support simply described the practical necessities of frontier economics.

Informal networks of colleagues and familial relationships often preceded official Methodist church structures in California. Taylor's position in San Francisco, the entry port and center of commerce for the state, made him a central node in a developing network of California's Methodists. As new argonauts arrived and converts joined Methodist societies, he used his position to integrate Methodists into the church at local and statewide levels. When members of his congregation in San Francisco moved elsewhere, for example, Taylor wrote letters to the preachers in those communities both commending his parishioner's "spiritual welfare," but also encouraging those preachers to support their businesses or to employ them as teachers.[54] Methodist preachers with business in the city visited or stayed with the Taylor family, and he hosted meetings to conduct statewide church business. The most significant of these meetings was in 1851 when he, Owen, and others met to found California Wesleyan College, now known as the University of the Pacific, California's first institution of higher learning.[55]

When additional missionaries did arrive in port, Taylor welcomed and initiated them to life in California. Some of those were Taylor's own family members. In October 1851, Taylor's brother- and sister-in-law, Adam and Ellen (Kimberlin) Bland, arrived as missionaries. Bland was first appointed to serve all of Nevada and then all of southern California. A few months later, Anne's brother and wife, James and Katie Elizabeth (Reed) Kimberlin, arrived with plans to start a school in San Jose. James later taught at the University of the Pacific. In September 1852, Taylor's brother Archibald arrived. Also a Methodist preacher, over the next twenty years he served churches in California, Oregon, and Nevada.[56]

In contrast with this informal network that grew with each new arrival, the basic body of official Methodist ecclesiology, the annual conference, took some time to develop. Until 1853, California and Oregon were a part of the same mission conference. Despite California's booming population, most Methodist preachers on the Pacific coast were in Oregon. Conference meetings were held there, and California was never represented in those meetings. By August 1851, enough preachers were in California to justify an informal gathering. Roberts came for the purpose, but the meeting held no official standing. Only after the General Conference of 1852 established California as an annual conference were such official meetings held.[57]

At all of these gatherings, Taylor played a prominent role. The details of his participation varied from year to year, but two recurrent themes emerged that foreshadowed a conflict he would have with church leaders late in his career. First, until 1853 he—and other California Methodists—found California's status as a mission conference troubling because it excluded them from participation in denominational decisions. Second, he became increasingly frustrated with what he saw to be the slow and inadequate response of the church leaders to the missionary needs of California. Both themes surfaced in the politics surrounding the status of the California book depository.

A part of the mission strategy adopted for California, in early 1850, Taylor established a book room in San Francisco to sell and distribute Methodist publications. He managed it for several years, often paying its expenses out of his pocket. As the 1852 General Conference approached, California's preachers were eager to become a full annual conference, and Taylor was ready to turn responsibility for the book room over to others.[58] The General Conference complied with California's requests by creating the California Annual Conference, separate from Oregon and embracing California and everything west of the Rocky Mountains. It also directed the Book Concern in New York, the publishing department of the church, to establish a branch in San Francisco.[59] The Book Concern's managers in New York, however, found the expense involved too great and refused to act on the resolution. Learning of this, a furious Taylor authored an extensive resolution adopted by California's Methodists at their first conference meeting in 1853 seeking to appeal that decision to the next General Conference in 1856.[60] Even so, the Book Concern only finally fulfilled its mandate in 1860.[61]

Outside of such church politics, Taylor also established church institutions in the developing city of San Francisco and himself became an institution of the city's life. He oversaw the construction of churches in San Jose, Santa Cruz, and two more churches in San Francisco, the first on Market Street and the second a Seamen's Bethel. Taylor would not be remembered in the city for his association with any building, however, but with the outdoors. On December 2, 1849, Taylor preached his first sermon on the city plaza (Portsmouth Square). He continued to do so weekly in this and other outdoor settings throughout his California ministry.[62] Decades later, a portrait of Taylor was included in a monumental arch constructed in San Francisco for the 1915 Panama-Pacific International Exposition.[63]

In his first book, *Seven Years' Street Preaching in San Francisco, California; Embracing Incidents, Triumphant Death Scenes, etc.* (1856), Taylor presented his first sermon in Portsmouth Square as momentous and dangerous decision to take the battle against sin to the enemy's ground. The plaza was home to several gambling establishments and saloons, and Sunday was their busiest day. Drinking, swearing, gambling, prostitution, and Sabbath-breaking were rampant, and he feared his sermon would incite some to violence.[64]

That decision loomed larger in retrospect. Although he was concerned for his safety, it was not clear Taylor believed he was doing anything particularly novel at the time. George Whitefield pioneered field preaching among Methodists in the mid-eighteenth century.[65] Taylor had regularly preached in public markets in both Georgetown and Baltimore.[66] Later Methodist preachers who came to California saw such preaching as a traditional Methodist practice well suited to their new context and also preached outdoors.[67] The real import of Taylor's street preaching was not that Taylor did it, but that he became good at it, and it brought him widespread notoriety.

The basic contours of Taylor's outdoor sermons were fairly uniform. He sang a hymn, often with Anne, to draw a crowd, and stood on an elevated surface, such as a carpenter's bench or a barrel to preach. The messages were evangelistic in focus, illustrating the visible effects of sin, the need for repentance, and God's offer of salvation. Beyond this template, however, lay considerable flexibility. Unlike his sermons on the *Andalucia*, Taylor developed by practice a preaching style that was inviting and sensitive to the whims of his audience. Like a good busker, Taylor knew that crowds needed to be enticed and that attention could be fickle if a more entertaining spectacle came along. He used humor to keep his audience engaged, and if they became distracted, Taylor sang to gather the crowd back. When he resumed, he tried to incorporate the distraction into his message, a practice he called setting his "sails to take the breeze."[68] A cry of "fire!" could lead to reflections on the warning of hell, for example.[69] A disruptive spectator would find himself used as a sermon illustration or the butt of a joke. On one occasion, a man tried to drive his donkey through the crowd. Taylor joked that the man lacked only "the ears of being the greater ass of the two," and when the animal refused to comply, Taylor compared it favorably to Balaam's animal for its fear of the Lord (cf. Numbers 22).[70] Apart from any interest his audience may have had in the religious content of his message, Taylor consistently drew an audience because his sermons were an entertaining and free way to pass leisure time.

Most of Taylor's listeners were respectful and genuinely interested in his message, however. He intended these sermons to be evangelistic efforts to reach those who would not otherwise come to his church. Some evidence exists that his listeners considered themselves to be a part of a regular, if outdoor, congregation. Oscar L. Shafter, who later became a justice on California's Supreme Court, for example, wrote in 1854 that he "numbered [himself] in the congregation of old Father Taylor, a street preacher. . . . I like him, and have elected him my Minister."[71] According to church membership records, however, Shafter was never a member of Taylor's congregation.[72]

"THE WORLD IN MINIATURE"

Before the Mexican War and the discovery of gold, Alta California was a distant and unimportant province to the Mexican capital. Convicts were sent there and trade regulations loosely enforced. In many respects, the most significant Mexican policy toward California was disengagement from the religious and economic life of the state. In 1833, the Mexican government secularized the Franciscan mission stations along the Pacific coast that had been founded in the eighteenth century. Mission property was to have been distributed to emancipated Indian converts. In practice Spanish-speaking residents appropriated the lands. Secularization diversified the economy and made California more attractive for American settlement.[73] By 1848, when Mexico ceded Alta California to the United States there were roughly 100,000 people in the state. Most were Indians, with about 7,000 Spanish-speaking Californians and about 6,000 Americans completing that number.[74]

This demographic change was minor compared to that wrought by gold. San Francisco's transformation was particularly dramatic. In 1845, it was known as "Yerba Buena" and had a population of about 150. Renamed "San Francisco," five years later it was home to about 35,000 people from around the world. It housed substantial communities of American Indians, Mexicans,

Chileans, Pacific Islanders, both European and Aboriginal Australians, Chinese, representatives of several nations of Western Europe, as well as both white and black, slave and free Americans.[75] As early as 1850, it was clear that Anglo-Americans would shape the state's social institutions. Nevertheless, the presence of substantial numbers of foreign-born immigrants created new possibilities for cross-cultural encounters.[76] Many American ministers feared this cosmopolitan society would overwhelm Anglo-Protestant culture and endanger the spiritual welfare of white Americans in California for gold.[77]

Taylor took a different view. He became excited about the diversity he encountered, and this excitement transformed his outlook on missions. Taylor had become a missionary out of a sense of fidelity to his salvation and in submission to God's will, but cross-cultural encounters in California prompted Taylor to adopt a perspective on mission that focused less on his own salvation and more on his hopes for the salvation of the world. He developed his first missiological reflections in this context as he interwove biblical analogies with his experiences in California.

The first signs of this shift were evident in March 1850 when Taylor began comparing life in California with a biblical story found in Acts 10. In that text, Peter, the leader of Jesus's disciples, had a vision of a sheet bearing different animals being lowered to earth and then raised up again. God told Peter that none of the animals contained therein were unclean. As a result of this vision, Peter realized that the Christian gospel was for all humanity, and not only Jews. In one of the fullest articulations of this comparison, Taylor wrote:

> What St. Peter saw in vision . . . we see now, in fact, here in California, with this difference, that when the "great sheet" was let down on these shores, it was not drawn up again, as when St. Peter saw it; but the attraction of our gold mountains produced such a commotion in the heterogeneous mass contained in it, that the sheet was rent from one end to the other, and out tumbled the whole concern, and every fellow of them grabbed a pick and shovel and went to digging, and here they are to-day. Nor is one of them called "common or unclean," but all of them are embraced in the covenant of promise.[78]

As a justification for cross-cultural evangelism, this text matched well with a Methodist concern for sharing the gospel with all people, and Taylor often returned to this analogy to describe California society.

In early 1851, Taylor tried another biblical image in a letter to a friend. He described Methodist class meetings with members from every part of the United States sharing the faith with members from Buenos Aires, New Zealand, New South Wales, North Wales, Paris, Great Britain and Ireland, Sweden, and Denmark. Rapturously evoking images from Revelation, he wrote, "I should like to show you the world in miniature, to introduce you to the representatives of every kindred and tongue under Heaven" (cf. Revelation

5:9).[79] Taylor often celebrated the diversity he encountered. In one outdoor sermon, rather than preaching from a scripture passage, Taylor took as his "text" the French, Spanish, Hawaiian, Chinese, and Irish people that made up his congregation. His message was that the Christian gospel was for them as it was for all people of the world. Unlike those who feared the effect of immigration on the nation, Taylor found it inspiring and filled with missionary potential.[80]

Few of Taylor's ideas about mission were novel or unique at this stage, nor was his enthusiasm about the diversity he encountered a deep appreciation for cultures other than his own. He was as ethnocentric as other white Americans of his day, unable to separate his understanding of Christianity from his culture. He believed, for example, that educational and industrial missions should be established on Indian reservations to protect them from exploitation from whites and to civilize them.[81] Rather, Taylor's excitement illustrates his own curiosity about other peoples and the power of the Methodist belief that God desired the salvation of all.

In years to come, one of the more innovative aspects of Taylor's missionary approach would be his reliance on women in leadership. While in California, however, he operated under the assumption Methodists shared with other American evangelicals that men and women operated in separate spheres. This ideology asserted the importance of public male leadership and that women were naturally religious and responsible for domestic nurture.[82] This ideology was so powerful that it influenced the practice of mission in California even in the absence of significant numbers of women.[83] Most gold rush migrants were men; as late as 1870, women comprised only 37 percent of the state's population.[84]

In mid-nineteenth-century America, health care was usually provided by women in the home. In the winter of 1849–1850, the absence of domestic health care, San Francisco's transient population, and unhealthy living conditions created an acute health crisis.[85] In those days, Taylor recalled seeing sick men languishing in the streets with no one to care for them. They were taken to a hospital where many died. Taylor began to make weekly visits to the hospital to visit, sing, pray, and distribute religious tracts to these patients. Disturbed by the lack of care even those in the hospital received, on occasion, he changed bandages, adjusted beds, or brought food to them. With his weekly sermons, Taylor's hospital visitations were a regular feature of his work in California.[86]

The absence of women also loomed large in the most colorful anecdote of Taylor's time in California. In January 1851, he was asked to preach a funeral for a man who had been shot in a saloon. He claimed such invitations were fairly commonplace, but on this occasion, standing next to the deceased in the bar, Taylor sang a hymn and read a scripture passage on the theme of God's judgment. In his sermon, Taylor rhetorically used the absence of women to call his listeners to repentance. He supposed they had "pious mothers" at home and so were not ignorant of their duty to God.[87] If they had faith in Christ, they would be happy, and as regenerated men they would transform California to "make this fair land a safe and happy home for your wives and children."[88] As for the deceased, Taylor proclaimed,

> Look at that bloody corpse! What will his mother say? What will his sisters think of it? To die in a distant land, among strangers, is bad; to die unforgiven, suddenly, unexpectedly, is worse; to be shot down in a gambling-house, at the midnight hour—O, horrible![89]

But, he proclaimed, such a death was the fruit of the depravity of his congregation.

Consistent with missionary practice of early Protestant missions and the gender role ideology of the time, Anne's primary role in their mission was to create a Christian home to serve as a model for others to witness.[90] This task was, a challenge for a number of reasons. Before coming to California, Anne's slaves had done the work of keeping house. As Anne remembered later in life, in California she "had to learn how to work."[91] William helped with housework when home, but prolonged absences visiting other Methodist communities in the state made him an unreliable aide. One attempt at hiring a servant ended with the servant attempting to take possession of the whole house in William's absence. In addition to Anne's bout with what was probably cholera, the family endured two break-ins, and their first home became infested with rats. Eventually, they moved to an apartment on board a ship that Taylor converted into a church. This situation proved no better, as in foul weather the ship could smash into neighboring structures. By 1853, Anne and the children finally made a home across the bay in Alameda.[92]

Far more serious than all these troubles was the condition of the Taylor children. In addition to Morgan and Oceana, in California Anne gave birth to William, Jr. (Willie), in June 1851 and Charles Reid in May 1853. Of these children, only Morgan would survive to adulthood. Oceana died when she was only thirteen months old. The baby had never been well, and may have suffered more from her care than any disease. For a time, her parents fed her a chalk and water mixture as a milk substitute.[93] Twice while living on the ship's apartment, Morgan fell into the bay. On the first occasion, William saved the boy from drowning, but on the second, in May 1853, his parents only learned of the fall after he came in wet. They never knew how he had been saved. This second incident could have been deeply tragic, as at that moment they were attending to Willie as he died.[94]

William interpreted these deaths, and all vicissitudes, as works of God's providence. They called for deeper commitment and faith and were a reminder that in his sanctification he had given them up to God. At Oceana's death, Taylor wrote to Roberts, "We feel the bereavement keenly, but submit gladly to the decisions of God's providence."[95] After Willie's death and Morgan's near tragedy, he reflected,

> I have long since consecrated myself, & wife & boys all to the Lord, and hold all subject to his order, and I shall certainly not complain if He take one, or any, or altogether. . . . I feel that my Savior is sanctifying this bereavement to my good. Yesterday was good training in theological study. There are lessons learned in experience which cannot be spread out on paper, and yet of infinite advantage in the details of Christian duty.[96]

Through it all William believed God was benevolently at work. Anne's feelings about the loss of her children are not recorded.

On the few occasions when Anne assumed more public role in the mission, it was always in ways consistent with the separate spheres ideology. When she accompanied William to his outdoor sermons, she sat near him while he preached in the expectation that a female presence would calm the men who gathered.[97] On another occasion, she prepared a scroll for men to sign pledging to abstain from alcohol while in California, and she solicited donations to support his ministry, sometimes raising money more effectively than her husband.[98] One source that provides a likely sample of her voice was an article in the Methodist paper by a "Sister Anne." The author argued too many California wives used domestic needs as an excuse to neglect their own spiritual lives. Both should be attended to. Cobwebs were "disagreeable to house-wives," but "many if not most of them have hearts, like deserted closets or rooms, filled with cobwebs."[99]

Some of Taylor's early missiological reflections were innovative, however. The biblical story of Pentecost was particularly fruitful in this regard. In that story, Peter and Jesus's other disciples received the Holy Spirit and were sent into the world. Before they went, however, the disciples preached the Christian message to Jews who had gathered in Jerusalem from all over the Roman Empire. Taylor often boasted that the crowds he preached to in San Francisco were more diverse than Peter's, and based on this story, he identified two different models for mission—sending and receiving. The apostles were sent into the world, but before they went, Jerusalem had already received people from around the world.[100]

In this idea, Taylor believed, lay the missionary potential of California. Immigrants could be converted and return to their native lands as Christians. By the 1850s, Methodist missions of this sort had already experienced some success, but Taylor offered a theological rationale for it. European converts in America had returned to establish Methodist missions in Germany and Scandinavia.[101] Indeed, one of Taylor's converts in San Francisco, Georg Goess, returned to Germany as a Methodist missionary.[102] Taylor also believed California offered the opportunity for a similar mission to China. Since 1847, the Methodist Missionary Society had supported a few missionaries in China who had to learn the language.[103] "But in the mean time," Taylor wrote, "God in his providence has forty thousand long-cued fellows in California, at no expense to anybody, studying the English language."[104] He believed Christianity could spread not only through the sending of formal missionaries but through the global movement of ordinary people. Taylor's reflections blurred any line that may have existed between domestic and foreign missions. To be sure, California was a place where religious institutions like those in the east were to be reproduced but it was not only that. It was also a center for Christian world mission. He gloried that there "within the compass of a single voice, the Gospel may be proclaimed to 'all nations,' or, at least, to the subjects of all nations."[105]

Taylor's grandiloquent enthusiasm, however, was frustrated by the same obstacle he hoped those immigrants could overcome—language. He became frustrated by the language barriers he encountered. On hospital rounds, he brought laymen with him who could speak Spanish or French, but he came to believe that as much as he wanted to reach those who did not speak his language, he could not. The barriers were too great. Taylor never made any concerted effort to learn another language himself. Later in life, he would express the view that language learning was extremely difficult and physically taxing for all but the young. As a result, in February 1851, he called on the Missionary Society in New York to send missionaries to San Francisco to work exclusively with Spanish, French, and Chinese-speaking communities.[106] In this matter, Taylor would again be disappointed by what he perceived as the failure of the Missionary Society to meet the opportunity California offered. Methodists did not send a missionary to work with the Chinese in California until 1868.[107]

For the rest of his career, Taylor's hope that a way might be found to bridge the linguistic divide in missions would resurface. For the remainder of his California ministry, however, Taylor let that hope rest. By early March 1851, he identified a group of people in the city with whom he could communicate and who he believed could, in turn, reach the world with his gospel: sailors.

SEAMEN'S BETHEL

Early in Herman Melville's 1851 novel *Moby Dick*, the reader encounters Father Mapple, a preacher on Nantucket. His sermon on the book of Jonah foreshadows the disaster to befall the Pequod at the end of the story, and explores themes such as the dangers of sin, the need for repentance, and his duty to preach. This fictional character was partially based on Edward Thompson Taylor, better known as "Father Taylor." Of no relation to William and a generation older, Edward was converted as a young sailor in the port of Boston, became a Methodist preacher, and, in 1828, began a ministry to seamen in that city.[108]

In the same year that Melville's novel was published, William Taylor initiated a seamen's ministry in San Francisco, and he soon inherited Edward Taylor's nickname. For several years, two "Father Taylors" ministered on opposite coasts of North America. Like the fictional Mapple, William Taylor believed it was his duty to preach to sailors about sin and the need for repentance. Even so, disaster would befall him, forcing him to abandon his ministry and leave California.

It is not clear where Taylor's inspiration to start a seamen's ministry came from. Evangelicals began outreach to sailors in many of the world's port cities following the Napoleonic wars. Not all Seamen's Bethels, as they were called, were run by Methodists such as the Fathers Taylor, but Methodists embraced this method of outreach in many American ports, leaning heavily on local initiative, as one way to couple evangelism and social reform, as well as for its broader missionary potential.[109] During his year in Baltimore, Taylor may have encountered the Bethel Methodists started there in 1846 when they converted a ship in the Baltimore harbor into a church and ordained its former captain.[110]

Taylor's only known association with this type of mission was in Chile on his way to California. In Valparaiso, Taylor worshipped with the Presbyterian missionary David Trumbull in the morning, and preached at Trumbull's invitation that evening. Trumbull had been sent to Valparaiso in 1845 by the Foreign Evangelical Society and the Seamen's Friend Society to serve both English-speaking merchants and sailors in port. From this brief meeting, the two men left with favorable opinions of the other.[111] Trumbull would become an important figure in Latin American Protestantism, and decades later the two would reconnect when Taylor started new missions in South America.

Whatever his inspiration, Taylor became excited about the missionary potential of sailors who came through the port of San Francisco. He thought sailors converted through his ministrations could serve as pioneers of Christianity in the world's ports, much as lay migrants had laid the foundations for Methodism in California. Beginning in March 1851, he threw himself into the project. He ran the idea by several ship masters who endorsed it, and San Francisco's Methodists passed their own resolutions of support.[112] Taylor also expanded his outdoor preaching schedule to the city's Long Wharf. That effort led to an invitation to preach onboard a ship the following week, an offer that he considered propitious. As he wrote, "I regard this as the entering wedge to a Seamen's Bethel enterprise which shall vie in importance with any in the world, not many years hence."[113]

As these plans developed, Taylor remained deeply committed to his life and work in California. On May 2, 1851—his thirtieth birthday—he predicted in his journal that "Thirty years of labour in California will probably end the strife and bring me to my home in Heaven."[114] In fact, he would have many more years of work and would travel many more miles than he could conceive at that moment.

The night after Taylor's birthday, disaster struck the city of San Francisco. The fire that burned was the most destructive catastrophe to hit the city until 1906. Flames were said to have been visible as far south as Monterey.[115] The morning after the blaze, Taylor considered forgoing his usual plaza sermon. At Anne's encouragement, however, the couple sang a hymn and a larger than normal audience of survivors gathered to listen. From the porch of the adobe custom house, Taylor preached that this tragedy was a chastening punishment for the city's sins. Taylor's jeremiad on Psalm 127:1 inverted the question "Why did this happen?" and instead asked, "Why hadn't it happened before?" There had been ample opportunities for catastrophe, Taylor argued, but it had not occurred before because, as the psalmist said, the Lord had kept the city. But the city had not honored the Lord in turn. Sabbath desecration, intemperance, fornication, adultery, and blasphemy were rampant. "It is this . . . ," proclaimed Taylor, "Which lays our city in ruins."[116]

Taylor's belief that God providentially allowed tragedies to chastise people for sin and bring them to repentance was unchanged from his time on the *Andalucia*. Nor was it that unusual. Indeed, the persistence of that theology partially explains why when disaster struck Taylor Bethel's ministry, he fielded challenges to his own character. Taylor's colleagues would assume God was disciplining him through those disasters for some unknown sin. But punishment for sin was only one dimension of this theology. Taylor and others believed tragedies were allowed by a loving God to inspire greater faith. For some, greater faith required repentance from sin. For others, it called for a deeper level of trust and consecration to God's will. Anything less than total commitment to God betrayed a lack of faith.

Taylor's commitment to his Bethel idea was so great that he began his work with sailors without any official sanction or funding from his church, embracing the risks involved and trusting that God would provide. Taylor purchased a lot on which to moor a ship on Davis Street, near the Long Wharf months before Roberts appointed him to start a Bethel in August 1851. After August, Taylor began canvasing for donations. By November, Taylor had raised enough to buy a ship, the *Panama*, moor and refit it to house a congregation. Eventually a church structure would be built on the deck, and an apartment added for the Taylor family.[117]

Taylor's speed contrasted with the slower, more cautious approach practiced by other Protestants. In early 1849, the American Seamen's Friend Society (ASFS) considered starting a Bethel in San Francisco but the effort stalled.[118] Finally, in January 1852, Eli Corwin, a Presbyterian minister sent by the ASFS, arrived in the city. Learning that Taylor had already done what he was sent to do, Corwin was uncertain how to proceed. For his part, untroubled by a sense of competition, Taylor graciously welcomed Corwin and encouraged him to start another Bethel, but Corwin opted to wait for instructions from the east.[119]

Taylor developed a three-pronged plan for his Bethel. He would build the aforementioned church, work to convert individual sailors, and open a seamen's home. The principal method Taylor used to bring new converts into his faith was to host "protracted meetings" on the Bethel. An urban extension of the camp meeting, protracted meetings sought to continue revivals after participants returned home. Taylor publicized these meetings by distributing tracts or handbills, attracting congregations averaging thirty to forty people a night, six nights a week, for several weeks at a time.[120]

Those who professed faith in these services were admitted to Methodist membership as "Probationers." After a six-month trial period and examination by Taylor, they could be admitted into full membership.[121] This two-tier system was rooted in a Methodist theology that following conversion a Christian must then evidence of growth in God's sanctifying grace. Although Taylor hoped Bethel converts would function as lay missionaries spreading their new faith elsewhere, in practice he found many disappeared before their probationary period was completed. Such was the transient nature of the gold rush and work with sailors. Of the 118 converts Taylor received in the Bethel, only 47 were admitted as full members. Only a few of these were dropped for failure to keep their faith. Most converts just "Went Away."[122] Years later, he lamented that new converts rarely stayed in one location long enough to be nurtured in faith.[123]

The third prong of Taylor's strategy, a home for sailors, was intended to address an acute social problem in the city. During the gold rush, many seamen entering San Francisco deserted their ships for the mines. Captains wanting to leave struggled to enlist crews. Organized crime, backed by business leaders who believed without shipping economic development would lag, filled the void by drugging and involuntarily impressing sailors into service. Boardinghouse masters—referred to by Taylor as "landsharks" for their predatory practices—were key players in this human trafficking. Generally known as "crimping," in San Francisco this practice became known as "shanghaiing" because the Chinese city of Shanghai was a distant destination from which it would be difficult to return. By providing sailors safe lodging, Taylor hoped they could escape the traps of the landsharks.[124]

In the summer of 1853, Taylor relocated the Bethel ship and erected a hotel on the old lot. Isaac Hillman, a Methodist hotelier, agreed to operate it at $1,000 a month rent. Problems plagued the project from the start. Costs associated with the move and construction soon reached almost $33,000, more than double the projected figure. Because creditors were unwilling to loan money to a church corporation, Taylor personally assumed this debt until it could be repaid and the property deeded to the Bethel trustees. Through rental income and occasional donations, Taylor regularly paid the loans, but the responsibility for doing so weighed heavily on him.[125]

By February 1854, Taylor was ready to divest himself of the burden. He secured an offer to buy the hotel for $40,000 and presented the plan to the California Annual Conference of that year. The presiding bishop, Matthew Simpson, and others, however, dissuaded Taylor from selling. Simpson stayed at the hotel while in San Francisco, experiencing that aspect of Taylor's ministry first hand. He was also impressed by Taylor's street preaching and came to agree with Taylor's assessment in the missionary potential in California. He wrote, "All nations and tongues seem to be congregating in California, and I trust that here is to be the centre of a great good."[126] In all, the ministry was judged too important, the income reliable, and the sale price lower than the estimated value of the property. Taylor acceded but finances continued to be a concern.[127] Nevertheless he remained confident that God would provide for he was "doing business for the Lord, and I know He does not want for funds. . . . I am the Lord's all I have is the Lord's."[128]

The decisions to assume personal responsibility for the Bethel debt and to retain ownership of the hotel had fateful consequences. One year later, on February 18, 1855, the Hillman hotel was destroyed by fire. Without its rent, Taylor could not repay his loans. The crisis compounded just four days later when San Francisco's banks failed. Merchants who one day sympathetically offered to contribute the next day found themselves bankrupt. Property values plummeted, including those owned by the Bethel and Taylor. After years of booming growth, the California economy fell into depression, and Taylor was left without aid and personally responsible for the ministry's debt.[129]

The local and entrepreneurial initiative that was so critical to the quick start of new Methodist ministries had this downside. Such endeavors often lacked backing or institutional support to sustain them. Ironically, the 1854 conference that counseled Taylor to retain ownership of the hotel was far more concerned with the continued viability of another ministry, the *California Christian Advocate*. It was one of several, regional newspapers modeled on the New York-based, flagship Methodist periodical the *Christian Advocate*. Started in 1851 by two Methodist preachers, its editors had struggled to make it a viable concern. Taylor had done his part; he served as a subscription agent, helped mail issues, and provided it with copy.[130] The General Conference of 1852 directed the *Christian Advocate* in New York to take over management of the paper but, as with the book depository, they did not do so. In 1854, publication of the California *Advocate* was suspended.[131]

Taylor could not so easily escape his debt, and his situation was exacerbated by a particularly Methodist form of professional shame. Preachers were expected to be free of debt or risk losing their ministerial credentials.[132] Although Taylor had taken on the Bethel loans with the blessing of his colleagues and Simpson, now it was unclear if the debt could be repaid. When the California conference met for the first time following the hotel fire, in May 1855, the body duly investigated Taylor's case to see if he had acted dishonestly. While the investigation found no reason to question Taylor's integrity, the conference also offered no money. The only assistance given Taylor was the permission to travel to the east to raise money.[133]

This Taylor planned to do until his professional shame became a public disgrace. Henry Matthews, most likely a merchant to whom Taylor owed money, had Taylor arrested to prevent him from leaving the state. Taylor was soon released but missed an opportunity to travel east for free. Taylor had to remain in California.[134] Throughout 1855, public disputes over the Bethel properties continued to surface. Creditors sued Taylor and the Bethel trustees. Newspapers reported altercations between members of the Bethel and attempted buyers. Eventually, a court ruled that the Bethel trustees owned the church-ship, but that the debt incurred by the ministry was Taylor's alone to bear.[135]

For Taylor, this crisis was both humiliating and a transformational experience. He would be in California for another year soliciting donations, but the character of his work was forever changed. He traveled in wider and wider circuits around the Methodist world raising money to redeem his debt and honor. In time, Taylor would come to believe that the same initiative and trust in God's providence that allowed him to start the Bethel also allowed him to emerge from the shadow of its debt. But it would take another tragedy, the assassination of a friend, to inspire Taylor to the idea that eventually cleared the debt, provided him with a means of support, and become a cornerstone of his legacy. William Taylor would become an author.

TRIUMPHANT DEATH SCENES

Taylor and the unusually named James King of William met in California but the friends shared similar backgrounds. They were the same age, from Virginia families, and had lived in Georgetown. For a time, King had even joined a Methodist church there. As a young man, King adopted his father's name as a suffix to differentiate himself from other James Kings. He moved to California in 1848 and opened San Francisco's first bank. The financial collapse that left Taylor in debt also brought down King's institution. King's next venture was a newspaper, the *Daily Evening Bulletin*.[136] After the hotel fire, Taylor sought out King's advice and help, and King used his paper to publicize opportunities for the public to aid Taylor.[137]

King is remembered today for other reasons. His paper established a reputation for its opposition to political corruption and crime. In sensational editorials, King argued that a confederacy of gamblers, prostitutes, and criminals ran San Francisco. In one article, King showed that city supervisor James P. Casey had been incarcerated in New York. Thus provoked, on May 14, 1856, Casey shot King as he left his office.[138]

When Taylor heard the news, he rushed to minister to his friend. For several days, Taylor remained with King until he died.[139] Taylor and two other ministers presided at the funeral. He read scripture passages and spoke of King's last days. Following the service, a procession of about 6,000 people including family, clergy, attending physicians, fire companies, musicians, Masonic and other voluntary societies followed King's body to the cemetery.[140] That night, Taylor eulogized his friend in his journal as "one of natures [*sic*] noblest men, ordained by Providence of God for the position of leader of the reforming hosts of California for the defence [*sic*] of which he lay down his life."[141]

King's murder was an important event in San Francisco's history. A committee of vigilantes took over the city, hanged Casey, and for several months resisted efforts to reestablish the city government.[142] While Taylor supported King's platform of reform, he doubted that such societal reforms could be lasting without personal regeneration. In a sermon to a crowd gathered outside the Vigilance Committee headquarters, Taylor proclaimed "Do not imagine that by ridding the city of a few murderers, thieves, and 'ballot-box stuffers,' you will reform society. . . . To reform society, we must have the individual members composing society reformed."[143] This view reflected Methodism's pietistic origins and illustrated a pattern that would be replicated in missions in other political contexts. Methodists often prioritized the need for individual redemption over the creation of a Christian society.

In the short term, however, King's successful turn to writing and public interest in his death prompted Taylor to consider writing a book himself. He alluded to this in his remarks at King's funeral, and a few days later Taylor mailed Bishop Simpson a book proposal. He asked for the bishop's help and patronage in bringing a book of death narratives to press. On his visit to California, Simpson had encouraged Taylor to write a book on street preaching. Taylor believed he did not have anything original to say on that subject but offered to include some thoughts on it to please the bishop and to dedicate the book to him. The main thrust of the book, Taylor insisted, would be death scenes. He believed they would provide hope to those who had lost touch with gold-seeking family members by testifying to the possibility of a faithful death on the California frontier.[144]

Accounts of holy dying were a staple of Methodist devotional literature. Informed by an Arminian theology that did not take perseverance in faith for granted, these stories testified to the efficacy of faith in the face of death and the value of a holy life lived to its completion.[145] Taylor had long demonstrated an interest in death narratives. In 1848, he wrote one about his sixteen-year-old sister Martha, testifying to her conversion and persistence in faith until death.[146] Death narratives also represented a subsection of a larger genre of published autobiographies and biographies that formulaically traced Methodist understandings of salvation and spiritual experience—beginning with a life of sin, conversion, continued struggles with sin, and, often, to entire sanctification—through individual lives.[147] Such biographical works were a part of an even larger world of Methodist print culture. In some respects, it is no surprise Taylor would venture into this world. Methodists were avid producers and consumers of religious books, hymnals, newspapers, and magazines. Preachers doubled as salesmen, earning commissions to supplement their salaries.[148]

Nor was it surprising when Taylor's critics took to press aspersions against him for the debt he bore, or that Taylor responded in kind. He was acutely concerned with his reputation and often sought public forums to defend it. A few years earlier he had written newspaper articles to answer those who charged him with visiting a Unitarian church and with owning slaves.[149] In the case of his debt, Taylor was particularly concerned when his situation was mentioned in the *Christian Advocate* as leading to a "wreck of confidence among brethren."[150] Taylor promptly responded to that article with his own letter, incensed that the author had attacked his good name and published false insinuations to "the church at large."[151] Taylor and the author of that article would reconcile. Yet another critic in the church, John Daniel, found the *California Christian Advocate* would not print his article, so he turned to the Presbyterian newspaper, the *Pacific*, to accuse Taylor of financial misconduct.[152]

When the 1856 California Conference met in August 1856, two separate committees were again convened to consider Taylor's case. The first, chaired by Owen, investigated the Bethel itself. The second, chaired by Daniel, considered Taylor's moral character. The report of Owen's committee detailed the history and status of the Bethel and acknowledged that Taylor had taken on a debt that now stood at $22,015.35 at the request of that body. Despite this claim of responsibility, the report fell to a weak conclusion: "Resolved that we deeply sympathize with Bro. Taylor in the said involvement, and regret that it is not in our power personally to assist him."[153] Taylor was on his own, and he would have to find a way to pay his debt himself. Daniel's committee considered nine accusations against Taylor. He responded to the charges in turn and offered his personal financial records for examination. This report has been lost, but the conference minutes recorded that it cleared Taylor's character and passed unanimously. Taylor was elated at his vindication and could not have hoped for a better outcome since even Daniel voted to clear him.[154]

Following the vote, Taylor took to the floor to ask for permission to travel east to raise money. He announced that he had again been offered free passage to New York and, for the first time, shared that he was writing a book for publication that he hoped would pay off his debt. Approval was granted unanimously. To their credit, some of Taylor's colleagues were unsatisfied with this closure. That afternoon, the body passed a resolution declaring "that Rev. Wm. Taylor has our confidence, our sympathy, our commendations, and our prayers; and he shall find willing hands to clasp him, and warm hearts to receive him on his return."[155] The family quickly sold their belongings, leased their home in Alameda, and sailed for New York. Taylor would never return to California as a regular Methodist preacher.[156]

This chapter has explored Taylor's work as a missionary in California to illustrate some dynamics of the Methodist missionary tradition in contexts of nineteenth-century American expansion. Methodists like Taylor worked to establish their presence, either in person or through their institutions, wherever they could within the growing nation. Taylor asserted his presence onboard ship, in the streets of San Francisco, saloons, and hospitals to bring those he met to repentance. He also worked with others to create a Methodist presence in California such as society meetings, schools, and published reading material, believing that through such means the souls and lives of people would grow in God's holiness. In its own way, even Taylor's book idea was a manifestation of this Methodist missionary strategy; it was to be an assertion that a holy life and death was possible even in California.

The development of Californian Methodism would go on in Taylor's absence. Others continued the mission of establishing a Methodist presence in the state. Another minister was appointed to continue the Bethel in Taylor place, for example.[157] Others attempted to take up his work with seamen, as well. A group known as the Ladies Aid and Protection Society for the Benefit of Seamen opened a boardinghouse called the Sailor's Home in 1856. Unfortunately it was run by a series of corrupt managers who were accused of stealing money from sailors and shanghaiing.[158]

This chapter also highlighted the importance of connection to Methodist missionary outreach. Taylor and others began building connectional networks among laity and preachers even before formal structures mandated by the denomination came into being. Once in place, such ecclesiological structures, however, provided very little support for ongoing ministry. Missionaries like Taylor were encouraged to take entrepreneurial risks trusting in God's providence. As Taylor discovered, however, Methodists may have believed that God would provide, but the church rarely did. Even formal missionary structures such as mission conferences offered little aid.

Taylor had not gone to California to make his fortune, but like many argonauts who joined the gold rush, he returned home penniless. But his odyssey was just beginning. On arriving in the east, he would take on new roles as an author and itinerant evangelist. These roles would take him almost around the world. He would find ways to use Methodist connectional structures to his own benefit. The vision Taylor had of reaching the world through his ministry would be realized not through sailors but his own life. The next chapter will describe that development and his encounters with British Methodism as he traveled to Canada, the British Isles, through Palestine to Australasia.

NOTES

1. Andrew F. Walls, "The American Dimension of the Missionary Movement," in *The Missionary Movement in Christian History: Studies in the Transmission of Faith* (Maryknoll: Orbis Books, 1996), 227.

2. "For California," *The Sun*, February 10, 1849; *Missonary Society of the Methodist Episcopal Church, Missions Minutes 1819–1916*, Scholarly Resources ([Wilmington, DE][1979]), February 21, 1849; William Taylor, *Story of My Life; an Account of What I Have Thought and Said and Done in My Ministry of More Than Fifty-Three Years in Christian Lands and among the Heathen. Written by Myself* (New York: Hunt & Eaton, 1896), 104.

3. Taylor, *Story of My Life*, 105.

4. "Local Matters: For California," *The Sun*, April 19, 1849.

5. Cynthia Lynn Lyerly, *Methodism and the Southern Mind, 1770–1810* (New York: Oxford University Press, 1998), 39–41; Tetsuo Scott Miyakawa, *Protestants and Pioneers: Individualism and Conformity on the American Frontier* (Chicago: University of Chicago Press, 1964), 54–58.

6. Anne W. Booth, *Journal of a Voyage from Baltimore to San Francisco. . . On Ship*, Andalusia, F. W. Wilson, Master, Bancroft Library, University of California, April 21, 1849; Charles W. Turner, "California' Taylor of Rockbridge: Bishop to the World," *Southern California Quarterly* 62, no. 3 (1980): 238; David Bundy, "Bishop William Taylor and Methodist Mission: A Study in Nineteenth Century Social History (Part 1)," *Methodist History* 27, no. 4 (1989): 200–1.

7. William Taylor to Charles B. Tippett, May 3, 1849, William Taylor Collection, Lovely Lane Museum and Archives.

8. Ibid.

9. Ibid.

10. Ibid.

11. Booth, *Journal*, May 20, 1849.

12. Ibid., May 20–27, 1849.

13. Nathan O. Hatch, *The Democratization of American Christianity* (New Haven: Yale University Press, 1989), 41.

14. Booth, *Journal*, June 3, 1849.

15. Taylor to Tippett, May 3, 1849.

16. Booth, *Journal*, June 21–23, 1849; Robert F. Lay, ed., *Lessons of Infinite Advantage: William Taylor's California Experiences. With Isabelle Anne Kimberlin Taylor's Travel Diary, 1866–67, Written During a Voyage with Her Family En Route from the Cape of Good Hope, South Africa, to London and Subsequent Travels Throughout Europe* (Lanham: Scarecrow Press and The Center for the Study of World Christian Revitalization Movements, 2010), 122. About four decades later, Taylor wrote that Oceana was born June 3, 1849, "off Cape Horn." Taylor, *Story of My Life*, 105.

17. Booth, *Journal*, August 29, 1849; Lay, ed., *Lessons*, 55.

18. Booth, *Journal*, July 15, 28, August 2 & 4, 1849; Taylor, *Story of My Life*, 105–6.

19. Booth, *Journal*, August 5, 1849.

20. Alexis McCrossen, *Holy Day, Holiday: The American Sunday* (Ithaca: Cornell University Press, 2000); Karen B. Westerfield Tucker, *American Methodist Worship* (New York: Oxford University Press, 2011), 44–47.

21. John Mack Faragher, *Women and Men on the Overland Trail* (New Haven: Yale University Press, 1979), 95–97.

22. John R. Jr. Purdy, "Isaac Owen—Overland to California," *Methodist History* 11, no. 4 (1973): 46–54.

23. Winton U. Solberg, "The Sabbath on the Overland Trail to California," *Church History* 59, no. 3 (1990): 340–55.

24. C. V. Anthony, *Fifty Years of Methodism: A History of the Methodist Episcopal Church within the Bounds of the California Annual Conference from 1847 to 1897* (San Francisco: Methodist Book Concern, 1901), 201; Booth, *Journal*, August 6, 11–12, 1849.

25. William Taylor, *California Life Illustrated* (New York: Published for the author by Carlton & Porter, 1858), 14.

26. Booth, *Journal*, August 19, September 2, 16, 1849.

27. Wade Crawford Barclay, *Early American Methodism, 1769–1844: To Reform the Nation*, vol. 2, History of Methodist Missions (New York: Board of Missions and Church Extension of the Methodist Church, 1950), 200–62; Bruce David Forbes, "'and Obey God, Etc.': Methodism and American Indians," *Methodist History* 23, no. 1 (1984): 12–14.

28. Luke Schleif, "That Her Religion May Be Uprooted: The Methodists and the Mexican-American War," *Methodist History* 52, no. 1 (2013): 19–32.

29. "Journal of the General Conference of the Methodist Episcopal Church, 1848," in *Journals of the General Conference of the Methodist Episcopal Church, 1848–56* (New York: Carlton & Porter), 32, 39–40.

30. Wade Crawford Barclay, *The Methodist Episcopal Church, 1845–1939: Widening Horizons, 1845–95*, vol. 3, History of Methodist Missions (New York: Board

of Missions and Church Extension of the Methodist Church, 1957), 166–70; Russell E. Richey, "Organizing for Missions: A Methodist Case Study," in *The Foreign Missionary Enterprise at Home: Explorations in North American Cultural History*, ed. Daniel H. Bays and Grant Wacker (Tuscaloosa: University of Alabama Press, 2003), 75–89.

31. *Missonary Society . . . Missions Minutes 1819–1916*, January 17, 1849; Taylor, *California Life*, 31.

32. Barclay, *Widening Horizons*, 166–70.

33. Anthony, *Fifty Years*, 9–21; Elizabeth M. Smith, "William Roberts: Circuit Rider of the Far West," *Methodist History* 20, no. 2 (1982): 60–74.

34. David Hempton, *Methodism: Empire of the Spirit* (New Haven: Yale University Press, 2005), 30.

35. Leon L. Loofbourow, *In Search of God's Gold: A Story of Continued Christian Pioneering in California* (San Francisco: Historical Society of the California-Nevada Annual Conference of the Methodist Church, and in cooperation with the College of the Pacific, 1950), 35–36; Taylor, *California Life*, 23, 26–29, 43, 46, 56, 89, 91–92.

36. Frank K. Baker, *Fifty-Fifth Anniversary History of First Methodist Episcopal Church*, Souvenir ed. (San Francisco: N.p., 1902), 15; William Roberts, *The Roberts Letters: Book Three: Additional Letters* (Salem: The Commission on Archives and History, Oregon-Idaho Conference, 1998), 103; Taylor, *California Life*, 25.

37. Booth, *Journal*, September 23, 1849; Taylor, *California Life*, 25–29.

38. Booth, *Journal*, August 29, 1849; H. W. Brands, *The Age of Gold: The California Gold Rush and the New American Dream* (New York: Doubleday, 2002), 211–12.

39. Taylor, *California Life*, 25, 30–31.

40. Ibid., 35–48.

41. Ibid., 49.

42. William Taylor to Charles B. Tippett, November 29, 1849, William Taylor Collection, Lovely Lane Museum and Archives.

43. Loofbourow, *God's Gold*, 36; Taylor, *California Life*, 57–58; Taylor to Tippett, November 29, 1849.

44. John Wigger, *American Saint: Francis Asbury & the Methodists* (New York: Oxford University Press, 2009), 388–90; Russell E. Richey, Kenneth E. Rowe, and Jean Miller Schmidt, *The Methodist Experience in America: A History* (Nashville: Abingdon Press, 2010), 103–6.

45. Isaac Owen to Bishop Waugh, November 7, 1848, Isaac Owen Papers, 1830–1866, Bancroft Library, University of California, Berkeley.

46. Taylor, *California Life*, 113.

47. Ibid., 112–13, 19–31.

48. Anthony, *Fifty Years*, 31–33; Taylor, *California Life*, 110–11.

49. Laurie F. Maffly-Kipp, *Religion and Society in Frontier California* (New Haven: Yale University Press, 1994), 99–102.

50. Robert W. Sledge, *Five Dollars and Myself: The History of Mission of the Methodist Episcopal Church, South, 1845–1939* (New York: General Board of Global Ministries, United Methodist Church, 2005), 62.

51. Taylor to Tippett, November 29, 1849.

52. Taylor, *California Life*, 34.

53. Baker, *Fifty-Fifth Anniversary*, 17–18; Taylor, *California Life*, 77; *Doctrines and Discipline of the Methodist Episcopal Church, 1848* (New York: Lane & Scott, 1848), 166.

54. Wm. Taylor to G. S. Phillips, May 16, 1853, May 24, 1853, June 16, 1853, G. S. Phillips Collection, California State Library.

55. "University Charter," University of the Pacific, accessed January 21, 2011, web.pacific.edu/Administration/Board-of-Regents/University-Charter.html; Lay, ed., *Lessons*, 49.

56. Lay, ed., *Lessons*, 48–49, 54, 90, 117; Anthony, *Fifty Years*, 79–80, 92–93; Archibald Taylor File, California Conference Papers, California-Nevada Conference Archives, Pacific School of Religion; William Taylor, *The Model Preacher: Comprised in a Series of Letters Illustrating the Best Mode of Preaching the Gospel* (Cincinnati: Swormstedt & Poe, for the author, 1860), 3.

57. Anthony, *Fifty Years*, 41–52; Minutes of the First Annual Meeting of the Members of the Oregon & California Mission Conference Stationed on the California District, California Conference Papers, California-Nevada Conference Archives, Pacific School of Religion.

58. Taylor, *California Life*, 139–42; Wm. Taylor to Henry Slicer, September 30, 1853, William Taylor Collection, Lovely Lane Museum and Archives.

59. "Journal of the General Conference of the Methodist Episcopal Church, 1852," in *Journals of the General Conference of the Methodist Episcopal Church, 1848–56* (New York: Carlton & Porter, 1856), 63, 153.

60. Minutes of the California Annual Conference 1853, California Conference Papers, California-Nevada Conference Archives, Pacific School of Religion.

61. Matthew Simpson, *Cyclopedia of Methodism: Embracing Sketches . . . .* (Philadelphia: Everts & Stewart, 1878), 782.

62. William Taylor, *Seven Years' Street Preaching in San Francisco, California Embracing Incidents, Triumphant Death Scenes, Etc* (New York: Published for the author by Carlton & Porter, 1856), 52–53.

63. "Description of Mural Paintings," *Municipal Record: City and County of San Francisco*, November 19, 1925. For a copy of the mural containing the portrait, see James A. Ganz, ed. *Jewel City: Art from San Francisco's Panama-Pacific International Exhibition* (San Francisco: Fine Arts Museums of San Francisco/University of California Press, 2015), 104–5.

64. Taylor, *Seven Years'*, 52–55.

65. Harry S. Stout, *The Divine Dramatist: George Whitefield and the Rise of Modern Evangelicalism* (Grand Rapids: W. B. Eerdmans, 1991), 66–86.

66. Taylor, *Seven Years'*, 26–27.

67. Roberts, *Roberts Letters: Book Three*, 122.

68. Taylor, *Seven Years'*, 42.

69. Ibid., 45–46.

70. Ibid., 130.

71. Flora Haines Loughead, ed., *Life, Diary and Letters of Oscar Lovell Shafter* (San Francisco: Blair-Murdock, 1915), 173.

72. San Francisco Bethel Church Records, California Conference Papers, California-Nevada Conference Archives, Pacific School of Religion.

73. J. S. Holliday, *The World Rushed In: The California Gold Rush Experience* (New York: Simon and Schuster, 1981), 27–29; Robert H. Jackson and Edward Castillo, *Indians, Franciscans, and Spanish Colonization: The Impact of the Mission System on California Indians* (Albuquerque: University of New Mexico Press, 1995), 87–111.

74. Doris Marion Wright, "The Making of Cosmopolitan California: An Analysis of Immigration, 1848–1870 (Pt. 1)," *California Historical Society Quarterly* 19 (1940): 323, 33 note 1.

75. Doris Marion Wright, "The Making of Cosmopolitan California: An Analysis of Immigration, 1848–1870 (Pt. 2)," *California Historical Society Quarterly* 20 (1941): 73–74.

76. Barbara Berglund, *Making San Francisco American: Cultural Frontiers in the Urban West, 1846–1906* (Lawrence: University Press of Kansas, 2007), 6–9.

77. Maffly-Kipp, *Religion and Society*, 50–51.

78. Taylor, *Seven Years'*, 348.

79. William Taylor to James Sewell, January 30, 1851, William Taylor Collection, Lovely Lane Museum and Archives.

80. Taylor, *California Life*, 324–5.

81. Ibid., 73–76.

82. Colleen McDannell, *The Christian Home in Victorian America, 1840–1900* (Bloomington: Indiana University Press, 1986), 7.

83. Maffly-Kipp, *Religion and Society*, 150–2.

84. Francis A. Walker, *The Vital Statistics of the United States . . . .* (Washington, DC: Government Printing Office, 1872), 560. On the presence of women in gold rush California, see JoAnn Levy, *They Saw the Elephant: Women in the California Gold Rush* (Hamden: Archon Books, 1990).

85. Susan Lee Johnson, *Roaring Camp: The Social World of the California Gold Rush* (New York: W.W. Norton, 2000), 129.

86. Taylor, *California Life*, 217–22, 29–30.

87. Wm. Taylor, "Missionary Department: From our Mission-Rooms," *Christian Advocate*, March 20, 1851; Taylor, *Seven Years'*, 82–86.

88. Taylor, *Seven Years'*, 84.

89. Ibid.

90. Dana L. Robert, *American Women in Mission: A Social History of Their Thought and Practice* (Macon: Mercer University Press, 1997), 39–80.

91. [Anne Taylor] to Bro. Leonard, January 27, 1892, Taylor, W. (Bishop) 1886–1890, Missionary Files (Microfilm Edition), United Methodist Church Archives—GCAH.

92. "Local Intelligence: City Improvements," *California Christian Advocate*, April 8, 1852; Taylor, *California Life*, 44–48, 118–19, 37–38; Lay, ed., *Lessons*, 25, 93, 134–35.

93. Taylor, *California Life*, 50.

94. William Taylor, "Memoirs: Little Charley Taylor," *Western Christian Advocate*, January 4, 1860; Lay, ed., *Lessons*, 117–23.

95. William Roberts, *The Roberts Letters: Book Two: The Carbonic Copy Book* (Salem: The Commission on Archives and History, Oregon-Idaho Conference, United Methodist Church, 1998), 37.

96. Lay, ed., *Lessons*, 122–3.

97. Taylor, *Seven Years'*, 53.

98. Lay, ed., *Lessons*, 52, 94–95.

99. "Sister Anne, "Cobwebs—California Housewives," *California Christian Advocate*, April 7, 1854.

100. Taylor, *California Life*, 304–6, 324–5.

101. Barclay, *Widening Horizons*, 932–95.

102. F. A. Schumann to S. N. Matthews, May 25, 1925, W. S. Matthew Papers, California Conference Papers, California-Nevada Conference Archives, Pacific School of Religion.

103. Barclay, *Widening Horizons*, 367–69.

104. Taylor, *California Life*, 313.

105. "Missionary Department: From Our Mission Rooms: San Francisco," *Christian Advocate*, April 17, 1851.

106. Wm. Taylor, "Missionary Department: From our Mission-Rooms," *Christian Advocate*, March 20, 1851.

107. Anthony, *Fifty Years*, 295.

108. Sargent Bush, "The Pulpit Artistry of Father Taylor: An 1836 Account," *American Literature* 50, no. 1 (1978): 106–9; George Duncan Campbell, "Father Taylor the Seamen's Apostle," *Methodist History* 15, no. 4 (1977): 251–260; Curtis Dahl, "Three Fathers, Many Sons: Ecclus. 44:1," *Methodist History* 15, no. 4 (1977): 234–50.

109. Roald Kverndal, *Seamen's Missions: Their Origin and Early Growth* (Pasadena: William Carey Library, 1986), 485–99; Henry C. Whyman, *The Hedstroms and the Bethel Ship Saga: Methodist Influence on Swedish Religious Life* (Carbondale: Southern Illinois University Press, 1992), 58–76.

110. Kverndal, *Seamen's Missions*, 492.

111. Taylor, *Story of My Life*, 664; Journal of Sabbaths (July 4, 1849–January 1, 1850), David and Jane Wales Trumbull Manuscript Collection, Princeton Theological Seminary Library.

112. Taylor, *Seven Years'*, 220–22; Baker, *Fifty-Fifth Anniversary*, 31–32; Lay, ed., *Lessons*, 27, 51.

113. Lay, ed., *Lessons*, 27.

114. Ibid., 34.

115. Frank Soulé, John H. Gihon, and James Nisbet, *The Annals of San Francisco* . . . . (New York: D. Appleton, 1855), 329–33.

116. Lay, ed., *Lessons*, 48; Taylor, *Seven Years'*, 112.

117. Roberts, *Roberts Letters: Book Three*, 158; Lay, ed., *Lessons*, 65–67, 90, 93, 117; Taylor, *California Life*, 333; Isaac Owen to J.P. Durbin, November 25, 1851, Isaac Owen Papers, 1830–1866, Bancroft Library, University of California, Berkeley; "Local Intelligence: City Improvements," *California Christian Advocate*, April 8, 1852.

118. Kverndal, *Seamen's Missions*, 484.

119. Lay, ed., *Lessons*, 71, 90; "Twenty-Fourth Annual Report of the American Seamen's Friend Society," *The Sailor's Magazine*, June 1852, 667.

120. Westerfield Tucker, *American Methodist Worship*, 79; Lay, ed., *Lessons*, 52, 94, 135.

121. *The Doctrines and Discipline of the Methodist Episcopal Church* (New York: Carlton & Porter, 1856), 30–31.

122. San Francisco Bethel Church Records, California Conference Papers, California-Nevada Conference Archives, Pacific School of Religion.

123. Taylor, *Seven Years'*, 343.

124. Kverndal, *Seamen's Missions*, 485; Taylor, *California Life*, 333; Lay, ed., *Lessons*, 52; Lance S. Davidson, "Shanghaied! The Systematic Kidnapping of Sailors in Early San Francisco," *California History* 64, no. 1 (1985): 10–17.

125. Report of the Committee Investigating the Seamen's Bethel 1856, California Conference Papers, California-Nevada Conference Archives, Pacific School of Religion; Lay, ed., *Lessons*, 133.

126. Journals—California [no date, page 94], Matthew Simpson Collection, Drew University Methodist Collection, Drew University.

127. Lay, ed., *Lessons*, 133–7; Report of the Committee; Taylor, *California Life*, 335.

128. Lay, ed., *Lessons*, 163.

129. Taylor, *California Life*, 335–37; Brands, *Age of Gold*, 291–2.

130. Richey, Rowe, and Schmidt, *Methodist Experience*, 107–11; Isaac Owen to Bishop Waugh, November 7, 1848, Isaac Owen Papers, 1830–1866, Bancroft Library, University of California, Berkeley; Taylor, *California Life*, 113, 39–42; Lay, ed., *Lessons*, 69, 96; Taylor to Slicer; Anthony, *Fifty Years*, 76–77.

131. Simpson, ed. *Cyclopedia*, 159; Minutes of the California Annual Conference 1854, California Conference Papers, California-Nevada Conference Archives, Pacific School of Religion; "Journal . . . , 1852," 63.

132. *Doctrines and Discipline of the Methodist Episcopal Church, 1852* (New York: Carlton & Phillips, 1852), 102.

133. Minutes of the California Annual Conference, 1855, California Conference Papers, California-Nevada Conference Archives, Pacific School of Religion.

134. Lay, ed., *Lessons*, 208.

135. "Row about a Church," *Daily Democratic State Journal*, October 12, 1855; "Malicious Mischief," *Daily Evening Bulletin*, October 13, 1855; "Seamen's Bethel," *Daily Evening Bulletin*, December 22, 1855; Wm. Taylor, "California Correspondence," *Christian Advocate*, April 3, 1856; Lay, ed., *Lessons*, 167.

136. *A True and Minute History of the Assassination of James King of Wm. At San Francisco, Cal. . . .* (San Francisco: Whitton, Towne, 1856), 3; Taylor, *Seven Years'*, 248–253.

137. "Donation Visit," *Daily Evening Bulletin*, December 31, 1855; Lay, ed., *Lessons*, 185.

138. *True and Minute History*, 3–4; Brands, *Age of Gold*, 350–1.

139. Taylor, *Seven Years'*, 255–6.

140. *True and Minute History*, 23–25.

141. Lay, ed., *Lessons*, 206.

142. Brands, *Age of Gold*, 350–8.

143. Taylor, *Seven Years'*, 258.

144. *True and Minute History*, 23; William Taylor to Matthew Simpson, June 4, 1856, Matthew Simpson Papers, Manuscript Division, Library of Congress.

145. Hempton, *Methodism*, 65–68.

146. Wm. Taylor, "Biographical," *Christian Advocate*, April 26, 1848.

147. Ted A. Campbell, "Spiritual Biography and Autobiography," in *The Cambridge Companion to American Methodism*, ed. Jason E. Vickers (New York: Cambridge University Press, 2013), 252–7.

148. Richey, Rowe, and Schmidt, *Methodist Experience*, 107–11.

149. Wm. Taylor, "Taylor and Bland—the Slave-holding Ministers," *California Christian Advocate*, June 10, 1852; Wm. Taylor, "Brother Taylor Speaks for Himself," *Christian Advocate*, December 22, 1853.

150. E. T., "Letter from San Francisco: Its Religious Interests," *Christian Advocate*, January 17, 1856.

151. Wm. Taylor, "California Correspondence," *Christian Advocate*, April 3, 1856.

152. Lay, ed., *Lessons*, 207.

153. Report of the Committee.

154. Minutes of the Fourth Session of the California Annual Conference, California Conference Papers, California-Nevada Conference Archives; *Lessons*, 207–8.

155. Minutes of the Fourth Session.

156. Lay, ed., *Lessons*, 209.

157. Minutes of the Fourth Session.

158. Bill Pickelhaupt, *Shanghaied in San Francisco* (San Francisco: Flyblister Press, 1996), 86–88.

Chapter 3

Dominions of the Divine Sovereign

The nineteenth century witnessed a transportation revolution. Technological advances in steam power enabled faster and more reliable movement around the globe. Rail lines were laid on land, and more and faster steamships plied the waters of the world. Taylor lived through this transformation; it made his global career and the missionary movement he inspired possible. For example, it took five months for the Taylors to reach California by sail in 1849. In 1856 the family returned east in only about six weeks sailing by steamship and crossing Panama by railroad.[1] Speed of travel continued to accelerate and become more reliable as the century progressed.

Taylor marveled at the power of steam. He assumed something so incredible and beneficial to the spread of his religion could only have a godly origin. Soon after launching new Methodist missions in South America in the 1870s, he wrote that steam-powered travel was made possible by the "emancipating power of the Gospel."[2] Because Anglo-Saxon peoples of England and America "more than any other people of the modern era" had embraced evangelical Christianity, God both liberated the inventive powers of those nations to develop such innovations and gave them dominion over much of the world to further the spread of his faith.[3]

Taylor's evaluation named intertwined factors that contributed to the spread of nineteenth-century Methodism. As noted by historian David Hempton, Taylor illustrated the way "American and English Methodism embraced the world in a kind of pincer movement of expanding empires."[4] Taylor's missionary career began in California, an area of American conquest and settlement. This chapter will explore how from 1856 to 1866, Taylor moved into and engaged with Methodism elsewhere in America and the British imperial world. After establishing himself as a revivalist and author in the northern United States, he moved into Canada and the United Kingdom. He toured the

Near East on his way to the British colonies in Australia and New Zealand. This tour was possible because Taylor took advantage of steam travel and a growing network of imperial and ecclesiastical contacts around the world.

Although Taylor's assessment of Anglo-American civilization was partially born of his own ethnocentrism, it was also a theological statement to be understood alongside his other beliefs. Like other evangelicals, Taylor saw all political authority to be under God's superintendence, and God intended the salvation of the world, not its political subjugation. What ultimately mattered was not the spread of empire but the spread of the gospel. Missionaries like Taylor generally sought to avoid political entanglements but were willing to embrace opportunities presented by empire to pursue their own objectives. Such openings were believed to have been brought about by the mysteries of God's providence. In this process, missionaries were often blind to the degree to which they became identified with colonizing powers by indigenous persons.[5] Moreover, it was understood that even Anglo-American civilization was not entirely Christian and many in the Anglo-American world who claimed to be Christian did not take that commitment seriously. As historian Andrew Walls noted, evangelicalism emerged as "a religion of protest against a Christian society that is not Christian enough."[6] This chapter will also explore some ways Methodists sought to fulfill their missionary calling in contexts not usually understood as missionary—contexts where church institutions were established and Christian identity taken for granted. In Taylor's career, this facet of mission primarily took the form of mass revivalism as he transitioned from being a Methodist preacher to an itinerant evangelist.

THE REVIVAL OF 1857–1858

The Taylors arrived in New York in November 1856. They hoped to continue on to family in Virginia. Publication of William's book, family tragedy, and winter weather, however, kept them in the city for several months. During this time, Taylor began transitioning into new roles. He had been a Methodist preacher and missionary in the American far west; now he became a revivalist and an author. For the next decade, Taylor traveled in wider and wider circles in the Methodist world, both leading revivals and selling books to pay off his debt.

Taylor's plan for redemption through book sales, however, almost floundered at the start. Abel Stevens and W. P. Strickland, leading editors of Methodist publications at the Methodist Book Concern in New York, met with Taylor. Strickland agreed to edit Taylor's manuscript for $200, and the publishers, Carlton and Porter, asked for a thousand dollar advance. Taylor was destitute but without that outlay, he could not proceed. Fortunately,

Taylor met a merchant he had known in California who advanced him the needed money.[7]

While waiting for his book to be printed, Taylor led revival services in the New York area. Individuals met in these ministrations came to the family's aid when their seventeen-month old boy, William Osman, died on Christmas day. The Taylors could not afford to bury their son, but laymen donated a coffin, transport to the cemetery, and a burial plot in Brooklyn. Taylor both grieved the death and feared additional tragedy. Letters sent to family in Virginia had gone unanswered.[8] As he wrote to his sister and brother-in-law, "I really do not know whether you are all dead or not. If you are not dead, please write by return mail and let me know. Doth my father & mother yet live, & are they well?"[9] They were alive, but it would be some time before the Taylors could travel south to be reunited.

The extended stay in New York allowed Taylor to become better acquainted with one of the leading lay Methodists of the period, Phoebe Palmer. Palmer and her sister Sarah Lankford were key figures in the mid-century holiness movement. In 1835, Lankford claimed an experience of entire sanctification and began holding women's prayer meetings on Tuesdays at her home in New York. She encouraged her sister to seek the experience as well. In 1837, following the death of a daughter, Palmer surrendered everything to God and received the assurance that consecration was the blessing she sought. Palmer took over leadership of the Tuesday meeting and began to include men in the fellowship. By the 1850s, many prominent Methodists, and other Protestant clergy and laity, attended the Tuesday meetings. As a young preacher, Taylor had met Palmer at a camp meeting near Baltimore.[10] Her theology had been influential in shaping Taylor's theology and call to become a missionary. Now Taylor participated in the meetings as a returned missionary.[11] Palmer recalled that Taylor shared with those gathered "a thrilling account of various trying, triumphant experiences" of his ministry in California.[12]

Palmer was not alone in her interest in California. The American public was eager for stories of life there. When Taylor's first book, *Seven Years' Street Preaching in San Francisco, California; Embracing Incidents, Triumphant Death Scenes, Etc.*, came out in early 1857, it joined a growing body of literature about the state. In this writing, California often functioned as a metaphor of a link between moral danger and potential prosperity.[13] Middle-class, polite culture was also critiqued. The worst thing one could be was an "over-civilized easterner."[14] Taylor's book shared these themes. As one reviewer observed, Taylor's book demonstrated that a successful evangelist must not put on "airs of superiority" or be "enslaved to propriety and routine."[15] In this respect, *Seven Years'* not only launched Taylor's literary career but also fostered a change in his identity. William adopted the nickname

"California" Taylor and gradually embraced the idea that his evangelistic success was due, in part, to his lack of civilized refinement.

Unlike other books about California, Taylor's also contained theological content that made it appealing to evangelical readers. The driving theme of the book was perseverance in faith. Despite its title and Bishop Simpson's encouragement, *Seven Years' Street Preaching* was not a treatise on the practice or a collection of sermons, although it contained some introductory chapters on street preaching and summarized some sermons. The book was a series of anecdotes and reflections about Taylor's work in California. Death scenes only comprised the final 10 percent of the book. It is not clear why Taylor chose to shift the focus away from these stories but those included fit the larger theme. The same faith featured individuals exhibited in death, Taylor presented himself as demonstrating in life while surrounded by depravity in California.

Strickland was probably responsible for making Taylor's prose more assertive. Just before working on Taylor's book, Strickland edited the autobiography of Peter Cartwright, an important early Methodist preacher. Literary scholar Robert Bray concluded that Strickland made Cartwright sound more confident and removed a tone of "apologetic anxiety."[16] Taylor's full manuscript is not available, but in a draft death scene sent to Bishop Matthew Simpson, Taylor used the first-person plural, indicating he visited the deceased in the hospital with others. The published version adopted the singular and gave the false impression that Taylor acted alone.[17] However these changes were introduced, the greater focus on Taylor in the book would anger his colleagues in California because it ignored their contributions to establishing Methodism in the state. Taylor also later recalled that he was unhappy with Strickland's work for his own reasons. In some cases, he preferred his own prose and "corrected the doctor's corrections, and clothed all my facts in my own homespun attire."[18] Nevertheless, Strickland's name remained on the book as editor.[19]

Contemporaries outside California read *Seven Years'* as a testimony of Taylor's own heroic and steady faith. They also saw it as a call to mission. By early March, the Taylors traveled south to Baltimore to attend the annual meeting of the Baltimore Conference of the Methodist Episcopal Church. Taylor addressed his former colleagues in that conference, and the conference adopted a report commending *Seven Years'* as a model for Methodist mission and evangelism.[20] This report of the Committee on Street and Field Preaching noted that the missionary commission that Methodists had been given for the whole world could also be also filled close to home through methods such as street preaching. Preachers and churches were encouraged to find ways to seek "the non-church goers" among their neighbors and bring them to God.[21]

While the adopted report commended street preaching as an evangelistic technique, revival services and prayer meetings were a more common way Methodists attempted to meet their missionary commission close to home.[22] Taylor's presence in Baltimore prompted Ben Brooke, the preacher appointed to Charles Street, to plan a revival campaign with Taylor's help. Brooke observed that the same interested congregations that had sent the Taylors west now crowded churches to hear their former preacher and returned missionary address Sunday schools, a missionary society, and give a benefit lecture to help a free black man buy the freedom of his family. Brooke realized the interest Taylor generated could also attract crowds to revival services.[23]

With these services Taylor's work as a revivalist began in earnest as did his participation in what has been called the Revival of 1857–1858. As historian Kathryn Long noted, traditional accounts of this revival portrayed it as a spontaneous event among New York's businessmen in September 1857. These accounts were shaped by a Calvinist theology that understood revivals to be an act of divine providence periodically visited by God on people. Methodists, however, saw revivals as an essential part of true religion and a useful evangelistic technique. Long also found that the revival began in many localities with little sense at the time that they represented a larger, national social trend.[24] Reflecting this broader and Methodist perspective, the account of the Baltimore revival in the Methodist press and Taylor's recollection emphasizes clerical initiative, the use of specific strategies to promote revival, the initial reluctance of businessmen to participate, and the early prominence of women and youth. The Baltimore revival also predated the one in New York.

Brooke and Taylor developed a plan in which Brooke retained responsibility for his duties as the appointed preacher at the church. He preached to the congregation Sunday morning and interviewed prospective members about their conversions. Taylor took on additional duties demanded by the revival schedule—preaching every day at prayer meetings. Laymen of the church were initially resistant because April was a difficult month to leave work, and Baltimore's Methodists traditionally held their revivals in the fall. Such lay support was necessary, because exhorters were needed to encourage potential converts. Attendees would be invited to give names of those "under an awakening of the Spirit" to be visited by Taylor or Brooke.[25]

Brooke and Taylor pushed ahead with their plan. By the end of April one report estimated that between 60 and 100, mostly young, men and women had been converted and sanctified. Women represented the bulk of the congregations at first but as the Baltimore revival gained momentum, men and prominent members of the community participated. Reports eventually noted the appearance of "numbers of *men of business*" in the meetings, and other congregations and denomination in the city began to hold special revival services.[26]

Most of the Baltimore revival took place without Taylor's help. He remained in the city for only three weeks before continuing south to Georgetown. There Taylor repeated the process for two weeks. He preached twice daily in the church and public markets and addressed Sunday school students.[27] In all his work as a revivalist, Taylor rarely remained in any location for more than three weeks. As a result, he rarely observed the long-term effects of his revivals, such as whether converts remained faithful or directed their energies to social reform.[28] Nevertheless, Baltimore's Methodists credited Taylor with sparking the city's revival.[29] Beyond any impact he had in that community, however, Taylor and Brooke's template became the basic model Taylor used for revivals for much of the next decade. It featured daily preaching by Taylor and prayer meetings at which potential converts were identified. These individuals were exhorted by lay leaders to have faith in Christ or to consecrate themselves to Christ and receive entire sanctification.

When the family finally arrived in Virginia, Taylor was impoverished, exhausted, and depressed. Revival work had tired him, but continued grief and financial strains certainly added to the pressure Taylor felt. "I felt the reaction telling upon me," he wrote, "Causing great lassitude of mind and body."[30] Back at home, Taylor rested, visited with family, and renewed boyhood diversions such as rolling rocks down hillsides. He also made a pilgrimage to the field in Panther Gap where he had been converted. There Taylor knelt and prayed in thanksgiving for all that God had done for him.[31]

In the summer of 1857, William left Anne and the children in Virginia to tour Methodist camp meetings and northeastern cities. He preached at twelve camps ranging from one in his native Rockbridge County, Virginia, in the south, to New Hampshire in the north. Taylor discovered that camp meetings offered opportune settings to sell his book. By assisting with the preaching, Taylor was exposed to a large number of potential buyers. In the midst of this camp meeting campaign, Taylor also spent several months leading revivals in Philadelphia and Boston. When in New England, William met Edward Thompson Taylor. For several years the two "Fathers Taylor" had worked with sailors on opposite sides of the continent. Now, William preached at the Boston Bethel and elsewhere in that city.[32]

Quite by accident, Taylor had found his way into an ambiguous place in the structure of his church. Methodists believed in itinerant evangelism. But that evangelism was practiced within conference boundaries at the direction of a bishop. Preachers were expected to remain in the annual conferences to which they belonged. Taylor, however, moved from conference to conference at his own initiative, traveling much greater distances across the Methodist connection than regular itinerant preachers ever would. There was no provision in nineteenth-century Methodism for an evangelist like Taylor who roamed the country, and eventually the world, as he did, while also retaining his position as an ordained preacher in good standing in his church. The contemporary evangelist, James Caughey, for example, left the ordained Methodist ministry as a career as a revivalist in Canada and the British Isles opened to him.[33]

Taylor was able to maintain his ordination and position in the church, in part, because the California Conference continued to list Taylor as a preacher in good standing on the expectation that he would return when his debt was paid. For his part, Taylor continued to profess a desire to return. *Seven Years'* sold well but to raise over $22,000 through the sale of one dollar books, minus expenses, was daunting.[34] For the next decade, until events in South Africa changed his mind, a return to California and the regular Methodist ministry continued to be Taylor's goal. As he told people, "I suppose it is there that I naturally belong."[35]

BECOMING AN AUTHOR

In the meantime, Taylor embraced a new identity as an author. One slow week in Philadelphia, in the interest of introducing a new book to market, Taylor wrote *Address to Young America, and a Word to the Old Folks* (1857).[36] This short, eighty-one-page booklet contained stories about the life of children in California, Taylor's own childhood, and accounts of other childhood faithfulness. He sought to convince children they were spiritual agents and authorities, responsible for both their own salvation and that of others. To the "old folks" he argued that children were a mission field they had neglected. He called on churches and Sunday schools to work for the conversion of "all our children before they leave their teens."[37]

While Taylor's stories were his own, his representations of children's spirituality were consistent with Methodist views of the time. Believing that the Christian faith was for all, Methodists saw no age or maturity barrier to receiving or testifying to God's salvation. While other nineteenth-century evangelicals either adopted or rejected Horace Bushnell's argument that Christian nurture made conversion unnecessary, Methodists like Taylor did not see nurture or conversion as an either-or proposition. They believed God's grace could work through the nurture of Sunday schools, for example, to spark a necessary conversion experience.[38]

Ironically, William's travels made him increasingly less involved in the nurture of his own children. While he was in New England in September 1857, Anne gave birth in Virginia to their son Ross. William returned south in late fall, and the family relocated to Newark, New Jersey, for the winter. When possible, William preached in the New York area but for most of that season they were quarantined with small pox. Sons Charley and Ross caught the disease, while William and Anne were struck with a recurrence of vario-loid. Thus isolated, Taylor prepared a third book.[39]

While *Seven Years'* was well received and sold well in the east, Taylor's California colleagues were less pleased. They felt the book implied that Taylor was the lone hero of the California mission. They also noted a significant omission. *Seven Years'* made no mention of the Bethel disaster or Taylor's debt. It only alluded to his desire to provide safe lodging for sailors to protect them from shanghaiing and vaguely noted that this desire had been frustrated "owing to an extraordinary train of reverses."[40]

Word reached Taylor of these concerns, and he took some steps to allay them in his third book. He wrote his California colleagues to ask for stories of their work. Some responded, but these sources did not arrive by the time Taylor felt compelled to write. Working from his own recollections and material at hand, Taylor finished *California Life Illustrated* in early 1858.[41] Like Taylor's earlier books, it enhanced his reputation as a rugged, frontier preacher. In the glowing words of one reviewer, it commended "the author as a Christian hero."[42]

In *California Life*, Taylor adopted the style that would characterize his most popular books. He employed first-person narratives to describe and highlight features of his travels and missionary life. Taylor added reflections on the social life and economic potential of the region to create a missionary memoir-cum-travelogue. Woodcuts depicted scenes such as cityscapes of San Francisco, swarms of rats on the street, the interior of a saloon, a public hanging, and Chinese women and men. In the first edition of this book, Taylor also concluded with a chapter entitled "Bit of Experience" in which he defended his continued debt and his unusual ministry as an author and traveling evangelist.[43]

From 1858 until the outbreak of the Civil War, Taylor preached and sold books in western Pennsylvania and New York, and the states of Ohio, Indiana, Illinois, Wisconsin, and Iowa. He and his family adopted a seminomadic lifestyle, and most of their comings and goings during these years are unclear. But reports of Taylor's revivals in these states surfaced in the press giving a broad scope of his travels. In November 1858, he assisted at a revival in Peru, Indiana. By the end of that month, he was in Mount Carmel, Illinois. In early 1859, he led revivals in Versailles and Dillsboro, Indiana. In May 1859, he visited Isaac Owen's mother in Vincennes and, that fall, Indiana Asbury (now DePauw) University. In early 1860, Taylor led revivals in Cincinnati, before relocating to Elmira, New York, where his son Edward was born.[44]

Although Taylor's own position in his church was unusual, he exploited the Methodist connectional structure that linked churches within regions into conferences and districts to create opportunities to lead revivals and promote book sales. Like camp meetings, annual conference gatherings provided occasions to make contacts with church leaders. Conferences brought all the Methodist preachers of a region together, and Taylor's presence was often noted at these meetings.[45] As a former missionary of the church, he was invited to address these gatherings to bring "a Pacific greeting" and to preach.[46] Relationships built at these events developed into invitations to conduct revivals in cities, smaller towns, and regional camp meetings.

By 1858, Taylor and others believed they were experiencing a nationwide revival. The Methodist church structure both served Taylor's cause and the desire of Methodists to join the revival. Often the key for Taylor was to get a presiding elder who wanted to bring the revival to churches in his district to sponsor Taylor's efforts. For example, in November 1859, Taylor spent almost a month with Granville Moody, the presiding elder of the Urbana, Ohio, District and held twice daily services in Urbana. For the following six weeks, Taylor traveled hundreds of miles within the district following a schedule prepared by Moody that took Taylor to twenty-three different communities. Moody used his authority as presiding elder to notify churches involved to prepare for Taylor through a notice in a church newspaper: "Let me by this medium advise all to hear him. Parents! be sure to bring your children. And send special invitations to all the hard cases to be present. Invite every shape and form of infidels and careless ones. Brother Taylor is a wonderful man of God."[47]

In this travel, Taylor moved at a breathtaking speed, preaching at countless Methodist congregations throughout the north. As he wrote to his California colleague Isaac Owen, "I preach every week from 8 to 15 sermons."[48] When possible, Taylor preached a special sermon to children in the community.[49] In small communities, he preached only once or twice but in larger towns he stayed longer. By early 1860, Taylor claimed that he had visited thirteen annual conference meetings and had met about 800 Methodist preachers.[50]

Some of these relationships developed into greater significance years later. Two names, in particular, are worthy of mention. In July 1858, Methodists in Pittsburgh who Taylor had known in California and Baltimore invited him to lead revivals in that city. A few years later, one of these, J. A. Swaney, went to South America to work with sailors through the American Seamen's Friend Society.[51] In the 1870s, Swaney convinced Taylor to start new missions in South America. In addition, while Taylor was in western Pennsylvania, a young preacher named James Mills Thoburn heard Taylor preach and came away impressed. "Infidelity seldom has received such blows in these parts," Thoburn wrote.[52] Thoburn later volunteered for missionary service in India, and he would invite Taylor to work in the Methodist mission there.[53]

By the eve of the Civil War, Taylor's transformation into a self-styled, rugged revivalist and author was complete. Through visits to annual conferences, camp meetings, and churches Taylor polished his own homiletic craft. His earlier belief that he had nothing to say on the subject of preaching vanished. In 1860, he wrote his fourth book overall, and the first to depart from the subject of California, *The Model Preacher: Comprised in a Series of Letters Illustrating the Best Mode of Preaching the Gospel.* The title preacher was Jesus, who, Taylor argued, contemporary preachers should emulate. Written as a series of letters to his brother Archibald, then a Methodist preacher in Oregon, Taylor identified five essential characteristics to Jesus' preaching: clearness, earnestness, naturalness, literalness, and appropriateness.[54] In summary, Taylor argued a preacher must have a clear understanding of his topic, earnest zeal directed to a concern for people, particularly their souls. A preacher should speak in a natural manner, avoid metaphysics, and select appropriate topics to his audience. Taylor argued the apostles adopted Jesus' model of preaching, and successful sermons always conformed to this "Master's model."[55]

Taylor's book was representative, not revolutionary. Almost one hundred pages were extracts of sermons from another book, reproduced to show their conformity to the "Master's model."[56] In his own text, Taylor also advocated for several features of American Methodist preaching that had already moved into the mainstream of American Christianity in the 1840s. This style followed a free-flowing pattern that used narrative illustrations and humor instead of theological jargon. Preachers sought to inspire and move the emotions of their congregations, rather than educate.[57]

Taylor's fourth book was most significant as another example of Taylor's biblical hermeneutic. He read the Bible and saw his own experiences paralleled in its stories. Just as he had once seen Pentecost in the streets of San Francisco, in *The Model Preacher*, he looked at Jesus and his apostles and saw a preaching style resembling his own. Ultimately, however, it was neither Peter nor Jesus who Taylor would most identify with in the pages of his Bible. It was Paul.

Taylor's turn to finding parallels between the stories of the apostle Paul and his own experiences represented a similar process. Paul, or Saul as he was also known, was a Jew and an early persecutor of Christians. Following a dramatic conversion to Christianity, however, he became a zealous Christian evangelist. A large portion of the New Testament was written by Paul or in his name. Taylor first became enamored of those portions of the biblical book of Acts that narrated Paul's travels through the eastern Mediterranean to Rome because he believed Paul's travels mirrored his own. In Taylor's mind, like the apostle he was traveling from city to city, holding daily revival meetings in churches, and preaching in the streets.[58] Taylor's identification with and reading of the Pauline example continued to develop in years to come and eventually resulted in his most innovative and enduring missiological insights.

As much as he admired the Pauline example, in one key respect, Taylor was unlike the apostle. Paul was unmarried and childless. For most of these antebellum years in the United States, the Taylor family traveled together. Anne made a temporary home with the children in a central location while William preached in neighboring communities before they moved together to the next region. The toll this lifestyle took on the family became evident in December 1859 when seven-year-old Charles Reid ("Charley") died from scarlet fever in Loveland, Ohio. William was about forty miles away in Oxford when he received word of his son's illness. By the time William arrived, he found Charley had been dead for a day and Anne and Ross incapacitated from the disease.[59]

In a memoir for his son, William celebrated Charley's faith, recalling his interest in prayer and that the child had come forward to seek assurance of his salvation at a revival. He also remembered that Charley wanted his father to stay with the family and not leave to attend camp meetings or conferences. He related a conversation about their constant movement.

> Seeing no end to the going, the tears started in [Charley's] eyes as he said, "Well, where is ma going to stay?" "My dear boy, I cannot tell," was the only reply I could make. My little fellow-pilgrim has found a home with his little sister and two little brothers in heaven, leaving his parents and two little brothers to finish their pilgrimage, and their join our little missionaries in their heavenly home.[60]

Anne's experience of this lifestyle and the loss of another child is not recorded.

As unusual as William's position in the church was, Anne's was even more extraordinary. It was extremely rare for Methodist preacher's wives to itinerate with their husbands as she did. It was also exceedingly difficult to maintain family life in this fashion. Just eight months after burying Charley in Ohio, Anne gave birth to a sixth child, Edward Kimberlin, in Elmira, New York.[61] Some Methodist preacher's wives traveled with their husbands as a way of fulfilling their own call to preach.[62] There is no sign this was the case for Anne. As historian Leonard Sweet noted, other women traveled because it allowed them to experience the adventure of travel while embodying "female virtues of suffering and servanthood."[63] Most certainly, the Taylors' nomadic lifestyle was probably driven both by family finances—Anne and the children could live off the hospitality of their different hosts—and an attempt to keep her family together.[64]

For his part, William continued to profess a hope for a more stable life in California and a return to a conventional Methodist ministry. In a letter to his old colleague Isaac Owen, he professed that he "I have no home, but Cal. is my ideal home, and I sometimes get very homesick, but I have crossed the rubicon and can't retreat till I shall have redeemed my paper."[65] The following year Taylor predicted that by 1861 he would be back in California, but noted, "if the Lord has a different design and reveals it, I'll be of his mind."[66] Time would prove that prediction faulty. By the winter of 1861–1862 Taylor would come to believe that the Lord desired him to visit the British colonies of Australia and New Zealand.

CAUSE AND PROBABLE RESULTS OF
THE CIVIL WAR IN AMERICA

In early 1861, the Taylors were in Illinois while the nation mobilized for war. A poor economy hindered book sales, and fundraising became difficult as the nation faced the looming conflict. Secession exacerbated Taylor's financial problems. Bank notes backed by southern securities devalued to cents on the dollar. Faced with these economic challenges, Taylor moved north to Canada. Canada, of course, was not at war and had more stable currency. As Taylor wrote years later, he decided he "could serve the cause of God and my financial interests better by a visit to my friends in Canada."[67]

For almost a full year from the spring of 1861 to 1862, Taylor worked in British North America between Sarnia in the west and Montreal in the east. As in the United States, he was received by a conference gathering of Canadian Methodists, and he used connections made there to preach in Canadian churches and camp meetings.[68] Taylor's time in Canada was brief but highly significant. His time there allowed him to expand his social network to include individuals from the British Methodist tradition. These connections would be Taylor's first ticket of entry into a Methodist fellowship that was expanding around the globe, in part by piggybacking on British expansion.[69]

Canadian Methodism had ties to the United States, England, and the wider British imperial world. A lasting Methodist presence first entered Canada with Loyalist laity after the American Revolution. In New York, Barbara Heck and her cousin Phillip Embury had started one of the first Methodist societies in North America. By 1791, they had settled in what would become Ontario, and they established a Methodist community there.[70] Other Loyalist Methodists settled in the Maritimes, including a substantial community of freed slaves in Nova Scotia.[71] After the war, American Methodists sent preachers to Canada and included it in their field of operations. The War of 1812 and its aftermath, however, prompted Methodists in Britain's North American colonies to break formal connections with Methodism in the United States and to request preachers from Britain. Through a series of mergers and reorganizations, Canadian Methodists remained a part of the British Wesleyan Methodist Connection until it became its own denomination in 1874.[72]

These historic, geographic, and political connections south to the United States and east across the Atlantic made Canadian Methodism a bridge in the Methodist world of the nineteenth century while also developing its own identity. Other American revivalists with Methodist ties, such as Lorenzo Dow, James Caughey, and Phoebe Palmer also preceded Taylor into Canada, and from there traveled to the British Isles. Such revivalism, however, represented one of the ways Canadian Methodism differed from that in Britain. Unlike American Methodism, the British Methodist tradition viewed revivalism of the sort practiced by Taylor with suspicion as a potential source of disorder and conflict. It adopted revival practices and received revivalists only tentatively. At the confluence of these two Methodist traditions, Canadian Methodists created their own cultural hybrid that adopted both American revivalism and British concerns for order.[73] As a result, Taylor was able to find in Canada both a welcome reception and recommendations for future work elsewhere in the empire.

That opening came from Taylor's host in Peterborough, James Brown. A doctor who had previously lived in Australia, Brown suggested that Taylor take his revival campaigns there, probably because of Taylor's fame as a preacher in California's gold rush.[74] Beginning in 1851, several gold finds in Australia and New Zealand sparked rushes in those colonies. Whatever the case, Taylor claimed that Brown's suggestion so weighed on his mind that he went out into the Canadian winter to pray. He later wrote that kneeling in the snow he "was certified by the Holy Spirit that the Lord wanted me in Australia."[75] Taylor did not elaborate the factors that led him to believe this claim, but once convinced such a trip was God's will, Taylor was bound by his faith commitments to go. As with his missionary call to California, to refuse to submit to God's will would be to jeopardize his own salvation.

In the spring of 1862, the Taylor family separated. Anne and the children returned to California. William boarded a ship to Liverpool. He planned to circumnavigate the globe and return to California by way of Britain, Palestine, and Australia. Despite daunting economic prospects, by the time he left North America, Taylor had settled about $15,000 of his debt. It seemed reasonable the remainder could be met on this tour.[76] A few years later, William related a belief that his tour was a divine appointment that he was bound to accept, and he likened this separation to that experienced by whalers, the merchant marine, or navy. It was a separation mandated by the call of God and the nature of the work to which he was called.[77] Anne seemed to share the view that the short-term sacrifice of separation needed to pay the debt was worth the cost if it meant eventually ending their constant travel and maintaining family unity.[78]

When Taylor landed in England, he followed his now-standard pattern of networking by exploiting the structures of Methodist polity and relationships he had made in Canada. Taylor brought letters of introduction from Canadian churchmen to their British counterparts and attended the annual conference meeting of the Wesleyan Methodists, the largest of the Methodist denominations in Britain. There Taylor met Methodist leaders who invited him to preach in Ireland and England. The most important connection Taylor made at the conference, however, was William Arthur.[79]

At the time, Arthur was secretary of the Wesleyan Methodist Missionary Society and had recently published his book *The Tongue of Fire* (1856). Well read on both sides of the Atlantic in the nineteenth century, historians have found in Arthur's work the seeds of two diverse strands of twentieth-century Christianity—the Social Gospel thought of Walter Rauschenbusch and Pentecostalism.[80] Since some of Taylor's missionaries became key figures in early Pentecostalism, this later connection was particularly significant. In the 1880s, Arthur's daughter and son-in-law, Emily and Anderson Fowler, became officers in Taylor's missionary organization. Their role in selection of missionaries for Taylor's missions of the 1880s and 1890s represented a personal connection between Arthur's ideas and those of Taylor's missionaries who became first-generation Pentecostals.

While Taylor never directly cited Arthur's book, there were clear commonalities that suggest Arthur influenced Taylor's thought. In Arthur's reading of the New Testament, he found evidence the apostolic age was characterized by massive and widespread revival. He believed that his own day was witnessing both technological improvements and a greater openness to Christianity in Africa, China, and Muslim regions that created opportunities for a contemporary revival.[81] Both Taylor's interest in apostolic models for revivalism and his trust in the power of technology to aid in the spread of his gospel have been noted. Whatever theological influence Arthur may have had on Taylor, the two developed a strong personal relationship. In years to come, Taylor would consider Arthur his most loyal friend and supporter.[82]

Such developments lay in the distant future, however. In the short term, Taylor garnered enough preaching invitations in Ireland and England to delay his trip to Australia.[83] That said, Taylor was generally disappointed by the results of his revival work in the British Isles. Certainly, the British press deemed his lectures on social life in California, rather than his revival campaigns, to be more newsworthy.[84] Historian Richard Carwardine judged Taylor's impact in Great Britain negligible compared to the American revivalists who preceded him both because Taylor arrived on the waning edge of a period of growth and remained for only a short time.[85] Historians David Hempton and Myrtle Hill found that the 1859 Ulster revival yielded only short-term growth in church membership that was not sustained over the long-term. By the time Taylor arrived in Ulster, Wesleyan Methodists were reporting membership losses.[86] Other factors were probably also responsible, as will be seen when this account considers his returns to England several years later.

Taylor's own contemporary, and self-interested, assessment of his revivals in Ireland, however, are worthy of note as it was as perceptive a view of the position of Methodism in Irish society as it was devoid of introspection. Taylor led revival campaigns in Ulster and the cities of Dublin and Cork and found his work yielded few converts. Taylor's own evaluation assumed his own message and methods could not be to blame. He believed his message was universal and was as pertinent to an Irish audience as to any other. Rather, he judged that the social context of Ireland made revivals ineffective as an evangelistic technique. Religious identity in Ireland was tied to political and economic competition between Protestants and Catholics. As a result, most people already affiliated with a church.[87] Taylor wrote, "We can only, as a general rule, gain access to those who live within the 'lines' of Methodism."[88] Methodism in Ireland dated to the beginnings of the movement in the eighteenth century. By the first third of the nineteenth century, Irish Methodism was established most strongly in cities and areas with a preexisting Protestant population but without strong ties to an Anglican or Presbyterian churches. Methodists found few converts among the Roman Catholic majority but grew in areas where tensions between Protestants and Catholics were most acute.[89]

This observation that evangelism was difficult because religious identity was strongly fixed by social factors demonstrates one dimension of a pattern that emerged over Taylor's career. Revivals could bring in new converts, but revivalism was most successful as a missionary strategy when used with a population who already identified themselves as Christians but for whom that identity had weakened. For such individuals, radical changes in belief were not needed. Revivals invited them to prioritize their religious identity, not to adopt a new one. In California, the core membership of the developing Methodist church had been those who had been Methodists in the east but had migrated. Confessional identity in Ireland, however, was too strong to be broken by revivalism.

Nevertheless, Taylor loved his time in Ireland. It allowed him to explore his ancestry and to indulge his curiosity about other ways of life. He visited the home of his paternal ancestors and tried to establish his kinship with the people there. He attended a fair at Enniskillen to watch people go about their business and listened for hours as a woman sang traditional Irish songs. He was troubled by the poverty he saw among people still recovering from the worst of the great famine. He blamed their suffering on a combination of the devil, the Pope, and English landlords.[90]

Like many Methodists, Taylor sought to avoid politics in the belief that evangelism was more important. Divisive subjects could drive away prospective converts, and Methodists sought, above all, to reach people with their message. Avoidance of controversy, however, meant that Methodists could favor the status quo over social change. Occasional comments such as this one on Irish suffering, however, indicated that Taylor was often concerned about exploitation of common people by powerful elites.

Taylor also found it impossible to avoid comment on the American Civil War. In England, he led revivals in Manchester, Birkenhead, Crewe, London, and elsewhere, and the American war dominated public attention.[91] More than any other international event of the time, it affected economic and political life in Britain. The blockade of Confederate ports hurt the British textile industry. British political parties saw their own struggles for or against reform reflected in the course of American democracy. Specific events, such as the Union seizure of Confederate diplomats from a British ship, Confederate attempts at winning diplomatic recognition, and the Emancipation Proclamation, contributed to a loud public debate in Britain over the war.[92]

Taylor supported the Union. Two of his brothers served in the Union army, and his father, while living in the war-torn valley of Virginia, remained a vocal supporter of the Union. Taylor was also proud that his father remained a member of the northern church when other Methodists in his native Rockbridge County affiliated with the Methodist Episcopal Church, South.[93] Although American Methodists had split in 1844 over slavery, many churches and pastors in Taylor's region of Virginia remained in the northern church until the outbreak of hostilities.[94]

In the fall of 1862, Taylor entered the British political debate over the war with a pamphlet entitled *Cause and Probable Results of the Civil War in America: Facts for the People of Great Britain* (1862). He presented himself as a knowledgeable American correcting common misperceptions of his British friends. Taylor's audience was far greater than a small circle of friends, however, and reflected his populist sensibilities. He later admitted that the pamphlet was "for the enlightenment of the higher classes" and mailed 11,000 copies of it to members of the British nobility.[95] As far as Taylor was concerned, he was perfectly within his rights to correct the mistaken beliefs of a foreign aristocracy. Taylor later claimed with pride that President Rutherford B. Hayes told him his pamphlet served the Union cause more than "a regiment of soldiers at the front," but this was certainly flattery since the two men became friends.[96]

While there is no evidence that Taylor's voice moved British public opinion, Taylor's opinions were clearly heard. Reviews commending the publication and excerpts from it were widely reproduced in other periodicals.[97] The antislavery movement in Great Britain, in particular, found Taylor's writing to be a helpful piece of propaganda. Portions were cited in other publications as an authoritative description of the causes of the war and the brutality of slavery.[98]

Taylor wrote as a Virginian who had spent most of his life in the south and had visited almost every free state. He sought to educate British readers on American geography, federalism, politics, and history. He stressed that he was intimately familiar with slavery. He vividly described the pain of families separated by slavery and the physical abuse slaves endured. He also admitted that he and his wife had inherited and freed slaves. He wrote, "I was born and bred with a horror of slavery, and I believe I am one of a large class in the South" who "are looking for redemption for the slaves, and for themselves as well."[99]

As a work of political theology Taylor's pamphlet was representative of the views of many northern Protestants, British Methodists, and other evangelicals on God's providence and the sinfulness of slavery.[100] He believed that God had allowed the war to chastise America for the sin of slavery and to bring about the end of human bondage. While writing his pamphlet, news of the Emancipation Proclamation reached England. He thought this development confirmed God was at work through the war since "developments of Providence" have "all been in favor of human freedom."[101]

The pamphlet also illustrated that, like many Methodists of his era, Taylor held to a quiet postmillennial eschatology that focused more on the personal salvation of individuals from sin and damnation than on biblical prophecy and the direction of history. Unlike many northern Protestants, he asserted no unique millennial role for America in the war.[102] Of course, he was writing to a British audience who would not have appreciated assertions that elevated America's place in the world to a theological proposition. Nevertheless, his optimism about the progress of human freedom, like his enthusiasm for steam travel, is of a piece with a postmillennial view that expected a gradual advent of a thousand-year reign of peace followed by Christ's return. Absent from Taylor's writing, both in this pamphlet and elsewhere, were interpretations of biblical prophecy as a guide to his present. Historian David Hempton noted that British Methodists were often unconcerned with such "prophetical speculations."[103] While a few antebellum American Methodists engaged in millennial conjecture, there was no consensus within the tradition on the matter, and Methodists were far more concerned with other subjects.[104]

In the later part of the century, dispensational premillennialism would grow in popularity among evangelicals on both sides of the Atlantic. This eschatology anticipated the immanent return of Christ as foretold by biblical prophecy.[105] Historians have often emphasized this belief motivated foreign missions and sparked the formation of independent evangelical missions, separate from denominational boards, as evangelicals urgently sought to evangelize the world.[106] Eventually, Taylor would lead his own independent missionary venture. Unlike such premillennial missions, however, Taylor's were born not of eschatological urgency but a belief in entrepreneurial possibility and infinite potential.

Taylor most pressing concern was the call to conversion and sanctified living. He argued extensively in his pamphlet that slavery threatened the salvation of both slave and slaveholder. One could not participate in this, or any, sin without jeopardizing one's salvation. Taylor saw the moral danger in slavery illustrated in the history of the Methodist Episcopal Church, South. He argued its leaders had transformed from conservatives who didn't discuss slavery into defenders of the institution as one "of God, supported by biblical authority, extended over the nation and perpetuated forever."[107] He claimed that, at one time, many southerners believed slavery was wrong, but profits to be gained convinced them first to tolerate the evil and eventually to celebrate it as "a good thing to all concerned."[108] He scornfully wrote that to argue that slavery was good because it allowed for the introduction of Christianity to African slaves was to cast the slave trade as "the greatest missionary enterprise of the age in which we live."[109]

Taylor's wartime rhetoric also illustrated that even within the Methodist family of churches, divisions could be deeply acrimonious, and levels of cooperation or competition among Methodists could vary. Relations between northern and southern Methodists were tense even before the Civil War. The conflict only exacerbated that division. Taylor's efforts were welcomed by Wesleyan Methodists in Canada and the British Isles because his Methodist Episcopal Church and the Wesleyan Methodists had no grounds of conflict and saw their work as compatible. In time, some would come to question that assumption. As Taylor's career took him into new contexts and as other Methodist denominations expanded into new settings, the question of cooperation or competition among Methodist churches and missions would surface.

AN INNOCENT ABROAD

In early 1863, Taylor left Britain for Australia by way of the Near East. Just before he left London, a woman asked if her son, a young man preparing for the Baptist ministry named Jim (Taylor never gave his full name), could join Taylor on his tour to Palestine. She offered to pay her son's expenses, and Taylor agreed to the company.[110] In Taylor's accounts of the trip, Jim served as a comic foil to his own, more devout and practical tour. Reminiscent of the tropes of literature about California and consistent with the identity he now claimed for himself, Taylor portrayed Jim as a kind of overcivilized innocent. Jim was presented as lacking common sense, even though he hailed from the British imperial capital.

Through the spring of 1863, the companions traveled from London to Alexandria, where they parted company. Their journey took them across the Channel to Paris, then south to Marseilles, where they booked passage on a steamship for Beirut, stopping for several days at Smyrna. From Beirut, they traveled to Egypt by land.[111] Although the details of Taylor's travels are vague, on this tour Taylor encountered foreign missionaries in the field for the first time, was exposed to current issues in mission thought and practice, and encountered examples that foreshadowed future developments in missionary practice. The trip also cemented his sense of personal identification with biblical stories and the apostle Paul.

Taylor's tour also put him ahead of a wave of Americans who visited Palestine following the Civil War. Mark Twain's book *The Innocents Abroad* (1869) heralded the start of that interest. Twain traveled on the first organized tour of Americans to Palestine, planned by members of Henry Ward Beecher's congregation in 1866.[112] Given Taylor's demonstrated success as an author by the 1860s, it is somewhat surprising that unlike Twain and many others, Taylor never wrote a book about his time in Palestine. Taylor's only published account of his tour was printed years after the fact in his newspaper, *The African News*, and reprinted in his autobiography.[113]

At Smyrna, the travelers were entertained by missionaries of the American Board of Commissioners for Foreign Missions (ABCFM), an American missionary endeavor dominated by Congregationalists. The ABCFM began work in the Near East in 1818 when voluntary change of religion was illegal under Ottoman law. Although those missionaries made early attempts at evangelizing Muslims and Jews, by the 1830s, they turned their focus to eastern Christians.[114] The ABCFM hoped to spread evangelical Christianity among these historic Christian communities through preaching and exposure to the Bible and to inspire revived eastern churches to convert Muslims. To that end, missions were established in Constantinople for work among Armenians, in Smyrna and Athens among Greeks, and in Beirut among Arab Christians.[115] Taylor recalled that he learned a lot from these missionaries he met about their work in the Near East.[116] Much like these missionaries, a key component of Taylor's later mission theory would be a belief in the potential of reviving the faith of self-identified, indigenous Christians and develop them into a missionary force to reach other indigenous people.

Though Taylor did not encounter Methodist missionaries on his travels through this region, he was probably aware that his own church had recently begun work in Ottoman Bulgaria. Methodist missionary aspirations for Ottoman lands dated from the early nineteenth century when some British Methodists studied Arabic and hoped to send a preacher to Palestine. The Wesleyan Methodists even stationed a missionary in Alexandria, Egypt, for six years but then abandoned the work.[117] Though Methodists might aspire to share their message with everyone, practical limitations such as limited finances and staffing often constrained those efforts, creating a tension between theologically driven hopes and mundane realities. Over the next decades, Taylor would come to believe that he had rediscovered a missionary method to overcome that tension.

This very sort of conflict between idealistic missionary aspirations and practical financial limitations lay behind the origins of the Methodist mission to Ottoman Bulgaria. ABCFM missionaries encountered Bulgarian Christians but lacked funds to start a mission in Bulgaria, so in the 1850s, it invited the Methodist Episcopal Church to assume that effort. The ABCFM hoped to both meet an apparent missionary need and to channel Methodist missionary interest away from Ottoman areas they already occupied, thus preventing competition between the missions. In 1857, the first Methodist missionaries were appointed to Bulgaria. Like the ABCFM, they adopted the mission strategy of seeking to introduce evangelicalism to historic Christian communities.[118]

Cooperative efforts like this were possible because the Protestant missionary movement was always marked by a strong sense of unity and common purpose transcending confessional, denominational, and national boundaries. Protestant missionaries and mission societies believed they were engaged in a common task of sharing Christ with the world, saw evidence of the Holy Spirit at work in each other's missions, and hoped that they were a part of creating indigenous churches wherever they labored.[119] That underlying sense of unity allowed cooperation to take place, but as the mission strategy of American evangelicals in the Near East illustrated, the ecumenical spirit Protestant missionaries shared with each other did not extend to Orthodox Christians of the Near East.[120]

Nor did ideological unity, even among Protestants, preclude competition. Until the later part of the nineteenth century, when formal comity agreement among mission agencies divided mission fields into territorial regions, such arrangements were informal, unofficial, and made by missionaries on site.[121] As with any agreement, either party could understand its parameters differently. For example, while the ABCFM hoped the creation of a Methodist mission in Bulgaria would forestall conflict elsewhere in Ottoman lands, Methodists viewed Bulgaria as a foothold from whence they could expand their missions elsewhere in the region and, as historian Christina Cekov wrote, "return the Bible to Bible lands."[122]

That desire to bring their faith to the land of the Bible illustrated the powerful influence the idea of the Holy Land had on the thought of evangelicals. That impact was also demonstrated in the popularity of ABCFM missionary William McClure Thompson's *The Land and the Book* (1858). Thompson's book outsold all other American books of the era except *Uncle Tom's Cabin*, appeared in over thirty editions, and remained in print into the twentieth century.[123] In Beirut, Taylor met Thompson, and Thompson prepared an itinerary for the travelers to follow through Palestine.[124] Taylor probably did not write a book about his tour because he did not think he could improve on Thompson's. Thompson's book appealed to American Protestants like Taylor because it encouraged them to trust the land of Palestine as a source of authority over traditional Christian pilgrimage sites. As historian Heleen Murre-van den Berg noted, the land became "a source of divine revelation essential for understanding the Bible."[125]

Like many other visitors to the Holy Land, Taylor's experiences there confirmed in his mind the veracity of the Bible. He considered such personal experience a definitive source of knowledge. Occasional references in Taylor's writings indicate that he was aware of higher biblical criticism and Darwin's theory of evolution, but unlike many Christians of the era, did not see them as threats to his faith. In part, he thought these ideas were either too ridiculous for the intelligent to take seriously but he also believed they were unable to withstand the authority of personal experience.[126] For example, in 1862, the Anglican Bishop John William Colenso of Natal published a book casting doubt on the validity of several biblical claims.[127] On his tour of Palestine, Taylor tested Colenso's assertion that the Israelites could not have gathered between the neighboring hills of Mts. Ebal and Gerizim and hear what was said to them.[128] He concluded that Colenso's argument was invalid because he made assertions about Palestinian geography that Taylor knew from his own experience to be wrong.[129]

Taylor's tour also strengthened his sense of personal identification with biblical stories. He found in the pages of his Bible the story he lived as he traveled. The land of Palestine and its people became a way for Taylor to feel as if he was experiencing stories of the Bible firsthand. In Nazareth, the travelers camped near a fountain where Taylor imagined Jesus' mother Mary had drawn water. On the west coast of the Sea of Galilee, they watched a sudden storm from over the water, as had happened with Jesus and his disciples. One night, they slept as near as possible to the place where Jacob dreamed his vision of a ladder. In the Garden of Gethsemane, Taylor and Jim read Mark's gospel, sang and prayed. In Bethlehem, they observed shepherds keeping watch over their flocks. At Joppa, they visited a home purported to be that of Simon the tanner where Peter had the vision Taylor had once used to describe life in California, as well as a contemporary tannery.[130]

In Jerusalem, Taylor also crossed paths with two other unique Protestant missionary endeavors. He was entertained in that city by Bishop Samuel Gobat. Gobat's mission originated in 1841 when King Friedrich Wilhelm IV hoped to persuade the Prussian church to accept bishops by creating a joint English-Prussian bishopric in Jerusalem. English evangelicals backed the proposal because they hoped to foster the advent of a millennial age through conversion of the Jews, Jewish restoration in Palestine, and the formation of a Jewish national church under British protection. In practice, Gobat's mission aroused hostility from all quarters. As with the ABCFM, facing Jewish opposition and legal barriers to Muslim conversion, Gobat opted to work among the local Christian population. This move offended Gobat's Anglican backers who opposed proselytism among Orthodox Christians and disappointed his sponsors who expected Jewish conversions.[131]

Gobat was able to inform Taylor of the fate of a friend, Alfred Roberts. A native of Connecticut, as a young man Roberts decided to become became an independent missionary. Early in life, he worked for several years among both Pawnee Indians and southern slaves before he had a vision in which God told him to go to California. There Taylor and Roberts met, and Roberts told Taylor he had seen him in that vision. Until 1851, when he took ill himself, Roberts ministered to cholera patients in California. After regaining his health, two members of Taylor's church paid for Roberts' passage to New York. A few years later, Roberts wrote Taylor from Jerusalem where he continued his work among the sick and distributed Christian tracts. Taylor learned that Roberts had died in Jerusalem and was buried there.[132]

The missions of Gobat and Roberts were each unique, as well as portended future changes in Protestant missions in the late nineteenth century. Gobat's work foreshadowed increased entanglements between Christian missions and European imperial expansion. The relationship between missions and the European colonial and imperial project was complex, and varied from context to context. In many settings, colonial officials were initially reluctant to tolerate a missionary presence for fear it would unsettle indigenous populations and threaten profits. In the second half of the century, however, as European powers extended their control over more of the globe, they simultaneously opened new areas for Christian mission and enabled an intertwining of Christian mission and the politics of empire. Missionaries increasingly operated with assumptions of the superiority of European civilization. The late century also saw the rise of independent "faith missions," prefigured by Roberts. Exemplified by the English missionary to China, Hudson Taylor, faith missionaries operated independently without the guarantee of a salary or support from a home missionary board. They trusted that God would provide for their needs in faith.[133]

Taylor's relationship to these developments will be explored in future pages, and in many ways defies easy description. On the one hand, he enthusiastically embraced the idea that an Anglo-American empire providentially encompassed the globe. Just as the Roman Empire had for Paul, he came to believe this empire provided opportunities to spread the gospel. But he also believed the gospel relativized any notion of European superiority.

Civilization would save no one. It was, at best, a means to an end. Taylor shared the racial prejudices of many of his time but he also believed God desired the salvation of all people and that his message was universal. In addition, while Taylor became an eager supporter of independent missions, separate from the direction and control of missionary boards, his own independent missions were born more of his own sense of pride and frustration that his own church's board was failing its missionary commission. He certainly did not believe it was sufficient for missionaries to simply trust in God's provision. The sense of providential self-sufficiency that sustained him in California was too strong for that. For Taylor, a faithful missionary must both work and trust God to provide.

DOWN UNDER

In Egypt, Taylor and Jim parted. Jim returned to London, and Taylor sailed by steamship from Suez to Australia by way of Ceylon. When he arrived in Melbourne in June 1863, Taylor found Australian Wesleyan Methodists eagerly awaiting him.[134] Taylor's work in Ireland and England had impressed his hosts who sent word ahead to their colleagues in Britain's Australian colonies to anticipate the arrival of Taylor as "one of the most eloquent and successful ministers of the Church."[135]

Part of this anticipation was due to Taylor's novelty. Traveling evangelists had plied the waters of the North Atlantic for generations, but until Taylor, none had made the journey to Britain's Australasian colonies. Many soon followed. After Taylor, countless itinerant evangelists toured the colonies that make up the present-day countries of Australia and New Zealand.[136] Successive preachers were not always as welcome as Taylor, however. Historian Ian Breward noted that Australian clergy often had other priorities than the evangelists' fundraising or "hobbyhorses of holiness and eschatology."[137] While Taylor certainly preached a holiness message and raised money to pay his Bethel debt, he found both evangelistic and financial success in his tour by deemphasizing his personal objectives. He worked with Wesleyan Methodists to meet his hosts' needs and interests, and by the time he left the continent, Taylor had successfully met his own debts.

In addition to using Methodist ecclesial networks to his advantage, Taylor had also developed a network of British commercial contacts. He brought letters of introduction from Wesleyan Methodist leaders to their Australian counterparts and a letter from an English merchant to his partners in Melbourne. On landing, Taylor sought out this business and learned that an employee was the brother-in-law of a Wesleyan preacher Taylor met in Belfast. Taylor's contact arranged a meeting with the local Wesleyan leadership. John Symonds, editor of Victoria's Methodist newspaper, the *Wesleyan Chronicle*, was present and lent his support by promoting Taylor's services in the paper, offering a sympathetic account of the Bethel disaster and an explanation that Taylor was selling his books to cover his debt. Daniel Draper, the chair of the Melbourne District, a position somewhat comparable to a presiding elder of American Methodism, was also present. He had read Taylor's books and insisted that Taylor commence his campaign by preaching the coming Sunday at his church in Melbourne.[138]

Australian Methodists were eager for Taylor's visit because they hoped for a revival. British emigrants to Australia had come from a society shaped by eighteenth- and early nineteenth-century evangelicalism. Methodists expected regular revivals, were aware that other lands had experienced large-scale awakenings, and wanted their own. They had considered holding special services of the kind Taylor would offer but had not done so. Taylor's presence provided that opportunity.[139] It was simple question of labor. Taylor was burdened by debt but free of pastoral responsibility. While Australian clergy were busy caring for parishioners, administering, and developing their churches, Taylor had the flexibility and time to offer special revival services.

Taylor began with a three-week campaign at Wesley Church on Lonsdale Street in Melbourne. His hosts were given their first glimpse of the revivalism that Taylor would introduce to most of Australia and New Zealand.[140] He immediately drew large congregations. Every evening, hopeful converts remained after his sermon for prayer meetings where many claimed they were "brought into glorious liberty," "found peace," or "found mercy," and local clergy and lay leaders prayed with and exhorted these potential converts.[141] In the mornings, others called on Taylor at the Draper home for spiritual counsel.[142] One evening was dedicated to promoting the "experience of entire sanctification to God," and an evening was set aside for converts to give testimonies.[143] Finally in early July, Taylor closed work at this church and moved to other communities in Victoria. For the remainder of 1863, he preached in churches near Melbourne, in outlying areas of Victoria, and eventually gold mining towns to the northwest.[144]

Victoria's Wesleyans saw Taylor as a new herald of a familiar message. His theology was consistent with their own, and not worthy of comment. Rather, they remarked on the novelty of his American speech and evangelistic style, and they credited him with sparking long-awaited revivals in their churches. Joseph Nicholson, who was converted during Taylor's visit and entered the Wesleyan ministry, remembered Taylor's "direct method of speech, flavored with an American accent and telling illustrations."[145] Draper commented, "Mr. Taylor, a *real live Yankee* from California, has been holding revival services, and *many hundreds* have been awakened to seek the Lord [emphasis in original]."[146] The *Wesleyan Chronicle* reported that Taylor preached in a "homely but telling style," with many illustrations.[147] Another Wesleyan preacher, James Bickford, observed that attendance at class meetings on his circuit more than doubled and circuits in Victoria received 797 new members from Taylor's revivals.[148]

Whatever growth Wesleyan churches experienced, however, church leaders were apprehensive that Taylor's fundraising would drain money from their ministries. His tour coincided with a new period in Australian church history. Early colonial authorities generally avoided religious matters, and transported convicts often rejected religious outreach as an attempt at social control. But large-scale, free European settlement to Australia and New Zealand began in the 1830s and accelerated with the discovery of gold. From 1851 to 1861, the European population of Australia tripled. With this large influx of free settlers, churches grew and developed as institutions.[149]

This development was aided by a relationship between church and colonial governments that benefited Wesleyan Methodists. First enacted in the Botany Bay colony (New South Wales), the 1836 Church Act offered subsidies for clerical salaries, and church and school construction to Anglican, Catholic, Presbyterian, and Wesleyan churches. The law spread to other Australasian colonies.[150] Wesleyan Methodists were both willing to accept government assistance and had developed traditions of voluntary giving. As a result, they were able to maximize the available financial resources. The Methodist system of itinerant clergy was able to send preachers to communities proactively to organize churches and raise necessary funds.[151] Taylor observed that Methodism in Victoria benefited from this arrangement. It allowed Wesleyans to hold a relatively favorable social position in the colony compared to other denominations and compared to his experience in California. While both were settler societies marked by rapid population growth, in Victoria churches were offered large and favorable grants of property for churches, parsonages, and schools.[152]

Taylor's hosts enlisted him both to lead revivals and aid in this institutional development. He was often asked to serve as a special preacher at church anniversaries or dedications, school fundraisers, missionary societies, and other benevolent causes. At times, revivals were scheduled to build on these events. For example, he eventually returned to Wesley Church to preach at an anniversary of that Gothic-style church building and to address a tea-meeting called to help pay the building debt. The next day, he began a week of revivals at a newly opened church in the Emerald Hill neighborhood, and he took part in the opening of a new church in Sandhurst. Reports of similar efforts in support of the church's ministries surfaced throughout his tour. To name two examples, in Sydney, he raised money to support flood victims in the interior, and Taylor convinced one of his converts, Thomas Waterhouse, to pay a church debt and endow a new school, the Prince Alfred College.[153]

Taylor's willingness simultaneously to win converts and develop church institutions muddles an interpretive framework often applied to American Christianity, and by historian Jay Riley Case, to Taylor himself. This framework sees a tension in American evangelicalism between "formalists" and "anti-formalists." According to this scheme, formalists developed voluntary societies, schools, publications, and other institutions to create the apparatus of a Christian society. Antiformalists prioritized conversions and an emotional response and sought to Christianize society from below. Although Case offers Taylor as the prime example of an antiformalist evangelical, Taylor's work in Australia, like his development of church institutions as a missionary in California, blurs that distinction.[154]

In early 1864, Victoria hosted the conference meeting of Wesleyan Methodists in the Australasian colonies. Taylor was invited to preach at the gathering and to speak to his financial need. The body passed a resolution that recognized "with gratitude to Almighty God the piety, zeal, and very remarkable pulpit labors of Rev. William Taylor, and also his remarkable success in winning souls to Christ."[155] At the same time, it sought to regularize his work. The Conference ruled that Taylor was to work only with the permission of the responsible district chairmen and circuit superintendents. Finally, it strongly recommended that no future visitors be allowed to raise money in the colonies.[156] Taylor's fundraising was to be a one-off affair.

While the Conference highlighted the sensitivity surrounding Taylor's fundraising and the need to keep his evangelistic work separate, more than anything, it opened new doors. Taylor developed new relationships and again used Methodist connectional polity to his advantage. Although the British colonies in Australia and New Zealand were separately administered, the Australasian Wesleyan Methodist Connection had been self-governing since 1855 and spanned these colonial jurisdictions. As a result, Wesleyan preachers from all the Australasian colonies heard firsthand about Taylor's revivals in Victoria. They heard him preach on "Perfect Love," and read a serial essay published in the *Chronicle* revisiting his thesis in *Address to Young America* on the necessity of both Christian nurture and evangelical conversions of children.[157] In addition, preachers who met Taylor in Victoria received new appointments to other colonies.[158]

After the close of the Conference, Taylor traveled to Tasmania. In early 1864, he led revivals in Launceston, Hobart, Longford, and smaller towns. In Tasmania, opposition to Taylor from outside the Wesleyan Methodist orbit crystallized around two issues. First, reports emerged in Launceston of "numerous cases of fainting and hysteria on the part of young females" at his revivals.[159] Taylor was not troubled by the response of the young women. Such reactions would not have been out of place at an American camp meeting, and he would defend similar ecstatic expressions in his revivals elsewhere. In Australia, however, Taylor was concerned that such actions would offend more than it would inspire. He took pains to offset any negative reactions and pointedly said this behavior was unique to Launceston, and "not characteristic of his meetings."[160]

Taylor's disclaimer was a mark of sensitivity to the concerns of his hosts. Respectability was a major concern for mid-century Australian evangelicals as they applied their values to a developing society. Emotional exuberance and physical displays, particularly by women, were seen as lacking dignity. While some historians have characterized this dimension of Australian evangelicalism as "unrelentingly and mercilessly moralizing," historian Stuart Piggin pointed out that for those who had been transported to Australia as criminals, the moral code of evangelicalism and Victorian mores provided a path to improved social standing.[161] In addition, gold rush-era settlers in Australasia, both male and female, provided the core of colonial middle-class society. Historian Anne P. O'Brien argued that Methodism was an attractive faith for these emigrants because it linked ideas of self-control and salvation.[162]

Australian Wesleyans were generally pleased by the behavior of those who attended Taylor's revivals. Taylor was no model of Victorian refinement, however, and even sympathetic observers could be shocked by Taylor's seeming irreverence. John Watsford remembered his surprise the first time he and Taylor met. The two happened to kneel by each other for prayer. When a congregant began to pray loudly in an unknown language, Taylor nudged the praying Watsford and joked that the man sounded as bad as "a cross-cut saw."[163]

The second critique of Taylor concerned his fundraising; some were concerned that he was exploiting people. Although this criticism shadowed Taylor, it failed to gain much traction because of the careful separation of evangelism and book sales pressed on him by the Wesleyans. His integrity on this account seemed to be confirmed when a report surfaced that he had repaid a creditor from California now living in Melbourne.[164] When asked, Taylor declared that he operated "on the principle of business equivalents."[165] Taylor meant by this phrase that he took no collections at his revivals and accepted no gifts of money. The gospel he preached was free to all, but he allowed that those who wished could give money in exchange for an equivalent thing of value—a book. Nothing was taken or given, only exchanged.

Taylor also raised money through lectures. When possible, he offered these soon after his revivals closed in a community. He thus separated his evangelistic work from his fundraising, while also building on the goodwill he had gained from preaching gratis. Standard lecture topics included California, Palestine, and the "Life and Times of St. Paul." Judging by newspaper reports, contemporaries may have been more surprised by Taylor's behavior in his lectures than his sermons. Reviews noted that Taylor did not adhere to the "stiff, formal style" characteristic of lectures, and he laced his talks with humor.[166] One joke came following Taylor's discussion of the biblical Herod who took his brother Philip's wife, Herodias. Taylor quipped it was not clear who was hurt in the deal more, Philip for losing Herodias or Herod for gaining her. The story reminded him of a headstone that read:

Underneath this sod doth lie,
Back to back, my wife and I,
Happier far than when in life—
Free from care and free from strife.
When the last trump the world shall fill,
If she gets up, I'll just lie still.[167]

Unfortunately, accounts of these lectures did not record the nature of his reflections on Paul except to note that, on one occasion, he spent a lot of time discussing the story of Paul in Athens.[168] That biblical episode was becoming very important to Taylor. In a few years while in South Africa, he would develop these reflections on Paul into a mission theory.

Taylor's next stop was New South Wales. In Sydney, he continued to hold multiple services on Sundays and weekday evening sermons with prayer meetings. He recorded the number of "converts" and "seekers" each night for about a month in June and July of 1864, claiming 864 total converts from his preaching in that span.[169] Unfortunately, beyond these raw numbers there are few clues as to who these converts were. Many were probably already members of the Wesleyan Methodist church but were persuaded by Taylor's preaching that they lacked a dramatic conversion experience. A significant number, however, seem to have been members of other churches, perhaps contributing to the hostility to Taylor's revivals by non-Wesleyans.[170] A study of church membership in New South Wales found the percentage of Wesleyan Methodists in the colony increased from 1861 to 1891 by drawing members from other denominations through revivals.[171] Australia never experienced a continent-wide, interdenominational revival, but local awakenings like Taylor's gave the Wesleyans an edge over other denominations in recruiting new members.[172] Some evidence also suggests that Taylor's revivals were a youth movement. Observers commented on a generational aspect to his work and noted his skill in dealing with youth.[173] Taylor estimated that more than half of his converts in Sydney were between 15 to 20 years old. He guessed that only about a third were over twenty. The conversion of older, established people of status was atypical and noted as an unusual occurrence.[174]

Taylor was occasionally encouraged to build on his fame as a street preacher and preach outdoors. He rarely did so, usually only when a building could not contain the congregation.[175] Taylor probably refrained from this practice out of respect for his Wesleyan Methodist hosts. In the early nineteenth century, another British Methodist denomination, the Primitive Methodists, had endorsed the use of American-style camp meetings. The resulting split from the Wesleyans over the issue had been carried to the colonies.[176] For their part, Primitive Methodists in Australia observed Taylor's success in open-air preaching and argued he proved their case that it was an effective evangelistic method.[177]

One notable exception took place in Sydney, when Taylor offered two weeks of evening sermons in the city's Hyde Park. A preaching platform was erected and temporary gas lighting installed. An estimated 10,000 people gathered to hear Taylor the first night. Prospective converts were invited to a prayer meeting afterward at nearby York Street Church.[178] Concerns about respectable behavior at his revivals persisted, but observers were generally pleased that decorum was maintained throughout these revivals. A description of the Hyde Park services noted with approval that the meetings saw over 300 converts, and although there was a great deal of "earnestness," "there was nothing of that excitement and enthusiasm which has sometimes characterized similar meetings."[179]

In late 1864, Taylor sailed north to Queensland. His time in that colony was spent primarily in Brisbane but he also toured further north by steamship and preached at stops along the way.[180] Although Taylor never ventured further into Oceania than Australia and New Zealand, he made several important contacts there with Wesleyan missionaries from Tonga. Nathaniel Turner, an important pioneer missionary who developed the Tongan alphabet and whose respectful approach to Tongan culture led to the first significant breakthrough in Christian conversions, had retired to Queensland.[181] Turner was in the final stages of his life during Taylor's visit. Taylor called on the dying missionary and celebrated a last communion with him. Turner gave Taylor's work a dying blessing, and Taylor remained until Turner passed to pray, sing hymns, and tell stories of other faithful deaths.[182]

Taylor also began a correspondence with Peter Turner. Of no relation to Nathaniel but also a missionary to Tonga, Peter Turner was notable for his role in promoting the Tongan revival of 1834 resulting in mass conversions to Christianity. At the time, Turner's use of revivals as a missionary method was controversial. Most of his missionary colleagues opposed the idea, believing catechetical instruction a better approach. Turner was concerned that without revivals, however, Tongan Christian commitment would be superficial. Turner's stories of the Tongan revival reinforced Taylor's belief in the importance of revivalism as a missionary method, a conviction Taylor would implement in southern Africa and around the world.[183]

The bulk of Taylor's time in Australasia was spent with British settlers. He seemed to have little interaction with Aboriginal people of Australia or the

Maori of New Zealand, but that conclusion may be a reflection of available sources. In New Zealand, Taylor's opportunity to meet Maori was probably limited. He spent his time in colonial cities and colonists were at war with the Maori on the North Island at the time.[184] In late 1864, Taylor crossed to New Zealand where he led revivals in the cities of Auckland, Wellington, Christchurch, and Dunedin, and smaller communities.[185]

In New Zealand, Taylor may have interacted with the Paheka-Maori, descendants born of European and Maori marriages. If so, based on patterns elsewhere in Taylor's travels, they may have been among those most receptive to his message and style of revivalism. People who experienced social disruption and marginalization and whose religious commitments had weakened were often open to Taylor's message and methods. Early successes of both Church Missionary Society and Wesleyan missionaries meant that by the 1840s most Maori identified themselves as Christian. Few Europeans had settled there, and unions between Europeans and Maori were common. At the time of Taylor's arrival a generation later, however, an influx of British settlers, including women, had marginalized the Pakeha-Maori, and Christian adherence among the Maori weakened.[186]

Unfortunately, few details are known about Taylor's time in New Zealand, the composition of his congregations, and his reception except that his revivals were less successful there than elsewhere in Australasia. This failure was probably due to the fact that the services began over the Christmas holidays. For his part, Taylor knew "that he had preached in Auckland the same gospel

Figure 3.1 "Portrait of William Taylor." *Source:* Methodist Church of New Zealand Archives Photographs Collections, General Portraits, Reverend William "California" Taylor, ca 1865, photographer Swan & Wriggleworth, Wellington, New Zealand.

that he had preached else where, and had had the consciousness of the present influences of the Holy Spirit."[187] In other words, since his message was universal and he felt God's blessing on him, external factors were responsible. Always confident, however, Taylor declared he was not worried that he left New Zealand just as the revival seemed to gain traction. He had come to see this as the nature of his ministry:

> To assist the church in developing, applying, exercising, and employing more efficiently her own resources . . . to get them to work, and then slip out. For the work that they might accomplish themselves without any foreign influence was better . . . it would have a better effect in giving them confidence in their resources and appliances than if the work were brought about by foreign support only.[188]

In other words, he saw his role as an evangelist not only to win conversions, but to cultivate the development of local resources necessary to carry on the work of revivals without his presence.

Taylor's efforts to develop local church leadership may have been the most significant long-term impact of his time in Australasia. In 1869–1870, Taylor returned to Australia for fourteen months. He discovered sixteen ministers serving Wesleyan churches in Australia had been converted during his revivals the previous decade. The actual number may have been higher.[189]

These figures point to the importance of revivalism not just as a mechanism for conversion but for leadership development. Taylor's revivals were structured in such a way that they cultivated new church leaders. Converts were expected to give a public testimony to their experience. They were also called on to exhort others to experience the sense of assurance they had felt. Individuals could discern in that process that they possessed gifts for professional ministry. In nineteenth-century Australasia, all Christian denominations looked to Britain for ministerial leadership, but the Wesleyans also had a system of developing, training, and ordaining preachers locally. Historian Ian Breward argued that the ability of Wesleyans to develop local leadership contributed to an increase in Wesleyan membership in proportion to the Australian population.[190]

PARTINGS AND REUNIONS

Through early 1865, Taylor remained in the Sydney area, leading revivals in towns throughout the colony. News of Lincoln's assassination arrived in early July, and about 6,000 people gathered to hear Taylor give a funeral sermon for the late President. The audience closed by singing the American

Figure 3.2   (Left to right) **Edward K. Taylor, Isabelle Anne Taylor, Ross Taylor. Photo of Mrs. William Taylor and Sons, W. S. Matthew Papers, California-Nevada Conference Archives, Pacific School of Religion, Berkeley, CA.** *Source:* Used with the permission of the Archives of the California-Nevada Annual Conference of The United Methodist Church.

patriotic song "My Country 'Tis of Thee." For many in the colony, Taylor had become a trusted religious voice and representative of the United States. The following evening, the Wesleyans of Sydney held a farewell service for Taylor. They expressed their thanks for his "untiring and successful labours" on virtually every circuit of their church in the colony and for the "mysterious . . . ways of Providence" that brought him there.[191] The women of the York Street congregation surprised the men presiding by presenting Taylor with a hand-made purse filled with gold coins for Anne in thanks for her consent in allowing Taylor to visit them.[192]

Little is known about how Anne and the children fared after parting from William in 1862. Money was an ongoing concern, but like this unexpected gold, they were partially supported by this and other gifts sent from Australia. William's supporters regularly circumvented his restrictions on accepting money by sending money directly to Anne in California.[193] There is also some evidence the California Conference of the Methodist Episcopal Church assisted her. California conference minutes listed Taylor as a "supernumerary preacher," giving it the authority to disburse money to the Taylors from the "beneficiary funds of the church," and Anne alluded to a financial arrangement of uncertain nature in a letter to William's old colleague, Isaac Owen.[194]

This letter also contained an example of Anne's humor. At the time Owen was preparing to leave California to visit Washington, D.C. She wrote that Owen would enjoy himself so much there that he would forget his family. He would be like the preacher who once exclaimed that on meeting Jesus he "would not think of his wife & children for a thousand years."[195] In a few years, this joke would perhaps cut close to home for Anne. William would eventually choose to continue work as a globe-trotting revivalist and missionary rather than return to his wife and children. The separation that had taken William to Australasia alone portended a deeper, looming split in the family.

First, however, William sought to bring his family along on his travels. In mid-1865, he proposed Anne and the children meet him in Australia. He hoped three months of revivals and sales in Calcutta and Madras would allow him to sell surplus books. Together they could return to California by way of India, Palestine, and New York.[196] While waiting for his family to join him, William carried his revival campaign to South Australia. His visit was much anticipated. Many Cornish Methodists had settled there, and an excited congregation crowded the Pirie Street Wesleyan Church in Adelaide in anticipation of Taylor's arrival by ship. He was brought straight from the docks to begin a prolonged revival.[197]

Taylor's South Australian campaign, however, was cut short when he learned his family had arrived in Sydney sooner and in a different colony than expected. Moreover, his eldest son, Morgan, was seriously ill, possibly with yellow fever. When the family was reunited after two weeks of anxious travel, William discovered the younger boys' memory of him had faded. Ross had to be introduced to his father, Eddie recognized him from a photograph, while Morgan, the eldest, remembered his father through his fever.[198]

Morgan's doctor counseled removing him to a cooler climate. The doctor had previously been a surgeon based in the Cape Colony, and he recommended a voyage across the southern Indian Ocean to expose Morgan to cool sea air and to winter in the Cape. William found a ship sailing from Adelaide to Cape Town. Representing the transportation revolution taking place, this would be the last ocean voyage William took by sail. As steamships

dominated more well-traveled routes, sailboats were relegated to the interco-
lonial trade.[199]

Taylor's brief return to South Australia allowed him to attend the 1866
meeting of the Australasian Wesleyan Conference there. It was a moment of
triumph for him. He presented the body with an itemized financial statement.
It detailed that Taylor had arrived on the continent owing just over £3,432.
With income from book sales and lectures, and deducting the cost of books,
donations, and travel, Taylor's debt had been reduced to just over £68. Since
he gave a £50 donation for mission work with the report, Taylor's debt had
been essentially covered.[200] He deposited his earnings at a bank in New York
and advertised that his creditors could receive repayment of forty cents on the
dollar. Not all heard of the offer, but as late as 1875, Taylor repaid a creditor.[201] From 1866 onward, however, Taylor no longer tried to raise money
for the Bethel debt. He believed he had acted honorably at the cost of great
hardship. He no longer felt encumbered by its burden. When the Taylors set
sail for South Africa in February 1866, William was, for the first time in his
adult life, free of professional and financial obligations. He had redeemed his
honor and been reunited with his family.

This chapter has charted Taylor's transformation from a missionary in
California into a revivalist preacher and author in the eastern United States
and parts of the British world. It has shown that Methodists like Taylor did
not see their mission as something that only existed beyond the scope of or to
extend "Christendom." They also believed they had a mandate to share their
faith with those within Christian lands to revive faith commitments that were
insufficiently strong or had lapsed. Such a concept of mission is, perhaps, not
surprising since Methodism began as a revival movement within the Church
of England. Camp meetings and revivals in towns and cities were preferred
methods for this missionary work, but Sunday schools and Christian education also had a role in evangelizing future generations and bringing them to
faith in Christ. This chapter has also shown that in some contexts such methods were ineffective, such as in Ireland where religious identity was already
strong. In newly settled, fluid contexts, such as Australia, however, revivals
could serve not only to retain and recruit new members but also to cultivate
future leadership.

Taylor's tour through the Near East and encounters with Christian missions
there foreshadowed his own future of missionary engagement beyond "Christian" lands. Events in South Africa would revive Taylor's vision of reaching
the world with the gospel that dated from his time in San Francisco. His
nascent interest in the apostle Paul would bloom, and Taylor would become
convinced that barriers to world evangelization such as language, finances,
and other religions could easily be overcome by adopting a Pauline model for
missionary work.

NOTES

1. William Taylor, *Story of My Life; An Account of What I Have Thought and Said and Done in My Ministry of More Than Fifty-Three Years in Christian Lands and Among the Heathen. Written by Myself* (New York: Hunt & Eaton, 1896), 215; William Taylor to Thomas & Eliza Kirkpatrick, January 3, 1857, Taylor, William. Papers, 1857–1867, Rockbridge Historical Society Manuscript Collection, Washington, DC & Lee University.

2. William Taylor, *Our South American Cousins* (New York: Nelson and Phillips, 1878), 85.

3. Taylor, *Our South American Cousins*, 87.

4. David Hempton, *Methodism: Empire of the Spirit* (New Haven: Yale University Press, 2005), 171.

5. Andrew Porter, *Religion versus Empire: British Protestant Missionaries and Overseas Expansion, 1700–1914* (Manchester: Manchester University Press, 2004), 12–13; Brian Stanley, *The Bible and the Flag: Protestant Missions and British Imperialism in the Nineteenth and Twentieth Centuries* (Leicester: Apollos, 1990), 67–70.

6. Andrew F. Walls, "The Evangelical Revival, the Missionary Movement, and Africa," in *The Missionary Movement in Christian History: Studies in the Transmission of Faith* (Maryknoll: Orbis Books, 1996), 81.

7. Taylor, *Story of My Life*, 217; William Taylor, *California Life Illustrated* (New York: Published for the author by Carlton & Porter, 1858), 344.

8. "Religious Summary: Methodist Episcopal Church," *Christian Advocate*, January 15, 1857; Taylor to Kirkpatrick; Taylor, *Story of My Life*, 218–19.

9. Taylor to Kirkpatrick.

10. Melvin E. Dieter, *The Holiness Revival of the Nineteenth Century*, Second ed. (Lanham: Scarecrow Press, 1996), 22–24; Jean Miller Schmidt, *Grace Sufficient: A History of Women in American Methodism, 1760–1939* (Nashville: Abingdon Press, 1999), 133–7; Taylor, *Story of My Life*, 100.

11. Taylor, *Story of My Life*, 218.

12. Richard Wheatley, *The Life and Letters of Mrs. Phoebe Palmer* (New York: W. C. Palmer, Jr., 1876), 247.

13. Brian Roberts, *American Alchemy: The California Gold Rush and Middle-Class Culture* (Chapel Hill: University of North Carolina Press, 2000), 55; Susan Lee Johnson, *Roaring Camp: The Social World of the California Gold Rush* (New York: W.W. Norton, 2000), 322.

14. Roberts, *American Alchemy*, 57.

15. "The Pioneers of American Methodism," *London Review*, April 1858.

16. Robert C. Bray, *Peter Cartwright, Legendary Frontier Preacher* (Urbana: University of Illinois Press, 2005), 237.

17. William Taylor, *Seven Years' Street Preaching in San Francisco, California Embracing Incidents, Triumphant Death Scenes, Etc* (New York: Published for the author by Carlton & Porter, 1856), 387–8; Taylor to Simpson, June 4, 1856, Matthew Simpson Papers, Manuscript Division, Library of Congress.

18. Taylor, *Story of My Life*, 217.

19. Taylor, *Seven Years'*, title page.

20. "Baltimore Conference," *Christian Advocate*, March 12, 1857; "Letter from Baltimore," Ibid., April 30, 1857; *Annual Minutes of the Baltimore Conference of the Methodist Episcopal Church, 1857* (Baltimore: Armstrong & Berry, 1857), 5.

21. *Annual Minutes*, 38.

22. David Bebbington, *Victorian Religious Revivals: Culture and Piety in Local and Global Contexts* (New York: Oxford University Press, 2012), 9–11.

23. "The Anniversary of the Baltimore Conference Missionary Society," *The Sun*, March 9, 1857; "Baltimore Conference," *Christian Advocate*, March 12, 1857; "Religious Summary: Methodist Episcopal Church," Ibid., March 12, 1857; "To the Benevolent," *The Sun*, April 22, 1857; Beta, "Letter from Baltimore, *Christian Advocate*, April 30, 1857; Taylor, *Story of My Life*, 219–23.

24. Kathryn Teresa Long, *The Revival of 1857–58: Interpreting an American Religious Awakening* (New York: Oxford University Press, 1998), 17, 60.

25. Taylor, *Story of My Life*, 220–3.

26. Taylor, *Story of My Life*, 223. Beta, "Letter from Baltimore," *Christian Advocate*, April 30, 1857; Beta, "Letter from Baltimore," *Christian Advocate*, June 11, 1857. "Revivals in Baltimore," *Christian Advocate*, June 25, 1857.

27. Mercury, "Correspondence of the Baltimore Sun. Washington, May 18," *The Sun*, May 18, 1857; Taylor, *Story of My Life*, 244.

28. Timothy L. Smith, *Revivalism and Social Reform: American Protestantism on the Eve of the Civil War* (New York: Abingdon Press, 1957), 146–62.

29. Beta, "Letter from Baltimore," *Christian Advocate*, August 5, 1858.

30. William Taylor, *Address to Young America, and a Word to the Old Folks* (Philadelphia: Higgins & Perkinpine, 1857), 65.

31. Ibid.; William Taylor, *How to Be Saved and How to Save the World. Vol. 1* (Adelaide: Alfred Waddy, 1866), 331.

32. "Letter from Philadelphia," *Christian Advocate*, August 20, 1857; "Newmarket Camp Meeting," *Zion's Herald*, October 7, 1857; William Taylor, "Camp-Meeting Campaign," *Christian Advocate*, October 22, 1857; Taylor, *Story of My Life*, 224–7.

33. Neil Semple, *The Lord's Dominion: The History of Canadian Methodism* (Montréal: McGill-Queen's University Press, 1996), 138–43; "Minutes of Conferences for 1842–3," *Minutes of the Annual Conference of the Methodist Episcopal Church, for the Years 1839–45* (New York: T. Mason and G. Lane, 1840), 257.

34. "Letter from Philadelphia."

35. "Religious Summary," *Christian Advocate*, November 26, 1857.

36. "Letter from Philadelphia."

37. Taylor, *Address to Young America*, 49.

38. Sean A. Scott, "'Good Children Die Happy': Confronting Death During the Civil War," in *Children and Youth During the Civil War Era,* ed. James Marten (New York: New York University Press, 2012), 98–103; Sydney E. Ahlstrom, *A Religious History of the American People* (New Haven: Yale University Press, 1972), 610–13.

39. Taylor, *Story of My Life*, 229–30.

40. Taylor, *Seven Years'*, 238.

41. William Taylor to Isaac Owen, August 13, 1858, Isaac Owen Papers, 1851–1865, Bancroft Library, University of California, Berkeley.

42. "Literary Items," *Christian Advocate*, July 1, 1858.

43. Robert F. Lay, ed., *Lessons of Infinite Advantage: William Taylor's California Experiences. With Isabelle Anne Kimberlin Taylor's Travel Diary, 1866–67, Written During a Voyage with Her Family En Route from the Cape of Good Hope, South Africa, to London and Subsequent Travels Throughout Europe* (Lanham: Scarecrow Press and The Center for the Study of World Christian Revitalization Movements, 2010), 231–8; Taylor, *California Life*, 333–48.

44. William Taylor, "A Criticism," *Western Christian Advocate*, January 12, 1859; "Revival Correspondence," Ibid. January 19, 1859; "Revival Correspondence," Ibid. January 26, 1859; "Revival Correspondence," Ibid. March 9, 1859; "Revival Correspondence," Ibid., November 18, 1859; "Church Items: Methodist Episcopal Church," Ibid., February 8, 1860; "Church Items: Methodist Episcopal Church," Ibid., February 27, 1860; "Church Items: Methodist Episcopal Church," Ibid., March 28, 1860; William Taylor to Isaac Owen, May 18, 1859, Isaac Owen Papers, 1830–1866, Bancroft Library, University of California, Berkeley; Taylor, *Story of My Life*, 240, 251–2.

45. "Cincinnati Conference," *Western Christian Advocate*, September 15, 1859; "The Delaware Conference," Ibid., September 28, 1859.

46. "South-Eastern Indiana Conference," Ibid., October 6, 1858.

47. "Revival Correspondence," Ibid., November 16, 1859.

48. Taylor to Owen, May 18, 1859.

49. Wm. Taylor, "Letter from Ohio," *Christian Advocate*, January 26, 1860.

50. "Letter from Ohio."

51. "Letter from Rev, Mr. Taylor," *Christian Advocate*, July 29, 1858; C. V. Anthony, *Fifty Years of Methodism: A History of the Methodist Episcopal Church Within the Bounds of the California Annual Conference from 1847 to 1897* (San Francisco: Methodist Book Concern, 1901), 95–96.

52. J. M. Thoburn, *Diaries & Journals, 1857–1918* (Lake Junaluska: Commission on Archives and History, United Methodist Church, 1975), microfilm, September 14, 1858.

53. Guy Douglas Garrett, "The Missionary Career of James Mills Thoburn" (Ph.D. diss., Boston University, 1968), 5–10.

54. William Taylor, *The Model Preacher: Comprised in a Series of Letters Illustrating the Best Mode of Preaching the Gospel* (Cincinnati: Swormstedt & Poe for the author, 1860), 3.

55. Taylor, *The Model Preacher*, 251–74.

56. Henry C. Fish, *History and Repository of Pulpit Eloquence*, 2 vols. (New York: M. W. Dodd, 1856); Taylor, *Model Preacher*, 275–372.

57. Frederick V. Mills, Sr., "Methodist Preaching 1798–1840: Form and Function," *Methodist History* 43, no. 1 (2004): 3–16; David S. Reynolds, "From Doctrine to Narrative: The Rise of Pulpit Storytelling in America," *American Quarterly* 32, no. 5 (1980): 481–5; Ronald E. Sleeth, "Roots and Influence of Early American Methodist Preaching," *Perkins School of Theology Journal* 37, no. 4 (1984): 2–4.

58. William Taylor, "Street Preaching—Philadelphia," *Christian Advocate*, June 10, 1858.

59. "Church Items: Methodist Episcopal Church," *Western Christian Advocate*, December 28, 1859; William Taylor, "Memoirs: Little Charley Taylor," *Western Christian Advocate*, January 4, 1860.

60. Taylor, "Memoirs."

61. *The Bay of San Francisco: The Metropolis of the Pacific Coast, and Its Suburban Cities: A History*, vol. 2 (Chicago: Lewis Publishing, 1892), 63.

62. John H. Wigger, *Taking Heaven by Storm: Methodism and the Rise of Popular Christianity in America* (Urbana: University of Illinois Press, 2001), 154–6.

63. Leonard I. Sweet, *The Minister's Wife: Her Role in Nineteenth-Century American Evangelicalism* (Philadelphia: Temple University Press, 1983), 62.

64. Ibid., 61.

65. Taylor to Owen, August 13, 1858.

66. Taylor to Owen, May 18, 1859.

67. Taylor, *Story of My Life*, 250.

68. Ibid.; "Personal Items," *Christian Advocate*, June 12, 1862.

69. Hempton, *Methodism*, 176.

70. Ibid., 20.

71. James W. St G. Walker, *Black Loyalists: The Search for a Promised Land in Nova Scotia and Sierra Leone 1783–1870* (Toronto: University of Toronto, 2017), 197–8, 290–5.

72. Todd Webb, *Transatlantic Methodists: British Wesleyanism and the Formation of an Evangelical Culture in Nineteenth-Century Ontario and Quebec* (Montreal: McGill-Queen's University Press, 2013), 17–101; Semple, *The Lord's Dominion*, 30–52, 71–99; Wade Crawford Barclay, *Early American Methodism, 1769–1844: Missionary Motivation and Expansion*, vol. 1, History of Methodist Missions (New York: Board of Missions and Church Extension of the Methodist Church, 1949), 175–200.

73. Semple, *The Lord's Dominion*, 127–47; Webb, *Transatlantic Methodists*, 3–16; George A. Rawlyk, *Wrapped up in God: A Study of Several Canadian Revivals and Revivalists* (Burlington: Welch Publishing, 1988), 103–7.

74. William Taylor, *Christian Adventures in South Africa* (London: Jackson, Walford, and Hodder, [1867]), 1–2.

75. Taylor, *Story of My Life*, 255.

76. Ibid.; "Personal Items," *Christian Advocate*, June 12, 1862.

77. Taylor, *Christian Adventures*, 3.

78. Lay, ed., *Lessons*, 259.

79. Taylor, *Story of My Life*, 256.

80. Donald W. Dayton, *Theological Roots of Pentecostalism* (Peabody: Hendrickson Publishers, 1987), 73–80; Donald W. Dayton, "From 'Christian Perfection' to the 'Baptism of the Holy Ghost'," in *Perspectives on American Methodism: Interpretive Essays*, ed. Russel E. Richey, Kenneth E. Rowe, and Jean Miller Schmidt (Nashville: Kingswood Books, 1993), 289–97; John Brittain, "William Arthur's the Tongue of Fire: Pre-Pentecostal or Proto-Social Gospel?," *Methodist History* 40, no. 4 (2002): 246–54.

81. Norman W. Taggart, *William Arthur: First among Methodists* (London: Epworth Press, 1993), 57–59.

82. William Taylor, *Ten Years of Self-Supporting Missions in India* (New York: Phillips & Hunt, 1882), 427–8.

83. "Sermons," *The Express* (Dublin), August 23, 1862; "Re-Opening Services," *Armagh Guardian*, October 10, 1862; *The Constitution* (Cork), December 6, 1862; "Editorial Notes: Brother Taylor in Ireland," *Christian Advocate*, December 11, 1862; Taylor, *Story of My Life*, 257.

84. "Lecture on California," *Belfast News-Letter*, September 27, 1862; "Social Life in California," *Northern Whig*, November 5, 1862; "California," *The Constitution* (Cork), December 15, 1862.

85. Richard Carwardine, *Transatlantic Revivalism: Popular Evangelicalism in Britain and America, 1790–1865* (Eugene: Wipf & Stock, 1978), 174–5.

86. David Hempton and Myrtle Hill, *Evangelical Protestantism in Ulster Society, 1740–1890* (London: Routledge, 1992), 155–6.

87. John Ranelagh, *A Short History of Ireland*, third ed. (New York: Cambridge University Press, 2012), 97–117; Carwardine, *Transatlantic Revivalism*, 110.

88. "Letter from Ireland."

89. Hempton, *Methodism*, 27–29; David Hempton, "Methodism in Irish Society, 1770–1830: Proxime Accessit for the Alexander Prize," *Transactions of the Royal Historical Society* 36 (1986): 117–42.

90. "Letter from Ireland."

91. Taylor, *Story of My Life*, 256–8.

92. R. J. M. Blackett, *Divided Hearts: Britain and the American Civil War* (Baton Rouge: Louisiana State University Press, 2001), 7, 154.

93. Taylor, *Story of My Life*, 31, 250.

94. Homer L. Calkin, "The Slavery Struggle, 1780–1865," in *Those Incredible Methodists: A History of the Baltimore Conference of the United Methodist Church*, ed. Gordon Pratt Baker (Baltimore: Commission on Archives and History, The Baltimore Conference, 1972), 218–24.

95. Taylor, *Story of My Life*, 258; Wm. Taylor Membership Document, Daniel Steele Collection, 1824–1914, Manuscript History Collection, Boston University School of Theology.

96. Taylor, *Story of My Life*, 258.

97. "America," *North Devon Journal*, November 6, 1862; "Summary of News," *Whitehaven News*, November 6, 1862; "Notice of Publications, *Weston-Super-Mare Gazette*, November 8, 1862; "The Civil War in America," *Heywood Advertiser* 5 (November 15, 1862); "Notices of New Publications," *Western Times*, November 22, 1862; "Literary Notices," *Leicester Guardian*, November 22, 1862; "Literature," *Fife Herald*, December 3, 1863; "American Slavery, *Perthshire Advertiser*, December 3, 1863; "Slavery As It Is," *Dundee, Perth, and Cupar Advertiser*, December 4, 1863; "Reviews," *Cambridge Independent Press*, December 6, 1862; "Pamphlets on the American Question," *Northern Whig*, December 17, 1862.

98. *Anti-Slavery Advocate*, December 1, 1862; "Address of Committee of Correspondence on Slavery in America," *Anti-Slavery Reporter and Aborigines' Friend*, February 5, 1863; Charles Adams, *Slavery, Secession, and Civil War: Views from*

the United Kingdom and Europe, 1856–1865 (Lanham: Scarecrow Press, 2007), 197–202.

99. William Taylor, *Cause and Probable Results of the Civil War in America. Facts for the People of Great Britain* (London: Simpkin, Marshall, 1862), 22–23.

100. W. Harrison Daniel, "The Reaction of British Methodism to the Civil War and Reconstruction in America," *Methodist History* 16, no. 1 (1977): 3–20; James H. Moorhead, *American Apocalypse: Yankee Protestants and the Civil War, 1860–1869* (New Haven: Yale University Press, 1978); Mark A. Noll, *The Civil War as a Theological Crisis*, Steven and Janice Brose Lectures in the Civil War Era (Chapel Hill: University of North Carolina Press, 2006), 95–123.

101. Taylor, *Cause and Probable Results*, 19.

102. Moorhead, *American Apocalypse*, 56–64.

103. D. N. Hempton, "Evangelicalism and Eschatology," *Journal of Ecclesiastical History* 31, no. 2 (1980): 189.

104. E. Brooks Holifield, *Theology in America: Christian Thought from the Age of the Puritans to the Civil War* (New Haven: Yale University Press, 2003), 262.

105. Crawford Gribben, *Evangelical Millennialism in the Trans-Atlantic World, 1500–2000* (New York: Palgrave Macmillan, 2011), 92–101.

106. Dana L. Robert, "'The Crisis of Missions': Premillenial Mission Theory and the Origins of Independent Evangelical Missions," in *Earthen Vessels: American Evangelicals and Foreign Missions, 1880–1980*, ed. Joel A. Carpenter and Wilbert R. Shenk (Grand Rapids: William B. Eerdmans Publishing, 1990), 29–46; William R. Hutchison, *Errand to the World: American Protestant Thought and Foreign Missions* (Chicago: University of Chicago Press, 1987).

107. Taylor, *Cause and Probable Results*, 7.

108. Ibid.

109. Ibid.

110. Taylor, *Story of My Life*, 258–9.

111. Ibid.

112. Lester Irwin Vogel, *To See a Promised Land: Americans and the Holy Land in the Nineteenth Century* (University Park: Pennsylvania State University Press, 1993), 44–45.

113. Wm. Taylor, "Story of My Life," *African News*, February 1894; Taylor, *Story of My Life*, 259–75.

114. Joseph L. Grabill, *Protestant Diplomacy and the Near East: Missionary Influence on American Policy, 1810–1927* (Minneapolis: University of Minnesota Press, 1971), 7–8; Habib Badr, "American Protestant Missionary Beginnings in Beirut and Istanbul: Policy, Politics, Practice, and Response," in *New Faith in Ancient Lands: Western Missions in the Middle East in the Nineteenth and Early Twentieth Centuries*, ed. Heleen Murre-van den Berg (Leiden: Brill, 2007), 218–19.

115. Grabill, *Protestant Diplomacy*, 7–8.

116. Taylor, *Story of My Life*, 259.

117. John Pritchard, *Methodists and Their Missionary Societies 1760–1900* (Farnham: Ashgate, 2013), 81.

118. Paul Benjamin Mojzes, "A History of the Congregational and Methodist Churches in Bulgaria and Yugoslavia" (Ph.D. diss., Boston University, 1965), 56–62,

196–204; Wade Crawford Barclay, *The Methodist Episcopal Church, 1845–1939: Widening Horizons, 1845–95*, vol. 3, History of Methodist Missions (New York: Board of Missions and Church Extension of the Methodist Church, 1957), 1018–19.

119. R. Pierce Beaver, *Ecumenical Beginnings in Protestant World Mission: A History of Comity* (Thomas Nelson & Sons: New York, 1962), 18–41.

120. Mojzes, "History", 50–55.

121. Beaver, *Ecumenical Beginnings*, 43–44.

122. Christina Cekov, *Bible Women in the Balkans* (Strumica: United Methodist Church in Macedonia, 2011), 4, quoted in Paul W. Chilcote and Ulrike Schuler, "Methodist Bible Women in Bulgaria and Italy," *Methodist History* 55, no. 1–2 (2016–2017): 111.

123. Vogel, *Promised Land*, 105; John Davis, *The Landscape of Belief: Encountering the Holy Land in Nineteenth-Century American Art and Culture* (Princeton: Princeton University Press, 1996), 45; Bilal Ozaslan, "The Quest for a New Reformation: Re-Making of Religious Perceptions in the Early History of the American Board of Commissioners for Foreign Missions to the Ottoman near East, 1820–1870" (Ph.D. diss., Boston University, 2010), 450.

124. Taylor, *Story of My Life*, 259.

125. Heleen Murre-van den Berg, "William McClure Thompson's *The Land and the Book* (1859): Pilgrimage and Mission in Palestine," in *New Faith in Ancient Lands: Western Missions in the Middle East in the Nineteenth and Early Twentieth Centuries*, ed. Heleen Murre-van den Berg (Leiden: Brill, 2006), 62.

126. Taylor, *How to Be Saved*, 142.

127. Jeff Guy, *The Heretic: A Study of the Life of John William Colenso, 1814–1883* (Johannesburg: Ravan Press, 1983), 34, 64–66, 80–82, 121–8.

128. See Deuteronomy, 27–28; John William Colenso, *The Pentateuch and Book of Joshua Critically Examined* (London: Longman, Green, Longman, Roberts & Green, 1862), 35–37.

129. Taylor, *How to Be Saved*, 117.

130. Taylor, *Story of My Life*, 260–5.

131. John S. Conway, "Jerusalem Bishopric: A 'Union of Foolscap and Blotting-Paper'," *Studies in Religion* 7, no. 3 (1978): 306–13; Sybil M. Jack, "No Heavenly Jerusalem: The Anglican Bishopric, 1841–83," *Journal of Religious History* 19, no. 2 (1995): 181–4, 92–93; Taylor, *Story of My Life*, 134.

132. T. Seavill, ed. *The Christian "Brave", or, Some Remarkable Passages from the Life of Mr. A. Roberts of Connecticut, U.S* (London: Elliot Stock, 1865), 132–4; Taylor, *Story of My Life*, 132–4.

133. Stanley, *Bible and the Flag*, 85–132; Andrew Porter, "An Overview, 1700–1914," in *Missions and Empire*, ed. Norman Etherington (Oxford: Oxford University Press, 2005), 40–63.

134. "Rev. William Taylor," *Wesleyan Chronicle*, June 18, 1863; Taylor, *Story of My Life*, 266–8; John C. Symons, *Life of the Rev. Daniel James Draper . . . .* (London: Hodder & Stoughton, 1870), 264.

135. "Probable Visit to Australia," *Wesleyan Chronicle*, November 25, 1862.

136. H. R. Jackson, *Churches and People in Australia and New Zealand: 1860–1930* (Wellington: Allen & Unwin/Port Nicholson Press, 1987), 57.

137. Ian Breward, *A History of the Australian Churches* (St. Leonards: Allen & Unwin, 1993), 63.

138. "Rev. William Taylor," *Wesleyan Chronicle*, June 18, 1863; Symons, *Life*, 82–83, 263–5; Taylor, *Story of My Life*, 267–8.

139. "Religious Intelligence: Victoria," *Wesleyan Chronicle*, July 14, 1863; A. D. Hunt, *This Side of Heaven: A History of Methodism in South Australia* (Adelaide: Lutheran Publishing House, 1985), 22–23; Jackson, *Churches and People*, 5–6, 49.

140. Glen O'Brien, "Australian Methodist Religious Experience," in *Methodism in Australia: A History*, ed. Glen O'Brien and Hilary M. Carey (Farnham: Ashgate, 2015), 172.

141. Symons, *Life*, 265.

142. "Religious Intelligence: Victoria," *Wesleyan Chronicle*, July 14, 1863; Symons, *Life*, 264–6.

143. Taylor, *Story of My Life*, 279.

144. "Rev. William Taylor," *Wesleyan Chronicle*, August 8, 1863; "Religious Intelligence: Victoria," Ibid.; Ibid., September 4, 1863; Ibid., November 19, 1863; Ibid., December 14, 1863; *The Argus*, June 21, 1864; Taylor, *Story of My Life*, 286–90.

145. J. E. Carruthers, "California Taylor in Australia," W. S. Matthew Papers, California-Nevada Conference Archives, Pacific School of Religion.

146. Symons, *Life*, 267.

147. "Religious Intelligence: Victoria: Sandhurst Circuit," *Wesleyan Chronicle*, September 30, 1863.

148. James Bickford, *James Bickford: An Autobiography of Christian Labour* . . . .(London: Charles H. Kelly, 1890), 181–2.

149. Hilary M. Carey, *Believing in Australia: A Cultural History of Religions* (St. Leonards: Allen & Unwin, 1996), xvi, 1; Roger C. Thompson, *Religion in Australia: A History* (Melbourne: Oxford University Press, 1994), 11; Breward, *History*, 48; Stuart Macintyre, *A Concise History of Australia* (Cambridge: Cambridge University Press, 2004), 86–87.

150. Hilary M. Carey, "Religion and Society," in *Australia's Empire*, ed. Deryck. M. Schreuder and Stuart Ward (Oxford: Oxford University Press, 2008), 189.

151. Breward, *History*, 37; Hunt, *This Side of Heaven*, 40–45; Jackson, *Churches and People*, 32.

152. William Taylor, "Methodism in Australia," *Christian Advocate*, January 14, 1864.

153. "Religious Intelligence: Victoria," *Wesleyan Chronicle*, July 14, 1863; "Religious Intelligence: Victoria," Ibid., September 4, 1863; "Religious Intelligence: Victoria," Ibid., September 30, 1863; *The Argus*, September 1, 1863; "Public Meeting in Sydney," *Maitland Mercury & Hunter River General Advertiser*, June 30, 1864; Taylor, *Story of My Life*, 317.

154. Jay Riley Case, *An Unpredictable Gospel: American Evangelicals and World Christianity, 1812–1920* (New York: Oxford University Press, 2012), 103–55; Curtis D. Johnson, *Redeeming America: Evangelicals and the Road to Civil War* (Chicago: Ivan R. Dee, 1993), 7–8.

155. *Minutes of Several Conversations between the Ministers of the Australasian Wesleyan Methodist Church at Their Tenth Annual Conference* (Melbourne: Wesleyan Book Depot, 1864), 28.

156. *Minutes of Several Conversations between the Ministers of the Australasian Wesleyan Methodist Church at Their Tenth Annual Conference.*

157. See W. Taylor, "Papers on Youthful Training," *Wesleyan Chronicle*, March 8, 1864; April 2, 1864; May 24, 1864; July 14, 1864; November 19, 1864; December 20, 1864; January 20, 1865; and March 20, 1865.

158. Bickford, *James Bickford*, 188–9.

159. "Summary of News," *The Mercury*, March 23, 1864.

160. Ibid.

161. Stuart Piggin, *Spirit of a Nation: The Story of Australia's Christian Heritage* (Sydney: Strand, 2004), 33.

162. Anne O'Brien, *God's Willing Workers: Women and Religion in Australia* (Sydney: University of New South Wales Press, 2005), 28–29.

163. John Watsford, *Glorious Gospel Triumphs: As Seen in My Life and Work in Fiji and Australasia* (London: Charles H. Kelly, 1900), 140.

164. "Religious Intelligence: Victoria," *Wesleyan Chronicle*, January 16, 1864; *The Argus*, January 12, 1864.

165. "Telegraphic," *Brisbane Courier*, November 11, 1864.

166. "Victoria," *The Mercury*, November 3, 1863; *Sydney Morning Herald*, August 9, 1864.

167. "Lecture by the Rev. W. Taylor," *Sydney Morning Herald*, August 10, 1864.

168. *The Argus*, September 5, 1863; Ibid., September 12, 1863.

169. William Taylor, "Rev. Wm. Taylor's Australian Journal," *Christian Advocate*, November 24, 1864.

170. "Religious Intelligence: Tasmania," *Wesleyan Chronicle*, April 28, 1864.

171. R. B. Walker, "The Growth and Typology of the Wesleyan Methodist Church in New South Wales, 1812–1901," *Journal of Religious History* 6, no. 4 (1971): 333–6.

172. Jackson, *Churches and People*, 49–50.

173. *Tasmanian Messenger*, March 1864; Ibid., April 1864; *Christian Advocate and Wesleyan Record*, July 19, 1864, quoted in Robert Evans, *Early Evangelical Revivals in Australia: A Study of Surviving Published Materials About Evangelical Revivals in Australia up to 1880* (Adelaide: Openbook Publishers, 2000), 41.

174. Taylor, "Taylor's Australian Journal."

175. "Correspondence: To the Rev. W. Taylor," *Wesleyan Chronicle*, September 30, 1863.

176. Ian Breward, "Methodist Reunion in Australasia," in *Methodism in Australia*, ed. Glen O'Brien and Hilary M. Carey (Farnham: Ashgate, 2015), 119–20.

177. "Parramatta," *Sydney Morning Herald*, August 10, 1864.

178. Evans, *Early Evangelical Revivals*, 45; "Notes of the Week," *Sydney Morning Herald*, August 27, 1864.

179. *Christian Advocate and Wesleyan Record*, July 19, 1864, quoted in Evans, 41.

180. "Telegraphic," *Brisbane Courier*, October 28 1864.; Ibid., October 31, 1864; Ibid., December 3, 1864.

181. Sione Latukefu, *Church and State in Tonga:The Wesleyan Methodist Missionaries and Political Development, 1822–1875* (Honolulu: University Press of Hawaii, 1974), 51.

182. Taylor, *Story of My Life*, 312; J. G. Turner, *The Pioneer Missionary: Life of the Rev. Nathaniel Turner, Missionary in New Zealand, Tonga, and Australia* (London: Published for the author at the Wesleyan Conference Office, 1872), 320, 25–28.

183. Taylor, *How to Be Saved*, 91; Latukefu, *Church and State*, 69–72.

184. Donald Denoon, Philippa Mein Smith, and Marivic Wyndham, *A History of Australia, New Zealand, and the Pacific* (Malden: Blackwell, 2007), 130–34; Taylor, *Story of My Life*, 315–16.

185. William Morley, *The History of Methodism in New Zealand* (Wellington: McKee, 1900), 470.

186. J. M. R. Owens, "Christianity and the Maoris to 1840," *New Zealand Journal of History* 2, no. 1 (1968): 39–40; M. P. K. Sorrenson, "Maori and Pakeha," in *The Oxford History of New Zealand*, ed. W. H. Oliver and B. R. Williams (Oxford: Clarendon Press, 1981), 169–72.

187. "Farewell Soiree to the Rev. Wm. Taylor," *Daily Southern Cross*, January 18, 1865.

188. Ibid.

189. Taylor, *Story of My Life*, 515; W. L. Blamires and John B. Smith, *The Early Story of the Wesleyan Methodist Church in Victoria* (Melbourne: Wesleyan Book Depot, 1886), 105; Morley, *Methodism in New Zealand*, 214, 393, 418–19.

190. Breward, *History*, 57; Carey, "Religion and Society," 194.

191. "Valedictory Service to the Rev. William Taylor," *Sydney Morning Herald*, July 11, 1865.

192. Ibid.

193. "Correspondence," *Wesleyan Chronicle*, January 20, 1865.

194. *Minutes of the Annual Conferences of the Methodist Episcopal Church* (New York: Carlton & Porter, 1864–5), 229, 31; *The Doctrines and Discipline of the Methodist Episcopal Church, 1864* (New York: Carlton & Porter, 1864), 102–3; Anne Taylor to Isaac Owen, April 2, 1864, Isaac Owen Papers, 1851–1865, Bancroft Library, University of California, Berkeley.

195. Taylor to Owen, April 2, 1864.

196. Letter to "the Bishop & members of the California Annual Conference," September 16, 1865, California Conference Papers, California-Nevada Conference Archives, Pacific School of Religion.

197. "Wesleyan Church: The Arrival of Rev. W. Taylor," *South Australian Advertiser*, 28 July 1865; Hunt, *This Side of Heaven*, 117–27.

198. Taylor, *Christian Adventures*, 5–8.

199. Ibid., 2–3, 8–9; "Topics of the Day," *South Australian Advertiser*, February 17, 1866.

200. "The Conference," *Wesleyan Chronicle*, February 20, 1866.

201. "E. O. Bass, "Rev. Wm. Taylor—An Incident," *Christian Advocate*, April 26, 1877.

Chapter 4

An "Evangelical Sherman" Crosses the Seas

Today eucalyptus trees are fixtures of the California landscape. Native to Australia, they are also a contemporary legacy of Taylor's worldwide travels. In 1863, perhaps recalling the difficulty he had finding wood to build a home in San Francisco, Taylor mailed a packet of eucalyptus seeds to his wife in Alameda. Her neighbor, James T. Stratton, was impressed by the fast-growing trees and asked Taylor to send more. Stratton sold the saplings he grew and may have distributed more around the state in his work as Surveyor General. Investigations into various claims for the introduction of the eucalyptus to California found that the first extensive cultivation and distribution of eucalyptus trees in California was by Stratton from Taylor's seeds.[1]

Toward the end of his life, Taylor used his introduction of eucalyptus trees to California as a metaphor for his missionary career. In his own hand, Taylor boasted in the frontispiece to his autobiography, *Story of My Life: An Account of What I Have Thought and Said and Done in My Ministry of More than Fifty-three Years in Christian Lands and Among the Heathen. Written By Myself*, that just as he had sent seeds from Australia to California where the tree flourished, he had also introduced the Christian gospel seed in settings around the world. Others continued the work, but he had started the growth "in the variety of fields, methods of work, and skillful rendering of the word of God."[2]

Taylor's boast was not just a statement of pride and reminiscence about the global scope of his evangelism. It was also the last example of a pattern Taylor increasingly demonstrated over the later stages of his life. The image of planting seeds and giving growth as a metaphor for Christian evangelism was one used by the apostle Paul. As Taylor traveled the world and took his evangelism into cross-cultural settings, he increasingly saw his own identity and experience reflected in the Pauline example. In ways large and small,

Taylor appropriated that example and came to believe that New Testament accounts of Paul's missionary work were not simply descriptive accounts of early Christian mission but proscriptive models for missionary outreach. Taylor found in Paul inspiration for new approaches to mission that he implemented in his evangelistic travels.

This chapter explores the beginnings of that process as Taylor visited southern Africa, England, and the Caribbean, made a return trip to Australia on his way to Ceylon and India, before returning to England. In this period, Taylor's missionary career moved into more identifiably cross-cultural and non-Christian settings. Many of those contexts were regions where Methodist missionaries had been at work for decades. His work and engagement with missionary practices in those settings illustrate some recurring themes in the Methodist missionary tradition. Methodists believed that their gospel was for all people but restricted leadership to some based on paternalistic assumptions of Western superiority. Methodist missions also often engaged with indigenous peoples by building on a Methodist colonial presence. These factors created an inherent tension in their missions. But a preexisting Methodist presence also enabled the use of revivalism and teachings on the doctrine of sanctification to identify and empower new leadership. In addition, Methodist acceptance of Taylor's new, "Pauline" approaches to mission illustrates that Methodists equally valued evangelistic methods that seemed biblical and effective.

Taylor's itinerant global revivalism was unique, but he was embraced and welcomed by Methodist missionaries from both the British and American traditions because he was seen as a faithful and successful representative of their tradition. He preached a theology those Methodists recognized as similar to their own. While some British Methodists were initially reluctant to adopt Taylor's American-style revivalism, they were usually persuaded his methods were both apostolic and fruitful. American Methodist missionaries in India also embraced his ideas when he visited the subcontinent. In the United States, California's Methodist preachers continued to claim Taylor as one of their own, but Taylor came to believe that California was too small a field in which to confine himself. As he wrote to his former California colleagues toward the end of his time in Australasia: "The facts are patent here, and thousands of new born souls are praising God for having me burn out in California, and sent to these Colonies."[3]

HOW TO BE SAVED

Before leaving Adelaide, Taylor published the first of what was intended as a two-volume work *How to Be Saved, and How to Save the World*. He dedicated it "as a memorial, and partial embodiment" of his preaching in Australasia and hoped it would continue his legacy in the region after he left.[4] As the title implied, the book's overarching theme was soteriology. It drew on Taylor's experience as an evangelist and reflected his interest in shepherding individuals through a process of salvation. Although a product of his revivalism in the Anglo-American world, this book illustrated the theological grounding for Taylor's evangelism. *How to Be Saved* also described Taylor's driving beliefs, the spirituality he thought was necessary for Christian missions, and his very high view of human freedom and potential.

Much of Taylor's soteriology followed contours familiar to Methodists. The first step in bringing a person to salvation was to convince the "unawakened sinner" that he or she was "in a state of spiritual death."[5] Taylor often did this in his revivals with an exposition on each of the Ten Commandments, identifying ways his listeners had broken them.[6] The hearer would be alerted to two forces at war within—the Holy Spirit drawing him or her toward Christ and Satan repelling the person. Taylor identified this essential step in the process of salvation as the "baptism of the Spirit and fire."[7] Unlike early Pentecostals who described the "baptism of the Spirit" as an empowering event, for Taylor this was a terrifying ordeal of spiritual conflict.[8] Next, the repentant must submit to God, confess their sins and reconcile personal relationships. Only then would one find peace.[9] Once one submitted to God's will, he or she became justified and could expect to feel of assurance of their salvation.[10]

Likewise consistent with traditional Methodist soteriology, Taylor argued the justified believer was expected to pursue entire sanctification or Christian perfection. To do otherwise was "not optional."[11] In his own articulation of this doctrine, Taylor identified two prerequisites for Christian perfection: "perfect submission of the will to God," and perfect faith demonstrated by "perfect confidence in God."[12] The fulfillment and maintenance of these would bring the believer into perfect love. This love was not an act of the will or an emotion but the experience of God dwelling in the believer in union. Taylor argued that sanctification might not happen immediately, but it would not take long. For Taylor, true holiness involved living and the only way to get through life was by putting oneself "fully under the leading of the Holy Spirit."[13] Taylor closed the book by alluding to the theme of the planned second volume, "How to Save the World," asserting that as long as the church fell short of this holiness, it would fail in its mission to share the gospel with the world.[14]

Although Taylor's theology followed traditional Methodist themes, in his specifics Taylor rested in an increasingly contested theological location. He described sin as a voluntary act, rejected the concept of total depravity, and insisted on the necessity of sanctification defined, in part, as subjection of the will to God. In the nineteenth century, a theological division had begun to emerge among Methodists over these issues. Those who became leaders of the Wesleyan holiness movement in America saw sin as a voluntary transgression of God's law, but, unlike Taylor, viewed depravity as inherent in human nature. Nevertheless, Taylor concurred with the theologians of this movement in emphasizing the necessity of two works of grace: justification to pardon the guilt of voluntary sins and entire sanctification to remove depravity. Holiness was necessary to eradicate sin in believers, and was considered an instantaneous gift of God.[15] In contrast, those whom historian Myung Soo Park called "progressive Methodists" rejected the doctrine of total depravity believing it to be a sinful inclination within humans that required God's help to overcome. Taylor concurred with this view. Sanctification was not an inward transformation, but "voluntary conformity to moral law," and since no second act of grace was necessary to transform human nature, it took the form of a gradual growth in holiness.[16] While Taylor wrote of the need for entire sanctification, his emphasis was less on God's work of grace than on the need of humans to conform their will with the will of God. Taylor, therefore, claimed ground on both sides of this emerging divide, giving his audiences both cause to appreciate and question his message.

Embedded in his description the process of salvation, Taylor devoted two long chapters to refuting a doctrine of election that asserted God only elected certain individuals for salvation and a doctrine of foreknowledge that claimed God knew who would be saved.[17] As a Methodist, Taylor's rejection of election as thus articulated was not unusual. This belief was anathema to the theological heirs of John Wesley. Moreover, like many Americans, the teaching offended Taylor's populist sensibilities.[18] Taylor's rejection of foreknowledge, however, was somewhat surprising. Methodists generally believed foreknowledge reconciled a belief in God's sovereignty and human freedom. Taylor, however, claimed that if God were to know who would be saved, it would limit human freedom.

This concern for human freedom and agency was Taylor's fundamental theological principle. He was no great theologian, and some of his beliefs could be inconsistent and statements careless. But an interest in human freedom and potential was the thread that tied Taylor's theology together. He articulated theological beliefs that maximized human ability. For Taylor, human nature was both untainted by total depravity and potentially empowered by sanctification. Human will was naturally free, inviolable by God, and, unconstrained by even the implication that God could know what people would do in the future. For Taylor, the experience of Christian perfection had less to do with sin and its eradication or overcoming its effects in the believer, and more to do with the believer making his or her will one with the will of God. This perfect union of wills enabled believers to undertake heroic actions, and, for Taylor, the failure of the church to draw on this power explained past failures of Christian evangelization.

It is worth noting that Taylor's rejection of election also illustrated his increasing admiration for the apostle Paul. In *How to Be Saved*, Taylor asserted that Jesus's disciples, erroneously believing that as Jews they were an exclusively elect people of God, were slow in starting missions to Gentiles. In this, they were corrected by Paul, lauded by Taylor as "God's great exponent of the doctrine of unlimited atonement and provision of salvation for the whole world."[19]

Within this work, Taylor also offered a brief theology of religion that he would soon have cause to develop further. Eventually, this approach to other religions would become a part of Taylor's Pauline theory for mission. At this stage, however, Taylor's theology of religion was derived from the language of the market. Religion, for Taylor, was a matter of supply and demand. God supplied every human demand. These demands included food, water, and air for bodies and the world around for the intellect. There were also spiritual demands in human nature that manifested in a fundamental "'religiousness' disposing [a person] to be a worshipper" evident in human love for poetry, music, the existence of a conscience, and "ancient heathen temples, and hecatombs of slain beasts, and all the varieties of modern expedients among Heathen, Mohamedeans, Jews, and formal Christians."[20] Taylor believed all these phenomena were human creations while his own evangelical Christianity was of God and perfectly matched human spiritual demands.

How to Be Saved was only published in Australia where it was harshly criticized. Taylor's view of foreknowledge was panned, as was a passage that discussed the Trinity in ways described by one reviewer as "not consonant with . . . the views held by all orthodox Trinitarians."[21] Despite great affection for Taylor and appreciation for his work in Australasia, the author wrote, "We are free to confess that the book has both pained and disappointed us; . . . We never thought, and never felt, the way 'to be saved' so difficult as since we have read this volume."[22]

This critique was important because it prompted Taylor to rework *How to Be Saved*. He would publish three books in its place that reproduced portions of the original and were supplemented with new material: *Reconciliation: Or How to Be Saved* (1867), *Infancy and Manhood of Christian Life* (1867), and *The Election of Grace* (1868).[23] In his revisions, Taylor backed away from any Trinitarian controversy.[24] These changes were most consequential because they resulted in Taylor's theology of sanctification being placed in one book, making it accessible to readers interested in the doctrine. When Taylor returned to the United States in 1875, he was welcomed by the postwar Wesleyan holiness movement as one of its own partially on the strength of his description of sanctification in *Infancy and Manhood*.[25]

CHRISTIAN ADVENTURES IN SOUTH AFRICA

Taylor never wrote volume two of *How to Be Saved, and How to Save the World*. Instead in South Africa he was able to test his emerging theories of mission and to develop new ones through his participation in the South African Revival of 1866. This event, that saw some 6,000 Africans professing evangelical conversions within the span of a few months, was a pivotal experience in Taylor's life. His experiences shaped and confirmed his developing "Pauline" theory of mission. It also gave Taylor's life new direction. He became convinced that the entire world was open to his evangelism, and that God would use him to accomplish great things. Part of that newfound enthusiasm stemmed from Taylor's belief that in South Africa he discovered a way around linguistic barriers to evangelism.

Taylor's inability to communicate with speakers of other tongues had frustrated some of his attempts at evangelism in San Francisco. Southern Africa also contained a complex mix of languages and cultures. First populated by the hunter-gatherer San, pastoralist Khoikhoi, and mixed farmers who spoke different Bantu-language dialects, such as Xhosa, Zulu, Pedi, and Tswana, in 1652, Dutch merchants and colonists established a base on the Cape. They introduced that language and culture, and those of slaves brought from around the Indian Ocean. As the Dutch presence grew, Khoikhoi society disintegrated and, with significant intermarriage, became known as the Cape Coloured. During the Napoleonic Wars, the British occupied the Cape, and large-scale British migration began in 1820. Most Britons settled in the Eastern Cape, but another wave colonized Natal on the Indian Ocean in 1849–1851. In addition, in the 1820 and 1830s, a process known as the *Mfecane* further disrupted African populations as an expanding Zulu kingdom and refugees known as Mfengu moved to the Eastern Cape and as far north as the contemporary nations of Malawi, Zambia, and Tanzania. Tensions between British officials and Dutch colonists, who were developing into a distinct Afrikaner culture, also prompted large migrations into the African interior.[26]

With this mix of cultures and peoples, southern Africa was one of the first settings for Methodist cross-cultural missions outside the north Atlantic. These emerged first out of British imperial expansion and engaged with indigenous populations as a secondary movement. British soldiers brought Methodism to southern Africa in 1806. Early attempts by Methodist missionaries to regularize the religion of these soldiers encountered government opposition on the grounds that soldiers had chaplains from the established church and preaching to slaves would offend Dutch colonists. In 1815, the missionary Barnabas Shaw, after being denied permission to preach, left Cape Town to start a mission to the Namaquas.[27] A lasting, formal Methodist presence in the Cape was established in 1820 and became bilingual with services for English soldiers and colonists and Dutch services for the slave and Coloured populations.[28] Among those who settled in the Eastern Cape in 1820 was William Shaw (of no relation to Barnabas), the pioneer organizer of Methodism there and a missionary to the Xhosa. He established a "chain" of Wesleyan mission stations to Africans stretching to Natal that Taylor would follow in his revival tour.[29]

When the Taylors arrived in Cape Town on March 31, 1866, William assumed he would find large populations of English speakers in the city and its environs to evangelize. He led a few small revivals but discovered the English-speaking population there was too small to occupy him. An invitation by the Grahamstown district chair of the Wesleyan Methodists to take his revivals to the Eastern Cape and the discovery that Methodists he had known in Ireland had settled there, convinced him to visit that region.[30] Taylor soon left his family, including the now pregnant Anne, in Cape Town and sailed for the Eastern Cape.[31]

As in Cape Town, Taylor initially worked among whites in Wesleyan Methodist churches. Most historiography of Taylor's time in South Africa has characterized this revival work as a failure. For example, historian David Bundy described colonial Europeans as being "unresponsive" to Taylor's preaching.[32] Historian Daryl Balia called Taylor's impact "rather limited."[33] To be sure, his revivals among whites never reached the magnitude of what Taylor would witness among Africans but after a slow start were comparable to what he had experienced in Australasia. South African whites were unfamiliar with and carried negative stereotypes of American revivalism. Only after Taylor was able to persuade a critical mass to accept his methods did his work among whites succeed in any measure.

Taylor convinced people to accept his revivalism by arguing that it followed a biblical and apostolic model and by allowing success to build on success. Taylor always began revival meetings with a description of how the evening would proceed and a biblical justification for that procedure. He explained that prayer, exhortations, and hymn singing were consistent with the "old simple methods of the Gospel" illustrated in the Acts of the Apostles.[34] As Taylor's itinerary took him through different communities in the Eastern Cape, exhorters frequently followed from one community to the next, thus contributing to the spread of the sense of a revival beyond a local context. In Port Elizabeth, for example, the Wesleyan Methodist superintendent, John Richards, with whom Taylor would later work in India, confessed he initially doubted any penitents or exhorters would come forward in response to Taylor's appeals. He felt "rebuked" when several did. Later, when Taylor moved on to Uitenhage, Richards, his wife, and several other laypeople went to assist in the revival work there.[35]

Although Taylor's language was not yet explicit, he had begun to identify the use of daily revival meetings, like those he had led almost constantly since early 1857, as a part of a Pauline model for missionary work. This model would soon grow to include other practices. The gradual acceptance of this revivalism by South African Methodists illustrated that part of the appeal of Taylor's Pauline models were that they seemed both biblical and successful. As Grahamstown's Methodists declared some months after Taylor left South Africa, Taylor had taught them "God's own instrumentality for saving souls is to be trusted as of incomparable efficacy.'"[36]

The Arminian theology of the Wesleyan Methodists made them theologically predisposed to adopt these revival techniques. Aware also of Taylor's reputation in Australia, they were willing to trust his expertise.[37] Most outright opposition to Taylor's revivalism came from Dutch Reformed Calvinists in the colony. At Uitenhage, a Dutch man protested Taylor's introduction of "blasphemous proceedings" in town.[38] Such opposition only confirmed in Taylor's mind the danger posed by Calvinist theology, and in particular, its doctrine of election. It should be noted, however, that Taylor left Cape Town with a favorable impression of Andrew Murray, Jr., after the two addressed a Sunday school meeting on the importance of both evangelical conversion and Christian education. Murray was a Dutch Reformed pastor who would introduce to that church a strong evangelical piety and become a major figure in the Keswick movement.[39]

After Taylor left Queenstown on his tour of the Eastern Cape, the Wesleyan minister there, H. H. Dugmore, lectured on Taylor's work in a way that managed to be both supportive and condescending. Dugmore described Taylor as a hardworking, disinterested (Taylor no longer raised money for his debt), earnest, and courageous man. Taylor reportedly violated some standards of propriety but only because he was American. Dugmore asserted that Taylor's nationality should not be held against him; rude behavior was acceptable in "the pulpits, the senate, and the drawing rooms of the United States."[40] Whatever Taylor did to confirm the worst stereotypes of Americans, he did not fit the caricature of revivalists. Dugmore noted that Taylor did not cast God as "a vengeful tyrant," and his sermons had "nothing of the 'fire and brimstone' character."[41] This was to his credit. Dugmore also defended emotional responses to Taylor's sermons as within the scope of what was appropriate and biblical for those seeking salvation. Most who felt sorry for their sins against God wept quietly, except for a few "youths from the country," who lacked refinement.[42]

Dugmore's lecture also revealed that while some opposition to Taylor's revivals were rooted in theological differences or a concern for respectability, as in Australasia, in the South African context, there was also a racial factor. Some were concerned that revivalism could undermine white control of the

African population. In a footnote, Dugmore haughtily defended emotional responses of Africans to Taylor's preaching. He asserted that like Americans and rural youth, Africans were "unrestrained by the conventionalities of civilized life," nevertheless the spread of revival among Africans was to be celebrated.[43]

Dugmore's defense of African Christian worship was necessary because as Taylor began his work among whites, a revival also started among blacks. That revival was sparked by the African Christian leader and candidate for the Methodist ministry, Charles Pamla. Taylor and Pamla partnered for several months to spread the revival more broadly. While Pamla was the driving force behind the African revival, Taylor helped catalyze it by normalizing ecstatic expressions among whites and placing the revival meetings within the auspices of the Wesleyan Methodist mission. The African revival was thus encouraged to spread without fear of white repression.[44] Unlike a catalyst, however, Taylor would be changed by the experience.

By all accounts a remarkable man, Pamla's parents were Mfengu who had converted to Christianity under the ministry of a Wesleyan missionary. Pamla served as a class leader, a lay preacher, and was fluent in five languages.[45] Pamla sparked the African revival when he became convinced that he should seek entire sanctification after reading John Wesley's sermons. Pamla prayed for the experience, and felt

> ease from the different thoughts, ease from the world, and from all the cares of the flesh. I felt the Spirit filling my soul, and immediately I was forced to say in my soul, "For me to live is Christ. And I gave up my body, soul, thoughts, words, time, property, children, and everything that belongs to me, to the Lord, to do as He pleases."[46]

Before Taylor reached the area, Pamla had begun to evangelize more aggressively and shortly claimed new converts.[47]

Taylor and Pamla first met in King William's Town where both led separate revival services among the English and Africans respectively. Because of his sanctification and evangelical zeal, Taylor would see in Pamla a kindred spirit. When Wesleyan missionaries invited Taylor to preach at the Annshaw mission station, the two men were given the first opportunity to work together.[48]

Mission stations such as Annshaw were a common model for Christian mission in Africa. Pioneered by Moravian missionaries of the eighteenth century, stations sought to create a community where converts could withdraw to live a Christian life. Unable to separate Western civilization from their understanding of Christianity, other missionaries adopted stations, complete with homes, churches, schools, and small industry, as a way to introduce both Christianity and civilization to Africans.[49] Annshaw had been built and settled by people from Wesleyville, the first mission station started by William Shaw, after it had been twice destroyed.[50]

Another African candidate for the Methodist ministry, William Shaw Kama, seemed to demonstrate the efficacy of the mission station model. Kama was the son of William Kama, a Xhosa chief baptized by Wesleyan missionaries in 1825. Despite the opposition of other Xhosa leaders, Chief Kama remained a Christian and ascended to his position while non-Christian rivals were unseated. He took only one wife and adopted European dress. In 1857, an African girl named Nongqawuse prophesied that if the Xhosa killed their cattle, their ancestors would destroy the British. The famine that resulted when many did so catastrophically weakened Xhosa society. Because of his faith, however, Kama's people did not participate in and were spared the worst effects of the cattle-killing.[51]

Taylor went to Annshaw with low expectations. He doubted his ability to preach through a translator because previous attempts to do so had been unsuccessful. This time, however, Taylor rehearsed his sermons for Pamla, who clarified any uncertainties. Taylor shared his theory in *The Model Preacher* that effective preaching followed the example of Jesus; he encouraged Pamla to speak with "naturalness," that is using a range of vocal expression and gestures.[52] Twice that day, Taylor and Pamla addressed a congregation that included Chief Kama and about 600 Xhosa and Mfengu. At the close of his second sermon, Taylor sang the Charles Wesley hymn, "Sinners, Turn: Why Will Ye Die?" Surprising everyone, Pamla sang along, translating as he went. The effect was remarkable, and when Taylor invited people for prayer, over a hundred surged forward.[53]

In a scene that repeated itself when Taylor and Pamla preached together elsewhere, the missionary on site initially sought to end the meeting, afraid the Africans would be unable to control their emotions. This concern, like Dugmore's, stemmed from a European cultural tradition that saw such enthusiasm as opposed to reason and a dangerous, disruptive force to be contained.[54] Taylor argued, however, that the African response was rational and to be expected. They had been under missionary instruction for years. This was the Holy Spirit at work, and penitents should not be dismissed and left without aid but be guided with the help of exhorters. The missionary at Annshaw, as elsewhere, relented to Taylor's advice and allowed the prayer meeting to proceed.[55]

Reports of the evening rapturously compared it to the first Pentecost as a miraculous work of God. Taylor was more restrained. He believed God was at work but not in an extraordinary way. Pamla was a gifted translator and speaker, revivals naturally followed the use of appropriate methods, and Pamla's sanctification empowered his work. The revival was "the Spirit's work . . . perfectly adjusted the human conditions employed, and did not miraculously rise above, or suspend any physical law."[56] In Taylor's view, Pamla was highly competent translator and public speaker, had a good memory, knew his theology, and had consecrated himself to God. Moreover, Pamla followed his advice on speaking with "naturalness."[57]

Taylor's evaluation was important because it meant that he believed the revival at Annshaw was replicable. Just as there was a right way to manage a prayer meeting to bring about conversions, Taylor came to believe there was also a right way to use a translator. He wrote,

> I felt an indescribable joy, not simply on account of the great work of God in the salvation of the Kaffirs,[58] which was an occasion of great joy to "the angels of God," but especially because the spell that bound me within the lines of my native language was broken. I could now preach effectively through an interpreter, and the heathen world seemed suddenly opened to my personal enterprise, as an ambassador for Christ.[59]

As never before, Taylor believed the world was open to his evangelism.

In the aftermath of this epiphany, Taylor and Pamla made arrangements to tour the chain of Wesleyan mission stations across the Transkei to Natal together. Taylor invited his son Morgan along, thinking the time together would renew their relationship.[60] While waiting for him to arrive from Cape Town, Pamla and other African leaders continued the ongoing revival at Annshaw. Taylor kept to his previously arranged preaching schedule among whites but now added sermons to his schedule requiring a translator. Continued success confirmed Taylor's conclusion that by rehearsing his message and instructing his translator to speak naturally, language would be no barrier to evangelism.[61] Once, at Craddock, two translators rendered Taylor's sermon into Dutch and Xhosa. He rapturously celebrated that "for over an hour the piercing light and melting power of the Gospel flowed out through the medium of three languages at once."[62]

By July 12, Morgan arrived, and Taylor and Pamla reunited for their tour. At multiple stations along the way, the partners spread the revival to new communities. This trip also allowed Taylor to learn about missionary practices in Africa and to engage firsthand with African culture. In this effort, Pamla served as his primary informant. Taylor also read what he could and interviewed community elders.[63] Although Taylor would come to criticize the use of mission stations, he agreed with most standard missionary practices he encountered and the ways missionaries had engaged with African culture. Like most missionaries, he judged polygamy to be a serious obstacle to the spread of Christianity in Africa. At Warners, he informed a potential convert that he could not be saved unless he sent his second wife back to her family.[64]

Taylor also objected to a proposal that the Thembu, a Xhosa-speaking people, consider converting to Christianity en masse. Despite ample historical precedents for national conversions reaching back into antiquity, most evangelical missionaries rejected mass conversions out of a concern that they would be superficial. Individual experience of God's salvation was paramount. Taylor thought the interest in Christianity behind the proposal should be encouraged but that it might also be "a trick of Satan" to prevent "personal acceptance of Christ to-day."[65] Both he and Pamla sought to persuade the Thembu chief to convert despite the opposition of other Thembu leaders, to no avail. Pamla even attempted to convince the chief's brother to convert, suggesting God would allow him to supplant his brother. In the end, neither sibling converted.[66] Without the option for a collective change of religion, the Thembu opted for social stability over dynastic struggle. [67]

While Taylor convinced himself that his newfound method of working with a translator allowed him to carry his revivals anywhere, it was clear, even from Taylor's own account of the tour, that Pamla, and not he, was the indispensable member of the evangelistic team. The party split up as they approached the Natal border to visit different mission stations. While Pamla led a revival at Emfundisweni, Taylor's services at Palmerston were "crippled" by his inability to communicate through the interpreter there.[68] In Natal, Taylor again devoted himself to English-language revivals. Pamla, meanwhile, continued to work among Africans.[69]

Interracial partnerships such as that between Taylor and Pamla were unusual. Taylor certainly held a paternalistic attitude toward Africans. He took for granted that they would accept the leadership of whites until such time as that leadership was unnecessary. For a while, following his epiphany, Taylor dreamed that he would personally direct the Christianization of Africa with Africans under his authority.[70] Eventually, he came to realize that Pamla's ability to evangelize Africans surpassed his own. It was best to step aside and let Pamla do the work. One reason the two split up in Natal was Taylor hoped that Pamla's evangelistic successes would "break down a foolish 'caste' and 'colour' prejudice" against African preachers who he believed would be agents "for the conversion of the millions of this continent for God."[71]

Taylor's optimism was unwarranted. Reflecting the racist assumptions of the time, missionary accounts focused on the revivals led by the white Taylor and attributed the revival to his leadership. They also expressed fascination and hope in the interlingual dimension of the revival. One Wesleyan missionary celebrated that converts had become evangelists, "Many young Englishmen have got Kaffir tongues and renewed hearts, and they are using both for God. I wish some of them had Tamil and Hindustani tongues."[72] Seth Stone, an American Board of Commissioners for Foreign Missions missionary in Natal, described his own fascination with Taylor and desire to learn the secret of Taylor's success. He wrote,

Rev. Wm. Taylor of the Methodist Episcopal Church in America has been to this country; Revival has followed in his track among white and black, though he stayed not long in any place. Has God such special agents? in what lies their power? do they preach more eloquently than others? do they use better schemes? are they better men at heart? He seemed to think he could produce the same results even among new tribes could he but get a medium of communication. Where lies the secret? I have thought of this. We want to be able to use it.[73]

For his part, Taylor believed that while Pamla could continue the work in Africa, since he had figured out how to overcome language barriers, perhaps God would take him "to some other part of His vast dominions."[74]

Taylor's published reflections of his time in Natal focused not on his revivalism but on his encounter with Bishop John Colenso. As noted earlier, Taylor was familiar with Colenso's work. The two met in Durban and shared a brief, cordial conversation. At the time, the bishop's wife, Frances Colenso, recorded her surprise that unlike most revivalists, Taylor did not denounce her husband.[75] Although Taylor did not hesitate to refute Colenso's assertions, he saw no reason to express any condemnation.

Unlike many evangelicals, Taylor saw little threat to his faith in either the theories of Charles Darwin or higher criticism of the Bible. He thought these ideas were too ridiculous to be of deep concern.[76] To illustrate that point, Taylor published a conversation Pamla had with a white traveling companion during their tour. Colenso was said to have first doubted biblical claims about the size of Noah's ark when questioned about it by a Zulu assistant. Inverting that story and racial hierarchies about the relative capacities of Europeans and Africans, Taylor approvingly told how Pamla proved himself the intellectual superior to Colenso by arguing that Colenso had made faulty assumptions in his analysis.[77]

Ultimately, however, for Taylor the weakness of Colenso's ideas and the strength of his own were best proved by comparing their tours of Natal. While he and Pamla claimed over 320 white and 700 African converts in the colony, Colenso only caused "a lively stir among the newspaper reporters . . . and baptized two babies."[78]

PAULINE METHODS

As Taylor returned to Cape Town, he wrote an essay detailing a "Gospel theory for evangelizing the world."[79] Although Taylor never wrote volume two of *How to Be Saved*, this piece, included in his book about his South African tour, *Christian Adventures in South Africa*, and published in several other forums, picked up where his previous book ended. At the close of *How to Be*

Saved, Taylor had claimed that in its missions the church had neither drawn on the full power of God's sanctifying work nor employed God's methods for saving the world. Failing both, the church had been unfaithful and would be called to account by God.[80] But, Taylor believed, his tour with the sanctified Charles Pamla had demonstrated the way forward for the church.

Taylor had long sought biblical parallels to match his experiences and his interest in the apostle Paul had been building for some time. Now, for the first time, he used his reading of the New Testament example of Paul to articulate a "Pauline" theory of Christian mission. Taylor's thesis was that the Pauline example offered a superior model for Christian mission than had been used in the recent past. New "Pauline" ideas would be added later, but those presented in this essay were revivalism, the formation of an elite team of native preachers, and voluntary giving. A fourth element—engagement with non-Christian religion—was not discussed in this essay but was illustrated in a sermon he frequently preached in his tour of the Transkei.[81]

Mission stations such as those he had toured, Taylor asserted, were ineffective methods of evangelism. Instead, he proposed leading a revival campaign into the African interior following "the old plan so successfully worked by St. Paul and his fellow-missionaries."[82] Stories in the Acts of the Apostles were not simply historical accounts but illustrations of "God's own methods of spreading the Gospel."[83] Referencing descriptions in Acts 5:42 and elsewhere of "daily" apostolic preaching, Taylor asserted that daily protracted revival meetings like those he had led since leaving California were the methods used by the apostles to win converts.[84] The second element of Taylor's "apostolic plan" could be executed by selecting "a few of the best native preachers in the country."[85] With them, he would go to population centers, and (referencing Paul's work described in Acts 17:17) "'dispute with them daily,' till the God of battles would give us 1,000 or 3,000 souls"—figures drawn from Acts where the conversion of thousands from apostolic preaching was related (2:41; 4:4).[86] Once a church was organized, the preaching cadre would set off to the next population center, and if necessary divide as Paul and Barnabas had. The final component of Taylor's plan expected that after a "multitude" had been converted, they would be instructed to voluntarily support the church with a tithe of their income. Paul's churches modeled this by not only supporting themselves but by sending money to Judea. In this way, the new churches would be taught to be "self-sustaining from the start."[87]

Taylor's ability to convince others of the biblical foundation for his revival practices has already been noted. Beyond this, Taylor's contemporaries saw his proposal to employ African preachers as the most innovative aspect of his plan, in part because it illustrated a fundamental tension that existed in Methodist missions. Methodists believed the gospel was for all, but mission structures often restricted leadership to white, male missionaries who held power in most aspects of mission work. Methodist missionaries only brought indigenous converts into leadership slowly and in subordinate roles. Pamla, for example, was approved as a candidate for ministry just before Taylor arrived. Despite his critical role in the revival, Pamla and two other Africans would only be ordained five years later, in 1871.[88] Historian Daryl M. Balia noted that although missionaries believed this policy was cautious and prudent, it was probably also a "ploy to protect their own power and safeguard their privilege."[89] In another generation, the continued hesitancy of Methodist missionaries to let Africans take leadership became a source of frustration and conflict that led to the formation of new black churches separate from white control.[90]

Methodist missionaries, like other Europeans and Americans in the late nineteenth century, increasingly embraced racial and civilizational hierarchies that privileged whites and Western civilization. They believed their task was to "elevate" converts toward Western norms from a presumed "depravity," and they linked understandings of Christianity with Western civilization. Ironically, some past missionary successes in Africa, such as the story of the Kama family mentioned earlier, were interpreted in ways that bolstered that belief. For example, recaptive Africans who had been taken into slavery, freed by British naval intervention, and resettled in Sierra Leone adopted both Christianity and many aspects of English culture.[91]

The fact that many missionaries saw the "civilizing" of non-Western peoples as a part of their missionary objective should not obscure the agency of indigenous peoples in this complex intercultural process. Africans and indigenous people elsewhere adopted and adapted resources offered by missionaries for their own purposes. Historian Wallace Mills, for example, argued that the South African Revival was a search by Xhosa-speaking people for "secondary forms of resistance" to white colonialism and conquest.[92] Traditional cultural resources were unable to deal successfully with changes Europeans had brought, the cattle-killing episode undermined confidence in African cultural resources, and Christianity seemed to offer superior supernatural and material benefits. Over time, conversion to Christianity also led to the training of new African leaders and the development of free associations that allowed for resistance.[93]

For his part, Taylor believed rapid deployment of African preachers was possible because of the universal nature of the gospel he preached and the empowering potential of entire sanctification. He wrote, the "Gospel is adapted to humanity in all its forms, from the most learned philosopher to the most degraded heathen. All the knowledge essential to the salvation of a poor heathen may be acquired in a very short time."[94] Moreover, since entire sanctification could follow soon after justification, Taylor saw no reason why a person could not be converted to Christianity and, very soon thereafter, be fully empowered as a preacher. This native preacher would be at least the equal of any foreign missionary—if not his superior—because of his linguistic advantages. Any further education was unnecessary. More than any other quality, Taylor believed Pamla's experience of Christian perfection enabled his evangelism.[95]

The last element of Taylor's emerging Pauline model, and one not addressed in this essay, was theological engagement with African religion. The biblical account of Paul's visit to Athens found in Acts 17 served as a template for Taylor's exploration of the relationship between traditional African beliefs and his Christian message. He developed his thoughts in a sermon he regularly preached on his Transkei tour he called his "Sermon to Kaffir Heathens."[96] It represented the only substantial way Taylor tried to adapt his evangelism to the culture of his African audience.

In the biblical story, Paul noted that the Athenians had an altar dedicated "TO THE UNKNOWN GOD," and the apostle identified the unknown deity as the Christian God of his proclamation. Likewise, Taylor sought to establish that the Christian God and the traditional African high god of his audience were one. He asserted the high god called by his audience Dala ("the Creator"), Tixo ("the preserver of all things"), or Inkosi ("the Lord, the Great Chief who ruled all things") was the "one Great God who made the world, the sun, moon, and stars, and every living thing; and who made man."[97] Taylor also invoked the memory of African ancestors to confirm his claims and to affirm a common belief in life after death.[98] He likened another African deity to the devil who tempted humans and introduced sin and corruption into the world.[99] As in his evangelism in the Anglo-American world, Taylor presented an extended exposition on Decalogue but in this context applied the commandments to African practices. Reliance on ancestors or objects of power violated the first commandment by showing a lack of trust in the one God.[100] Polygamy was a form of adultery. Witchcraft was a form of theft, since accusations of witchcraft robbed people of their reputations.[101] In the final movement of his sermon, Taylor introduced the Christian Trinity as one God that exists in "three distinct personal spirits."[102] These spirits developed a plan whereby one of them, called the Son of God, took on a human body and spirit, lived a good life, and gave it as a sacrifice so that those who believe in him would be saved. Taylor closed with an appeal for his audience to believe his message and to be saved from their sins. Those who did would receive "power, renewing their hearts, and making them 'the sons of God.'" but those who did not would "die in [their] sins."[103]

Taylor's attempt to develop connections between his Christian message and African religion were significant in three ways. First, it was an irenic attempt to establish common ground across differences of belief. Historian David Bundy noted Taylor did not argue for the total replacement of traditional African religion with Christianity so much as he sought to redefine its meanings and introduce Jesus Christ into that belief system.[104] As such, Taylor was somewhat ahead of his time. Missionary "fulfillment theologies," in which it was argued Christ fulfilled the aspirations of other religions, became common in the early twentieth century. In addition, such theologies were most common in India, where Hinduism offered beliefs and practices that fit the definition of religion held by most missionaries.[105] In this point lay the second importance of Taylor's sermon. It was an implicit recognition that there was such a thing as African religion. Westerners rarely saw in Africa anything approaching a religious belief structure. They were more likely to ascribe to Africans a collection of primitive "superstitions" rather than a religion. Finally, this sermon became a template for Taylor as he encountered other religious beliefs in his travels. As will be seen, outside of this African context, Taylor would use variations of this sermon to adapt his message to the religious beliefs of different audiences.

LONDON

Before leaving Cape Town, 120 Wesleyan laymen presented Taylor with a letter expressing their belief that his visit was by "the order of [God's] providence" and rejoicing that Taylor was "the chosen instrument in the hands of God" to bring salvation to so many.[106] The spread of revival among Africans, it declared, heralded "a new era in the history of modern Missions, and we cannot but recognize the finger of God in this leading you to those lands."[107] Taylor shared their conviction that providence had brought him to South Africa and that a new day in missions had dawned. He boasted in a letter to Walter and Phoebe Palmer, "God gave us about 6000 souls in Australia in 2½ years and over 5500 in Africa in 7 months."[108] The South African Revival convinced Taylor that God had something even greater in store for him. According to his wife, Taylor believed that "the Lord must have a larger field for him elsewhere, or he would not have allowed him to depart" Africa.[109]

This grandiose conclusion, however, did not answer the obvious follow-up question: Where did God want him to go? It was also becoming less clear how William could reconcile his own sense of mission with stable family life. A month before he returned to his family in Cape Town, Anne gave birth to a boy, first named Africanda or Africanus.[110] Departing Cape Town with this new addition, the Taylors arrived in England shortly before Christmas 1866. William had promised to show his family London's sights, but word of his evangelistic successes in Australasia and South Africa preceded him. His schedule filled. Invited to lead revivals in London, William left sightseeing to his family.[111]

In contrast with his first visit to the United Kingdom when Taylor preached primarily in Ireland and scattered communities around England, on this visit he was invited to preach at several locations in London, including the prestigious City Road Chapel. For about two weeks in January 1867, Taylor led a revival at the building that was built by Methodist founder John Wesley and had served as his London base. Anne was proud that her husband preached there "to full houses."[112] The Methodist press noted that the meetings drew curious members of other congregations and Wesleyan chapels, interested to hear the preacher lauded as a missionary and evangelical hero. It declared, "The most valuable result of the services consists in the revival and quickening of the society and congregation attached to the chapel" including a number of young people who had recently joined, but now "have professed to find 'the peace which passeth all understanding.'"[113] In addition, the paper noted approvingly, that Taylor's preaching style was lauded as "original," with "nothing . . . approaching to rant."[114]

From City Road, Taylor branched out to other Wesleyan circuits around London. For the first time, he also fielded invitations from outside the Methodist world. Charles Spurgeon, the noted English Baptist preacher, invited Taylor to teach students at his school the "best method of preaching the gospel."[115] Spurgeon was impressed by Taylor's evangelistic ability but was as troubled by Taylor's theology as Taylor was by Spurgeon's Calvinism. In a review of *Infancy and Manhood*, Taylor's book on sanctification, Spurgeon declared, "We have not a particle of faith in its main doctrine."[116] British Methodists were proud that other evangelicals were interested in Taylor, feeling it reflected well on them. Ultimately, however, Taylor's unwillingness to mute his strong antipathy toward Calvinism and his promotion of entire sanctification limited his appeal to Methodist circles. In this, Taylor resisted the nineteenth-century trend toward a synthesis in revival traditions among diverse evangelicals identified by historian David Bebbington.[117]

Now free of debt, Taylor's book sales served only to support him. Taylor also broadened his self-identification with Paul to include this method of support. Taylor refused compensation for his preaching but encouraged people to buy his books. Alluding to a description of Paul's occupation in Acts 18:3, he said, "Like St. Paul, he was engaged on an extensive ecclesiastical expedition, preaching Christ and doing good; but he was also a tent-maker, and did not wish to be chargeable upon the people among whom he laboured."[118] Taylor used similar language when Elliot Stock, a London publisher abridged *The Model Preacher* and sold it for half Taylor's price. Taylor appealed to public sympathy to avoid that edition by stressing the apostolic nature of his ministry. "Instead of building tents to meet the financial demands of my mission, as did St. Paul, I have written and published a few books" that were sold "on the principle of business equivalents."[119] Taylor thus merged the market-oriented rationale for his publishing that he offered in Australia and a new apostolic description of self-support. The self-sufficiency that had been instilled in Taylor as a young boy, served him well as a missionary in California, and that Taylor valued was, thus, elevated to the level of Christian principle.

Although Taylor believed he was supporting himself through the sale of his books, he was heavily supported by others. The Christian philanthropist and Wesleyan lay preacher Henry Reed was a major patron. The two men had heard of each other through church and family connections in Tasmania and Africa but did not meet until 1867 when Reed invited Taylor to lead a revival at his home in Tunbridge Wells.[120] After Taylor refused to accept payment for his sermons, Reed offered to make occasional book purchases through Taylor's publisher and give the books away.[121] Taylor agreed to this arrangement. The full extent of Reed's support may not be known, his patronage was evidently so critical the family renamed their African-born son after him![122]

Reed's philanthropy and distribution of Taylor's books probably extended Taylor's influence to other evangelicals. Reed was a supporter of evangelical missionary endeavors such as Hudson Taylor's China Inland Mission, and William and Catherine Booth of the Salvation Army.[123] Although sharing a surname and pioneering roles in late nineteenth-century Christian missions, it is unlikely that William Taylor and Hudson Taylor ever met. William and Catherine Booth, however, met at the Reed mansion. During Taylor's week at Tunbridge Wells, she exhorted during his services.[124]

While such invitations kept William busy, Anne and the children were eager to return home. William, however, was no longer certain that God wanted him in California. The tension these conflicting desires placed on the family were evident in Anne's journal:

> When I left California . . . for Australia . . . it was with the expectation of proceeding with him [on] the overland route via Palestine to England and home to California instead of the "overprogramme." We had much affliction instead of pleasure, wearisome months of watching by the bed of a dear son in the burning heat of Australia, and instead of the trip to Palestine [we] went to South Africa [and] came to London en route to California. We have been here three months, waiting! and now! unless I say to my husband "I cannot go without you," after circumnavigating the globe, I must return alone! . . .[125]

Her reflections end abruptly; the page below this entry was torn from her diary. On the next page, Anne continued to struggle with the issue. She believed that God had other purposes for her husband than a return to pastoral ministry in California, rejoiced in his role in the South African Revival and evangelistic work in England, and trusted that these events were part of God's plan. She confessed, however, "that on the subject of 'necessary continued separation' of my husband from his family 'for the sake of God's cause,' I am not now so able to endure as twenty years ago."[126] In the end, the family split up. Anne and the younger boys left for the United States. Morgan enrolled in school in Lausanne, Switzerland, and in late 1867, William sailed for the Caribbean with plans to continue on to California. It would take nearly a decade for Taylor to return home for a visit.[127]

CROSSING THE SEAS

Methodism in the Caribbean had a long history. In 1758, Nathaniel Gilbert heard Wesley preach while visiting England. When he returned to Antigua, Gilbert formed Methodist societies—the first outside the British Isles—although two female slaves, Mary Alley and Sophia Campbell, probably led evangelization of the slave population.[128] As in North America, slaves in the Caribbean were both highly receptive to Methodism and active in promoting its spread. On his many visits to the region, Thomas Coke, the pioneer of Methodist missions, both established formal missions and discovered Methodist slaves carried their religion with them when they were involuntarily transported.[129]

From this early date, Caribbean Methodism was characterized by predominantly black members served by white missionaries. Even after emancipation in 1838, ministerial leadership in Wesleyan Methodist missions was overwhelmingly white. Nevertheless, emancipation sparked rapid growth as former slaves, now free to associate, joined Methodist societies. Membership doubled by 1844, and in some places growth was even more dramatic. Methodist membership on Barbados grew 166 percent in the decade after emancipation.[130] This growth, however, gave way to decades of decline. Economic stagnation meant that wage laborers could not afford the contributions required of full members of the society.[131] By the 1850s, Wesleyan missionaries were discouraged by membership decline and the inability of local communities to support them.[132]

Taylor's success as a revivalist was now well-known among Wesleyan Methodists who encouraged him to visit the West Indies. They hoped he could reverse flagging membership and finances.[133] As such, Taylor's unexpected arrival on Barbados surprised and pleased Henry Hurd, the Wesleyan missionary in Bridgetown.

How many times, since reading, at our Missionary prayer-meetings, the letters of the brethren in South Africa, have I wished that Mr. Taylor would visit the West Indies! And now at a time when we least expected him, but perhaps when we most needed him, God has sent him to us.[134]

Others concurred that Taylor's visit was an answer to prayer for a revitalized membership, and for almost six weeks, Taylor led revival services around Barbados, stopping only briefly for the Christmas holidays.[135]

Taylor's primary focus during these revivals was to renew the faith of those who had not been faithful, had not experienced a sense of assurance, or who had not been sanctified. His sermons focused on traditional Methodist doctrines such as "Justification by Faith, the New Birth, the Witness of the Spirit, and Entire Sanctification."[136] While revivals were suspended for Christmas, Taylor met with class leaders to revitalize these leaders of local societies. In the end, both Taylor and Hurd were pleased with the results. As many as 150 people claimed conversion, as Hurd testified, "Many believers have been quickened and sanctified; and many sinners have been awakened and converted."[137]

Elsewhere, Taylor's revivals had cultivated new leadership among Methodists. In the West Indies, as in South Africa, however, this potential was limited by racial politics. The Wesleyan Methodist mission there adopted the social and racial hierarchy that privileged white, British-born missionaries over locally born whites, mixed-race descendants of white men and slave women, and blacks, in that order. For decades after emancipation, Wesleyan Methodists were reluctant to develop West Indian ministerial leadership. Although some local whites and people of color were admitted into the ministry, only in the early twentieth century were black ministerial candidates received in significant numbers.[138] The lack of locally available ministerial education also depressed leadership development; the first school for West Indian preachers opened in the 1870s.[139]

From Barbados, Taylor sailed to British Guiana where he spent about seven weeks in George Town, Essequibo, and Berbice. Like the African Cape, British Guiana had been a Dutch colony until the Napoleonic Wars. It experienced one of Taylor's few ecumenical revivals as the Wesleyan Methodists and the London Missionary Society, a missionary society dominated by British Congregationalists, cooperated, with new converts divided between the missions.[140]

Taylor abruptly interrupted his Caribbean tour in mid-1868 when Morgan, alone in Switzerland, again became ill. Taylor returned to Europe and removed him to the care of Dr. Ralph Grindrod in England.[141] Given Grindrod's interests, it is not surprising Taylor looked to him to help his son. The two shared an evangelical Christianity, an interest in missions, and Taylor had long espoused the health benefits of vigorous exercise and total abstinence from alcohol. Grindrod's hydrotherapeutic facility in Great Malvern treated patients with a variety of water wraps, baths, and showers. Patients were well-fed, engaged in vigorous exercise, and attended daily prayer. His facility also hosted meetings of British missionary societies, and he was an early English advocate of total abstinence from alcohol and industrial reform.[142]

Taylor's interest in hydrotherapy was also illustrative of his deeper theological commitments. Hydrotherapy was one of several new approaches to the treatment of illness and healing embraced by late nineteenth-century Protestants.[143] Although Taylor consistently espoused a strong belief that all afflictions, including illness, were sent by God for the spiritual edification of believers, he did not counsel passive resignation to illness. His belief in God's providence was coupled with a high view of human agency. He believed both illness and health could also be the result of human action, an opinion historian James Whorton called "physical Arminianism."[144] In this view, a failure to actively pursue health was considered a violation of one's religious obligations.[145] This perspective explains why, unlike some contemporaries, Taylor had little confidence in miraculous "faith" cures.[146] As with steam travel, Taylor placed his confidence in technological advancements as manifestation of God's work through people.

While in England, Taylor's now weak formal relationship with the Methodist Episcopal Church in the United States began to break. His own sense of apostolic authority conflicted with increasing bureaucratization of his church. For years, Taylor had been listed as a supernumerary preacher in the California Conference. In 1864, his denomination legislated that only those with health problems or a disability could be considered supernumerary.[147] Taylor's California colleagues delayed action on this rule until 1867, when they passed a resolution asking Taylor to return. From England, Taylor replied that he would be unable to do so. He had planned to following his Caribbean tour but had been "providentially hindered" by Morgan's illness. Now he doubted a return was God's intent.[148]

Instead, Taylor declared his belief that British Methodist missions needed help. Its preachers and missionaries were too busy to hold the revivals necessary for missionary success. Taylor clearly thought he was the man for the job.

> Now why should not God raise up an evangelical Sherman, who can command the respect and confidence of those missionaries, old and young, and so bind them to him, as to lead them out of their old lines into the more thoroughly apostolic methods of aggression.[149]

Since this commission was directly from God, ordination would be helpful but not necessary. Taylor wanted to remain an ordained Methodist preacher and member of the California conference, but not under the condition that he return. Rules were important, but since his was "a special work of worldwide importance," he asked that an exception be made.[150]

Soon after Taylor sent this letter, he was invited to India by the American Methodist missionary James M. Thoburn. Soon after meeting Taylor in 1858, Thoburn joined the Methodist mission there. Now, Thoburn hoped Taylor could spark a revival in the subcontinent as he seemed to have done in Africa.[151] For Taylor's part, the conversion of several Indian indentured servants in Guiana made him consider that God wanted him to go to India.[152] The response of Anne and the younger Taylor boys to William's decision was not recorded, but clearly, William felt more bound by his faith commitments than to his familial relationships.

While Morgan convalesced, Taylor led revivals in nearby English towns. After touring the Scotland together, Morgan went home to California, and his father returned to the Caribbean to complete his preaching commitments there.[153] In one summation, Taylor wrote he visited "Tobago, Trinidad, Grenada, St. Vincent, Nevis, [St. Kitts],[154] and Jamaica."[155] He planned to board a steamship from Panama to New Zealand, Australia, and India, but this plan to circumnavigate the world did not materialize. Taylor's global career was made possible by reliable steam travel across the oceans, but here its absence hindered him. While Taylor completed his revivals in the Caribbean, ships stopped running from Panama to New Zealand. To meet his schedule of reaching Sydney by mid-May 1869, Taylor ended his revivals in Jamaica early and sailed to Australia via London and Suez.[156] Despite Taylor's impressive global travel, he never crossed the Pacific.

Taylor spent fourteen months in Australia in 1869–1870. This visit to the continent received considerably less news coverage than his first. For this reason, some historians have concluded that it was an evangelistic failure.[157] Historian Eric G. Clancy cast it in a more positive light and argued Taylor built on his earlier work.[158] Most likely, Taylor was newsworthy on his first visit because he was a novelty. By 1869, traveling evangelists were commonplace in Australasia. Time had also tempered expectations. Although, as noted earlier, at least sixteen of Taylor's converts entered the Methodist ministry in Australasia, others had lapsed in their faith.[159]

As on his first tour, Taylor's revivals often coincided with major events in the life of churches. For example, in late September 1869, he led two weeks of revivals at Wesley Church in Melbourne coinciding with the congregation's anniversary. He returned to Melbourne in early 1870 to participate in the dedication of the building and to continue revival meetings. His role in fundraising and other benevolent causes was also valued.[160] The *Wesleyan Chronicle* summarized, "The Rev. W. Taylor is still pursuing his evangelistic efforts in our midst, and with considerable success. To many of the circuits his labours have been of considerable pecuniary advantage."[161]

While in Australia, Taylor received a decision from the California Annual Conference regarding his ministerial status. His former colleagues celebrated his evangelistic successes around the world, but they noted the church's *Discipline* was clear. No exception could be made. "At the same time that we submit to this necessity, laid on us by authority, we heartily commend you to God and to the confidence of all Christians of every name and place."[162] Taylor would be welcome to return to the ministry if he ever returned to California. In Methodist parlance, they granted him a location; Taylor's status as a Methodist preacher was terminated. At Taylor's request, this letter was reprinted in newspapers around Australia.[163]

En route to Australia, Taylor landed briefly in Ceylon. He was invited to return by the chair of the Wesleyan Methodist Mission of South Ceylon to hold revivals, and on his way from Australia to India he returned to preach in communities on the southwestern coast of the island between Galle and Colombo but also inland at Kandy.[164] Ceylon was only a brief stop on the way to India, but it allowed Taylor the opportunity to confirm, at least in his own mind, the efficacy of his "Pauline" missionary methods such as daily revivals, methods of working through a translator, and engaging with other religions.

Like the Caribbean and South Africa, Ceylon had a long Methodist history. Methodist mission leader Thomas Coke and other Methodist missionaries departed England for Ceylon in 1814. Coke died at sea, but his colleagues continued on and started missionary work there. By 1870, Ceylonese Methodism was well established, and missionaries reported that they had been in the midst of a revival since 1865.[165]

Wesleyan Methodist missionary reports of Taylor's revivals often cast his work as a construction on foundations they had laid through many years of hard labor. In his study of Taylor's work in South Africa, historian Daryl Balia quoted one missionary report that Taylor was "reaping where others have sown."[166] While such claims were partially rhetorical efforts to cast their own past labor in a favorable light following the successes of a newcomer, they were also certainly true. Converts at Taylor's revivals were largely those who already considered themselves Christians. These patterns were true in Ceylon, as elsewhere. Taylor claimed a total of about 1,000, mostly Sinhalese, converts during his time on the island. By Taylor's own accounting, only about one-tenth of these had been Buddhist; the vast majority were "from the ranks of nominal Christians, who had before received Christianity, but now received Christ and salvation in Him."[167] Testimonies of converts he recorded described education in Christian schools, baptism, reading the Bible or Christian devotional texts, as well as a failure to find "peace with God" before the revival.[168]

As indispensable as Taylor and other Methodists believed the evangelical conversions experienced by people at his revivals were, they built on a foundation laid by more prosaic methods that Methodist missionaries engaged in such as education, distribution of the Bible and Christian literature, and preaching. But as with Taylor's embrace of both Sunday schools for children and his stress on the imperative of evangelical conversions, Christian nurture through diverse means and conversions through revivalism were seen as complementary efforts. Taylor's introduction of American revivalism and his theology of conversion and sanctification provided a mechanism and ideology by which a preexisting Christian identity could be strengthened. His employment of reinvigorated laity as exhorters in his meetings contributed to the development of new, indigenous leadership. One Ceylon missionary, James Nicholson, noted that one of the most significant results of Taylor's work was "the effect that it produced upon our native ministers. Their views of faith, their closer fellowship with God, and expectations of success in soul-winning, have made a deep mark upon their ministry."[169]

One of the most distinguishing characteristics of the Methodist mission in southern Ceylon, however, was not revival and growth but interreligious controversy. With the advent of British rule in 1796, civic benefits associated with Christian conversion and restrictions on the public practice of Buddhism introduced by Catholic Portuguese and Reformed Dutch missionaries ended. Sinhalese Buddhism became resurgent.[170] By the mid-nineteenth century, a combination of Christian evangelism and Buddhist renewal created what historians R. F. Young and G. P. V. Somaratna called a "state of virtually unremitting and relentlessly reactionary hostility" between Christians and Buddhists.[171] Methodist missionaries were often at the forefront of this conflict. They were both among the leading scholars of Buddhism and its strongest critics. Representatives of both faiths engaged in a pamphlet war and held major public debates between Christian missionaries and Buddhists, culminating in an 1873 debate between the Buddhist Mohottivattē Gunānanda and a Ceylonese Wesleyan minister David de Silva.[172]

Unfortunately, there is no evidence of the details of Taylor's engagement with Sinhalese Buddhism, or any other religion in Ceylon, comparable to that of his encounter with African religion. There is some indication, however, that following his Pauline missionary model, Taylor took a more irenic approach than was typically the case in Ceylon. Taylor wrote that he modeled his sermons in Colombo after Paul's in Athens as a way of finding common ground. He claimed that by using this "Pauline method" he was able "to command a respectful hearing" from Buddhists, Hindus, Muslims, and Christians.[173] Beginning his sermons with points of agreement earned him a far more receptive audience than outright confrontation. As he wrote, "No controversy challenged, nor offered, from the other side. This is St. Paul's method, and I'm sure it's the thing."[174]

Taylor's encounter with Buddhism, however, did lead him to make one change in his evangelistic strategy and illustrated the increasing importance of apostolic models for Taylor's work. After a Buddhist convert was prohibited from returning to the mission by his father because he might be baptized, Taylor consulted the Book of Acts and found instances where baptism was performed immediately after conversion. Neither Taylor nor the missionary on hand had considered doing this, probably in the interest of providing catechesis. The loss of this Buddhist convert troubled Taylor. He wrote it taught him "the importance of following strictly the apostolic precedent, in this as in everything else."[175]

Taylor's Ceylonese revivals also marked the first time since South Africa that Taylor used a translator to preach. If Taylor did not experience the same spectacular effects as in South Africa, neither did he doubt that the principles he thought he discovered in South Africa were valid. Commenting on his interpreters, he wrote, "Some were better than others, but they all did well."[176]

CAMPAIGN IN INDIA

The American Methodist mission in India was relatively new when Taylor arrived, founded by William and Clementina Butler in the northwestern city of Bareilly in 1856, shortly before the Uprising of 1857.[177] That revolt was sparked by a rumor among Hindu and Muslim soldiers in the employ of the East India Company (EIC) that their rifle cartridges were greased with a mixture of cow and pig fat. The rebellion spread through northwest India before the British reasserted control, and in 1858, took over administration of India from the EIC.[178] The Butlers reestablished themselves in the aftermath, and other missionaries followed them. By 1870, American Methodists claimed 468 members spread across twenty circuits or stations around Bareilly, Lucknow, and Moradabad.[179]

William Butler served as superintendent of the mission until 1864, eventually becoming a missionary in Mexico. During his tenure, several lines of tension developed that persisted in years that followed. Butler's authoritarian leadership style bothered colleagues who expected to play a greater role in decision making. He also angered the Methodist Missionary Board in New York by appealing directly to Methodists in America and India for money and missionaries. By the end of Butler's tenure, missionaries in India were eager for greater autonomy, and the Board was keen to establish firm oversight of its missions in India.[180]

Both of these contradictory desires were frustrated. The hope of missionaries for more autonomy was stymied when the Methodist General Conference organized India as a mission conference in 1864. As in California, the designation as a "mission" conference was disliked by those forced to live under it. In this case, the General Conference enacted the qualifier because it was reluctant to place Indian preachers on par with American missionaries.[181] Mission conferences marginalized people of color by incorporating them into the church but in a subordinate status.

The desire of the Missionary Board for greater control was challenged by Methodist women in the United States. In 1869, two returned India missionary wives, Lois Stiles Parker and Clementina Butler, and six other women organized the Woman's Foreign Missionary Society (WFMS). Concerned that male missionaries could not reach women in gender-segregated societies such as India and China, the WFMS sent single women to serve as missionaries. The first two WFMS missionaries, Isabella Thoburn, sister of James, and Clara A. Swain, the first woman medical missionary, arrived in India in early 1870. The WFMS insisted it was an independent, Methodist missionary society that would manage its own affairs and refused to allow the mission board to take over the selection and sending of missionaries.[182]

Taylor arrived at the American Methodist mission in Lucknow in late November. His first revival services there were, by all accounts, a failure for reasons that ranged from the mundane to the significant. Sick at the time, Taylor's preaching was uncharacteristically subdued.[183] His translators at Hindi services were either not fluent in English or Hindi.[184] At English-language services, he offended the Victorian sensibilities of his congregation with stories that made people laugh, causing a scandal.[185] Taylor had encountered such mores before, however, his hosts in Australasia and South Africa had simply excused Taylor's behavior as "American." In India, for the first time in almost a decade, Taylor was surrounded by other Americans. That excuse no longer held.

Whatever the case, convinced that God desired a revival and that his revival methods were God's own as revealed through the model of the apostle Paul, Taylor arrived at two conclusions. First, he needed a better translator. His search for a better one would eventually bring him to another "Pauline" missiological insight. Second, the English-speaking population in India was to blame for the lack of revival. These ostensible Christians lacked a sanctified faith and by their immoral behavior drove Hindus and Muslims away. Surrounded by "the paralyzing influence of heathenism, formalism, and caste," they had seen their souls "mildew."[186] The conversion and reformation of the English-speaking population in India, Taylor concluded, was prerequisite for evangelistic success in the whole of India.

To address this second concern, at Taylor's suggestion, the American missionaries decided to allow English-speaking converts to join their churches. This change in policy was significant since the missionaries had been given to understand that representatives of the British colonial presence fell outside their commission. They were to convert Indians to Christianity, not representatives of so-called Christian nations. The quick adoption of this new policy, however, suggests that the missionaries concurred with Taylor's assessment and opinion that it was unwise to limit the scope of their mission. Their message was intended for all people, and reformation of the English colonial presence was necessary for missionary success.[187]

This new policy was also not without precedent in India and elsewhere. The British-run EIC had been in India since the early seventeenth century, but it prohibited missionary activity in its area of control until 1813. Wesleyan Methodist missionaries entered south India from Ceylon in the years that followed, ministering first to English colonists and their families. Aside from fleeting attempts to start missions in Bombay and Calcutta, Methodism in the north was known primarily among European civil servants. Only after 1858 did increased British interest in India result in a significant increase in Wesleyan Methodist mission activity throughout India.[188] In addition, as in the Near East where Taylor had met missionaries who adopted a similar strategy, social antagonism encountered by converts to Christianity made work among self-identified Christians less controversial than converting Hindus, Muslims, or Zoroastrians to Christianity.[189]

British colonists and soldiers, however, were not particularly receptive to Taylor's revivalism. Nevertheless, this shift to include English-speaking, self-identified Christians in the scope of Methodist outreach tapped into a segment of Indian society that was—people of mixed European and Indian ancestry known today as Anglo-Indians.[190] In the 1870s there were over 100,000 persons of mixed ancestry in British India.[191] In the early history of European engagement in the subcontinent, Anglo-Indians served as cultural intermediaries as both EIC traders and noncommissioned officers. By the late eighteenth century, however, they found themselves marginalized and despised by both English and Indians alike. Antagonism between the English and Indians after 1857 provided renewed opportunities for Anglo-Indians who had been fiercely loyal to the English during the fighting. They again found employment in the lower Indian civil service, army, and the railway system.[192]

Much of this history was exemplified by one of Taylor's first converts in India, George Bailey. Bailey's great-grandfather was a Frenchman who had served as an officer in the Persian and Mughal armies. Later generations of the family served in the military of different Indian principalities. In 1857, at the age of sixteen, Bailey distinguished himself fighting with the English at the siege of Lucknow. He was fluent in English and Hindi and had married an Indian woman. Before his conversion, probably because of his French heritage, Bailey identified himself as Roman Catholic.[193]

A decision to include English speakers in membership was only the first change in mission policy Taylor provoked. In his years of travel around the world, he had developed an extensive social network of individuals throughout the British Empire. A remarkable example of this network led to the expansion of the American mission beyond its previous boundaries. The doctor in Sydney who advised Taylor to take his son to South Africa had also asked Taylor to visit a nephew in London. Taylor had tried to find the man but was mistakenly taken to the home of another man with a similar surname. The person he sought, however, just happened to be visiting at that home! Taylor was able both to pay the promised visit and make a new acquaintance. Since then, the new friend had become a British army surgeon stationed at Cawnpore, about fifty miles from Lucknow, and he invited Taylor to hold a revival there. For Taylor, this was no comical case of mistaken identity and chance meeting but a providential act of God allowing him to extend his ministry.[194]

Cawnpore was generally considered outside the boundaries of the India Mission Conference, however. Some Methodist missionaries were concerned that if Taylor were to preach there it would violate both Methodist polity and agreements with other mission bodies intended to limit conflict among missions. Also of concern was the possibility the cash-strapped mission would expand beyond its ability to care for converts. Since Thoburn had previously preached there, and Methodist founder John Wesley had once declared, "The world is my parish," however, most missionaries were unwilling accept these limits, provided Taylor did not financially encumber the mission.[195] A Methodist theology that sought to evangelize all people accepted restrictions only reluctantly.

Taylor's sermons to English soldiers and civilians and to Indians in Cawnpore did not yield the evangelical conversions Taylor sought, but he was quickly able to form a small and receptive congregation of twenty Anglo-Indians, a Hindu woman, and her adopted daughter. With the cooperation of James Thoburn and Henry Mansell, the presiding elder of Moradabad District, Taylor organized these followers into a church. Taylor collected commitments to pay a missionary salary, allaying financial concerns and making the church in Cawnpore self-supporting.[196] The January 1871 meeting of the India Mission Conference included Cawnpore in the conference's list of appointments, and earlier concerns were set aside.[197] The worry that a Methodist church in Cawnpore would intrude upon the territory of another mission was also dropped. It was determined that any previous commitments Butler had made to limit the area of Methodist work had since been declared void because Anglicans had already breached the agreement, and Presbyterians who had missions in the region gave their blessing to this Methodist expansion.[198]

Inclusion of Anglo-Indians in the mission churches also offered an unexpected solution to the problem of translation. Taylor stumbled into the discovery that Anglo-Indians were not only a reservoir of potential converts but often bilingual. Once while preaching at the Bailey home, Taylor attempted to work with a translator whose native language was Bengali. Since the congregation gathered were Hindi speakers, Bailey had to help with the translation.

Taylor realized that Bailey could be his translator instead.[199] Just as they had long served as cultural intermediaries for the EIC, Taylor discovered that Anglo-Indians could do so for missionary work. When, in early 1871, Taylor took tour to other sites in the American Methodist mission, Bailey traveled with him most of the way to translate.[200]

On this tour, Taylor and Swain met. Methodist women such as Swain were at the vanguard of a transformation in the Protestant missionary enterprise. In the earliest days of the missionary movement, many women who went abroad did so as the wives of male missionaries. These women saw their task to be the creation and modeling of a Christian home in "heathen" lands.[201] This was the role that Anne Taylor had adopted in California. The WFMS was one of several new women's mission organizations formed in the late nineteenth century that sent single women as missionaries. In the process, these organizations transformed the demographics of the missionary enterprise. By 1890, women accounted for 60 percent of all American missionary personnel.[202]

This new generation of women missionaries adopted a new mission theory known as "Woman's Work for Woman." Female missionaries sought both to convert non-Christian women and to improve their social status by giving them access to the benefits of Western civilization such as medicine and education. As historian Dana Robert noted, because they emphasized social change toward Western norms and held assumptions of Western superiority, these missions could be perceived as a form of cultural imperialism. Simultaneously, however, their ideological emphasis on the existence of a worldwide sisterhood of women and human unity countered widespread patriarchal assumptions and looked to an underlying human equality.[203]

The founders of the WFMS were concerned that because women in India were often segregated from men, male missionaries could not evangelize women. Certainly in India, Taylor's own revivalism was more effective at reaching men who operated in public spaces. He was impressed by the new model of mission Swain represented through both her medical skill and evangelization of Hindu women.[204] For her part, Swain perceived Taylor's now deep sense of self-identification with Paul. He was, she proclaimed, "a second St. Paul . . . . He fully believes in the Pauline method of doing the Lord's work."[205]

This brief encounter and mutual appreciation between Taylor and Swain pointed toward a much greater affinity than just one between two individuals. As Robert also argued, in years to come there would develop a "mutual admiration" between the WFMS and Taylor grounded in a shared holiness piety and desire for independence from their church's mission board. In time, Taylor eagerly recruited women to serve in positions of leadership as missionaries. Some of these moved fluidly between Taylor's own mission movement and that of the WFMS.[206]

INDIA BEYOND

Despite Swain's praise, Taylor was frustrated. He believed he moved through his tour of Methodist mission sites so quickly that he was unable to practice his Pauline theory by holding daily revival meetings. Time was too short "to 'dispute daily' . . . and pursue fully St. Paul's methods."[207] Nevertheless, he completed his commitment to tour American Methodist missions in Nainital, where he spent the remainder of the summer. Freed of his obligations, Taylor prepared himself for a new revival campaign that would follow his own vision and adhere to his latest understanding of Pauline methods.

Taylor believed his study of African culture and religion had improved his evangelism there. Consequently, he dedicated the month of September 1871 to visit the temples of Badrinath and Kedarnath with Hindu pilgrims. He hoped this experience would help him "learn what [Hindus] did and suffered to get rest for their souls."[208] Whatever Taylor hoped to learn on the pilgrimage, however, was limited by illness. Taylor developed malaria on the pilgrimage. His fever peaked every afternoon, so Taylor rose early to walk before looking for a large stone to use as a pillow. Then, he wrote, he "lay down in the path and shook for an hour or two" until falling asleep.[209] After ten days, the fever broke, and he recuperated with Presbyterian missionaries at Mussoorie and Lahore, in present-day Pakistan. When Taylor arrived in Bombay in late October, he had lost fifty-four pounds.[210]

Taylor tried other, less immersive, ways to learn about the religions of India. His book about his time there, *Four Years' Campaign in India*, mentioned visits to temples, mosques and a dakhma where Zoroastrian dead were exposed, and conversations with converts to learn about their original beliefs.[211] In all his observations, Taylor was a curious but not a careful student of religion. As noted before, his theology inclined him to consider all non-Christian religions as the product of a natural human desire for God for the salvation God supplied only through his own evangelical Christianity. He believed that study of these religions would aid his efforts to sell their practitioners on his form of Christianity by matching their demand to God's supply. These beliefs made Taylor predisposed to view other religions with sympathy and interest but less disposed to note religious differences. For example, on several occasions, Taylor likened Hinduism to Roman Catholicism as if the two religions were the same phenomenon.[212]

To self-identified Christians, Taylor's message was twofold—a conversion experience of "new birth" was essential for all Christians and entire sanctification was necessary to empower Christian life and witness. These were the messages Taylor shared in late 1871 when invited to address Indian pastors associated with the American Board Maratha Mission.[213] Those present were impressed by Taylor and convinced by him that his American revival methods were "Bible methods, to advance the kingdom of Christ."[214] Some also embraced the Methodist doctrine of sanctification. One wrote that "we who call ourselves Christians were greatly enlightened in regard to our spiritual state," and he realized that to be an effective evangelist he needed to be "endued with power from on high."[215]

After that meeting, Charles Harding, an ABCFM missionary in Bombay, invited Taylor to lead a revival in that city. With this invitation, Taylor began a prolonged revival campaign there. Other than Harding's own, however, most churches in Bombay were unreceptive to Taylor's revivalism. For the first time in his career, Taylor held revivals without church sponsorship. For months, Taylor preached in any hall or theater he could rent.[216] Even without significant church backing, Taylor found two critical allies in Harding and George Bowen, the American editor of a Christian newspaper in India, the *Bombay Guardian*, both of whom assisted in the exhortation at his revivals.[217]

Bowen also led the defense in the *Guardian* and other papers when Taylor's revivals attracted negative press. A sensational description of a revival meeting printed in the *Times of India* claimed that people tearfully repented for sins such as going to picnics. These confessions were accompanied by emotional shouts. Taylor's sermon on the occasion was said to be a reflection on how it was "sinful to have religious meetings in churches."[218] Bowen and other writers offered rejoinders. Some embraced this criticism as a form of persecution, while others encouraged people to attend meetings and judge for themselves. Most importantly, several pointed out that the initial article was a second-hand description.[219] In a follow-up article, the instigating author admitted that he had never attended one of Taylor's revivals. His story was based on something once told him by a friend and the common knowledge that revival meetings were always accompanied by emotional excess and indelicate behavior of women. The embarrassed *Times* published a retraction.[220]

A lack of church sponsorship, however, presented a problem. By the end of December, Taylor had accumulated about sixty converts. Taylor was concerned that clergy who did not share his evangelical Christianity, view of entire sanctification, or had not welcomed him to lead revivals in their churches would not care for his followers adequately. He initially organized his converts into "fellowship bands" based in private homes but they petitioned him to organize a Methodist church in Bombay and serve as their pastor until a replacement could be found.[221] Taylor accepted their call with a letter published in the *Guardian*.[222]

Taylor would later portray this act as consistent with long-established Methodist practice but this was only partially true. To be sure, Taylor saw himself as a faithful Methodist, sought to instruct the church in Bombay on Methodist doctrine and the Methodist *Discipline*, and worked to bring it into an organic relationship with the denominational structure of the Methodist Episcopal Church. But the Bombay congregation was anomalous for several reasons. Methodists did not conceive of churches as congregations of individuals of assembled believers who called pastors. Methodist church polity was an organic network of institutions and offices. At least within American Methodism, clergy were dispatched by bishops to work with other preachers in regional conferences to organize and lead lay religious practice and to reach out to the surrounding community. Bombay existed in a Methodist no-mans-land, hundreds of miles away from the nearest American Methodist conference. Taylor had not been sent there by a bishop and was no longer clergy. For these reasons, Taylor's decision to organize this church would be considered irregular by some. From Taylor's perspective, however, it was the only justifiable response to the needs of his spiritual followers. They had been saved by his ministry, and the inability of other churches he thought they needed put that salvation in jeopardy.[223]

Taylor reported these events in a letter to Methodist Bishop Edmund Janes and the upcoming Methodist Episcopal General Conference. He claimed his work had grown to include over 130 members and ten "preaching places" around the city served by himself, Bowen, Harding, and twelve "Prayer Leaders." He asked for two missionaries to be sent and the General Conference to form a new Bombay Conference to regularize his actions with church discipline. While he asked for the Missionary Committee to pay the transportation expenses of these missionaries, he insisted that no further appropriations would be needed or welcome. He believed Paul had taught that new churches should support their leaders through voluntary contributions, and insisted this would be the case in Bombay. To accept financial support from America would put "this Mission on the list of *dependent* Missions" and bring it down to the "dead level" of others.[224] He wrote that he believed "the time has fully come when God wishes to demonstrate the soundness and practical utility of His own Gospel methods of aggression—one principle of which is self-sustentation."[225] In short, he wanted "the Holy Spirit [to] be allowed to test His simple Pauline methods."[226] Taylor also insisted that the conference not be designated a "Mission Conference."[227]

The 1872 General Conference took no action on Taylor's petition. Taylor thought this inaction was a mark of disbelief in his accomplishment.[228] In truth, the delegates had little information to act on. The only other report confirming the situation in Bombay arrived days before the Conference convened.[229] In addition, Taylor's petition was poorly worded. He employed many phrases such as God's "own Gospel methods" or "old Pauline track" that had become very meaningful to him but would have been incomprehensible to most American Methodists unless they had carefully read *Christian Adventures in South Africa*.[230]

The Methodist Missionary Board could respond more nimbly to Taylor's requests, however, than the church's large, legislative body. Some may have considered the Bombay church "irregular," but most Methodists also viewed it as a sign of God's work and sought to include it as best as possible within church structures. Evangelistic success was considered a mark of God's blessing that should be embraced. The Board did not have the authority to create or change conference boundaries but thought the opportunity in Bombay was significant. In July 1872, it sent two new missionaries to Bombay to work with Taylor.[231] This action by the Board would take on great significance later, as Taylor would eventually recast it as an attempt to supplant him, even though Taylor had requested the missionaries from the Board in the first place.[232] Albert Norton and Daniel O. Fox were appointed, and they arrived in India on December 1.[233]

If a committee was more responsive than a large legislative body, private individuals could act with even greater initiative. Much as Butler had once done, Taylor also wrote to the *Christian Advocate* in New York describing the need for missionaries who were "young men of our old heroic, self-denying type."[234] William E. Robbins evidently saw himself in that description, resigned his position as a Methodist preacher in Indiana, and sailed for Bombay, not unlike those Methodist preachers who migrated to California on their own. Robbins beat Norton and Fox to Bombay by ten days.[235]

Despite the arrival of missionaries from abroad, the success of Taylor's mission would ultimately hinge on the development of local leadership. Within the American Methodist mission, Anglo-Indians not only formed the heart its membership but also became key leaders.[236] Some converts in Bombay began the process to become Methodist preachers—C. W. Christian, W. Curties, and George Gilder, Jr.[237] Taylor did not specify, but based on their names and occupations, these men were probably Anglo-Indian. Unlike some other denominations in India, American Methodists did not differentiate between European, Indian, or Anglo-Indian preachers. As early as 1864, they admitted Indian preachers to Annual Conference membership. While it was a controversial decision at the time, while the Civil War raged at home, to admit nonwhite persons to membership, it allowed Methodists in India to avoid some of the problems with racial discrimination faced by others denominations.[238]

From Taylor's accounts, few Hindus, Muslims, or Zoroastrians attended or participated in the revival meetings or were among the converts, though many listened and engaged with Taylor when he preached outdoors.[239] Nevertheless, to illustrate that non-Christians could be converted and develop into Christian leaders, Taylor devoted several pages in his book about his time in India to the story of three Hindu brothers who did convert—Krishna, Trimbuk, and Ana Chowey. Krishna attended Taylor's meetings and was interested in converting but was reluctant to do so because he feared he would be disowned, lose his arranged marriage, and job.[240] Eventually, however, the brothers converted and were baptized.[241] Krishna regularly offered his testimony and served as an exhorter at revivals.[242]

The Chowey brothers' fears were not unfounded. All Christian missions in India grappled with the social sanctions faced by converts to Christianity. These issues often centered on the concept of caste and its impact on the church. The word "caste" described two related concepts, *jati*, a kinship group that traditionally held a specific job, and *varna*, a primordial division of humanity into four groups as described in the Rig Veda, and a fifth group of people considered subhuman, "outcaste," or to use the contemporary term "Dalit." Within this matrix of identities were strong social sanctions regulating interaction among groups, promoting endogamy, and prohibiting commensality.[243] With some exceptions, most Protestant missions expected that Christian converts would violate these sanctions, or "break caste," and become ostracized from their communities of origin.[244]

Accordingly, after Krishna's baptism a missionary recommended that he hide from his uncle, the head of the family. Taylor, however, persuaded him to maintain the relationship, even accepting martyrdom from his uncle, if necessary. To intentionally break kinship ties would benefit no one. He advised Krishna communicate to his uncle a desire to be both a faithful Christian and nephew.[245] Eventually, the uncle gave his blessing for his nephews and their families to become Christians.[246] The advice that converts should make every effort to maintain social relationships after conversion became another facet of Taylor's Pauline mission theory. As he wrote, freely mixing his own words with those of the apostle, "'Let every man abide in the same' secular 'calling wherein he was' engaged when 'called' by the Spirit of God."[247]

According to the Pauline theory Taylor developed in South Africa, after a church had been established in one population center, the missionary should move to another. In the summer of 1872, Taylor began to make short trips from Bombay to Poona. By fall, a church was organized there.[248] It consisted mostly, in Taylor's words, of "'Hindu Britons'—people born here, and fully identified with this country, the natives and their language."[249] One of these was William Fitzjames Oldham. Born and raised in India, Oldham was a surveyor with the Great Trigonometric Survey of India. He had never met an American before, and was curious when he heard that one "with a long beard like a preaching Arab" was speaking in the city.[250] Oldham eventually became a Methodist preacher and a missionary bishop in the Methodist Episcopal Church.[251]

In January 1873, with two circuits in two cities established and staffed, Taylor moved his work to Calcutta. Although it lay on the opposite side of the subcontinent, given the appeal of Taylor's work to English-speaking Indians, Calcutta was the next obvious choice for expansion. It was the capital of British India, had a large English-speaking population, and the Bengal

Presidency was home to about 18 percent of the subcontinent's Anglo-Indian population.[252] Taylor also had personal connections in the city. The doctor who invited Taylor to Cawnpore had been re-stationed there, as was John Richards, the Wesleyan Methodist missionary Taylor worked within South Africa.[253]

Taylor's time in Calcutta coincided with a major India missionary conference in Allahabad. Taylor was not present, but his work in India was discussed. J. Fordyce, the Commissioner of the Anglo-Indian Christian Union and pastor of a church in Simla, called on other missionaries to follow Taylor's example in ministering with Anglo-Indians and praised his work.[254] James Thoburn was also present at the conference. Both he and Fordyce offered the conference an important Pauline metaphor that Taylor eventually adopted. As Thoburn stated, Europeans and Anglo-Indians "stand in somewhat the same relation to us that the Jewish colonists did to Paul."[255] In their interpretation of biblical passages such as Acts 13:43, Paul, a Jew, began his Christian evangelism among the Jewish diaspora before reaching out to Gentiles of the Roman world. Missionaries, European expatriates, and Anglo-Indians, they reasoned, represented a contemporary diaspora with a shared national, linguistic, and religious identity that could be harnessed to evangelize Indians.

In time, this justification for work among English speakers would become a key addition to Taylor's own Pauline theory of mission, but Taylor had not yet drawn this same analogy. In a March 1873 letter describing his work, Taylor offered a strategic, rather than a biblical, argument for focusing his work among English speakers. Redeeming self-identified Christians would change Indian perceptions of Christianity that had been unfavorably shaped by the dishonorable actions of British colonial authorities and Anglo-Indians who made up "the most imperious of all Indian castes . . . the *Christian* caste."[256]

The only cautionary note from Allahabad emerged in the form of a "Resolution on Mutual Non-interference of Missionary Societies." It stated that, except in major cities, missions should refrain from proselytizing members of other churches.[257] Taylor's work had taken him well beyond the boundaries of the American Methodist mission, and his revivalism that sought to convert to evangelical Christianity those already identified as Christian was considered by some to be a form of proselytism. Thoburn considered opposing the motion. Harding, also present at the meeting, convinced him not to do so since the resolution was not directed at Taylor. Moreover, as Thoburn told Taylor when informing him of the debate, "We knew that you would not regard their resolutions in any case."[258] Thoburn knew his man.

Nevertheless, some missionaries were more concerned by the appearance of competition among missions than Taylor. Richards, for example, was pleased to welcome his old friend in Calcutta but preferred that the city be reserved for the Wesleyan Methodists. He noted with some regret that Taylor was now organizing American Methodist Episcopal churches instead of only holding revivals in support of existing missions.[259] While some did interpret Taylor's actions as intrusive, from Taylor's point of view that was a gross mischaracterization of both his motives and actions. He believed that as long as there were millions of people unreached by the Christian message, there was ample evangelistic work to be shared by all.

From his time in Calcutta, Taylor stopped recording events in his diary. Whatever notes he had were left behind in India when he wrote his book.[260] His actions become difficult to document. In a letter written at the time, however, Taylor described his weekly schedule in Calcutta as:

> I preach 7 sermons, with prayer mgs after 5 of them, hold 4 morning pr. mgs. & service of from ½ to one hour each in 30 families per week and enjoy it. God is leading I am following. Besides the above I lead a class of about 30 young converts.[261]

By early April, Taylor had gathered enough followers in that way to form a church in Calcutta.[262]

Taylor eventually moved his revivals and church organization south to Madras and Bangalore following the same pattern. Although Taylor was pleased that his meetings attracted curious Hindus, and that some were converted and baptized, Anglo-Indians continued to form the bulk of his constituency and were the leaders that developed within these congregations. While some were men who began the process to become Methodist preachers, many women also took on leadership roles. For example, Taylor entrusted oversight of a construction project in Calcutta to a woman. In Madras, several women started new schools for Indian children. When Taylor was in Bangalore, he entrusted pastoral care of the nascent church in Madras to a woman named Rosalina Raitt.[263]

The most significant of these new leaders to emerge was Grace Stephens. An Anglo-Indian woman, in 1873, Stephens underwent an evangelical conversion while reading. When Taylor came to Madras the following year, Stephens attended his revivals, and her father offered the use of their home for prayer meetings. At one, Taylor encouraged Stephens to stand and give a testimony. She had been taught that as a woman she should keep silent in such gatherings, but Taylor convinced her to whisper her story to him, which he repeated aloud.[264] From that tentative beginning, Stephens became convinced in Taylor's revivals that she was "called of God to be a missionary in my own land."[265] She eventually became a WFMS missionary, and was the only non-Western, female representative at the 1910 Missionary Conference in Edinburgh.[266]

For both men and women, Taylor modeled his own highly entrepreneurial style of leadership. Although he rarely missed an opportunity to tout his own accomplishments, Taylor counted it a sign of success when preachers or laity under his authority started new ministries at their own initiative. Taylor noted approvingly that Fox had converted several soldiers in Poona. When their unit was transferred to Karachi, Fox went with them to start a new church there.[267] After five members of the Calcutta congregation were transferred to Agra to work with the telegraph system, they organized themselves into a class meeting that Taylor visited and arranged to provide with pastoral care.[268]

Meanwhile, Methodist church leaders in the United States were eager to regularize Taylor's work in India and to situate both Taylor and the churches he had started within Methodist polity. Since Taylor had been out of the country for so long and was no longer connected to the California conference, however, church leaders did not know what to expect from him or how best to proceed. Some effort was made to convince Butler to return to India.[269] Taylor would later reinterpret this action as an attempt by the church in America to usurp his leadership.[270] There is no evidence that was the intent. By all accounts, mission leaders of Taylor's church took extraordinary measures to incorporate his work into church structures while also following church law.

Both Bishop Matthew Simpson and the secretary of the Methodist Episcopal Missionary Board, Thomas Mears Eddy, wrote Taylor to assess the situation. Simpson probably wrote Taylor since the two shared a history. Eddy wrote on behalf of Bishop William Logan Harris, who toured the world in 1873 to visit Methodist missions. Taylor's reply to Simpson expressed his commitment as a loyal Methodist to do whatever the Bishops or the Missionary Board "think necessary to harmonize my mission movement with the general working of our system."[271] He suggested that his work outside the Lucknow region could be designated as "Beyond the conference" since the Board that had sent Norton and Fox under that budgetary heading, or as he later abbreviated it, "India beyond."[272] As for his place within this structure, Taylor stipulated that he would not accept an appointment that would prevent him from going anywhere in the rest of India. He wanted to be "left entirely free to follow the leading of the Holy Spirit through this empire," and thought an appropriate title would be *Founder and General Sup't of Self-sustaining Methodist Missions in India.*[273] He offered that if the Missionary Board was willing to send more missionaries to work "on the Pauline self-sacrificing principle" and forego a salary from America in trust that God would provide one in India, they would be welcome.[274]

It was a mark of the eagerness of Methodist leaders to integrate Taylor's churches into the larger denomination that his recommendations were essentially accepted and implemented as proposed. Harris was met by Taylor and Thoburn when he arrived in Calcutta. Harris offered to make Taylor superintendent over the churches he started and agreed that if the Missionary Board contributed no funds to the work, they would not be concerned with its management.[275]

This decision was ratified at the January 1874 meeting of the India Mission Conference in Lucknow. Taylor was readmitted to the Methodist clergy and the Bombay and Bengal Mission of the India Mission Conference was established with Taylor as its superintendent. Nine preachers joined him and were appointed to take charge of the churches Taylor had started in Bombay, Poona, and Calcutta, as well as one Norton had started in Bhusawal. In addition to the three who had come from America—Robbins, Norton, and Fox—three converts from Taylor's revivals were accepted as new preachers—Christian, Gilder, and Charles R. Jefferies of Calcutta. Three others who had been in India for some time also cast their lots with Taylor. Bowen transferred his ordination from the Presbyterian Church. James Shaw, an Irish army "scripture reader" posted to India who helped with revivals in Bombay resigned his commission to become a Methodist preacher. Most notably, Thoburn transferred from the Mission Conference to join Taylor.[276] Thoburn would eventually rise to become a missionary bishop of his church in India.[277]

TO THE HEATHEN OF LONDON

Following the 1875 meeting of the India Conference, Taylor traveled to Lahore to lead revivals at a Presbyterian mission. There he received an invitation to join Dwight L. Moody and Ira Sankey in a planned London revival. By 1875, Moody and Sankey had become the most successful American revivalists to work in England.[278] Taylor believed the invitation was a providential opportunity since the organizing committee promised to cover his travel expenses to London. From there, it would be cheaper and easier to reach the United States, where he hoped to recruit additional missionaries for India.[279] He also had not seen his wife and sons in over seven years. Anne had written him in those years first encouraging, then outright asking him to return to his family.[280] These appeals may have finally convinced Taylor to do so when he learned of the death of his own father and mother in Virginia.[281] Taylor sailed from Bombay on March 1 and reached London by the end of the month.[282]

Beyond a brief mention that the invitation provided the occasion for leaving India, Taylor never wrote about his work with Moody and Sankey. Taylor's pride was probably hurt by the discovery that he had not been invited to partner with Moody but to "assist in the evangelistic work" of the younger and less experienced Moody.[283] The Islington Agricultural Hall was the principal location for Moody's sermons, but the revival's organizers booked several other halls for meetings in order to create the sense that a revival was spread throughout London. Taylor was one of the most prominent preachers invited to fill these satellite locations. On other occasions, Taylor substituted for Moody when he was not available.[284]

For this reason, two revivalists were often compared. With a degree of partiality, the Methodist press judged Taylor, on the whole, the better preacher of the two for his solidly Arminian theology, experience, and effective use of illustrations.[285] Moody's meetings, however, were better attended. His sermons were marquee attractions of the revival. One observer considered Moody better suited to a British audience than Taylor. While Taylor's reputation "as an evangelist and missionary from Polynesia, India, and the Western States" was honored, for he had preached in "the darkest places of earth" and the "worst places of horrid cruelty," but his rough-cut "appearance, manner, and bearing" were judged out of place in England.[286] Taylor's gifts were considered more appropriate for "savages living beyond the joyful sound of salvation" than those in the imperial metropole.[287]

If some thought that Taylor was better suited for an uncivilized audience than proper Britons, Taylor vehemently disagreed. He believed that his message was universal and that the spiritual status of an unconverted African was exactly the same as an unconverted Englishman. On at least one occasion in the Agricultural Hall, Taylor preached to a London congregation a version of his so-called "Kaffir sermon," adapted for his English audience.[288] On another occasion, Taylor paralleled the spiritual condition of Londoners with the Gerasene demoniac of Mark 5. He informed his audience that they were no different than so-called heathen idolaters.

> Man is a religious being, and must have a religion of some sort. In heathen countries where they have not the light, [the devil] gives them a religion that will be most insulting to God and most debasing to man. He gives them a dirty stone to which he bows down, saying, "This is my God;" but in enlightened countries his policy is to furnish every man with a religion as nearly like the real thing as possible. He would have you all belong to some church. The devil is ashamed of a man who won't join some church, and the more ceremony you attach to it the better, only you must stop short of submitting to God and receiving Christ.[289]

If Taylor's Victorian audience was not shocked by the claim they were not unlike "heathens," they probably were by his vivid illustration of the violent behavior of the demoniac, graphic description of a cholera patient, and a story of a visit to a "lunatic asylum" in Melbourne.[290]

The incongruities between Taylor's own manner and those of Victorian Britain illustrated by these episodes foreshadowed a greater divergence to come. Taylor found himself increasingly out of sync with cultural trends in the Anglo-American world. This disconnect would be highlighted when at the close of the London revivals, Taylor returned to America. Since he left his country at the start of the Civil War, Taylor's native country and church had changed in ways that he did not appreciate or understand. Those underlying differences would eventually erupt in a conflict between Taylor and some of his church's leaders. Many Methodists, however, continued to view him as a hero of their faith and would follow his lead into the mission field. The following chapter will point to some divergences and tensions in the Methodist missionary tradition as it explores those who followed Taylor into missionary work, that conflict, and those who sought to claim his legacy as his health failed.

This chapter has offered a view of Methodist mission in the nineteenth century, primarily within the British imperial world, by following Taylor's transoceanic voyages to southern Africa, the Caribbean, and Ceylon. These were some of the first contexts for Methodist cross-cultural missions. Although the American Methodist mission in India was not as old, similar dynamics were at play. Colonial populations offered a foundation for missionary outreach to colonized, enslaved, or otherwise marginalized peoples. Methodists welcomed such initiatives as opportunities to share their gospel with the whole world and uncritically accepted such colonial foundations as opportune movements of God's providence. If socially marginalized persons such as blacks in South Africa, the Caribbean, or Anglo-Indians responded favorably to the Methodist message, they also found that racial and colonial hierarchies existed within the church.

In each context he visited, Taylor employed revivalism as his preferred missionary method. While such revivalism was more representative of the American Methodist tradition, British Methodist missionaries accepted his ministrations because that revivalism affirmed shared core principles that drove Methodist missionary outreach, such as the need for all to be justified by God's grace, to experience new birth, and to continue on to entire sanctification. For persons who identified themselves as Christian, revivalism and a theology of conversion and Christian perfection offered a mechanism by which that identity could be strengthened. Moreover, Taylor presented his revivals as both biblical and effective methods for missionary outreach, confirming for Methodists such methods were, indeed, blessed by God, and illustrating that Methodists valued missionary means that were judged to be scriptural and successful. For Taylor, however, the definition of what was both scriptural and successful continued to change over time as his Pauline theory of mission developed and evolved. Indeed, reflecting this fundamental pragmatic orientation, Taylor would soon abandon revivalism as a missionary method.

NOTES

1. Charles H. Shinn to Dr. Mell, December 10, 1921, California-Nevada Conference Archives, Pacific School of Religion; W. S. Matthew to Charles H. Shinn, December 30, 1921, W. S. Matthew Papers; Robert L. Santos, *The Eucalyptus of California: Seeds of Good or Seeds of Evil?* (Denair: Alley-Cass Publications, 1997), under "Interest Continues," http://library.csustan.edu/sites/default/files/Bob_Sant os-The_Eucalyptus_of_California.pdf; Robin W. Doughty, *The Eucalyptus: A Natural and Commercial History of the Gum Tree* (Baltimore: John Hopkins University Press, 2000), 67.

2. William Taylor, *Story of My Life; an Account of What I Have Thought and Said and Done in My Ministry of More Than Fifty-Three Years in Christian Lands and among the Heathen. Written by Myself* (New York: Hunt & Eaton, 1896), frontispiece.

3. Wm. Taylor to "The Bishop & members of the California Conference," May 5, 1865, California Conference Papers, California-Nevada Conference Archives.

4. "The Conference," *Wesleyan Chronicle*, February 20, 1866; William Taylor, *How to Be Saved and How to Save the World. Vol. 1* (Adelaide: Alfred Waddy, 1866), v.

5. Taylor, *How to Be Saved*, 27.

6. Ibid., 9–13.

7. Ibid., 80.

8. Ibid., 76–82; Donald W. Dayton, *Theological Roots of Pentecostalism* (Peabody, MA: Hendrickson Publishers, 1987), 94.; Grant Wacker, *Heaven Below: Early Pentecostals and American Culture* (Cambridge: Harvard University Press, 2001), 62.

9. Taylor, *How to Be Saved*, 87, 125.

10. Ibid., 227.

11. Ibid., 249.

12. Ibid., 265, 284.

13. Ibid., 348.

14. Ibid., 365.

15. Myung Soo Park, "Concepts of Holiness in American Evangelicalism: 1835–1915" (Ph.D. diss., Boston University, 1992), 129–37.

16. Ibid., 142.

17. Taylor, *How to Be Saved*, chapters 6–7.

18. Ibid., 132; Nathan O. Hatch, *The Democratization of American Christianity* (New Haven: Yale University Press, 1989), 170–9.

19. Taylor, *How to Be Saved*, 136.

20. Ibid., 121–2.

21. "Literary Notices," *Wesleyan Chronicle*, June 20, 1866.

22. Ibid.

23. *Reconciliation* reproduced chapters 1 through 5, 8, and 9 of *How to Be Saved* with only a few changes. *Infancy and Manhood* copied chapter 10 and following of *How to Be Saved*, but also included about 18 pages of original text. Chapters 6 and 7 of *How to Be Saved* provided much of the text and formed the core of *The Election of*

Grace (1868). *Reconciliation: Or How to Be Saved* (London: S. W. Partridge, 1867); *Infancy and Manhood of Christian Life* (London: S. W. Partridge, 1867); *The Election of Grace* (London: Hodder and Stoughton, 1868).

24. "Literary Notices: *How to be Saved*. By Rev. W. Taylor," *Wesleyan Chronicle*, February 20, 1867; Taylor, *How to Be Saved*, 52; William Taylor, *Reconciliation*, 57, 62.

25. "Rev. Wm. Taylor," *Christian Standard*, September 30, 1876; "A Wonderful Book," *Christian Standard*, October 21, 1876.

26. Leonard Thompson, *A History of South Africa*, Rev. ed. (New Haven: Yale University Press, 1995), 6–16, 33–38, 52–53, 66–67, 80–81, 96–97, 100.

27. Leslie A. Hewson, *An Introduction to South African Methodists* (Cape Town: Standard Press, 1950), 12; J. Whiteside, *History of the Wesleyan Methodist Church of South Africa* (London: Elliot Stock, 1906), 35–40.

28. Hewson, *Introduction*, 36; Whiteside, *History*, 63–64.

29. Whiteside, *History*, 95, 100, 106–7, 170.

30. "Cape: Rev. W. Taylor," *Wesleyan Chronicle*, June 20, 1866; William Taylor, *Christian Adventures in South Africa* (London: Jackson, Walford, and Hodder, 1867), 34–37.

31. Taylor, *Christian Adventures*, 38–39.

32. David Bundy, "William Taylor as an Interpreter of African Culture: The Foundation for a Theory of Mission," University of Cambridge Currents in World Christianity position paper 52b, 3.

33. Daryl Balia, "Bridge over Troubled Waters: Charles Pamla and the Taylor Revival in South Africa," *Methodist History* 30, no. 2 (1992): 80; see also Jay Riley Case, *An Unpredictable Gospel: American Evangelicals and World Christianity, 1812–1920* (New York: Oxford University Press, 2012), 112–14.

34. Taylor, *Christian Adventures*, 56.

35. Ibid., 42–43, 137–8.

36. "Extract of the Minutes of the 43rd Annual Meeting of the Grahams Town District," W. S. Matthew Papers, California-Nevada Conference Archives, Pacific School of Religion.

37. "South Africa: Graham's-Town," *Wesleyan Missionary Notices*, October 25, 1866.

38. Taylor, *Christian Adventures*, 55–59.

39. Taylor, *Christian Adventures*, 35; J. Du Plessis, *The Life of Andrew Murray of South Africa* (London: Marshall Brothers, 1919).

40. H. H. Dugmore, *The American Preacher: His Preaching, and Its Effects, . . .* (Queenstown: David S. Barrable, 1866), 3.

41. Dugmore, *The American Preacher*, 6.

42. Ibid., 8.

43. Ibid.

44. Wallace G. Mills, "Taylor Revival of 1866 and the Roots of African Nationalism in the Cape Colony," *Journal of Religion in Africa* 8, no. 2 (1976): 113,

45. Balia, "Bridge over Troubled Waters," 78.

46. "Annshaw," *Wesleyan Missionary Notices*, September 25, 1866.

47. "Graham's Town District," Ibid., December 26, 1866.

48. Ibid.; Taylor, *Christian Adventures*, 91–95.

49. Robert Ross, "The Social and Political Theology of Western Cape Missions," in *Missions and Christianity in South African History*, ed. Henry Bredkamp and Robert Ross (Johannesburg: Witwatersrand University Press, 1995), 101; Jean Comaroff and John L. Comaroff, *Of Revelation and Revolution: The Dialectics of Modernity on a South African Frontier*, vol. 2 (Chicago: University of Chicago Press, 1991), 293.

50. Taylor, *Christian Adventures*, 110; Whiteside, *History*, 179, 200, 221.

51. Dictionary of African Christian Biography, s.v. "Kama, William," accessed January 18, 2017, https://dacb.org/stories/south-africa/kama-william/; J. B. Peires, *The Dead Will Arise: Nongqawuse and the Great Cattle-Killing Movement of 1856–7* (Johannesburg: Ravan Press, 1989), 78–100.

52. Taylor, *Christian Adventures*, 118; William Taylor, *The Model Preacher: Comprised in a Series of Letters Illustrating the Best Mode of Preaching the Gospel* (Cincinnati: Swormstedt & Poe, for the author, 1860), 150–75.

53. Taylor, *Christian Adventures*, 119–22; "Annshaw," *Wesleyan Missionary Notices*, October 25, 1866.

54. Taylor, *Christian Adventures*, 124–5; Case, *Unpredictable Gospel*, 114–17.

55. Taylor, *Christian Adventures*, 125; "Annshaw," *Wesleyan Missionary Notices*, October 25, 1866.

56. Taylor, *Christian Adventures*, 122.

57. Ibid., 122–3.

58. Offensive terms are retained only when quoting historical sources.

59. Ibid., 125–6.

60. Ibid., 225–6.

61. Ibid., 156–62, 216–17; "Heald-Town," *Wesleyan Missionary Notices*, October 25, 1866; "Annshaw," Ibid.

62. Taylor, *Christian Adventures*, 201

63. Bundy, "William Taylor as an Interpreter," 13–16.

64. Taylor, *Christian Adventures*, 260–2.

65. Ibid., 305.

66. Ibid., 305–12.

67. For an alternate interpretation of this episode, see Bundy, "William Taylor as an Interpreter," 15.

68. Taylor, *Christian Adventures*, 449–50.

69. Ibid., 469–75.

70. Ibid., 162, 413.

71. Ibid., 475.

72. "Natal," *Wesleyan Missionary Notices*, February 25, 1867.

73. Stone to N. G. Clark, December 1, 1866, Southern Africa, Zulu Mission, 1860–1872, Papers of the American Board of Commissioners for Foreign Missions (microfilm) (Woodbridge: Research Publications, 1994).

74. Taylor, *Christian Adventures*, 451.

75. Wyn Rees, ed., *Colenso Letters from Natal* (Pietermaritzburg: Shuter and Shooter, 1958), 122–3.

76. Taylor, *How to Be Saved*, 116, 142; Taylor, *Christian Adventures*, 474.

77. Taylor, *Christian Adventures*, 477–80; Jeff Guy, *The Heretic: A Study of the Life of John William Colenso, 1814–1883* (Johannesburg: Ravan Press, 1983), 90–91; Case, *Unpredictable Gospel* 117–19.

78. Taylor, *Christian Adventures*, 474.

79. Ibid., 505.

80. Taylor, *How to Be Saved.*, 364–5.

81. Bundy, "William Taylor as an Interpreter," 18–20.

82. Taylor, *Christian Adventures*, 509.

83. Ibid., 510.

84. Ibid., 511.

85. Ibid., 513.

86. Ibid.

87. Ibid., 515.

88. Hewson, *Introduction*, 74.

89. Daryl M. Balia, "Reaping Where Others Have Sown: William Taylor's Impact on Methodism," in *Perspectives in Theology and Mission from South Africa*, ed. Daryl M. Balia (Lewiston: Snow Lion Publications, 1993), 122.

90. James T. Campbell, *Songs of Zion: The African Methodist Episcopal Church in the United States and South Africa* (Chapel Hill: University of North Carolina Press, 1998), 116–25.

91. Case, *Unpredictable Gospel*, 119–27; Andrew F. Walls, "Black Europeans-White Africans: Some Missionary Motives in West Africa," in *The Missionary Movement in Christian History: Studies in the Transmission of Faith* (Maryknoll: Orbis Books, 1996), 103–4.

92. Mills, "Taylor Revival," 114.

93. Ibid., 114–20.

94. Taylor, *Christian Adventures*, 509–10.

95. Ibid., 514.

96. Ibid., 391–420.

97. Ibid., 391.

98. Ibid., 391–4.

99. Ibid., 395.

100. Ibid., 402.

101. Ibid., 405–7.

102. Ibid., 412.

103. Ibid., 420.

104. Bundy, "William Taylor as an Interpreter," 16.

105. Brian Stanley, *The World Missionary Conference, Edinburgh 1910* (Grand Rapids: William B. Eerdmans Publishing, 2009), 205–47.

106. "To the Revd. William Taylor Minister of the Methodist Episcopal Church America," W. S. Matthew Papers, California-Nevada Conference Archives.

107. Ibid.

108. Wm. Taylor to Dr. and Mrs. Palmer, January 25, 1867, William Taylor, Correspondence and Biographical Material, 1867–1901, United Methodist Church Archives—GCAH.

109. Isabelle Anne Kimberlin Taylor, "Isabel Anne Kimberlin Taylor's Travel Diary," in *Lessons of Infinite Advantage: William Taylor's California Experiences. With Isabelle Anne 1Kimberlin Taylor's Travel Diary, 1866–67, Written During a Voyage with Her Family En Route from the Cape of Good Hope, South Africa, to London and Subsequent Travels Throughout Europe,* ed. Robert F. Lay (Lanham: Scarecrow Press and The Center for the Study of World Christian Revitalization Movements, 2010), 245.

110. Taylor, "Isabel Anne Kimberlin Taylor's Travel Diary," 241–2; Taylor, *Story of My Life,* 500; Taylor, *Christian Adventures,* 506.

111. Taylor, "Travel Diary," 245.

112. Ibid.

113. "Revival Intelligence," *Methodist Recorder,* January 25, 1867.

114. Ibid.

115. Taylor, "Travel Diary," 258.

116. "C. H. Spurgeon and William Taylor," *The Earthen Vessel and Christian Record,* July 1, 1867; "Litereary Notices," *Wesleyan Chronicle,* May 20, 1869.

117. David Bebbington, *Victorian Religious Revivals: Culture and Piety in Local and Global Contexts* (New York, Oxford University Press, 2012), 11–13.

118. "Revival Intelligence."

119. "The Rev. W. Taylor's Publications," *Methodist Recorder,* February 22, 1867.

120. Australian Dictionary of Biography, s.v. "Reed, Henry (1806–1880)," accessed November 11, 2011, http://adb.anu.edu.au/biography/reed-henry-2582 (accessed November 11, 2011); Taylor, *Story of My Life,* 504.

121. Taylor, *Story of My Life,* 505.

122. In *Christian Adventures,* William called the child "Africanus." In his later autobiography, he called the child "Henry Reed." In her travel journal, Anne refers to the boy as their "blue eyed 'Africanda.'" Taylor, *Christian Adventures,* 506; Taylor, "Travel Diary," 241–2; Taylor, *Story of My Life,* 500.

123. Margaret S. E. Reed, *Henry Reed: An Eventful Life Devoted to God and Man* (London: Morgan & Scott, [1906]), 74, 179–80; Pamela J. Walker, *Pulling the Devil's Kingdom Down: The Salvation Army in Victorian Britain* (Berkeley: University of California Press, 2001), 48–49.

124. Catherine Bramwell-Booth, *Catherine Booth: The Story of Her Loves* (London: Hodder and Stoughton, 1970), 231–2; Taylor *Story of My Life,* 504.

125. Taylor, "Travel Diary," 259.

126. Ibid. Historian Robert F. Lay speculated the phrases Anne quoted above may have been William's words or those of another individual mentioned in the context of the entry. Robert F. Lay, "He Said/She Said: The Diaries of William and Anne Taylor" Bishop William Taylor Collection, Taylor University, accessed June 9, 2009); http://www.taylor.edu/academics/supportservices/archives/pdf/he_said_she_said.pdf.

127. William Taylor, *Four Years' Campaign in India* (London: Hodder and Stoughton, 1875), 3.

128. Sylvia R. Frey and Betty Wood, *Come Shouting to Zion: African American Protestantism in the American South and British Caribbean to 1830* (Chapel Hill: University of North Carolina Press, 1998), 104–5.

129. John A. Vickers, ed., *The Journals of Dr. Thomas Coke* (Nashville: Kingswood Books, 2005), 82–83.

130. Arthur Charles Dayfoot, *The Shaping of the West Indian Church, 1492–1962* (Kingston, Jamaica; Gainesville: The Press University of the West Indies/University Press of Florida, 1999), 174; Noel Titus, *The Development of Methodism in Barbados, 1823–1883* (Bern: Peter Lang, 1994), 73.

131. Dayfoot, *Shaping*, 183; Titus, *Development*, 78.

132. Titus, *Development*, 93, 137–49.

133. William Taylor, "Tour of Barbadoes and British Guiana," *Christian Advocate*, July 23, 1868; Taylor, *Four Years' Campaign*, 2, 8–9.

134. "Barbadoes," *Wesleyan Missionary Notices*, March 25, 1868.

135. Ibid.; Taylor, "Tour."

136. Taylor, "Tour"; "West Indies: Barbadoes," *Wesleyan Missionary Notices*, April 25, 1868.

137. Taylor, "Tour"; "Barbadoes."

138. Paula L. Aymer, *Evangelical Awakenings in the Anglophone Caribbean: Studies from Granada and Barbados* (New York: Palgrave Macmillan, 2016), 60–64.

139. John Pritchard, *Methodists and Their Missionary Societies, 1760–1900* (Farnam: Ashgate, 2013), 164.

140. Taylor, "Tour"; "Demerara," *Wesleyan Missionary Notices*, June 25, 1868.

141. Taylor, *Four Years'*, 3.

142. Janet Grierson, *Temperance, Therapy & Trilobites: Dr. Ralph Grindrod: Victorian Pioneer* (Malvern: Cora Weaver, 2001), 31–41, 71–75, 95–108, 112.

143. Heather D. Curtis, *Faith in the Great Physician: Suffering and Divine Healing in American Culture, 1860–1900* (Baltimore: Johns Hopkins University Press, 2007), 4.

144. James C. Whorton, *Crusaders for Fitness: The History of American Health Reformers* (Princeton: Princeton University Press, 1982), 5.

145. Curtis, *Faith*, 59–68.

146. Ibid., 68–79.

147. *The Doctrines and Discipline of the Methodist Episcopal Church, 1864* (New York: Carlton & Porter, 1864), 102–3.

148. Wm. Taylor to Bishop and Members of the California Conference, July 25, 1868, California Conference Papers, California-Nevada Conference Archives.

149. Ibid.

150. Ibid.

151. J. M. Thoburn, *My Missionary Apprenticeship* (New York: Phillips & Hunt, 1884), 11–14, 279.

152. Taylor, "Tour;" Taylor to Bishop and Members; Taylor, *Four Years'*, 3.

153. Taylor, *Story of My Life*, 510–13.

154. Taylor's quote here reads "St. Catharine's." There is no island named St. Catharine's. He probably meant St. Christopher or, as it is known, St. Kitts. During his visit there, he lectured at a schoolhouse. "West Indies," *Wesleyan Missionary Notices*, October 1871.

155. Taylor, *Four Years'*, 3.

156. Ibid., 3–4.

157. Ian Breward, *A History of the Australian Churches* (St. Leonards: Allen & Unwin, 1993), 62; H. R. Jackson, *Churches and People in Australia and New Zealand, 1860–1930* (Wellington: Allen & Unwin/Port Nicholson Press, 1987), 53–54. Jackson's argument is somewhat flawed since it rests on Taylor's penchant for self-promotion. While Jackson is certainly right about Taylor's self-promoting tendencies, elsewhere in his biography, Taylor implied that he was responsible for a large portion of the 21,000 members that joined the Wesleyan Methodist churches in Australasia in the periods covered by his two visits. Taylor, *Story of My Life*, 277–8.

158. Eric G. Clancy, "William ('California') Taylor: First Overseas Evangelist to Australia," *Church Heritage* 6, no. 3 (1990): 55.

159. John C. Symons, *Life of the Rev. Daniel James Draper. . .* (London: Hodder & Stoughton, 1870), 267–8.

160. "Correspondence," *Wesleyan Chronicle*, September 20, 1869; "Circuit Intelligence," Ibid., October 20, 1869.

161. "Editorial Notices," *Wesleyan Chronicle*, November 20, 1869.

162. California Annual Conference of the Methodist Episcopal Church to William Taylor, September 21, 1868, California Conference Papers, California-Nevada Conference Archives.

163. "The Rev. William Taylor," *Sydney Morning Herald*, July 31, 1869; "The Rev. William Taylor," *Cornwall Chronicle*, August 16, 1869.

164. Taylor, *Four Years' Campaign*, 4–6; "Christian Evangelization in Ceylon: Letter from Rev. Wm. Taylor," *Christian Advocate*, December 1, 1870.

165. Mary B. Barker et al., *A History of the Methodist Church in Ceylon, 1814–1964* (Colombo: Wesley Press, n.d.), 226.

166. Balia, "Reaping Where Others Have Sown."

167. Taylor, *Four Years' Campaign*, 6.

168. "Christian Evangelization in Ceylon."

169. Quoted in Barker, *History*, 226.

170. R. F. Young and G. P. V. Somaratna, *Vain Debates: The Buddhist-Christian Controversies of Nineteenth-Century Ceylon* (Vienna: Institute of Indology, University of Vienna, 1996), 38–40.

171. Young and Somaratna, *Vain Debates*, 40.

172. Ibid., 44–46.

173. "The Rev. Mr. Taylor in India," *Wesleyan Chronicle*, November 19, 1870.

174. Ibid.

175. Taylor, *Four Years'*, 170–1.

176. "Ceylon: Kandy," *Wesleyan Missionary Notices*, April 1871; "Christian Evangelization in Ceylon"; "Rev. William Taylor in Ceylon," *Christian Advocate*, February 1, 1871.

177. Wade Crawford Barclay, *The Methodist Episcopal Church, 1845–1939: Widening Horizons, 1845–95*. History of Methodist Missions, vol. 3 (New York: Board of Missions of The Methodist Church, 1957), 449–51.

178. Lawrence James, *Raj: The Making and Unmaking of British India* (London: Little, Brown, 1997), 233–53; Denis Judd, *The Lion and the Tiger: The Rise and Fall of the British Raj, 1600–1947* (Oxford: Oxford University Press, 2004), 70–90.

179. Barclay, *Widening Horizons*, 452–545, 470–2; *Minutes of the Annual Conferences of the Methodist Episcopal Church,* . . . 1870-1 (New York: Carlton & Lanahan, 1870), 41.

180. Barclay, *Widening Horizons*, 453–4, 470–2.

181. Ibid., 167; Case, *Unpredictable Gospel*, 136–40; J. M. Thoburn, *My Missionary Apprenticeship* (New York: Phillips & Hunt, 1884), 108.

182. Barclay, *Widening Horizons*, 139–45; Dana L. Robert, *American Women in Mission: A Social History of Their Thought and Practice* (Macon: Mercer University Press, 1997), 137–9.

183. Taylor, *Four Years'*, 10, 19, 22.

184. Ibid., 17–22, 26.

185. Ibid., 16; Thoburn, *My Missionary Apprenticeship*, 282.

186. Taylor, *Four Years'*, 25.

187. Taylor, *Four Years'*, 22–24; Thoburn, *My Missionary Apprenticeship*, 282.

188. Pritchard, *Methodists*, 96–97, 103–4.

189. Wilbert R. Shenk, "'Ancient Churches' and Modern Missions in the Nineteenth Century," in *India and the Indianness of Christianity*, ed. Richard Fox Young (Grand Rapids: William B. Eerdmans Publishing, 2009), 42–43, 53.

190. The term has also been used to describe English people living in India and people of mixed English (but not other European) and Indian ancestry. For a discussion of the use of "Anglo-Indian," see Evelyn Abel, *The Anglo-Indian Community: Survival in India* (Delhi: Chanakya Publications, 1988), 5–6.

191. Henry Waterfield, *Memorandum on the Census of British India of 1871–72* (London: Eyre and Spottiswoode for H. M. Stationery Office, 1871), 5, 28–29.

192. Abel, *Anglo-Indian Community*, 13–33; James, *Raj*, 220–1.

193. Taylor, *Four Years*, 21–22.

194. Ibid., 32–33.

195. Ibid., 28.

196. Ibid., 36–40.

197. *The Doctrines and Discipline of the Methodist Episcopal Church, 1868* (Cincinnati: Hitchcock & Walden, 1870), 296.

198. Taylor, *Four Years'*, 41–43; For his part, Butler insisted that he never entered into any comity agreements that would limit the freedom of Methodist missions to expand anywhere in India. William Butler, "A Correction," *Christian Advocate*, November 9, 1882.

199. Taylor, *Four Years'*, 43.

200. Ibid., 47–66.

201. Robert, *American Women in Mission*, 65–75.

202. Ibid., 130.

203. Ibid., 125–37.

204. Taylor, *Four Years'*, 63.

205. Clara A. Swain, *A Glimpse of India: Being a Collection of Extracts* . . . (New York: James Pott, 1909), 54.

206. Dana L. Robert, "Holiness and the Missionary Vision of the Woman's Foreign Missionary Society of the Methodist Episcopal Church, 1869–1894," *Methodist History* 39, no. 1 (2000): 25–27.

207. Taylor, *Four Years'*, 69.

208. Ibid., 86.

209. "The Rev. Wm. Taylor in India," *Wesleyan Chronicle*, December 20, 1871.

210. "The Rev. Wm. Taylor in India".

211. Taylor, *Four Years'*, 88–93, 181.

212. Ibid., 92, 95.

213. Ibid., 99.

214. *Report of the American Mission among the Marathas for 1871* (Bombay: Education Society's Press, 1872), 12.

215. *Report of the American Mission among the Marathas for 1871*.

216. "Local," *Times of India*, January 6, 1872; Ibid., January 15, 1872; "Local," Ibid., February 10, 1872; Taylor, *Four Years'*, 95–149.

217. Robert E. Speer, *George Bowen of Bombay: Missionary, Scholar, Mystic, Saint: A Memoir* (New York: Printed privately, 1938), 149–93.

218. "A Visit to a Revival Meeting," *Times of India*, January 23, 1872.

219. W. A. E. B., "The Rev. Mr. Taylor's Meetings," *Times of India*, January 23, 1872; "Mr. Taylor's Services, I," Ibid., January 24, 1872; D. N., W. G. T., "Revivals," Ibid., January 26, 1872; "Rev. Mr. Taylor," Ibid., February 7, 1872; Speer, *George Bowen of Bombay*, 261–2.

220. "Mr Taylor's Services. II," *Times of India*, January 24, 1872; "The Revivals—A Rejoinder," Ibid., January 27, 1872.

221. Taylor, *Four Years'*, 124–5; 150–1; Sampath Kumar, "The Impact of William Taylor's Urban Mission on the Methodist Church in India During the 19th Century," in *Doing Contextual Theology: A Festschrift in Honour of Bruce John Nicholls*, ed. Bruce Nicholls and Sunand Sumithra (Bangalore: Theological Book Trust, 1992), 139–52.

222. Kumar, "The Impact of William Taylor's Urban Mission on the Methodist Church in India During the 19th Century," 151–4; R. S. Maclay, "Letters from Dr. Maclay," *Christian Advocate*, April 25, 1872.

223. Taylor, *Four Years'*, 147–8.

224. Ibid., 164.

225. Ibid.

226. Ibid.

227. Ibid., 166–7.

228. Taylor mistakenly claimed the Committee on Foreign Missions tabled his memorial. *Journal of the General Conference of the Methodist Episcopal Church, . . . 1872* (New York: Nelson and Phillips, 1872), 114; Taylor, *Four Years' Campaign*, 167.

229. Maclay, "Letters from Dr. Maclay."

230. Taylor, *Four Years'*, 164, 166.

231. Missionary Society of the Methodist Episcopal Church, *Missions Minutes 1819–1916* ([Wilmington, DE]: Scholarly Resources, [1979]), July 16, 1872.

232. William Taylor, *Ten Years of Self-Supporting Missions in India* (New York: Phillips & Hunt, 1882), 452.

233. Taylor, *Four Years'*, 238–9.

234. "Letter from Bombay, India," *Christian Advocate*, May 9, 1872.

235. Taylor, *Four Years'*, 238.

236. Arun W. Jones, *Missionary Christianity and Local Religion: American Evangelicalism in North India, 1836–1870* (Waco: Baylor University Press, 2017), 232–6.

237. Taylor, *Four Years'*, 189–90.

238. Jones, *Missionary Christianity*, 87–88, 155–6.

239. Taylor, *Four Years'*, 207.

240. Ibid., 169.

241. Ibid., 190–3.

242. Ibid., 196, 199, 205, 214, 222.

243. Susan Bayly, *Caste, Society and Politics in India from the Eighteenth Century to the Modern Age*, ed. Gordon Johnson, The New Cambridge History of India IV 3 (New York: Cambridge University Press, 1999), 8–10; Stanley A. Wolpert, *India* (Berkeley: University of California Press, 1991), 118–28. For a survey of the extensive debate over the nature of caste, see Bayly, *Caste, Society and Politics*, 11–24.

244. Robert Eric Frykenberg, "Introduction: Dealing with Contested Definitions and Controversial Perspectives," in *Christians and Missionaries in India: Cross-Cultural Communication Since 1500 with Special Reference to Caste, Conversion, and Colonialism*, ed. Robert Eric Frykenberg (Grand Rapids: William B. Eerdmans, 2003), 11–17; Stephen Neill, *A History of Christianity in India, 1707–1858* (Cambridge: Cambridge University Press, 1985), 403–7.

245. Taylor, *Four Years'*, 194–5.

246. Ibid., 250–1.

247. Ibid., 308; cf. 1 Cor. 7:20.

248. Ibid., 219–20, 229–35.

249. "Rev. William Taylor in India," *Christian Advocate*, October 2, 1873.

250. W. F. Oldham, "God Keeps," *Christian Advocate*, November 1, 1917.

251. Barclay, *Widening Horizons*, 521–3.

252. Waterfield, *Memorandum on the Census*, 28.

253. Taylor, *Four Years'*, 255.

254. *Report of the General Missionary Conference Held at Allahabad, 1872–73* (London: Seeley, Jackson, and Halliday, 1873), 455.

255. *Report of the General Missionary Conference Held at Allahabad, 1872–73*, 474.

256. *Christian Advocate*, May 17, 1873.

257. *Report of the General Missionary Conference*, 485.

258. Taylor, *Four Years'*, 257.

259. Ibid., 255.

260. Ibid., 274, 317.

261. Wm. Taylor to Rev. Bishop Simpson, May 9, 1873, Box 9, Matthew Simpson Papers, Manuscript Division, Library of Congress.

262. Taylor, *Four Years'*, 272.

263. Ibid., 317–19.

264. Grace Stephens, *Triumphs of the Cross* (Baltimore: Baltimore Branch, Woman's Foreign Missionary Society, 1901), 9–10.

265. Grace Stephens, Mission Biographical Reference files, 1880s–1969, United Methodist Church Archives—GCAH.

266. Dana L. Robert, "Faith, Hope, Love in Action: United Methodist Women in Mission Yesterday, Today, and Tomorrow" (paper presented at Mission Forward event, UMW Assembly, St. Louis, MO, April 29, 2010), accessed February 15, 2012, http://new.gbgm-umc.org/umw/learn/studies/articles/item/index.cfm?id=616; Brian Stanley, *World Missionary Conference*, 91–97.

267. "From Our Mission Rooms," *Christian Advocate*, April 2, 1874.

268. Taylor, *Four Years'*, 327–8.

269. Clementina Butler, *William Butler, the Founder of Two Missions of the Methodist Episcopal Church* (New York: Eaton & Mains, 1902), 137.

270. Taylor, *Ten Years*, 252.

271. Taylor to Simpson, May 9, 1873.

272. Ibid.

273. Ibid.

274. Ibid.

275. Taylor, *Ten Years*, 293–4, 453; Thoburn, *My Missionary Apprenticeship*, 325–6.

276. *Minutes of the Tenth Session of the India Annual Conference of the Methodist Episcopal Church U.S.A. Held at Lucknow, January 7–13, 1874* (Lucknow: American Methodist Mission Press, 1874), 41–43, 52; Taylor, *Four Years'*, 295–6.

277. Barclay, *Widening Horizons*, 180.

278. Bruce J. Evensen, *God's Man for the Gilded Age: D.L. Moody and the Rise of Modern Mass Evangelism* (Oxford: Oxford University Press, 2003), 14–47; John Kent, *Holding the Fort: Studies in Victorian Revivalism* (London: Epworth Press, 1978), 132–68.

279. Taylor, *Four Years'*, 328–9.

280. Ibid., 265–6, 329.

281. J. E. Abrams, "Bishop Taylor's Boyhood Home," *Christian Advocate*, July 24, 1902; William Taylor, *Story of My Life*, 32.

282. *The Bombay Guardian*, March 6, 1875; "Monday's Noon Meeting," *The Christian*, March 25, 1875.

283. "Future Arrangements," *The Christian*, March 25, 1875.

284. W. H. Daniels, *D. L. Moody and His Work* (London: Hodder & Stoughton, 1876), 361–2; Kent, *Holding the Fort*, 144; "Evening Meetings: Agricultural Hall," *The Christian*, April 8, 1875; "The Work in Liverpool," Ibid., April 8, 1875; "Rev. W. Taylor's Work in Bristol," Ibid., May 20, 1875.

285. B. A. G., "Mr. Moody's Address," *City-Road Magazine* 6 (March 1876): 115–21.

286. "The Work in Liverpool."

287. Ibid.

288. "Evening Meetings, Agricultural Hall."

289. W. Taylor, "The Demoniac," *The Christian*, April 22, 1875.

290. Ibid.

Chapter 5

The Flaming Torch Burns

As her steamship crossed the Pacific in the spring of 1875 to return her to Foochow, China, the American Methodist missionary Susan Moore Sites was surprised to discover her cabin steward, a Chinese man, spoke English. While cleaning her room, the steward asked if Sites was married to a Wesleyan minister. She said that they were American Methodists, but basically the same as the British Wesleyans. He then asked if she knew William Taylor. She affirmed that she had heard of his work in India. The steward told Sites that he had once lived in Australia where he learned English and had been converted to Christianity at one of Taylor's revivals. Sites marveled at this information.[1]

By 1875, Taylor had developed a global reputation. That strangers who knew him—or knew of him—could meet on the other side of the world was not surprising. But Sites's comment about Taylor's work in India was also telling. American Methodists knew of Taylor—certainly some remembered his prewar revivals or had read of his exploits in the British Empire—but they did not really know him anymore. Nor did he know them. Taylor had been out of America for a period of time that had seen major changes in the life of his country.

Taylor landed in New York as Sites crossed the Pacific, and he found himself in a different America than he had left. Wounds of the Civil War were still fresh. Taylor's home region of Virginia had been ravaged by competing armies. The south was forced to abandon slave labor, and industrial development grew in the north. As Reconstruction ended in 1877, former slaves found their lives circumscribed in new ways. Immigrants entered the country to work in factories, and violent labor conflicts were common. Taylor never wrote about it, but the culture shock he experienced on returning home must have been profound.

Still, with his stories from around the world, Taylor instantly became a popular preacher at late-summer camp meetings across America. He struggled to balance invitations, dates, and distances as he gradually made his way across the county to be reunited with his family.[2] Few sources exist to reveal the lives of Taylor's wife and sons since they had parted in 1867. Those that do indicate that Anne managed life for her family alone, arranging legal representation for herself in a dispute and exploring career possibilities for her sons.[3] But Taylor's long absence made those sons strangers to him. William did not recognize his adult son Ross when they met at a camp meeting near Milwaukee in 1875.[4]

As Taylor became reacquainted with his church, he found two related segments of the church to be the most receptive to his message and methods: mission-minded Methodist women who had organized themselves into an independent Methodist missionary society—the Woman's Foreign Missionary Society (WFMS)—and a postwar network of camp meetings. Both groups were centers of the postwar holiness movement in American Methodism, in part because both existed outside official denominational structures.[5]

Taylor had been a part of the prewar holiness movement, but his primary contact in it—Phoebe Palmer—had died. John S. Inskip, one of the organizers of a seminal, 1867 holiness camp meeting in Vineland, New Jersey, and editor of the holiness periodical the *Christian Standard*, reintroduced and endorsed Taylor to the movement after hearing Taylor preach on sanctification. He commended Taylor's book, *Infancy and Manhood*, as "a most admirable work on the subject."[6] In short order, the *Christian Standard* became Taylor's unofficial organ, providing publicity and an administrative apparatus for Taylor's emerging missionary movement.

In this period, Taylor was reintroduced to American Methodism and became a significant force within it. This chapter will show that the holiness movement within American Methodism provided Taylor with both a community of support within his church and a pool of missionaries motivated by fidelity to doctrines of entire sanctification whom he sent around the world. It will also relate how Taylor's own sense of entrepreneurial, apostolic independence existed in tension with a Methodist desire for networked connection. For most of his career, Taylor had been free to act independently and use Methodist networks to support his work. Church leaders were initially highly supportive of Taylor's independent efforts and willing to bend church structures to accommodate him. But eventually, there came a breaking point. While the conflict that erupted burned hot for a number of years, Taylor's fame among grassroots Methodists was unabated. Even as it raged, lifted by his popularity and new interest in missions to Africa, Taylor was elected to be the Methodist Episcopal Church's missionary bishop for Africa. Bitter feelings between Taylor and others eventually dissipated. As Taylor's own abilities declined, others filled the void he left, and his mission initiatives were more fully incorporated within Methodism, dissolved, or became independent.

The conflicts central to the story of this chapter help illuminate more fully some persistent tensions in the Methodist missionary tradition. These tensions were present earlier in this account but now come into full view. The tension between individual action and networked connection has already been mentioned. Doctrines of entire sanctification continued to be an engine for missionary motivation, but shifting theologies foreshadowed the eventual emergence of Pentecostalism as a new religious movement. A desire to seize opportunities for missionary expansion and a pragmatic spirit also existed in tension. The willingness of Methodists to use uncritically whatever means were available to aid their expansion made them prone to be generally uncritical of the political dynamics or imperial or commercial expansion.

MISSIONARY RECRUITMENT

Officially the "Conference Agent" of the South India Conference, from 1875 to 1882 Taylor traveled North America enlisting missionaries at camp meetings and colleges to serve in India or South America. His recruitment tours were interrupted only by occasional visits to South America to start new missions there. By 1882, Taylor had sent 117 missionaries to both regions.[7] By the middle of the 1880s, when missionaries began to join him in Africa, the number of missionaries associated with Taylor exceeded 200. These missionaries were at the vanguard of a late nineteenth-century surge in American missionary involvement. From 1860 to 1900, the number of American missionary societies mushroomed from sixteen to ninety, and by 1910, Americans became the largest national missionary contingent.[8] Historians have offered several reasons for this upsurge in missionary enthusiasm. Sydney E. Ahlstrom argued that American Christians turned to foreign missions to "heal or hide" conflicts over the rise of historical criticism and evolutionary theory.[9] William Hutchison claimed that missions of this period sought to offer "a moral equivalent for imperialism."[10]

Like Taylor, his missionaries were driven by a belief that entire sanctification was the basic prerequisite for missionary service, that this gift of grace was available to all people, and that maintenance of one's full salvation demanded perfect fidelity to God's will. These beliefs led to a radical openness to potential missionary candidates since the primary qualification for becoming a missionary was freely offered by God to all who would receive it. In later years, for example, the blind and elderly hymnist, Fanny Crosby, spoke with Taylor about her desire to join him in Africa.[11] Neither age, gender, nor blindness were insurmountable obstacles, and Taylor's description of his missionaries often referenced their sanctification as their primary qualification. He called Robert E. Carter, a missionary to Rangoon, Burma, "one of our holiness men."[12] Henry Hoffman, a student from German Wallace College sent to minister to Germans in Valdivia, Chile, was "willing to go anywhere, and to do anything under the orders of the Savior of sinners, to whom he had consecrated his soul and body."[13]

Taylor judged this spiritual quality of his candidates by interrogating their willingness to sacrifice their lives and accept suffering and loss as God's will. When Taylor interviewed Sarah Longley, he asked if she was willing to go to Panama. Would she, a white woman, live with black Jamaican workers and share any discrimination they faced? She agreed. Taylor next told her that her own death was likely. Longley persisted. Taylor eventually sent Longley to Concepcion, Chile, and Charles and Lillie Birdsall to Panama. As expected, disease was a problem; Charles became fatally ill. As her husband died, Lillie wrote that she was able and willing to give him up because of her own sanctification. Because she had already sacrificed everything to God, her husband's death was bearable. Lillie returned to the United States after Charles's death, but within seven months, continued as a Taylor missionary in India.[14]

Taylor's own spiritual authority, derived from his past exploits and apostolic lifestyle, contributed to the lure of becoming a Taylor missionary. Taylor believed he was following God's will, and his candidates were convinced that God was working through him. Because their theology demanded fidelity to God in order to continue in a state of holiness, missionary candidates who saw Taylor as an agent of God believed the best way to maintain their own salvation was to follow Taylor's orders into the mission field. One missionary to Chile, Ira LaFetra, had not considered becoming a missionary before meeting Taylor. He recalled,

> It was in the parlor of a friend's house that I first met Mr. Taylor. After a brief conversation he said to me, "I want you to go to open the work at Valparaiso." His words came to me as a call from the Lord. I bowed my head on the chair before me in a moment of prayer to make sure I was not mistaken, and said, "I should like to see my parents before I go."[15]

Taylor told him there would not be time; LaFetra obediently left and never saw his parents again. Taylor asked Leila Waterhouse to be a teacher in Concepcion. She was not interested in missionary work, but believed she was bound by her sanctification to accept this call. She told her parents, "From babyhood you have taught me that God had a mission for me in the world. I have asked him to use me where I could do the most good. This may be simply a test of the sincerity of my consecration. The situation is none of my seeking."[16]

Taylor expected his missionaries to demonstrate an entrepreneurial spirit and respond to unexpected opportunities they believed God offered. As his missionaries identified new needs, Taylor supplied the missions with new recruits. One of Taylor's first missionaries, C. B. Ward, went to India. Several members of Ward's church started a home for orphans of famine victims. Christians in India supported the ministry financially, but Taylor sent Mary M. Miller to operate the orphanage.[17] Some of these initiatives led to new Methodist missions in regions Taylor never visited. E. L. Latham, a missionary Taylor sent to Colon after Birdsall's death, for example, was instrumental in developing two missions in Central America. He visited and started a church in Greyton, Nicaragua. Latham also met Arthur Morrell, American consul to Costa Rica and told him of Taylor. Morrell and Taylor later met in Washington, D.C. Over bowls of ice cream, the consul agreed to find financial support for a missionary if Taylor would send one. Taylor did so.[18]

Beyond a commitment to holiness, Taylor targeted individuals with qualifications that met particular missionary needs. He anticipated his missionaries to South America would both preach and teach school. Shortly before his first tour of South America, Taylor visited Boston University in search of ministerial students who possessed the holiness piety, missionary zeal, and higher education he sought.[19] After returning to the United States, Taylor selected his candidates. Three of these, Alexander P. Stowell, LaFetra, and William A. Wright were among the first party Taylor sent to South America. Two other graduates, Alexander T. Jeffrey and Lucius C. Smith, and their wives constituted the second group. Two younger students, Israel Derrick and Justus H. Nelson, completed their education before entering missionary service. Nelson went to Brazil, Derrick, an African American, was sent to Panama.[20]

One notable feature of Taylor's missionaries was that many saw their missionary service as a short-term commitment. Reliable steam transportation made it both easier to reach the mission field and easier to return home. Two Boston students suspended their education to become missionaries. Wright described both his missionary call and his plan to return to Boston in a letter to his sister:

> Mr. Taylor has charge of a mission on the Western coast and there are one or two at least of the brethren here that shall go the following Summer. I have been requested to go. . . . I do not know . . . but should probably have some preaching in English to do. Meanwhile I should take up the 3 languages that are there chiefly spoken, French, German and Spanish. I should only arrange to stay 3 yrs when I would expect to return here and finish my classical and theological courses.[21]

Wright completed his education in Boston in 1884.[22] Philip Price went to Guayaquil, Ecuador, but returned to graduate from Boston University in 1886.[23]

In general, Taylor preferred young missionaries because he believed they would be better able to learn new languages. This desire for youth could conflict with an interest in educated missionaries. Given a choice between youth and education, Taylor chose youth on the assumption that education was rarely necessary to be an effective missionary, but the ability to communicate was.[24] Taylor met Ward as he was preparing to enroll at Northwestern University. Ward recalled that Taylor

> cut short our interview by saying: "Brother Ward, go home and pray over the matter three days. If the Lord wants you to go to India, I would rather send you now than after you have spent six years more of the best part of your life in getting college stuffing after which you will have to learn your A.B.C. with any other barbarian boy out in India." With this he bade me good morning.[25]

Ward abandoned his education.[26]

Except in situations where Taylor hoped to send an ordained minister, neither gender nor race was a barrier in Taylor's recruitment. In many respects, Taylor had better success finding young, educated women than men. In 1880, Taylor visited Mount Allison Seminary in New Brunswick, Canada, to recruit missionaries from the faculty. The school president was a supporter of Taylor's work, and the trustees released the preceptress, Adelaide Whitfield, and two members of the faculty, Lizzie Kipp and Rosina Kinsman, to go to Chile.[27] For young women who became Taylor missionaries, the mission offered an opportunity to rise to a heroic challenge called for by their faith.[28] Of at least seventy-three missionaries sent by Taylor to South America from May 1878 to June 1882, thirty-seven were women.[29]

Taylor's missionaries saw him to be a person of great sanctity, and they desired a close relationship with him. As Oscar von Barchwitz-Krauser, a native German sent by Taylor to minister to Germans in Chile, rhapsodized, "There was something in all [Taylor's] movements and manners, and in all he said or sang, that impressed me deeply, . . . To say it: I fell in love with Father Taylor."[30] Their letters to Taylor often addressed him by this title, and they called themselves his children.[31] Taylor had long been addressed by this honorific, but now there was a different quality to the title as these missionaries were of a younger generation and looked to him as a mentor. Taylor, however, offered them very few benefits other than an outlet to act on their faith commitments.

Taylor did give his missionaries one characteristically home-spun word of advice. He told them to "root hog or die." As noted earlier, that American backcountry idiom celebrated the virtue of economic self-sufficiency. Individuals Taylor recruited for India, South America, and Africa used the phrase to describe their work with Taylor.[32] Taylor's message with his advice was clear. Once in the field, they would be responsible for their own survival. No money would be sent from a mission board to support them in their work. Their missionary work was to be self-supporting from the start.

Taylor's advice highlights his high view of human agency, particularly when contrasted with a parallel development in late nineteenth-century Protestant foreign missions. The late nineteenth century saw the rise of independent, faith missions such as the China Inland Mission. Like William Taylor's missionaries, faith missionaries went overseas without the guarantee of financial support from a mission board and trusted God would provide for their needs.[33] The difference was that Methodists like Taylor emphasized human action in that process. It was insufficient simply to trust that God would provide. To do so, in their view, was presumptuous. True faith, for Taylor, resulted in action, and a faithful missionary must be willing to work. His was a kind of economic Arminianism; God would provide but only to those for those willing to work for it.

SOUTH AMERICA

Taylor twice suspended his North American recruitment campaigns to visit South America. That continent was one of the earliest settings for American Methodist foreign missions. In 1836, the Methodist Episcopal Church sent missionaries to Rio de Janeiro and Buenos Aires. Despite this early beginning, the mission had remained small. By 1876 there were only three Methodist churches in South America, all on the east coast.[34] In that year, however, the Methodist Episcopal Church, South, initiated a new mission to Brazil, prompted by the migration of southerners to a country where slavery persisted and there was a desire to bring evangelical Protestantism to Catholic Brazilians.[35] Northern Methodists looked on the southern initiative with approval, and in September 1876, the *Missionary Advocate*, a publication of the northern church's Missionary Society, commended that enterprise and called for the establishment of a "South American Methodism from the Isthmus to Tierra del Fuego."[36] Methodists aspiring to reach all people with their message could not long abide the evangelistic neglect of an entire continent.

That article sparked a series of events that sent Taylor to South America. The spark was kindled by Taylor's own sense of apostolic authority and a miscommunication between J. A. Swaney, Bishop Matthew Simpson, and Taylor. Swaney and Taylor had worked together briefly in California and during a prewar revival in Pittsburgh. He had also served twice in South America with the American Seaman's Friend Society. The call issued by the *Missionary Advocate* rekindled Swaney's interest in the region, and he wrote Simpson to volunteer.[37] Simpson agreed Methodist expansion in South America was desirable but was concerned finances presented a practical difficulty. Missionary collections were down, and mission executives were wary of overexpansion. Nevertheless, in early 1877, the two met, and Simpson asked Swaney to prepare a report on the subject. Soon after, Swaney became seriously ill and asked Taylor to take over the project. Taylor initially demurred. When Swaney became convinced his own death was immanent, however, he made a dying request of Taylor to establish a new Methodist mission in South America. These appeals persuaded Taylor that the Holy Spirit was leading him to visit the continent.[38]

Simpson could not have expected that a noncommittal request for a report from Swaney would inspire Taylor into action, but Taylor was clearly encouraged by what he believed was the endorsement of a leading bishop of the church. Unlike Simpson, Taylor was confident that any financial obstacles could be overcome with missionaries who found support in the local economy as he believed both he and Paul had done. Taylor did not go to South America to test the efficacy of his missionary methods.[39] He believed his message and methods were God's own as demonstrated by the example of the apostle Paul and had been proven through a missionary career on five continents.

In the fall of 1877, Taylor sent Simpson several letters outlining his thoughts on a new South American mission. They illustrate that Taylor held conflicting desires at the start of this enterprise. He wanted to be a part of the Methodist Episcopal Church and to operate independently at the same time. Taylor considered himself a loyal Methodist who started Methodist churches; he wanted to proceed "in closer union with the church" than he had in India.[40] But, Taylor informed the bishop, he was subject only to God's direction and not that of church leaders. "My commission is from God, and by His will I go to do whatever work He shall appoint, whatever my church at home may do."[41] Just as Paul did not ask for permission from the church in Jerusalem before starting a new mission in Macedonia, he, as a "pioneer of the Pauline track . . . must be entirely free . . . to follow instantly the leading of the Holy Spirit."[42]

William and his brother Archibald, who had been serving a church in Texas, sailed from New York for the west coast of South America in October 1877. Unlike Taylor's work in the British imperial world, in this region, there were no preexisting Methodist, and few Protestant, churches or missions. In the absence of a friendly ecclesial network to structure his work, Taylor relied on commercial and diplomatic connections of English-speaking expatriates.[43] He obtained a letter of introduction from an executive of the Pacific Steam Navigation Company, a British steamship line operating in South America. Since every port of call would have an English-speaking shipping agent who could introduce him to other expatriates, he used their routes to plan his trip.[44]

Taylor also carried with him a letter from US president Rutherford B. Hayes. The president was familiar with Taylor's work; the First Lady, Lucy

Webb Hayes, was an active Methodist laywoman and served as the president of the Methodist Episcopal Woman's Home Missionary Society. In a meeting with President Hayes, one of Taylor's benefactors, Chauncey Schaffer, requested a letter of introduction for Taylor.[45] It stated,

> Understanding, that you are about to visit various countries in South America for the purpose of establishing Schools and for other purposes connected therewith, it affords me great pleasure to express my favorable regards for yourself as a man and as a Christian laborer; and to wish you a continuance of health and success in your new field of labor.[46]

Any reticence an American consul might have in helping Taylor would certainly be overcome by this presidential endorsement.

Taylor also had reason to hope this American political backing would also open doors with friendly Latin American governments. The first wave of Methodist missions in South America took place in the aftermath of revolutions against Spain that weakened the Catholic Church's authority and offered new freedoms to Protestants. Taylor's South American visits coincided with a similar period, as liberals promoted new educational opportunities to break Catholic control of schools and sought to attract British and American investment.[47] Indeed, at the end of this tour Taylor met with the Chilean president and minister of justice and public instruction who encouraged him in his work.[48]

Most of Taylor's interactions, however, were with English-speaking expatriates. Taylor targeted Callao, Peru, as the first destination of his tour because seventeen years earlier, Swaney started an English-speaking, Protestant congregation there. Taylor discovered en route, however, that Americans and Britons were not the only English-speaking people living in Latin America. When crossing Panama by train, Taylor learned that at Aspinwall and Panama City thousands of West Indians worked on the railroad and supporting industries. He even met some Methodists who had been members of a church in Jamaica where he had preached a decade earlier.[49]

Taylor did not preach or hold a revival in either Aspinwall or Panama City on his way south because train and ship schedules demanded he keep moving. As a result, Taylor probably missed an opportunity. Several factors associated with his most successful revivals elsewhere were present there. Like migrants to California or Australasia, the West Indians he met were English-speaking, self-identified Christians with commitments to Methodism that had weakened because of migration. There were no Methodist churches to serve them. In addition, like the Xhosa and Mfengu of South Africa and Anglo-Indians in India, West Indians occupied a marginal position as black laborers in Colombian society. On his return, Taylor did collect subscriptions for the support of missionaries, and he sent several there. He also held no revival on his return because events in Callao prompted him to abandon revivalism as a method of missionary organization.

At the start of his trip, however, Taylor hoped Callao would offer a platform from which to launch a revival campaign through the continent. Events did not go as planned. After six weeks of revival meetings in Callao, Taylor claimed only one convert. Taylor's account of his trip, *Our South American Cousins* (1878), published shortly after his return to New York, did not mention this failure and placed a positive spin on the experience. He claimed he contacted eighty-five English-speaking, Protestant families, developed a list of names for pastoral care, calmed conflicts in the community, and installed his brother as an interim pastor.[50] But privately Taylor confessed to Swaney both his failure and his resolve, "This is the hardest field I ever struck, yet none on earth more needy, and I believe the Lord through your agency sent me hither, and I am bound to give it a fair trial."[51]

Several factors contributed to Taylor's failure. The congregation was divided between evangelical and high church Anglican factions, some of whom were probably opposed to Taylor's revivalism. In addition, although liberal governments provided an opening for Protestant missions in this period, Catholic opposition to Protestant missions remained strong. During Taylor's time there, the Papal Nuncio tried, unsuccessfully, to have the church closed.[52]

Whatever the case, Taylor's failure and the absence of an existing church for English-speaking Protestants at his next stops in Molleno, Arica, and Tacna, Peru, led to a significant change in Taylor's missionary methods. Instead of holding a revivals, he gathered financial pledges from English speakers to support a missionary who would both preach and teach school until that school was self-supporting. He entrusted collection of money and the necessary arrangements to a committee and left town. In Tacna, Taylor experienced what he described as a "waking vision" that confirmed this course of action was best. The contrast between his failure to spark a revival in Callao and the apparent ease with which he organized these new missions seemed to prove the matter.[53]

This decision represented a major shift in and narrowing of Taylor's thinking. Revivalism had carried him around the world and formed the foundation for his Pauline theory of mission. Now Taylor approached mission as an economic, rather than revivalistic, enterprise. At the time, Taylor saw this shift as simply a pragmatic response to the South American context, but in time he would make the economic foundation for mission the defining characteristic of his work as other elements of his Pauline theory were deemphasized.

Since this form of organizing required very little time, as Taylor continued south along the South American coast, his work picked up pace. At each port of call, Taylor found English speakers and offered to send a man or a married couple to be a preacher and teachers in exchange for a pledge of financial support for a contracted period. At Antofagasta, Bolivia, Taylor committed to send a teacher and a preacher.[54] At a former whaling station called Talca-huana, Taylor found a few American families and collected subscriptions to pay someone to start a school and preach to sailors.[55] At Concepcion, Taylor met a nephew of the ship captain who had taken him to California in 1849, and he quickly gathered enough pledges to form a school.[56] Further south, at Valdevia, he found that a large settlement of Germans and decided that a German-American Methodist preacher would be well received by that community and could develop them into a "grand medium of access to masses of the natives" just as an English speaker might elsewhere.[57] South of Iquique, Taylor tried to organize a seamen's mission for ships involved in guano mining.[58] At Huanillos, Taylor attempted to accomplish the same feat in only one day but found the task too great.[59] Although he did not completely give up preaching or attempting to convert individuals through personal evangelism, he scaled back these efforts significantly. He stayed in Iquique, Peru, for ten days, a long stay in this whirlwind tour, but during that time, Taylor preached only four sermons to small congregations.[60]

As was always the case with Taylor, he enjoyed opportunities to observe local life and culture. In Callao, he attended the Christmas Eve Mass at the Lima cathedral. While baffled by the Latin liturgy, he wrote respectfully of the piety he witnessed of some in the congregation.[61] In Arica, he admired a church designed by Gustave Eiffel and built entirely out of metal.[62] He learned about South American independence leaders and spent evenings watching the *paseo* of young men and women.[63] In Tacna, he rapturously described the music played in the plaza as taking him "quite on the verge of heaven."[64]

Taylor's tour was also not without a measure of danger. One evening at Iquique, while counseling an Englishman who felt guilty for converting to Catholicism, an earthquake rattled the town. Taylor was alarmed that people and dogs responded to the tremors by fleeing uphill, away from the ocean. A decade earlier an earthquake and tsunami hit the region. Unlike the residents, Taylor did not know what to expect from such a disaster; their fear rattled him. Fortunately, no further disaster hit the town.[65] Not surprisingly, Taylor turned to his faith in this crisis. He prayed for the city, and later that night, Taylor considered the state of his own soul.

> I searched to see that I was wholly submitted to God, and quietly entrusted soul and body to the care of my Savior. I could not call to mind one act of my life on which I could base any hope of heaven, but sweetly resting my all in the hands of Jesus, I had sweet assurance that all was well.[66]

Convinced that his own salvation was secure and hopeful that God would spare the city, Taylor returned to his room. He counted ten aftershocks that night before he slept.[67]

One of Taylor's last stops in South America was Valparaiso, Chile. There he renewed his acquaintance with David Trumbull. The two had met at the beginning of their careers in 1849, and Trumbull's early ministry among sailors may have provided Taylor with the inspiration to start a Seaman's Bethel. In the intervening years, their lives had taken different paths. While Taylor traveled the world, Trumbull made Chile his home and became a Chilean citizen. He established schools, newspapers, an orphanage, and a church. On his death, the Chilean legislature suspended business to honor Trumbull's memory.[68] Now reacquainted, and at Trumbull's encouragement, the two partnered to restart a seamen's ministry in Valparaiso. Taylor agreed but insisted that it live by a lesson experience had taught him. The mission was not to be encumbered by ownership of land or a ship.[69]

By late March 1878, Taylor ended his whirlwind tour of South America and set sail for the United States. He wrote and published his account of his trip shortly after landing and resumed his work of missionary recruitment. Methodists at both the grassroots and in the leadership of his church would be excited by reports of Taylor's tour and encouraged that new Methodist missions seemed to have been started in South America with minimal effort or cost. Taylor, however, totally underestimated the changes that had taken place in his church and country, and attempts to integrate these new missions with the Methodist Episcopal Church did not go well.

SUPPORT FOR "SELF-SUPPORTING MISSIONS"

A long-standing goal of Protestant mission theory had been to create self-supporting, self-governing, and self-propagating native churches. This objective was shared by mission executives of different nationalities and ecclesiological traditions. The American Congregationalist Rufus Anderson and the Anglican Henry Venn each proposed the creation of "three-self" native churches to be the aim of foreign missions.[70] Late in Taylor's career, one of these legs of this theory, "self-support," became his battle cry in a fight to operate independent from his own denomination's Missionary Board. As has been seen, however, this principle had deep roots in Taylor's biography. Self-sufficiency was one of Taylor's core values rooted in his social origins in the backcountry south. He had lived by that value as a California missionary and as an itinerant, book-writing evangelist. With the gradual development of his Pauline mission theory, that value was raised to the level of Christian principle. For Taylor, a fight over "self-support" was not a debate over mission theory but his own identity.

But the belief that missionaries, once in the mission field, should be self-supporting, either through their own labor or voluntary contributions, left the problem of transport to the mission field unresolved. Taylor initially sought to cooperate with the Methodist Missionary Board in this effort. Before 1875, it sent five men to India to work under Taylor. In that year, he asked the Board to send a dozen additional missionaries. This number was ten more than budgeted. The Board instead agreed to pay fares of outgoing missionaries to London, provided Taylor paid their transit from London to India.[71] Taylor agreed and initially hoped to do so with book sales but realized he could not meet this commitment. Other arrangements were made. Some of Taylor's wealthy benefactors, such as Schaffer and Henry Reed, made large donations for the purpose, and the Rock River Annual Conference sent the Carter family to Rangoon, Burma.[72] Taylor agreed to this arrangement but would eventually feel that in this matter the Board failed both churches he started in India and missionaries he had recruited.

Having learned this lesson, Taylor's contracts in South America stipulated that those patrons would forward the cost of missionary passage to New York. Very little of that money was sent, however. Short on funds, most of Taylor's early missionaries to South America traveled by steerage.[73] Although some historians have asserted a strong linkage between a commitment to holiness and a rejection of class privilege, news that missionary women were traveling steerage caused a minor scandal among leaders of the holiness movement.[74] With Taylor's support, two of these, Inskip and William McDonald, mobilized their publications, *The Christian Standard* and *The Advocate of Holiness*, to publicize the need for missionary transit money and school equipment. Money soon flowed in to the *Standard* and was duly recognized in a weekly column.[75]

These donors illustrated both the base of Taylor's support and the possible extent of his influence. The names of prominent figures in the holiness movement were featured, as were two future Taylor missionaries, J. W. Spangler and B. F. Kephart. The vast majority, however, were significantly less prominent individuals. The median contribution was $5. More than two-thirds of the donors came from midwestern and northeastern states.[76] The donors included Pah Liang Fong, one of the first Chinese students to study in the United States. While in America, he and four other Chinese students converted to Christianity and committed to become evangelists when they returned to China. In 1879, Fong wrote to the *Christian Standard* to testify that he had found entire sanctification and contributed to Taylor's work.[77]

In addition to resolving the immediate problem of paying missionary passage, this funding campaign marked a step in the development of Taylor's missions as an organization independent from the official mission structures of the Methodist Episcopal Church and closely integrated with the American holiness movement. Another step in that process were commissions Taylor gave men sent to South America. Before his trip, Taylor had hoped to send ordained men as missionaries but did not hear from Bishop Simpson before he left.[78] After returning, Taylor corresponded with Bishop Gilbert Haven regarding ordinations. On the unanimous recommendation of the church's bishops, Haven offered Taylor exactly what Taylor had asked of Simpson. Any men selected by Taylor could be ordained, Taylor could be made superintendent of the South American mission, and the mission could be appended to any conference Taylor wished.[79]

Now, however, Taylor backed away from his request. He worried that his South American sponsors might be concerned if he sent ordained Protestant ministers. Taylor also felt obliged to dispatch the missionaries quickly, without waiting for candidates to be admitted to conference membership and ordained.[80] Nevertheless, Taylor did offer the men he sent to South America credentials of his own making. These he issued on his authority derived from God. Taylor's certificate to A. T. Jeffrey, for example, read:

> By virtue of my commission from God, as a Cosmopolitan Evangelist and founder of Gospel Missions in many lands, [I] solemnly set apart the said A. T. Jeffrey as one of my educational and evangelistic workers for South America, and do hereby authorize him, accompanied by his good wife, to proceed to Antofagasta.[81]

When they came to light, Taylor issuance of these credentials coupled with his rejection of offers to incorporate his missions into the church would eventually appear to some to be a schismatic act. Taylor seemed to be setting himself up on his own God-given authority independent from his church. In the meantime, however, Taylor convinced Haven of the prudence of avoiding formal ordination of his missionaries until 1881.

Taylor did, in fact, insist on independence on one issue. He refused any arrangement that included the church's Missionary Board in his missions. Past grievances dating from his time in California—the Missionary Society had failed to respond to opportunities there—and present ones—the lack of missionary passage to India accumulated in Taylor's mind. He also did not appreciate changes that had taken place in his church. After the war, a rising generation of Methodist leaders embraced the development of national church bureaucracies as the best way to administer outreach, instead of the old system of funding from a missionary society that resourced locally supervised missions. In 1872, the Methodist Episcopal General Conference assumed oversight of all missionary work of the church, designated the Missionary Board to manage it, and elected Corresponding Secretaries as supervisors.[82] Taylor refused to work with this bureaucracy and preferred to operate as he always had, through personal relationships and networking. In his correspondence to Haven, Taylor forcefully asserted the independence of his missions from any involvement of the Missionary Board.[83]

Taylor's concern for independence was also evident in his latest iteration of a "Pauline" mission theory. He aided the *Christian Standard* campaign with a series of articles entitled "Pauline Methods of Missionary Work," later reprinted as a book by that name.[84] Consisting mostly of letters and reports from his missionaries, Taylor set forth six points of his theory succinctly without elaboration or explanation.[85] The first principle was "to plant nothing but the pure gospel seed."[86] Second, Paul employed local leadership and "laid the entire responsibility of Church work and Church government upon his native converts."[87] Third, Paul kept peace with the churches in Jerusalem, but was unwilling to allow "the home Churches to put a yoke of bondage on his neck, or [lay] any restrictions on his foreign Churches."[88] Fourth, the Christian preacher could expect to be supported locally, and not from foreign missionary contributions, "on the principle of equivalents, or value for value."[89] Fifth, Paul began work among the Jewish diaspora who then evangelized "their heathen neighbors."[90] Finally, Paul stayed in one location only long enough to develop leadership and "the Christian character of each member up to the standard of holiness."[91] In this new formulation, revivalism, which had been the foundational centerpiece of Taylor's theory, was dropped entirely.

Taylor may have understood his relationship with Hayes as another way of mimicking Paul, who used his Roman citizenship to his advantage. Hayes's letter of introduction inaugurated a friendship between the men. Taylor regularly requested the president send letters of commendation for his missionaries like his own. Hayes did so throughout his presidency.[92] In addition, after Hayes appointed Henry Hilliard to a diplomatic post in Brazil, and encouraged by a favorable report on the missionary potential of that country, in 1880, Taylor founded a new mission in that country. Taylor and Hilliard had known each other in Georgetown before the war.[93]

Taylor was so optimistic about prospects in Brazil that he took the missionaries he hoped to appoint, Nelson, his wife Fannie, and Walter W. Gregg, with him. Despite theoretical formulations to the contrary, Taylor now decided it was not necessary for missionaries to work though English speakers as a way to reach native populations. Theory, for Taylor, was almost always driven by practical considerations, and in Para, he found only a few English-speaking expatriates. Nevertheless, Taylor appointed Nelson to preach to this small community and directed the other missionaries to start a school for Brazilian students.[94]

After establishing his missionaries in Para, Taylor sailed for Pernambucco, Bahia, and Rio de Janiero to reconnoiter other missionary prospects and returned to New York in early September.[95] Despite passing through a hurricane on the way, he completed a new book, a treatise on baptism published as *Letters to a Quaker Friend on Baptism* (1880).[96] His arguments for infant baptism and allowing for a variety of modes of baptism were unremarkable as a work of Methodist theology.[97] The fact that he wrote in response to the spiritual inquiry of a Quaker, however, indicated that Taylor's influence was spreading beyond his own Methodist church to others participating in the postwar holiness movement.[98]

By the start of the Brazilian mission, Taylor's missionary movement had grown beyond the size that he and the *Christian Standard* could manage. Taylor delegated the task of missionary recruitment for India to James M. Thoburn and South America to Asbury Lowrey, an active leader in the holiness movement.[99] Taylor also tasked Emily Fowler, the daughter of the English Wesleyan Methodist leader William Arthur, and her husband, Anderson, to be his secretary and treasurer in New York. The Lowrey and the Fowlers formed the administrative core of Taylor's missionary enterprise for years to come.[100] Despite his rejection of official structures provided by his church, Taylor developed his own. Bureaucracies had their advantages.

ISIKUNISIVUTAYO

In 1882, Taylor first claimed that from his time in Bombay, he was in a constant state of conflict with leaders of his church who sought to take over his work to place it under the oversight of the Missionary Board or discredit it. Historians David Bundy and Jay Riley Case followed this line of interpretation.[101] This portrayal, however, does not match contemporaneous sources, including Taylor's own writing prior to that date. A more accurate description would be to say that until 1881, when a combination of events sparked a major confrontation between Taylor and church leaders, the roots of a conflict existed, but church leaders were highly supportive of Taylor and willing to accommodate church structures to incorporate his initiatives. After 1881, however, once supportive leaders expressed vocal concerns, and Taylor's own evaluation of previous events changed.

Before 1881, leaders who became critics offered effusive public praise of Taylor and his work. They believed Taylor represented the best of the Methodist missionary tradition. A speaker at the 1872 anniversary celebration of the Methodist Missionary Society cited Taylor as an example for Methodist missions to follow because he did not wait for official sanction by church authorities but acted on his own initiative.[102] Daniel Curry, editor of the *Christian Advocate,* celebrated that, thanks to Taylor, missions in India were more vigorous than ever.[103] Mission Secretary J. M. Reid praised Taylor's work in India as being "worthy of all commendation" and extolled his decision to follow the "the call of the Spirit" to South America.[104] Bishop Haven called Taylor "the John Wesley of to-morrow," and Bishop Randolph Sinks Foster lauded Taylor as "the greatest man of his age."[105] At the 1880 General Conference, the church's bishops praised Taylor and his missionaries for extending Methodist missions in South America.[106]

Among this effusive praise, former missionary to India, John T. Gracey, offered a dissenting voice. A former missionary whose time in India preceded Taylor's, Gracey wrote a negative review of *Four Years'* that accused Taylor of "uncharitableness" toward the work of other Christian missions in India. Gracey also took issue with Taylor's confidence in claiming to know God's will, his description of the spiritual life of certain individuals, his concern with Anglo-Indians instead of Hindus and Muslims, and his expansion beyond the set bounds of the mission.[107] In addition to this review, Gracey wrote an article in the *Northern Christian Advocate*, a regional Methodist newspaper, that critiqued Taylor's assertion that missionaries should live simply and at a level consistent with the local economy.[108] While Gracey probably spoke for more than just himself, until 1881, such criticism of Taylor was the exception rather than the rule. Still, Taylor never took any criticism well. Almost a decade later, Taylor referenced Gracey's disapproval as proof he faced a massive campaign of opposition by church leaders, despite the fact that most church leaders defended him at the time.[109]

The first significant complaints about Taylor and his concept of missionary self-support surfaced in early 1881 and were voiced by his own South American missionaries. At that time, twenty-six of the thirty-three people Taylor had sent there remained and met in Santiago. They reported that their work had suffered from the lack of Taylor's supervision and that Taylor's vision of missionary self-support was not as effective as he thought. As pragmatic Methodists, they simply argued that Taylor's concept of self-support didn't work. They declared, "It would be a mistake for the church at home to receive the impression that all the work which needs to be done in foreign fields can be done by simply sending missionaries to those fields to find their own support."[110] They found schools were rarely viable. Anglo-American merchants with whom Taylor contracted withdrew their patronage when faced with social opposition to Protestant missionary work. In addition, the outbreak of war and between Chile and a Peruvian-Bolivian alliance prompted both expatriate families and missionaries to flee, leaving missionaries without a base of support.[111]

Taylor probably did not hear these complaints for some time. The first criticism to reach him was voiced at the Œcumenical Methodist Conference in London. This gathering brought together for the first time, representatives of twenty-eight Methodist denominations from around the world.[112] In a paper on foreign missions, Englishman James H. Rigg, a Wesleyan Methodist, harshly critiqued Taylor by name. Rigg asserted that Methodist missionaries and their sponsoring societies should avoid competition with each other.[113] Rigg illustrated the problem by contrasting William Butler and Taylor.

> With the name of Dr. Butler—an American Irishman, beloved and honoured on both sides of the Atlantic—is associated the observance of the established Indian rules of missionary procedure, and all that is brotherly and pleasant in experience and remembrance. With the name of the Rev. W. Taylor, of Californian and South African fame, is associated, at least in the minds of many, the thought of intrusion and irregularity, and much that is more or less disturbing and perplexing. . . . Dr. Butler represented the American Methodist Missionary Board, whereas Mr. Taylor represented only his own convictions and his own methods and enterprises.[114]

While Butler consulted with others before beginning his mission, Taylor acted of his own accord.[115]

Despite his reference to established missionary procedures, Rigg did not argue in favor of missionary comity agreements, as has been suggested.[116] His concern was less ecumenical. Rigg asserted that Methodist missionary initiatives taken without consultation with other Methodists violated a core Methodist ecclesiological principle. One of Rigg's recurring arguments, in this paper and elsewhere, was that a Methodist "connexional" ecclesiology, in which all clergy and laity cooperated with each other, was far superior to the "independency" of Congregationalists and Baptists.[117] For Rigg, Taylor's mission initiatives symbolized the independent ecclesiology he opposed.

Rigg had a point. A sense of networked connection had always been a part of the Methodist tradition. Indeed, Taylor's global evangelistic career had only been possible because he, as an individual, traveled along webs of Methodist connectional relationships. But entrepreneurial independence was also a part of that tradition. The Methodist missionary tradition operated in a dynamic balance between independent initiative and connectional accountability.

Still, Rigg's criticism was unusually personal. Representatives audibly expressed their disapproval of Rigg's attack but did not discuss Taylor's work further. Of greater concern to the delegates was Methodism in Germany where three different missions operated.[118] It didn't matter. When word of Rigg's paper reached Taylor, he understood the central message to be that his missions in India "had a bastard birth, and no legitimate family relationship in Methodism."[119] Furthermore, he believed he had been personally defamed in the most prestigious global gathering ever assembled of his fellow Methodists. His only defender had been William Arthur who, without naming Taylor, insisted that it was wrong for missionary committees to subvert the independence of native churches by managing their business.[120]

Another offense to Taylor quickly followed when the *Christian Advocate* published the minutes of the November 1881 meeting of the Missionary Committee of the Methodist Episcopal Church. The actual item of discussion—the appropriation of $500 to help a church debt at Allahabad—mattered less than the comments of the participants, many of whom were bishops. The recurring themes were that Taylor had sent unqualified men to India, contributions to Taylor's missionaries drew money away from other needs, and his missions in India did not evangelize non-Christians.[121] Taylor had his defenders at the meeting but they were in the minority. If such criticisms had been spoken privately before, they had never been printed in the church's flagship newspaper.

Taylor read the minutes while on a preaching tour and visit to his family in the west. He lashed out to defend his honor, first with a letter to the *Advocate*, then a book, *Ten Years of Self-Supporting Missions in India* (1882) that escalated the conflict.[122] *Ten Years* was largely derivative. Large portions had been previously published in *Pauline Methods* and *Four Years' Campaign in India*. Other chapters contained missionary reports to prove his missions were viable, successful, self-supporting, and expansive.[123]

The new text in *Ten Years* was highly personal. Taylor included an autobiographical chapter describing how he had come to found "self-supporting missions."[124] He lashed back at his attackers, sarcastically calling Rigg "a celebrated doctor of divinity" and "that little Englishman."[125] He sniped at bishops of his church, and recast past actions of the Missionary Board and other church leaders as a pattern of subversion. In his continuing identification with Paul, Taylor flexibly manipulated his metaphor. In one case the Missionary Board could be like the Sanhedrin persecuting Paul/him. In another the Board was like the Apostles in Jerusalem from whom Paul/he stood independent.[126]

Despite this Pauline rhetoric, Taylor showed the social origins of his missionary vision were clearly rooted in American expansion and superseded any biblical foundations. In this book, Taylor elevated the self-supporting aspect of his missions to be their defining quality and argued self-supporting missions were sustained by three economic principles. The pioneer principle was illustrated by California miners who risked everything to strike gold. Under it and the commercial principle, "the mountains are tunneled, the railroads built, the machine-shops run, the wheels of commerce turned."[127] These principles guide commerce and should guide missionary work as well. Paul, Taylor wrote, operated on the pioneer principle and taught the commercial principle. The danger of the charity principle was shown by "the cattle kings of Wyoming" who learned herds that relied on charitable meals of hay would not survive the winter.[128]

Reviews of *Ten Years* were deeply ambivalent. Methodists had come to see Taylor as a hero of their church and were troubled by his tone. The *Zion's Herald*, for example, read the book with "mingled feelings of admiration and grief" and worried that it would undermine confidence in the church's administration since the critiques came from "the nearest representative to St. Paul now upon the earth."[129] The *Christian Advocate* praised Taylor's past work and his description of Pauline methods but saw no evidence anyone sought to undermine him.[130]

For those outside church leadership, particularly those in the holiness movement, Taylor now became a populist hero whose tensions with church leaders reflected their own. In a contemporary parallel development, in late 1881, some of the leaders of the holiness movement in northern Methodism, including notable Taylor's supporters Asbury Lowery and Daniel Steele, petitioned the church's bishops to call a national holiness convention. While professing their commitment to the doctrine of entire sanctification, the bishops responded by asserting that holiness should be promoted within established church structures, and not through separate means. The result of the bishops' response was that the movement's leadership became confirmed in their belief that holiness publishing enterprises separate and independent from the church remained necessary. For many within the movement, Taylor's missions were of a piece with other holiness entities and functioned as the missionary wing of the movement.[131] Although Taylor wholeheartedly endorsed the doctrine of entire sanctification and saw the formation of independent, entrepreneurial initiatives as needed in response to the Sprit's calling, for his part, Taylor would never completely embrace those elements in the holiness movement that believed it necessary to "come-out" of the Methodist Episcopal Church.

As a living hero of the Methodist faithful, Taylor had no equal. By 1882, he had traveled the country for seven years speaking at countless church gatherings and camp meetings. Many Methodists had learned of his evangelistic exploits around the world. For over a generation he had been traveling the world and sharing his gospel. Collectors sought his autograph, which he signed with both his name and "Isikunisivutayo"—a nickname given him in South Africa meaning "flaming torch."[132] Mount Union College in Ohio and Hedding College in Illinois both awarded him a Doctorate of Divinity.[133] Taylor's rhetoric that past Christian missions had been hampered by a lack of holiness and his commitment to an apostolic model for that mission, matched the rhetoric of the late-century holiness movement that believed spiritual laxity bedeviled the church's leadership, sought to promote renewal through extra-ecclesial methods, and increasingly founded the doctrine of Christian perfection on biblical passages in the Book of Acts.[134]

A breaking point arrived the following November at another meeting of the Missionary Committee. Simpson suggested Taylor's South American missions should be added to a list of the church's missions. Taylor's initial moratorium on ordinations had expired; bishops were now ordaining men for South America, and Harris had visited the continent to ordain missionaries previously sent by Taylor.[135] For almost two days, the committee discussed the matter without resolution. Most were inclined to make arrangements that kept Taylor's missionaries connected with the church but that allowed Taylor maximum freedom. Curry, for example, praised Taylor's initiatives, but declared, "Missionary societies must be in the wake to gather up and establish the work. Red tape is necessary to bind up the bundles. We need more of it rather than less."[136] Harris, on the other hand, produced one of the certificates Taylor issued to his missionaries and related the dissatisfaction of Taylor's missionaries, one of whom had called Taylor "like a child at play, scattering his blocks along here and there."[137]

Unable to arrive at a consensus, the body appointed a subcommittee chaired by Simpson to meet with Taylor. That meeting went as badly as possible. Taylor would frequently repeat the claim that it was tasked to force him to surrender administration of his South America missions, but the committee probably did not make such demands. More moderate options, including maintaining the status quo, had been discussed in committee.[138] Taylor refused any arrangement that connected his missions to the Missionary Society.[139] A rupture was reached when an unnamed bishop suggested Taylor return to his appointment in India. Taylor allegedly declared, "Bishop I have just heard from your Master and he says I am to go to South America."[140] He resigned his ministerial credentials and insisted he would appeal the entire matter to the 1884 General Conference. Until then, Taylor said, he would remain in South America.[141]

BISHOP OF AFRICA

Taylor's decision in that moment was also an implicit decision not to return to his family in California. Long absences had led to an estrangement with his wife. Silent about such matters, Taylor instead portrayed his self-imposed exile as an act of sacrifice and solidarity with his missionaries as he served a church in Coquimbo, Chile.[142] In fact, Taylor's ten months in Coquimbo were discouraging. He thought the work beneath him. Since he had a divine commission "to preach to the nations . . . , to have my wings clipped and to be stuck down in a duck pond with the tadpoles for nearly a whole year is no joke."[143]

Nevertheless, Taylor did oversee the institutional development of the mission. With his church salary and contributions from the United States, he bought the first real property to be owned by the mission. He also started a school in Coquimbo with W. T. Robinson, a professor from Iowa Wesleyan College who Taylor had first recruited to found a school in Brazil. Taylor and LaFetra also sought legally to incorporate the mission with the Chilean government. Until it had legal status under Chilean law, property was titled to individuals, a practice that caused problems when missionaries left or moved.[144]

In retrospect, Taylor feared his impulsive resignation could prevent him from appealing the actions of the Missionary Committee to the General Conference. He was, once again, a layperson, and he worried that, as such, he might not be eligible to be elected a delegate.[145] This fear was another mark of Taylor's failure to appreciate changes in his church. American Methodism had gradually, and with much conflict, allowed some laity to participate in its governing conferences.[146] Fortunately for Taylor, his colleagues in South India perceived the problem and the solution without him. They elected him to the 1884 General Conference as their lay delegate.

Taylor returned to the States to attend that conference when it met in Philadelphia. He had never been a representative to his church's highest legislative body but played an active role from the beginning. He led devotions, introduced legislation, spoke for the South India Conference, and attempted, unsuccessfully, to replace J. M. Reid as corresponding secretary of the Mission Board with his own candidate. The conference acted favorably on Taylor's grievances by changing the *Discipline* to allow churches to be formed outside of the United States and conference boundaries and to permit bishops to ordain preachers to serve such churches.[147]

These actions were overshadowed, however, by Taylor's unexpected election to the episcopacy. Behind that event lay not only Taylor's place in the church but issues that had vexed the Methodist Episcopal Church for decades, such as race and the relationship of the church in the United States to that in foreign lands. It also incorporated developments emerging out of the new mission field in the American south created by emancipation.

Methodist mission strategy in the Reconstruction south varied by race and denomination and built on the Christianization of African Americans before the war. The possible Methodist identity of slaves in Taylor's own family illustrated the presence of black Christianity in the antebellum south. White Methodists had also sponsored plantation missions driven by a dual motivation to create obedient slaves and to share the gospel with them. After the war, black Methodist denominations sent missionaries south to offer freed people a message of freedom and black nationalism. The African Methodist Episcopal and African Methodist Episcopal, Zion, churches experienced spectacular levels of growth from these missions in the 1860s and 1870s. White Methodists in the south, sought to stem this membership loss and maintain a paternalistic relationship to southern blacks by forming the Colored Methodist Episcopal Church. Black leaders in that church rejected slavery and paternalism but otherwise embraced southern traditionalism. Northern Methodist Episcopal missionaries continued the crusade against slavery by seeking to dismantle racially based social hierarchies, often through educational missions such as the Freedmen's Aid Society.[148]

This "anticaste," as they called it, idea, however, l was rarely realized in northern Methodism. In 1864, that church created mission conferences for blacks in border states that, as elsewhere, allowed for ordination but denied resources and a role in the governance of the denomination to its members. Some progress was made when the church eliminated those constraints in 1868. The church retained an office, however, first created in 1856, known as a missionary bishop. The church had elected two African Americans to that office to give leadership to the church's missions in Liberia. Unlike other bishops, missionary bishops only presided over their limited field. This limitation allayed fears of white Methodists that they might have to submit to the authority of a black bishop. Since 1875, the position of missionary bishop for Africa had remained open, and by the 1880s, with a growing African American constituency, some Methodist Episcopal leaders were eager to elect another African American to that post.[149]

Interest in a new bishop for Africa also grew out of a renewed interest among Protestants in missionary outreach to Africa. Previous missionary endeavors had been hampered by the presence of tropical diseases, but new medical advances minimized such concerns. The exploits of Western explorers brought new regions of the so-called "dark continent" to light. Western nations began to map imperial designs onto these regions. Both white and black Protestants hoped for new energy and leadership for African missions.[150]

Taylor's speech to that effect at the General Conference and in favor of a new bishop for Africa most likely secured his nomination for the position. He called for an aggressive mission in Africa that not only would make efforts that already existed in Liberia a success but was expansive. He thought the church could draw on African American interest in Africa and send black men who had been educated in church schools as missionaries. Untroubled by threats of disease that had limited African missions in the past, Taylor insisted a bishop who worked hard, exercised, and ate well "would sweat the malaria out of him."[151]

When nominations for a missionary bishop for Africa opened, Curry proposed Joshua E. Wilson, an African American preacher from South Carolina. J. C. Hartzell, the corresponding secretary of the Freedmen's Aid Society who would replace Taylor as bishop in Africa, nominated another African

American, Marshall W. Taylor. Other names were also advanced, but when William Olin nominated William Taylor, the mood of the body shifted. His name was seconded from all parts of the room. Wilson's supporters unsuccessfully called into question William Taylor's eligibility to be a bishop since he was now a layman. Citing health concerns, Marshall Taylor withdrew his name. Wilson followed suit, and the balloting proceeded.[152]

Taylor's mistrust of church leaders was such that he initially believed his nomination was a plot to "interfere" with his missions in India and South America. He was assured, however, that was not the intention of the nominator. Taylor received 250 votes of 353, well over the 177 needed for election. Whatever conflicts Taylor had with church leaders, he was clearly a highly popular figure. He was well-known throughout the church, and may have met many of the delegates who voted for him on his tours around the United States. In addition, unlike other candidates, he was white. Dennis Osborne, one of Taylor's Anglo-Indian converts who had become a preacher, and Marshall Taylor escorted him to the platform where he was consecrated bishop.[153]

When the conference reconvened the following day, Taylor was invited to join the other bishops on the dais. He responded that, as a missionary bishop, he was only a bishop when in Africa. In Philadelphia, he was still a lay delegate from South India. Taylor expressed his thanks for the offer and promised that if "any Bishop visited him . . . in Africa he would reciprocate the courtesy."[154] Taylor's action was a clever one. It made him appear gracious and humble, while also clearly asserting his authority. The message conveyed was that any bishops to visit Africa would be welcomed out of politeness, but Africa was his charge.

AFRICAN BEGINNINGS

In the 1850s the Scottish missionary and explorer David Livingstone crossed Africa to scout out locations for a chain of mission stations. He hoped introducing Christianity and mapping African river systems for commerce would halt the African slave trade. Years later, Henry Morton Stanley's search for Livingstone became a sensational event avidly followed in America and Europe. With the words, "Dr. Livingstone, I presume?" Stanley joined the object of his search as a famed African explorer.[155]

Western knowledge of Africa was mediated through such accounts. Livingstone's story and Stanley's search sparked a great deal of Protestant interest in missions to Central Africa. Such accounts also aided European imperial expansion, and in the 1880s European powers began to assert control over previously independent regions of Africa, a process sometimes called the "Scramble for Africa." Indeed, Stanley's racist description of Central

Africa as a "forgotten and unpeopled country" well served European imperial designs.[156]

There was little in such a description as Stanley's, however, to attract Taylor's interest as a newly consecrated missionary bishop. There were no converts to be found in an unpopulated land. But shortly after Taylor's election, German explorers Hermann von Wissmann and Paul Pogge described finding the "Bashilange" country near the source of the Kasai River, about 1,000 miles east of Loanda, Angola. Taylor thought a large, well developed society such as this promised would be able to support his missionaries, and he decided this region would be his missionary objective. It promised, in Taylor's words, "a dense population, with large towns and fruitful fields approaching high up toward the standard of civilized life."[157]

Taylor returned to the task of missionary recruitment, this time for Africa. He consulted John Franklin Goucher, a leader in Methodist missions and higher education, for recommendations. He may have also hoped for a contribution toward the start of a new mission in Africa. Goucher and his wife, Mary, were generous contributors to Methodist mission work in Asia.[158] Taylor initially sought strong, healthy men who possessed the requisite faith— "men of good constitution, not corpulent men, but wirey & tough, sound Methodist men, wholly consecrated to God, who will feel it an honor to die for Jesus in Central Africa, if the Lord shall so order"—they could be white or black but would need to have construction and trade skills, since they would build pioneer settlements.[159]

Taylor quickly found two such young men in William Summers and Heli Chatelain. Summers was a Guernsey-born, former circus magician, Salvation Army evangelist, and student at Pennington Seminary in New Jersey. In 1881, he heard of Dwight L. Moody's Northfield conferences and sold portraits of the recently assassinated President Garfield to earn passage to New Haven. From there he walked along the Connecticut River to the conference and became convinced God wanted him to become a medical missionary in Central Africa. Through the New York Medical Missionary Society, he met Chatelain, a similarly entrepreneurial Swiss immigrant who wanted to become a medical missionary to Madagascar. Chatelain was fluent in several European languages. The friends worked as janitors to support themselves in school. Pennington's principal introduced Taylor to Summers who introduced Taylor to Chatelain. The friends agreed to join the new mission and were commissioned to go to Europe to gather the latest knowledge of Africa.[160]

Taylor's preference for young, single men quickly faded. Because the primary qualification for missionary success—sanctification—was available to all believers, almost anyone could become a missionary. Dr. Mary R. Myers became celebrated among Taylor's supporters for convincing him to accept women as missionaries to Africa.[161] Women became essential to the mission, and few barriers existed to participation. In 1887, Taylor enlisted an African American woman, Susan Angeline Collins, to serve in the Congo.[162] In 1890, Taylor declared that women managed the hardest missionary stations in Africa, and he was quoted as saying, "When I find a field too hard for a man, I put in a woman."[163]

Taylor's first missionary party to Africa also expanded to include children. Eleven-year-old Herbert Withey met Taylor at a camp meeting in 1884. He and his three sisters often play-acted Stanley's search for Livingstone.[164] Their father, Amos, was a Methodist evangelist in Lynn, Massachusetts, but the children's interest was a decisive factor in the family's decision to enlist with Taylor. Their mother, Irene, did not want to be a missionary. She became convinced, however, that God wanted her children to be missionaries and that she had to submit to God's will.[165] Taylor accepted the Witheys and five other families—with seventeen children among them—as missionaries in his first party. For Taylor, these children were not incidental additions to the enterprise but essential members.[166] Taylor had consistently advocated that children were spiritual agents and responsible to God for their own salvation and that of others. Taylor issued the children, just as the adults, certificates identifying them as his missionaries.[167] Taylor was especially proud that his son Ross, his wife, Ada, and his four grandchildren, the youngest only weeks old, joined the mission.[168]

In late 1884, when this pioneer band had been selected, Taylor left for Europe to arrange for provisions. He expected it would take some time for his mission to become self-supporting, and made sure his party would be well supplied with food, trade goods, tools, a printing press, a portable canvas boat, rifles, and specially printed Bibles.[169] Taylor, Summers, and Chatelain reunited in London at the home of William Arthur.[170]

To manage this enterprise, Taylor needed money and administrative support but stubbornly refused to deal with the Missionary Board.[171] Accordingly, Taylor's ad hoc administrative committee was incorporated as "The Transit and Building Fund Society of Bishop William Taylor's Self-Supporting Missions" and given responsibility to raise money to supply and send missionaries to India and South America and Africa while Taylor was overseas, but the society was prohibited from using its funds to pay either missionary salaries or domestic agents.[172] Missionary salaries were to come from the local economy. For other needs, the society solicited contributions. These came in from a number of sources. Bishop Simpson's widow gave $52 to buy a tent as a memorial to her husband. In Berlin, Summers and Chatelain preached at a small German Methodist church that offered a collection. Some of Taylor's friends in Sydney, Australia, sent £97.[173]

Although Taylor devoted most of his time since becoming bishop to starting a new central African mission, as Bishop of Africa Taylor had one clear

Figure 5.1 Photo and Missionary Cards of Lottie May, Mary Estella, and Florence Steele Withey. W. S. Matthew Papers, California-Nevada Conference Archives, Pacific School of Religion, Berkeley, CA. *Source:* Used with the permission of the Archives of the California-Nevada Annual Conference of The United Methodist Church.

responsibility: to provide episcopal leadership to the Liberia Conference. The origins of the Methodist Episcopal Church in Liberia were closely tied to the American Colonization Society and mixed desires to provide a home for freed American blacks outside of the United States and hopes that the colony might lead to the conversion of Africans to Christianity.[174] As the debate over new episcopal leadership for Liberia indicated, however, in America the Liberian mission was generally considered a failure.

Taylor arrived in Monrovia a week before that annual conference was scheduled to meet. He held twice daily revival services in Monrovia and, after the conference, led revivals at Cape Palmas and Grand Bassa County. In total, he preached almost sixty times on his month long visit to Liberia.[175] Despite a few attempts at missions to native Africans, the Methodist Episcopal Church in Liberia was dominated by Americo-Liberians whose ancestors had emigrated from the American south. They brought their religion with them, and Taylor found worship styles in Liberia very familiar to those he remembered from his youth.[176] He wrote that those converted in his revivals "all took it in the old way—awful screaming and crying for pardon, and when saved shouted all over the house, and all through the streets."[177] Taylor even met some of the slaves inherited by his wife and her siblings whom he had manumitted.[178]

Although Taylor felt a spiritual kinship with the Liberian Methodists, he did not navigate the racial and cultural dynamics of the context well. Many white missionaries in Liberia failed to respect Americo-Liberians as free people.[179] Taylor seemed to fall into the same pattern. When the African Methodist Episcopal Bishop Henry McNeal Turner visited Liberia in 1891, he offered praise for Taylor. His congregation, however, shared their opinion that Taylor "realizes himself as white, and does not fail to let them know it."[180]

Taylor was aided somewhat in navigating these waters by the African American evangelist Amanda Berry Smith. On several occasions in Liberia, Smith mediated between Taylor and black leaders. She was a former slave, but following her experience of entire sanctification, Smith quickly rose to become a prominent speaker in the holiness movement. She traveled Europe and India before going to Liberia in 1882. Smith was an ardent supporter of Taylor but had hoped for a black man to be elected bishop. Nevertheless, she noted Taylor's skin color did aid the expansion of African missions in ways that may not have been possible with a black bishop. Steamships transported Taylor and those with him when they would not carry those with black skin.[181]

On a return visit to Liberia in 1886, Taylor would expand the work there. He established an "industrial school farm" on 1,000 acres near Setta Kru. It was both to teach Africans trades and to support his missionaries. Since Taylor now prioritized the economic foundations of missionary work, he established such missions as he had in South America—by contracting with local leaders to provide financial support for his missionaries. As Taylor described the process, he met with an African chief and explained that he would provide ministers, teachers, and equipment to start a school. In exchange, the chief would prepare 1,000 acres of land, build houses and a school and pay a monthly tuition for schoolchildren. This quick and easy process allowed Taylor to claim by 1892 that he had established forty mission stations in Africa, twenty-four in Liberia, and the rest in Central Africa.[182]

In 1885, however, Taylor just used the Liberia Conference as an administrative base for a new expansion into in Central Africa. Taylor added the ordained members of his missionary party, and other men he would later ordain, to the membership of that conference, and he appointed them "missionaries in South Central Africa."[183] In 1888, the Liberia Conference would be changed to the Africa Conference to better encompass the scope of the missions that existed throughout the continent.[184]

CENTRAL AFRICA

Taylor's first band of missionaries to Africa left America in early 1885. In a practice that became a tradition with later parties, just before their departure they participated in a weeklong "Holiness Convention" at a Methodist church in the New York area. The missionaries gave testimonies linking experiences of entire sanctification and missionary call. For example, Henry McKinley of Raymore, Missouri, declared he would go to Africa because, "I am not ashamed of the Gospel of Christ, or of the doctrine of Holiness. I have been cleansed from all sin, and I cannot help speaking of the things I know."[185]

Lowrey was instrumental in these events, and his involvement marked a theological shift among the missionaries associated with Taylor. Taylor always interrogated potential missionaries about their sanctification using language rooted in Phoebe Palmer's theology of personal sacrifice and submission to God's will. Lowrey, however, employed theological language more common in the turn-of-the-century holiness movement and early Pentecostalism that described empowerment from the Holy Spirit. Lowrey called the first convention a "Pentecostal preparation for the missionaries."[186] Before the second group of twenty-three missionaries was sent to Africa in 1886, he invited guests to experience "the descent of the tongues of fire and the enduement [sic] of power."[187] The first question Lowrey asked missionary candidates was, "Do you trust you are moved by the Holy Ghost to take upon you the work of a foreign missionary?"[188] All of the "Taylor" missionaries who became first-generation Pentecostals, such as Willis C. and May Hilton Hoover in Chile and Samuel J. and Ardella Mead in Africa, were recruited by Lowrey.[189]

Interest in the mission was so broad that although Lowrey interviewed applicants, it was generally understood and celebrated that almost anyone who had found entire sanctification could become a missionary to Africa. As the *Christian Standard* opined: "That young lady who was rejected by a Missionary Board because she declared 'the blood of Christ cleanseth from all sin,' would doubtless be welcomed to Bishop Taylor's work. That is the kind he wants."[190] The second party sent to Africa would include a former slave, J. L. Judson, mechanics, farmers, surveyors, a school teacher, and a woman named Mary A. Clift. Clift had not been invited to join the mission but heard of it and traveled to New York from Iowa for that purpose. Two men exchanged their tickets for steerage passage and collections were taken to pay her way.[191] In a sign that perhaps Taylor was more judicious in his missionary selection than Lowrey allowed and Taylor's critics alleged, soon after she arrived in Africa, Taylor sent Clift home.[192]

Taylor was also known to collect new missionaries along the way. Several Liberians expressed an interest in joining his mission to Central Africa. Taylor initially deferred such requests, preferring they remain in Liberia. At some point, however, he relented, and a man named Henry Kelly joined the missionary band. At Gabon, a man from the Cape Coast named Albert Arthur, who had been educated in Wesleyan Methodist missions, joined the party. Europeans were welcome, too. A German merchant converted at worship onboard ship, Carl Steckelmann, enlisted with the mission. For various reasons, none of these individuals remained with the mission long, but for now the missionary enthusiasm was infectious.[193]

Taylor and his first missionary band reunited off the coast of Liberia and together they continued to Angola.[194] His presence with the group was a mixed blessing. On one hand, it allowed for flexible responses to new opportunities. For example, a merchant on the ship encouraged Taylor to open a mission at Mayumba, Gabon. When the ship stopped there Taylor dispatched Henry M. Willis, his wife Annie and child, Fred B. Northam, and Steckelman.[195] Taylor repeated this pattern other times in his episcopacy. In 1886, when the ship carrying Taylor and his second party called at Kabinda, Judson woke Taylor at night, convinced that God wanted him there. "Without taking time to put on my pantaloons," Taylor wrote, he appointed Judson and two other men to Kabinda.[196] Taylor thought this nimble adjustment to opportunity, or the Holy Spirit's leading, was a great thing. With himself as bishop in Africa, God would not have to wait for a yearly meeting of the Missionary Board on the other side of the world, or even pants, to start a new mission. The cost of this flexibility was that rather than developing a plan and sticking with it through persistence or institutional inertia, Taylor constantly moved on to what seemed to be the next great opportunity. Like those in South America, Taylor's Africa missionaries would complain of his inconstancy.[197]

The missionaries reached Loanda in March 1885. Summers and Chatelain had preceded them to rent a twenty room house. Although Taylor hoped to set off toward the Bashilange country immediately, Chatelain reported the Portuguese colonial governor was willing to offer land grants for mission stations. While Taylor and the missionaries waited for the governor, they established daily routines and formal structures of a Methodist church in Angola. Taylor officially organized a church made up of the lay missionaries and held a mass baptism of the unbaptized missionary children.[198] Everyone rose together and met for meals. Children had daily religious instruction, while the adults learned Portuguese and phonetics. He called together the clergy in the party and declared it to be a District Conference—"the germ of future conferences" that would one day extend from the Atlantic to the Indian Ocean.[199] Taylor embraced Livingstone's dream of crossing Africa with mission stations as his own.

Phonetics was Taylor's latest attempt to overcome the obstacle language presented to rapid evangelization. Developed by Isaac Pitman, the creator of English shorthand, it introduced new spellings of English words. Since Taylor did not expect to find English speakers in Central Africa to serve as interpreters, his missionaries would learn African languages while they taught English. As an article describing phonetics described,

> Bishop Taylor findz our English mōd ov speling wun ov the gratest drabaks in tēching the nativz; and also wun ov the grātist obstiklz in rēdūsing the native languajez to riting. Mishunarez evri whar have komplānd ov thēz difikultez. Bishop Taylor haz kut the Gordian not.[200]

Taylor believed phonetic writing would make it easier for mission students to learn English. The Bibles he brought for use in the mission were printed in this form.[201]

Figure 5.2 "First Party Loanda, 1885." *Source:* Angola Mission and Missionary Photos. Herbert Cookman Withey Collection, United Methodist Church Archives—GCAH, Madison, NJ.

While waiting, the group experienced two embarrassing setbacks. Four adults, including Taylor's son and family, returned home. Taylor bitterly lamented his son's decision and publicly stated it reflected poorly on his son's character.[202] Ross's involvement in African missions did not end here, however. In time he would take over parts of his father's missionary operations.

The second embarrassment was the death of Charles Miller. Although most of the party suffered from some illness in Africa, Miller believed in faith healing. He trusted that God would miraculously cure him, and refused medical treatment.[203] Taylor's opponents in America would seize on Miller's death as proof that his missionaries were unstable fanatics, but on this matter Taylor and his critics agreed. Taylor mourned Miller's death but also his theology. He thought the faith healing movement was a diabolical parasite within the holiness movement, where it had begun to flourish.[204] Taylor rejected faith healing for the same reason he advocated for self-supporting missions and told his missionaries to "root hog or die"; his understanding of faith always highlighted human agency. Missionaries must act while trusting God to provide. Taylor believed it was easy to remain healthy in Africa as long as missionaries took action with hard work, the use of quinine, healthy eating and drinking.[205]

When the Portuguese governor confirmed his willingness to grant the mission property, Taylor, Summers, and five other men set off on a several monthlong inland trek to select locations for six mission stations.[206] This trip introduced Taylor to two persistent and related economic problems that would hinder his missions in Central Africa and illustrated a limitation of his idea of self-support. For a missionary to find support in the local economy, it required full participation in the local economy. Since the height of the slave trade, alcohol had been a common item of trade in Angola, and it continued to be in high demand.[207] For Methodist missionaries, however, trade in alcohol violated a deeply held tenet of their faith that had only grown stronger following the Civil War. Missionaries found other trade items were less desirable. Without a medium of exchange, it was difficult to hire porters, and the mission was often stalled by the inability to move supplies.[208]

The persistence of slavery provided another option for finding labor. This too was not an option. Taylor's missionaries saw it as their religious duty to avoid entanglements with slavery and end the practice.[209] In 1887, Summers became the first of the missionaries to reach the Bashilange. He preached to the chief, Kasongo, and explained his desire to start a church. Kasongo welcomed Summers and offered to endow the church with land and slaves. Summers refused the gift of slaves, an action that seems to have confused the chief.[210]

For a mission that endeavored to support itself on the local economy and resist foreign aid, a principled refusal to use a predominant medium of exchange and a major source of labor was often an insurmountable obstacle. Missionaries found little demand for teaching. Some men Taylor stationed along rivers supported themselves by hunting hippopotami. Some of most persistent and enduring of Taylor's Africa missionaries, the Withey family regularly appealed to friends in America for help. By 1887, they had developed a substantial farm with 139 head of cattle, including twenty-one milk cows, with plans for a tannery and a small store.[211]

While Taylor was in Angola, Western diplomats met in Berlin to set new parameters for imperial expansion into Africa. Under the agreement, Angola was confirmed as a Portuguese colony, and the Congo River basin was designated the Free State of the Congo, under the control of King Leopold II of Belgium.[212] In late 1885, after receiving word of this decision, Taylor returned to Europe to call on the Portuguese king. En route, Taylor met both the European explorer Pierre De Brazza who told him of his explorations of the Congo River and Wissmann who told him more about the Kassai. These meetings convinced Taylor to create a new entry point at the Congo River and follow it to the Kassai as it turned south, rather than reinforcing the start already made in Angola and pushing east.[213] In Europe, he called on the royal palace in Lisbon for an audience with King Luis I, and met with Leopold II in Brussels, now that he had decided to start new missions on the Congo.[214]

Descriptions of Taylor's encounters with European royalty in Taylor's autobiography may have been revised to reflect a more positive opinion of European imperialism than Taylor's own. Those descriptions claimed that Taylor wanted nothing but "good will" from the monarchs and he "ever felt the benefit" of his interviews.[215] As will be noted, sources for Taylor's later career in Africa are suspect. A contemporary source indicated Taylor went to confront the Portuguese king on the persistence of slavery in Angola.[216] This agenda would be consistent with Taylor's democratic and populist orientation, his past opposition to slavery, and the problems his mission faced finding free labor. Taylor had not yet visited the Congo when he called on Leopold, and Leopold's genocidal exploitation of the Congo and its people to extract ivory and rubber was just beginning.[217] Confrontation would not have been on Taylor's agenda, but his Congolese mission would suffer from the meeting even before it began. Leopold promised free transport for Taylor's missionaries and their equipment on the river. Once he and his missionaries arrived in the Congo, however, Taylor learned that despite holding papers confirming this offer, Belgian colonial officials were ordered not to help him.[218]

The Sisyphean episode that followed showed again how dependent missionary expansion was on cheap and easy transportation. Encouraged by Leopold's offer, Taylor led his second band of missionaries to the Congo. He explored inland to Stanley Pool, but most of this band remained on the Lower Congo, unable to proceed upriver and around the 62 miles of cataracts without passage or porters. Taylor first decided he needed a boat, and he bought materials to build a schooner. Other missionaries advised him to get a steamship instead. English Baptists had one named for Taylor's late patron, Henry Reed.[219] Money was raised in America, and the *Anne Taylor,* was built in London, disassembled, and shipped to the Congo. Taylor appealed for missionaries with shipbuilding and sailing skills. Once delivered, however, there was still no way to get the disassembled ship past the cataracts. Taylor next proposed to draw the parts inland by a traction engine. While this machine was built in England, the missionaries made carts to be drawn by it, cleared and graded roads, and built bridges until halted by the start of the rainy season. The *Anne Taylor* only became usable over five years later, in 1892. It never made it to the Upper Congo.[220] This prolonged ordeal did yield the establishment of seven mission stations between the mouth of the Congo and Stanley Pool.[221]

Not all missionaries were as persistent as Taylor through that episode. A revealing example came from J. C. Waller. Converted at a Methodist church in New York, Waller enlisted to cook on the *Anne Taylor.* He thought life on the ship would provide food and shelter for his family and that through trade with Africans he could earn money to educate his children. By his life, Waller thought he could be "a good example" for Africans.[222] Whatever his hopes, Waller was informed that Taylor only committed to transporting his missionaries to Africa. After that, the bishop's advice was to "root hog or die."[223] The Waller family was delivered to the shores of the Congo and provided first a tent, and eventually a three-room adobe house. This Waller found unacceptable since it had a dirt floor and glassless windows. When his wife and children became ill, Waller asked Taylor to send them home. Taylor did so, and the family arrived in New York penniless.[224]

The return of this destitute missionary family became another small scandal. For some of Taylor's detractors, it was evidence illustrating Taylor's folly. Not everyone was completely sympathetic to Waller's experience, however. Other missionaries, such as Agnes McAllister and Clara Binkley, delivered by Taylor to Garraway, Liberia, in 1889, reported a similar experience and managed.[225] Even in America, the *Christian Advocate* noted, the Waller family's sufferings were "no harder than settlers in new countries have always had to endure."[226]

As this scandal illustrated, while Taylor was in Africa, a debate over his mission raged in America. His decision to take white women and children to Africa was denounced in the secular press, and *The New York Times* predicted the death of the entire party.[227] Many prominent Methodists tried to distance their church from Taylor to spare it embarrassment. An article in the *Christian Advocate* asserted that the church was only responsible for Taylor when he performed his official duties in Liberia. Anything he did elsewhere, he did as a private individual.[228] At the New York Preachers' meeting, Bishop Foster voiced his opposition to Taylor's expedition to Central Africa, and the body adopted a resolution declaring that it was not "apostolic or wise."[229]

The mass of people at less prominent levels of the Methodist Episcopal Church, however, saw Taylor as an epic hero. Prominent preachers in New York Methodism may have been ashamed of Taylor, but the Convention of Methodist Local Preachers, a gathering of laymen who preached at small, less prestigious churches, designated fifteen minutes of their agenda to pray for Taylor's mission to Africa.[230] One writer declared, "The march of Wm. Taylor and his little band of missionaries into the heart of Africa is the sublimest spectacle of modern times."[231] For their wiliness to die for a noble cause they were compared to the Greeks at Thermopylae, and it was predicted that if Taylor's band should die, "the church will chant in epic pentameters their vicarious heroism."[232] To capitalize on this interest, the Transit and Building Fund Society produced an engraving depicting a heroic Taylor, wide-brimmed hat in hand, standing in the African jungle.[233] Edward Davies published a biography of Taylor that surveyed his early life, described Taylor's election to the episcopacy, and reported on the early developments in Taylor's African missions.[234]

These conflicting opinions on the wisdom of Taylor's mission to Central Africa coalesced into a debate over his episcopal status and salary. The first salvo was fired when Taylor's name was omitted from the list of the church's bishops in the 1884 *Discipline* on the grounds that he had been elected a missionary bishop, and not to the regular episcopacy.[235] Curry, for example, argued church law identified two orders of bishops, regular and missionary, with the later exercising some episcopal responsibilities in limited jurisdictions. Curry also, with little subtlety, explained how one might use church law to charge Taylor with immoral conduct.[236] Taylor's defenders retorted with American, democratic, and Reconstruction era rhetoric on the equality of all people and the sanctity of elections. Future bishop J. W. Hamilton accused Taylor's detractors of seeking to undermine democratic processes that elected Taylor bishop, and he explicitly called out the racism implicit in some critiques of Taylor, "If men may be found who will say only little Bishops ought to go into Africa because the people are black, we simply want their names."[237]

Taylor did not mind being a missionary bishop until he learned that, as such, his salary would be paid by the Missionary Board. Taylor still refused any involvement with the Board and asked to be paid as other bishops were, by the Book Committee.[238] That committee refused, however, citing prior precedent.[239] This debate raged while Taylor was in Africa until 1887 when, in Liberia, Taylor found the aforementioned article by Curry. Offended, Taylor vowed that the next General Conference would resolve the issue of his episcopal status and salary.[240]

Figure 5.3 "Bishop William Taylor." *Source:* Angola Mission and Missionary Photos. Herbert Cookman Withey Collection, United Methodist Church Archives—GCAH, Madison, NJ.

When that conference met in 1888, opinion on Taylor's mission was still mixed. The Miller and Waller affairs gave his critics ammunition but neither did all his missionaries die. A few modest chains of mission stations had been established, but there had been no widespread revival. Taylor's popularity in the church remained unabated, and supporters from all over the country flooded the General Conference with petitions to resolve the issue of his episcopal status in his favor.[241]

The 1888 General Conference also became the first opportunity for Taylor to address his critics in public. Wounds from past conflicts had not healed, and tensions ran high. Taylor used his report to air his grievances stemming from the fateful 1882 meeting, review the status of missions in Liberia, Angola, and the Congo, argue for the legitimacy of self-supporting missions, and call for the adoption of the Transit Fund Committee as an agency of the church. Taylor here abandoned all claims to Pauline inspiration and declared that his missionary methods were those that had succeeded on the American frontier and would on the African frontier; they were those of "the pioneer founders of our Church in America, deep down in the shades of towering mountains and unbroken forests, in a continent of unknown boundaries, whose limits their field of vision could not exceed."[242]

The conference provided Taylor a small measure of vindication. It ruled that missionary bishops were full bishops, paid as others, and limited only by their jurisdiction. In addition, Thoburn was elected missionary bishop of India. The Transit Fund Committee was left as a separate organization from the church.[243]

ROSS TAYLOR

After 1888, Taylor's conflict with other church leaders gradually faded for no other reason than Taylor stopped fighting the battle. Instead his missionary operations became the source of internal turmoil and instability, with his son Ross at the center of that strife. The first step in that process came when the bishop returned to Africa in 1889. With no explanation, he placed his son in charge of American operations for Africa.[244] The following year, Taylor completely removed Africa from the responsibility of the Transit Fund Committee. He gave Ross power of attorney and designated a banker, S. A. Kean of Chicago, as treasurer for Africa. Problems surfaced almost immediately. Requests for disbursement went unpaid, and in December 1890, Kean's bank failed. The mission lost over $8,800 and lacked significant financial resources going forward.[245] The Transit Fund Committee continued to oversee the South American work without Taylor's help, and operated independently of the Methodist Episcopal Church until 1893 when the South American missions were organized as the Chile District of the South America Annual Conference. Over the subsequent years negotiations between the Transit and Building Fund and the Missionary Board eventually led to the transfer of all South American mission property to the Board.[246]

Taylor's launch of a magazine in January 1889 offered a second field of conflict. Taylor had sent out occasional circular letters to inform supporters of the status of his work, but a magazine could provide a regular, steady income from subscriptions and did not require personal promotion.[247] Taylor enlisted the Welch family of Vineland, New Jersey, for this project. Two decades earlier, Thomas B. Welch discovered pasteurization of grape juice prevented fermentation and offered it to Methodists as a nonalcoholic substitute for communion wine. Welch's son, Charles, was a friend of Chatelain and planned on joining Taylor's second party to Africa until poor health, family, and business commitments prevented him.[248] From January 1889 to April 1891, the Welch family published *The African News* from their home in Vineland, New Jersey. Like the missions themselves, the magazine was expected to be "self-supporting."[249] As with most serials of the time, the bulk of *The African News* was copy reprinted from other publications. Two unique, ongoing features, however, were contributions by Taylor—a monthly theological reflection and Taylor's own autobiography, published serially. Taylor's missionaries also offered letters describing their travel or missionary work.[250]

From the start, *The African News*, and its successor titles, existed under a cloud of charges and countercharges about its veracity and profitability. After one year of publication, Ross offered to relieve T. B. Welch of his editorial duties, claiming errors in the magazine. Soon, the offer became a demand, and he enlisted his father's help to get Welch to surrender the publication. Well after Welch complied, Ross Taylor accused the Welches of mismanagement and publishing misstatements. He claimed Welch undermined the bishop by depicting him as unwilling to take criticism and describing dissatisfaction among Taylor's missionaries. Welch admitted that the magazine did not meet its expenses, but argued that starting a new periodical was expensive. He believed he was forced out because Ross wanted to profit from the enterprise and the bishop was unhappy he reported on other Christian missions in Africa.[251] Furthermore, Welch doubted the *News* would be a reliable source of information under the bishop's son. As he wrote, "so I think the *African News* will likely now be used to give the sunny side of Bishop Taylor's Missions."[252] Time proved Welch correct.

Ross Taylor assumed publication of *The African News* in May 1891. Under his leadership, the magazine commercialized the bishop's fame. Its ads carried his explicit or implicit endorsement. Royal Baking Powder was approved as the only baking powder used by Taylor missionaries, because only Royal could be used in the African climate.[253] Taylor commended Bradbury Pianos as the instrument used in his South American schools.[254] In June 1894, the magazine was renamed *Illustrated Africa* and in July 1896 again renamed *Illustrated Christian World* until it closed publication in May 1898. Although William Taylor's name was always associated with these publications as the principal editor, and his picture was featured on the masthead, William Taylor's own contributions to the magazine were increasingly limited.[255]

Several other institutions arose in the 1890s that drew on Taylor as a source of inspiration. Although they carried his name, Taylor's involvement with them was minimal. The most lasting of these was Taylor University in Indiana. Taylor had visited the campus of Fort Wayne College during his prewar evangelistic tour. In 1890s, the National Association of Local Preachers renamed it after their hero, Taylor, but he had no formal role in the school.[256] Taylor played a small role in the development of the Union Missionary Training Institute, the brainchild of Lucy (Drake) Osborn. She had gone to India with Amanda Berry Smith. There she married one of Taylor's missionaries, William Osborn. When the couple returned to the United States, she opened a missionary training school in Niagara Falls.[257] Taylor helped relocate it to Brooklyn and arrange for a source of financial support. Some of his missionaries trained there.[258] There is no evidence that Taylor provided anything but a name to the short-lived Bishop William Taylor Tropical Training School that opened in Bridgetown, Barbados, in 1894.[259] Although Taylor lent his name to these institutions, such schools were a mark that a new era in the missionary movement had emerged.[260] Even the informal training these institutions offered was more than Taylor ever had himself.

Several historiographic problems, in addition to the unreliability of *The African News*, inhibit study of Taylor's later African episcopate. Although there are several errors in his evidence, historian David Bundy's central argument is sound.[261] As Ross Taylor assumed a greater role over his father's publishing business and enlisted other prominent figures such as Emil Holub and Henry Morton Stanley in the projects, Taylor's own voice and role became hard to identify, even in writing bearing his name. There were two books supposedly written by Taylor at this time: *Africa Illustrated: Scenes from Daily Life on the Dark Continent* (1895) and *The Flaming Torch in Darkest Africa* (1898). Bundy notes that one of these demonstrated knowledge of contemporary scholarship on Africa and would have required a dedication to research that Taylor had never before demonstrated as well as a more favorable perspective on European imperialism than was characteristic.[262] Bundy does not note that many of these later writings under Taylor's name were not autobiographical, as almost all of his previous writing had been. It is doubtful that the relentlessly self-promoting Taylor suddenly decided in his seventies to stop writing in the first person. Other articles under his name were often excerpts from his earlier books, indicating that Ross was mining his father's earlier writing for copy.[263]

There were a few episodes in Taylor's final years of ministry that revisited past concerns. His interest in the spiritual agency of children and desire to overcome language barriers surfaced in his celebration of the progress of "juvenile missionaries" in learning African languages. Amos Withey recalled Taylor's excitement when the Withey children translated for him in Angola.[264] An open attitude to non-Christian religions paired with a commitment to Christian evangelism in a sermon Taylor often delivered in his final years. He described ways non-Christians knew God and could be admitted into heaven, because such was not "God's highest ambition for humanity."[265] The task of Christian missions and evangelical preaching, Taylor declared, was to live "on the line of holiness, to develop the God-like power with which he has endowed us."[266]

The combination of excessive pride and humor that many thought inappropriate surfaced, as well. On a visit to Oregon, Taylor's host saw he wore a toupee. He advised that the bishop secure it during a particularly windy carriage ride. Taylor forcefully denied he wore a hairpiece. On another occasion, however, a missionary in Liberia, Charles Owens, recalled that Taylor enjoyed surprising Africans he met by casually removing his false hair and teeth in the course of conversation.[267] Taylor also remained eager to find new opportunities to expand his missions. Encouraged by Goucher to start a mission on the east coast of Africa, Taylor enlisted a returned American Board missionary, Erwin H. Richards, to go back to Portuguese East Africa, and use it as a base to start missions in Mashonaland.[268]

Some of these themes were present in Taylor's 1892 General Conference report. Unlike his bombastic tirade four years earlier, this time Taylor was winsome, hopeful, and engaging. He had mellowed, and one reporter described it as a typical "'William Taylor' address, . . . and what every person wishes to hear when he arises."[269] It was a sermon on the spiritual potential of African children. The climax of his message was his declaration "in the name of the Lord, that the countless millions of little children in Africa are not heathens, but are, in common with the children in Europe or America, the children of God."[270] He then electrified the body by introducing a three-year-old Grebo girl named Diana.[271] Originally named Tia Bralah, the girl's mother asked one of Taylor's Liberian missionaries, Elizabeth McNeil, to raise and educate her daughter. McNeil brought Diana to the United States to raise interest in African missions. Diana McNeil would grow up with her missionary parents in Liberia, Mozambique, and California, and became the first person of African descent to graduate from the University of Southern California.[272]

Although Taylor continued to travel to and from Africa, beginning in 1888, he began to show signs of declining physical and mental health.[273] The decline certainly accelerated following an incident in Rotterdam, on the night of October 7, 1891. The hotel manager where Taylor was staying heard a loud noise and found Taylor bleeding on the floor. Taylor recalled waking at night with pain in his face before passing out again. When Taylor finally regained consciousness, he found his face was bruised and bloody. With no memory of what happened, he concluded he fell while sleepwalking. Others drew more sinister conclusions and claimed Taylor had been attacked by a thief, but Taylor never did.[274] Confirming Welch's fear that *The African News* under Ross Taylor's direction would only print positive news, only the briefest note was made of the incident, celebrating Taylor's recovery.[275]

On Taylor's last official tour of Africa in December 1893, he was accompanied by his niece, Jennie Taylor. The daughter of Taylor's younger brother Andrew E. Taylor of Pennsylvania, Jennie graduated from Dickinson College, earned her MD from Women's Medical College in Philadelphia, and took further training as a dentist. In addition to providing any support and

Figure 5.4   Photo of "Diana" (or Bralah) and William Taylor. W. S. Matthew Papers, California-Nevada Conference Archives, Pacific School of Religion, Berkeley, CA. *Source:* Used with the permission of the Archives of the California-Nevada Annual Conference of The United Methodist Church.

care her uncle needed, she was also sent by the Methodist Missionary Board to provide dental care to Taylor's missionary families. As such, she was the first dental missionary. The fact that the bishop allowed his niece to be paid by the Missionary Board also revealed that Taylor was no longer fighting against the Board's involvement in his missions.[276]

Taylor and his niece traveled along the African coast, visiting missions and missionaries through most of 1894. He was in Ireland at the end of that year and made a short return to Africa in early 1895 before returning to New York in the spring of 1895.[277] A decade after declaring Taylor a menace, *The New York Times* now celebrated his return. "If ever there was a grand missionary," the paper declared, "Bishop Taylor is surely worthy of that distinction."[278] A reporter was dispatched to interview the bishop. Asked about his most recent trip, Taylor said,

> I have had a pretty long tour. I have encountered some trying experiences, but I do not think I feel any the worse for it. This is the fifth trip I have taken since I was made Bishop for Africa in 1884, and every journey has made me more deeply interested in Africa and more hopeful for its future. It is an enormous territory, and the missionary field is broad and difficult to cover; but the progress in the last ten years has been remarkable. Speaking for the Methodist mission, I can say that the Lord has richly blessed them.[279]

Taylor's response on that occasion could be applied to more than his most recent trip. He had traveled the world for most of his adult life. Few people in his day could claim to have seen as much of it as he had. It had been a long tour. Although Taylor had experienced his share of problems, some of them self-inflicted, he remained optimistic and buoyant. There were still new frontiers ahead, and he believed that blessed by God, missionary progress would continue. Taylor's role in that enterprise, however, was drawing to a close.

In the two decades since he returned to America, Taylor had become not only a representative of the Methodist missionary tradition but a force within it. He had recruited hundreds of new Methodist missionaries to serve in India, South America, and Africa. He had developed new fields for Methodist missions. Like Taylor himself, those missionaries had been motivated by a desire to reach all people with their gospel of God's salvation and doctrines of entire sanctification, though Taylor's articulation of sanctification as sacrifice differed from Asbury Lowrey's emerging notion of sanctification as empowerment. Taylor was both embraced by the late-century holiness movement and also struggled against theological shifts in it. This tension foreshadowed the emergence of Pentecostalism after Taylor's lifetime.

During this final period of Taylor's active life he was in conflict with many leaders of the Methodist Episcopal Church and the recipient of pointed critiques from Methodist voices. Such opposition might give a false impression that he no longer represented that tradition but was an eccentric rebel. This was not the case. Those conflicts and Taylor's role in them were, in fact, representative of core tensions in the Methodist missionary tradition. That tradition always celebrated both independent, entrepreneurial action following the Spirit's guidance and connected relationship among believers. Taylor often acted independently as he sought to follow God's will for him, but he was ultimately never willing to completely break from his church. Nor was his church ever willing to let him go. Taylor's independent, self-supporting initiatives were widely celebrated among Methodists. If voices were raised in critique, including those of his own missionaries, as was befitting a pragmatic Methodist missionary spirit, those complaints were usually practical in nature: "Self-supporting missions" in South America just didn't work, or missionaries to Africa would not survive. In the end, what else could be expected of a religious movement that worried simultaneously about what was practically possible while also wanting to count the entire world as its parish?

NOTES

1. "Letter from S. Moore Sites," *Heathen Woman's Friend*, September 1875.

2. Wm. Taylor to R. R. Lanahan, August 17, 1875, William Taylor Collection, Lovely Lane Museum and Archives; "Movements of Rev. William Taylor," *Christian Advocate*, August 19, 1875; "Missionary Items," *Christian Advocate*, January 13, 1876.

3. Isabelle Anne Kimberlin Taylor, "Isabel Anne Kimberlin Taylor's Travel Diary," in *Lessons of Infinite Advantage: William Taylor's California Experiences. With Isabelle Anne Kimberlin Taylor's Travel Diary, 1866–67, Written During a Voyage with Her Family En Route from the Cape of Good Hope, South Africa, to London and Subsequent Travels Throughout Europe,* ed. Robert F. Lay (Lanham: Scarecrow Press and The Center for the Study of World Christian Revitalization Movements, 2010), 269; Robert Ridgway to Anne Taylor, 26 June 1887, Division of Birds Records, RU 105, Box 1, vol. 3, Smithsonian Institution Archives.

4. "A Great Sacrifice," *Christian Standard*, November 11, 1882.

5. David Bundy, "Bishop William Taylor and Methodist Mission (Part 2)," *Methodist History* 28, no. 1 (1989): 20; Dana L. Robert, "Holiness and the Missionary Vision of the Woman's Foreign Missionary Society of the Methodist Episcopal Church," Ibid., 39, no. 1 (2000): 25–27; Melvin Easterday Dieter, *The Holiness Revival of the Nineteenth Century,* Second ed., Studies in Evangelicalism 1 (Lanham: Scarecrow Press, 1996), 79–89; Russell E. Richey, Kenneth E. Rowe, and Jean Miller Schmidt, *The Methodist Experience in America: A History* (Nashville: Abingdon Press, 2010), 247–8.

6. "Rev. Wm. Taylor," *Christian Standard*, September 30, 1876; "A Wonderful Book," Ibid., October 21, 1876.

7. William Taylor, *Ten Years of Self-Supporting Missions in India* (New York: Phillips & Hunt, 1882), 285.

8. William R. Hutchison, *Errand to the World: American Protestant Thought and Foreign Missions* (Chicago: University of Chicago Press, 1987), 91–93.

9. Sydney E. Ahlstrom, *A Religious History of the American People* (New Haven: Yale University Press, 1972), 733.

10. Hutchison, *Errand to the World*, 91–124.

11. Fanny Crosby, *Memories of Eighty Years: . . .* (Boston: James H. Earle, 1906), 140–1.

12. "Rev. Wm. Taylor," *Christian Standard*, March 29, 1879.

13. William Taylor, *Pauline Methods of Missionary Work* (Philadelphia: National Publishing Association for the Promotion of Holiness, 1879), 71–73.

14. William Taylor, *Our South American Cousins* (New York: Nelson and Phillips, 1878), 315–8; *Minutes of the Central Ohio Conference of the Methodist Episcopal Church, 1890* (Cleveland: Cleveland Printing & Publishing, 1890), 433–5; Taylor, *Pauline Methods*, 113–14.

15. Goodsil F. Arms, *History of the William Taylor Self-Supporting Missions in South America* (New York: Methodist Book Concern, 1921), 34.

16. Arms, *History of the William Taylor Self-Supporting Missions in South America*, 34–35.

17. "The Witnessing Church," *Christian Standard*, July 19, 1879; Wm. Taylor, "Letter from Rev. Wm. Taylor," Ibid., November 15, 1879; C. B. Ward, *Our Work* (Chicago: E.J. Decker, 1894), 19–34.

18. Taylor, *Ten Years*, 278–9.

19. Dana L. Robert, *American Women in Mission: A Social History of Their Thought and Practice* (Macon: Mercer University Press, 1997), 141–3.

20. Taylor, *Our South American Cousins*, 315; "Personal," *Christian Standard*, June 8, 1878; *Historical Register of Boston University, 1869–1891* (Boston: University Offices, 1891), 58; *Minutes of the Annual Conferences of the Methodist Episcopal Church, Spring Conferences of 1880* (New York: Phillips & Hunt, 1880), 88; *Minutes of the Annual Conferences of the Methodist Episcopal Church, Spring Conferences of 1882* (New York: Phillips & Hunt, 1882), 61; Wm. Taylor to President Hayes, October 23, 1879, Rutherford B. Hayes Papers, Manuscript Collection, Rutherford B. Hayes Presidential Center.

21. William A. Wright to Jennie Wright, February 1, 1878, copy of letter in a private collection.

22. *Historical Register*, 70.

23. Ibid., 74; Taylor, *Ten Years*, 482.

24. Wm Taylor, "The New Idea," *Christian Standard*, November 22, 1879.

25. Ward, *Our Work*, 11–12.

26. Ibid., 12.

27. "Letter from Rev. Wm. Taylor," *Christian Standard*, January 1, 1881; *Adelaide Whitfield LaFetra: A Teacher of Young Women* (Los Angeles: J. O. C. Class of the Bible School of the First Methodist Episcopal Church of Los Angeles, California), 37.

28. Arms, *History*, 60–61.

29. Taylor, *Ten Years*, 482–4.

30. O. von Barchwitz-Krauser, *Six Years with William Taylor in South* America (Boston: Published for the author by McDonald & Gill, 1885), 84–85.

31. Taylor, *Pauline Methods*, 95–96, 100.

32. "Mr. Waller's Statement, with Comments," *Christian Advocate*, January 19, 1888; Arms, *History of the William Taylor*, 49; Mrs. C. B. Ward to Bishop W. J. Oldham, December 10, 1912, Missionary Files: Methodist Episcopal Church, 1912–1949 (misfies), United Methodist Church Archives—GCAH, Madison, NJ.

33. Alvyn Austin, *China's Millions: The China Inland Mission and Late Qing Society, 1832–1905* (Grand Rapids: William B. Eerdmans' Publishing, 2007), 18.

34. Wade Crawford Barclay, *History of Methodist Missions: Early American Methodism, 1769–1844: Missionary Motivation and Expansion*, History of Methodist Missions 1 (New York: Board of Missions and Church Extension of the Methodist Church, 1949), 344–7; *Minutes of the Annual Conferences of the Methodist Episcopal Church, for the Year 1876*, vol. 16 (New York: Nelson & Phillips, 1876), 361.

35. Robert W. Sledge, *"Five Dollars and Myself": The History of Mission of the Methodist Episcopal Church, South, 1845–1939*, vol. 2 (New York: General Board of Global Ministries, United Methodist Church, 2005), 217–26.

36. "Missionary Items," *Missionary Advocate*, September 1876.

37. J. A. Swaney to Bishop M. Simpson, September 13, 1876, Box 10, Matthew Simpson Papers, Library of Congress.

38. J. A. Swaney, Account of the Beginnings of the Work in South America, Papers of Bishop John McKendree Springer, United Methodist Church Archives—GCAH; William Taylor, *Pauline Methods of Missionary Work* (Philadelphia: National Publishing Association for the Promotion of Holiness, 1879), 46.

39. David L. Bundy, "The Legacy of William Taylor," *International Bulletin of Missionary Research* 18, no. 4 (1994): 173.

40. Wm. Taylor to Rev. Bishop Simpson, October 9, 1877, Box 11, Matthew Simpson Papers, Library of Congress.

41. Ibid.

42. Ibid.; See also Wm. Taylor to Rev. Bishop Simpson, September 25, 1877, Box 11, Matthew Simpson Papers, Library of Congress.

43. Peter Feinman, "William Taylor in Chile: A Methodist Missionary Case Study (1877–1903)," *Methodist History* 47, no. 2 (2009): 88.

44. Taylor, *Our South American Cousins*, 180.

45. Ibid., 286–7.

46. R. B. Hayes to William Taylor, October 8, 1877, Rutherford B. Hayes Papers, Manuscript Collection, Rutherford B. Hayes Presidential Center.

47. Jean-Piere Bastian, "Protestantism in Latin America," in *The Church in Latin America, 1492–1992*, ed. Enrique Dussel, A History of the Church in the Third World 1 (Tunbridge Wells: Burns & Oates, 1992), 314–25; Frederick B. Pike, "Church and State in Peru and Chile Since 1840: A Study in Contrasts," *American Historical Review* 73, no. 1 (1967): 31–34; Hubert Clinton Herring and Helen Baldwin Herring, *A History of Latin America from the Beginnings to the Present*, Third ed. (New York: Alfred A. Knopf, 1968), 652; Howard J. Wiarda and Harvey F. Kline, "The Pattern of

Historical Development," in *Latin American Politics and Development*, ed. Howard J. Wiarda and Harvey F. Kline (Boulder: Westview Press, 1985), 24–25; Donald E. Worcester and Wendell G. Schaeffer, *The Growth and Culture of Latin America*, vol. 2 (New York: Oxford University Press, 1956), 182–4.

48. Taylor, *Our South American Cousins*, 261–5.

49. Swaney, Account; Taylor, *Our South American Cousins*, 17–20, 24–25.

50. Taylor, *Our South American Cousins*, 98.

51. Swaney, Account.

52. Taylor, *Our South American Cousins*, 96–99.

53. Ibid., 113–30.

54. Ibid., 182.

55. Ibid., 233.

56. Ibid., 237–42.

57. Ibid., 296–7.

58. Ibid., 161–7.

59. Ibid., 171.

60. Ibid., 149–52.

61. Ibid., 93–96.

62. Ibid., 116–18.

63. Ibid., 128–9; 237–40.

64. Ibid., 257.

65. Ibid., 153–6.

66. Ibid., 157.

67. Ibid.

68. Juan B. A. Kessler, Jr., *Conflict in Missions: A History of Protestantism in Peru and Chile* (Denver: iAcademic Books, 2001), 41–45.

69. Taylor, *Our South American Cousins*, 304.

70. Paul William Harris, *Nothing But Christ: Rufus Anderson and the Ideology of Protestant Foreign Missions* (New York: Oxford University Press, 1999), 112–32; Wilbert R. Shenk, *Henry Venn—Missionary Statesman* (Maryknoll: Orbis Books, 1983), 44–46.

71. Taylor, *Pauline Methods*, 42.

72. Ibid., 43–44; J. M. Thoburn, *My Missionary Apprenticeship* (New York: Phillips & Hunt, 1884), 386.

73. Arms, *History*, 35–37; Taylor, *Pauline Methods*, 51–52.

74. Jay Riley Case, *An Unpredictable Gospel: American Evangelicals and World Christianity, 1812–1920* (New York: Oxford University Press, 2012), 148.

75. Taylor, *Ten Years*, 305–6; Wm. Taylor, "India, South America," *Christian Standard*, September 7, 1878, "Contributions for the Rev. Wm. Taylor's Missions," Ibid., September 14, 1878.

76. Taylor, *Pauline Methods*, 166–78.

77. Ibid., 177; Edward J. M. Rhoads, *Stepping Forth into the World: The Chinese Educational Mission to the United States, 1872–81* (Hong Kong: Hong Kong University Press, 2011), 89–93; Joseph H. Sawyer, "Religious Intelligence: The Chinese Christian Home Mission," *The Independent*, July 5, 1894; "Letters from the Children," *Christian Standard*, January 18, 1879; Taylor, *Pauline Methods*, 177.

78. Taylor to Simpson, September 25, 1877; Taylor to Simpson October 9, 1877.

79. Taylor, *Ten Years*, 360–78.

80. Wm. Taylor to Bishop Simpson, June 16, 1878, Matthew Simpson Collection, Drew University Methodist Collection.

81. Certificate Commissioning Alexander T. Jeffrey, 1878, Alexander T. Jeffrey Papers, General Commission on Archives and History The United Methodist Church.

82. Wade Crawford Barclay, *The Methodist Episcopal Church, 1845–1939: Widening Horizons, 1845–95*, History of Methodist Missions 3 (New York: Board of Missions of The Methodist Church, 1957), 40–44, 115–19; William McGuire King, "Denominational Modernization and Religious Identity: The Case of the Methodist Episcopal Church," in *Perspectives on American Methodism: Interpretive Essays*, ed. Russell E. Richey, Kenneth E. Rowe, and Jean Miller Schmidt (Nashville: Kingswood Books, 1993), 349; Russell E. Richey, "Denominations and Denominationalism: An American Morphology," in *Reimagining Denominationalism: Interpretive Essays*, ed. Robert Bruce Mullin and Russell E. Richey, Religion in America (New York: Oxford University Press, 1994), 84–87.

83. Taylor, *Ten Years*, 360–78.

84. Wm. Taylor, "Pauline Methods of Missionary Work," *Christian Standard*, December 14, 1878; Ibid., December 21,1878; Ibid., December 28, 1878; Ibid., January 4, 1879; Ibid., January 11, 1879; Ibid., January 18, 1879; Ibid., January 25, 1879; Ibid., February 1, 1879; Ibid., March 15, 1879; Ibid., March 22, 1879; Ibid., March 29, 1879; Ibid., April 5, 1879; Ibid., April 12, 1879; Ibid., April 19, 1879.

85. Bundy, "Legacy," 173–4.

86. Taylor, *Pauline Methods*, 3.

87. Ibid., 4.

88. Ibid., 4–5.

89. Ibid., 5.

90. Ibid., 6.

91. Ibid., 7.

92. Wm. Taylor to President Hayes, July 2, 1879, Taylor to Hayes, October 23, 1879, Wm. Taylor to President Hayes, December 17, 1879, Wm. Taylor to President Hayes (March 1880), Wm. Taylor to President Hayes (June 1880), Wm. Taylor to President Hayes, November 8, 1880, James P. Gilliland to R. B. Hayes, August 29, 1879, Rutherford B. Hayes Papers, Manuscript Collection, Rutherford B. Hayes Presidential Center.

93. Wm. Taylor, "Letter from Rev. Wm. Taylor," *Christian Standard*, May 15, 1880; David I. Durham, *A Southern Moderate in Radical Times: Henry Washington Hilliard, 1808–1892* (Baton Rouge: Louisiana State University Press, 2008), 166–96; David I. Durham and Paul M. Pruitt, *A Journey in Brazil: Henry Washington Hilliard and the Brazilian Anti-Slavery Society* (Tuscaloosa: Bounds Law Library, University of Alabama School of Law, 2008), 41.

94. Wm. Taylor, "Letter from Rev. Wm. Taylor," June 19, 1880; Ibid., September 11, 1880; Justus H. Nelson, "Our New Work in Brazil," Nelson, Justus H., Mission Biographical Reference files, 1880s–1969, United Methodist Church Archives - GCAH; *Zion's Herald & Wesleyan Journal*, July 29, 1880; Wm. Taylor to President Hayes, June 28, 1880, Rutherford B. Hayes Papers, Manuscript Collection.

95. Taylor to Hayes, November 8, 1880; "Personal," *Christian Standard*, September 18, 1880.

96. "Personals," *Christian Advocate*, September 9, 1880; William Taylor, *Letters to a Quaker Friend on Baptism* (New York: Phillips & Hunt, 1880), 3–4.

97. Karen B. Westerfield Tucker, *American Methodist Worship*, Religion in America (New York: Oxford University Press, 2001), 99–100.

98. Dieter, *Holiness Revival*, 89–101.

99. Ibid., 108–10; William Kostlevy, "Lowrey, Asbury," in *Historical Dictionary of the Holiness Movement*, ed. William Kostlevy, Historial Dictionaries of Religions, Philosophies, and Movements 98 (Lanham: Scarecrow Press, 2009), 186.

100. "Letter from the Rev. Wm. Taylor, *Christian Standard*, July 10, 1880; "Letter from the Rev. Wm. Taylor," *Christian Advocate*, July 29, 1880.

101. Taylor, *Ten Years*, 448–9, David Bundy, "Bishop William Taylor and Methodist Mission: A Study in Nineteenth Century Social History (Part 2)," *Methodist History* 28, no. 1 (1989): 5; David Bundy, "Legacy," 173. Case, *Unpredictable Gospel*, 125–55.

102. "Missionary Breakfast," *Christian Advocate*, December 19, 1872.

103. "Our Church Work in India," *Christian Advocate*, April 10, 1873.

104. J. M. Reid, *Missions and Missionary Society of the Methodist Episcopal Church*, 2 vols., vol. 2 (New York: Phillips & Hunt, 1879), 248, 254

105. *Christian Standard*, October 5, 1878; "Maine Conference," *Zion's Herald*, May 8, 1879.

106. *Journal of the General Conference of the Methodist Episcopal Church, . . . 1880* (New York: Phillips & Hunt, 1880), 408.

107. "Rev. Wm. Taylor and India Missions," *Methodist Quarterly Review*, April 1877.

108. "Rev. W. Taylor on Missions," *Northern Christian Advocate*, May 29, 1873.

109. Taylor, *Ten Years*, 448–9; "Gracey vs. Taylor," *Christian Advocate*, June 5, 1873; Barclay, *Widening Horizons*, 464, 534.

110. Arms, *History*, 73.

111. Ibid., 51–52.

112. Lee F. Tuttle, "World Methodist Conferences," in *The Encyclopedia of World Methodism*, ed. Nolan B. Harmon, Albea Godbold, and Louise L. Queen (Nashville, TN: The United Methodist Publishing House, 1974), 2600–1.

113. *Proceedings of the Œcumenical Methodist Conference, Held in City Road Chapel, London, September, 1881* (Cincinnati: Walden and Stowe, 1882), 483.

114. *Proceedings of the Œcumenical Methodist Conference*, 487.

115. Ibid.

116. Bundy, "Legacy," 173, 175.

117. David Carter, *James H. Rigg* (Peterborough: Foundery Press, 1994), 23–24.

118. "General Missionary Committee." *Christian Advocate*, November 15, 1882; *Proceedings*, 492–7.

119. Taylor, *Ten Years*, 426.

120. *Proceedings*, 495; Methodist missionaries in India later passed a resolution repudiating Rigg as well. C. P. Hard, "Kind Words at Moradabad," *Christian Advocate*, April 6, 1882.

121. "Annual Meeting of the General Missionary Committee," *Christian Advocate*, November 10, 1881; "Meeting of the General Missionary Committee," *Zion's Herald*, November 17, 1881.

122. "Letter from the Rev Wm. Taylor," *Christian Advocate*, February 9, 1882; Taylor, *Ten Years*, iii.

123. William Taylor, *Four Years' Campaign in India* (London: Hodder and Stoughton, 1875), 150–67; Taylor, *Pauline Methods*, 1–36.

124. Taylor, *Ten Years*, 92–116.

125. Ibid., 426–7.

126. Ibid., 392, 431.

127. Ibid., 52.

128. Ibid., 55.

129. "Our Book Table," *Zion's Herald*, September 13, 1882.

130. "Literature," *Christian Advocate*, August 31, 1882.

131. Timothy L. Smith, *Called Unto Holiness: The Story of the Nazarenes: The Formative Years* (Kansas City: Nazarene Publishing House, 1962), 38–41.

132. Autograph cards dated January 5, 1880 and April 6, 1882, Box 1, Folder 11, Bishop William Taylor Collection, Taylor University Archives, Upland, IN.

133. *Mount Union College Alumni Catalogue, 1926* (Alliance: N.p., 1926), 49; *Christian Standard*, July 5, 1884.

134. Donald W. Dayton, "From 'Christian Perfection' to the 'Baptism of the Holy Ghost'," in *Perspectives on American Methodism: Interpretive Essays*, ed. Russell E. Richey, Kenneth E. Rowe and Jean Miller Schmidt (Nashville: Kingswood Books, 1993), 295–6; Timothy L. Smith, *Called Unto Holiness: The Story of the Nazarenes* (Kansas City: Nazarene Publishing House, 1962), 38–39.

135. *Minutes of the Annual Conferences of the Methodist Episcopal Church, Spring Conferences of 1880*, 89; Wm. Taylor, "Letter from Rev. Wm. Taylor," *Christian Standard*, June 18, 1881; Arms, *History*, 79.

136. "The General Missionary Committee," *Christian Advocate*, November 15, 1882.

137. Ibid.

138. "William Taylor and the Missionary Society," *Christian Advocate*, November 16, 1882.

139. "William Taylor and the Missionary Society"; Taylor, *Story of My Life*, 684, 687.

140. "Rev. Wm. Taylor," *Christian Standard*, May 31, 1884.

141. Taylor, *Story of My Life*, 687; Arms, *History*, 86.

142. Taylor, *Story of My Life*, 687.

143. Arms, *History*, 87.

144. Ibid., 86–90; Wm. Taylor to John F. Goucher, November 4, 1880, Series 5: Miscellaneous Countries, Box 15, John F. Goucher Papers, The Burke Library Archives, Columbia University Libraries; Taylor, *Ten Years*, 282–3.

145. Taylor, *Story of My Life*, 687.

146. Richey, Rowe, and Schmidt, *Methodist Experience*, 225–9.

147. "The General Conference: Synopsis of the Proceedings," *Christian Advocate*, May 29, 1884; *Journal of the General Conference of the Methodist Episcopal*

Church, . . . 1884 (New York: Phillips and Hunt, 1884), 102, 144, 210; *The Doctrines and Discipline of the Methodist Episcopal Church, 1884* (New York: Phillips & Hunt, 1884), 106–7, 280.

148. Sledge, *Five Dollars*, 23–28; Reginald F. Hildebrand, *The Times Were Strange and Stirring: Methodist Preachers and the Crisis of Emancipation* (Durham: Duke University Press, 1995), 15–27, 50–72, 101–18; Richey, Rowe, and Schmidt, *Methodist Experience*, 257–61.

149. Barclay, *The Methodist Episcopal Church, 1845–1939*, 171–4; James E. Kirby, *The Episcopacy in American Methodism* (Nashville: Kingswood Books, 2000), 178–81; Richey, Rowe, and Schmidt, *Methodist Experience*, 217–18.

150. Jay D. Green, "Africa Rediviva: Northern Methodism and the Task of African Redemption, 1885–1910" (Ph.D. diss., Kent State University, 1998), 182–3.

151. "The General Conference: Synopsis."

152. Ibid.; *Journal of the General Conference, . . . 1884*, 248; Taylor, *Story of My Life*, 695.

153. Taylor, *Story of My Life*, 692; *Journal of the General Conference, . . . 1884*, 248, 253.

154. "Bishop William Taylor," *Christian Advocate*, May 29, 1884.

155. Tim Jeal, *Stanley: The Impossible Life of Africa's Greatest Explorer* (New Haven: Yale University Press, 2007), 89–130, 159–215; Andrew Ross, *David Livingstone: Mission and Empire* (London: Hambledon and London, 2002), 82–119.

156. Lurton Dunham Ingersoll, ed., *Explorations in Africa, . . .* (Chicago: Union Publishing, 1872), 240.

157. Taylor, *Story of My Life*, 696.

158. Barclay, *Widening Horizons*, 134, 390, 421, 612.

159. Wm. Taylor to John F. Goucher, July 26, 1884, William Taylor Collection, Lovely Lane Museum and Archives.

160. George D. Dowkontt, *"Tell Them"; or, the Life Story of a Medical Missionary* (New York: Office of the Medical Missionary Record, 1898), 146–62.

161. "The Missionaries for Africa," *Christian Standard*, May 9, 1885; "The Taylor Band," Ibid., February 27, 1886.

162. Jan B. Van Buren, "Susan Angeline Collins Rediscovered: The First African American Missionary in Angola" (paper presented at United Methodist Women's History: Voices Lost and Found conference, Delaware, OH, May 29, 2015).

163. "The Dark Continent," *Christian Standard*, September 18, 1890; Caroline Atwater Mason, *Lux Christi: An Outline Study of India, a Twilight Land* (New York: Macmillan, 1902), 228.

164. Magazines, Articles, and Clippings 1891–1938, Herbert Cookman Withey Collection, United Methodist Church Archives—GCAH, Madison, NJ.

165. "Selections," *Christian Standard*, April 18, 1885.

166. E. Davies, *History of Silver Lake Camp Meeting, near Brandon, Vermont* (Reading: Holiness Book Concern, 1880), 9.

167. Certificates of Mary Estella Withey, Lottie May, Withey, and Florence Steele Withey, W. S. Matthew Papers, California-Nevada Conference Archives, Pacific School of Religion; South Central Africa Minutes, California-Nevada Conference Archives, Pacific School of Religion.

168. South Central Africa Minutes, California-Nevada Conference Archives.

169. "Bishop Taylor's Missionaries," *Christian Standard*, February 7, 1885; "General News," Ibid., February 14, 1885; Ibid., February 21, 1885 "Communications," Ibid., February 21, 1885.

170. Ibid., March 7, 1885.

171. "The General Missionary Committee," *Zion's Herald*, November 19, 1884.

172. *The Chile Mission of the Methodist Episcopal Church, 1878–1893* (Santiago: Published by the Mission, 1894, 32.

173. Taylor, *Story of My Life*, 684, 699; "General News," *Christian Standard*, January 10, 1885; "Brief Mention," *Zion's Herald*, January 7, 1885; "Religious Items," Ibid., February 25, 1885; Alida Chatelain and Amy Roch, *Héli Chatelain, L'ami De L'angola, Fondateur De La Mission Philafricaine* (Lausanne: Secrétariat de la Mission Philafricaine, 1918), 43–44.

174. Wade Crawford Barclay, *History of Methodist Missions: Early American Methodism, 1769–1844: Missionary Motivation and Expansion*, History of Methodist Missions 1 (New York: Board of Missions and Church Extension of the Methodist Church, 1949), 325–6; Lamin O. Sanneh, *Abolitionists Abroad: American Blacks and the Making of Modern West Africa* (Cambridge: Harvard University Press, 2001), 182–237.

175. Wm. Taylor, "Letter from Bishop Taylor," *Christian Standard*, March 21, 1885.

176. Wm. Taylor, "Letter from Bishop Taylor," *Christian Advocate*, May 14, 1885.

177. Wm. Taylor to Richard Grant, February 26, 1885, Taylor, W. (Bishop) 1886–1890 Microfilm Edition of the Missionary Correspondence of the Board of Missions of the Methodist Episcopal Church, United Methodist Church Archives—GCAH.

178. "The Taylor Band," *Christian Standard*, June 6, 1885.

179. Barclay, *Widening Horizons*, 875.

180. Henry McNeal Turner, *African Letters* (Nashville: Publishing House A.M.E. Church Sunday School Union, 1893), 68.

181. Amanda Smith, *An Autobiography: The Story of the Lord's Dealings with Mrs. Amanda Smith, . . .* (Chicago: Meyer & Brother, 1893), 362–4, 384, 435–6, 546; Adrienne M. Israel, *Amanda Berry Smith: From Washerwoman to Evangelist*, Studies in Evangelicalism 16 (Lanham: Scarecrow Press, 1998), 42–73.

182. "The Taylor Band," *Christian Standard*, April 10, 1886; Ibid., April 17, 1886; *Journal of the General Conference of the Methodist Episcopal Church,. . . 1892* (New York: Hunt and Eaton, 1892), 374–5.

183. *Minutes of the Annual Conferences of the Methodist Episcopal Church, Spring Conferences of 1885* (New York: Phillips & Hunt, 1885), 18.

184. *Journal of the General Conference of the Methodist Episcopal Church, . . . 1888* (New York: Phillips and Hunt, 1888), 405.

185. "The Missionaries for Africa," *Christian Standard*, March 21, 1885.

186. Ibid.

187. "The Taylor Band," Ibid., February 27, 1886; Ibid., March 6, 1886.

188. Ibid., October 16, 1886.

189. Walter J. Hollenweger, "Methodism's Past in Pentecostalism's Present: A Case Study of a Cultural Clash in Chile," *Methodist History* 20 (1982): 169–82; D.

William Faupel, *The Everlasting Gospel: The Significance of Eschatology in the Development of Pentecostal Thought*, Journal of Pentecostal Theology 10 (Sheffield: Sheffield Academic Press, 1996), 220.

190. "General News, *Christian Standard*, February 14, 1885.

191. "The Taylor Band," Ibid., March 27, 1886; Ibid., August 21, 1886.

192. Ibid., October 2, 1886.

193. "Latest from Bishop Taylor," Ibid., May 16, 1885; Kelly died in 1886. Arthur may have returned home. There was an Asante prince named Albert Arthur Owunsu Ansa matching his description. Steckelman returned to a trading career, and in 1888 he visited the United States with a substantial collection of African artifacts displayed in Cincinnati as probably the first collection of African art in the United States. "The Taylor Band," Ibid., March 13, 1886; Christine Mullen Kreamer, "The Cincinnati Art Museum's Steckelmann Collection: Late-Nineteenth-Century Collecting and Patronage Along the Loango Coast," in *Representing Africa in American Art Museums: A Century of Collecting and Display*, ed. Kathleen Bickford Berzock and Christa Clarke (Seattle: University of Washington Press, 2011), 20–22; Ivor Wilks, *Asante in the Nineteenth Century: The Structure and Evolution of a Political Order* (London: Cambridge University Press, 1975), 632–3.

194. "Letter from Bishop Taylor," *Christian Standard*, April 25, 1885; Ibid., May 30, 1885

195. P. Dodson, "Bishop Taylor's Company," Ibid., May 9; "Letters from Bishop Taylor," Ibid., May 23, 1885.

196. "The Taylor Band," Ibid., August 14, 1886.

197. Herbert C. Withey to W. S. Matthew, June 11, 1929, W. S. Matthew Papers.

198. "Letters from Bishop Taylor," *Christian Standard*, May 23, 1885; "The Taylor Band," Ibid., May 23, 1885; Ibid, May 30, 1885; Ibid., June 6, 1885; Ibid., June 13, 1885; Ibid., June 27, 1885; Ibid., August 8, 1885; South Central Africa Minutes; David Birmingham, *Empire in Africa: Angola and Its Neighbors*, Ohio University Research in International Studies Series 84 (Athens: Ohio University Press, 2006), 32–33.

199. South Central Africa Minutes.

200. "How Bishop Taylor Techez Speling," *The African News*, April, 1889.

201. *Christian Standard*, November 15, 1884.

202. "The Taylor Band," *Christian Standard*, July 11, 1885.

203. Ibid.; "The Taylor Band," Ibid., July 18, 1885.

204. Ibid., July 25, 1885; Heather D. Curtis, *Faith in the Great Physician: Suffering and Divine Healing in American Culture, 1860–1900*, ed. David D. Hall and Robert A. Orsi, Lived Religions (Baltimore: Johns Hopkins University Press, 2007), 194–5.

205. "The Taylor Band," Ibid., November 21, 1885; Ibid., April 10, 1886.

206. South Central Africa Minutes; "The Taylor Band," *Christian Standard*, August 8, 1888; Ibid., December 5, 1885; "Selections," Ibid., June 27, 1885.

207. Birmingham, *Empire in Africa*, 14–15.

208. Ibid., 33–34; "The Taylor Band," *Christian Standard*, October 10, 1885; Ibid., February 6, 1886; Ibid., February 13, 1886; Ibid., February 20, 1886; Ibid.,

September 26, 1886; Ibid., October 2; 1886; Ibid. December 18, 1886; Ibid., November 5, 1887.

209. Ibid., May 30, 1885; Ibid, January 30, 1886; Ibid., February 6, 1886; Adam Hochschild, *King Leopold's Ghost: A Story of Greed, Terror, and Heroism in Colonial Africa* (Boston: Houghton Mifflin, 1998), 119–20, 129–31, 161–1.

210. Diary entry for July 11, 1887, William Summers Papers, Miscellaneous Personal Papers Collection, Record Group No. 30, Special Collections, Yale Divinity School Library.

211. "The Taylor Band," February 6, 1886; Ibid., May 14, 1887; Ibid., August 6, 1887; Ibid., November 5, 1887

212. M. E. Chamberlain, *The Scramble for Africa*, Seminar Studies in History (London: Longman, 1974), 54–55.

213. Wm. Taylor, "The Taylor Band," *Christian Standard*, December 26, 1885; Ibid., January 16, 1886.

214. Taylor, *Story of My Life*, 713–14.

215. Ibid.

216. "Africa," *Christian Standard*, January 30, 1886.

217. Hochschild, *King Leopold's Ghost*, 188, 158–9.

218. "The Taylor Band," *Christian Standard*, August 7, 1886; Ibid., September 17, 1887.

219. Reed died in 1880. At the time, Taylor wrote a long tribute to his patron that was published serially in the *Christian Standard*. Wm. Taylor, "Reminiscences of Henry Reed," *Christian Standard*, April 16, 1881; Ibid., April 23, 1881; Ibid., April 30, 1881; Ibid., May 7, 1881; Ibid., May 21, 1881; Ibid., May 28, 1881; Ibid., June 11, 1881; Ibid., June 18, 1881.

220. "The Taylor Band," Ibid., November 9, 1886; Ibid., November 27, 1886; Ibid., December 11, 1886; Ibid., January 22, 1887; Ibid., January 29, 1887; Ibid., February 26, 1887; Ibid., May 14, 1887; Ibid., September 10, 1887; Ibid., October 15, 1887; Ibid., October 29, 1887; "The Taylor Band," Ibid., November 19, 1887; Ibid., April 9, 1891; Bradley L. Burr, "An Exciting Voyage," *The African News*, August, 1892.

221. "Letter from Bishop Taylor," *Christian Standard*, October 15, 1887; *Journal of the General Conference, . . . 1892*, 374–5.

222. "Mr. Waller's Statement."

223. Ibid.

224. Ibid.

225. Agnes McAllister, *A Lone Woman in Africa: Six Years on the Kroo Coast* (New York: Eaton & Mains, 1896), 22–27.

226. "Mr. Waller's Statement."

227. "A Dangerous Crank," *New York Times*, April 10, 1885.

228. "How Far is the Methodist Episcopal Church Responsible for Bishop William Taylor's Enterprises in Africa?" *Christian Advocate*, February 26, 1885.

229. "Letter from New York," *Zion's Herald*, March 4, 1885.

230. "The Local Preacher's Convention," *Christian Advocate*, October 8, 1885.

231. "Church Benevolences," *Zion's Herald*, June 3, 1885.

232. Ibid.

233. "Philadelphia Conference Notes," *Christian Advocate*, May 28, 1885.

234. E. Davies, *The Bishop of Africa; or, the Life of William Taylor, D.D. With an Account of the Congo Country, and Mission* (Reading: Holiness Book Concern, 1885).

235. *The Doctrines and Discipline of the Methodist Episcopal Church, 1884*, 375.

236. Daniel Curry, "Editorial Miscellany: Current Topics: 'A Missionary Bishop for Africa,'" *Methodist Review*, May, 1885.

237. J. W. Hamilton, "Lesser Bishops for Africa," *Christian Advocate*, July 16, 1885.

238. Wm. Taylor, "Bishop Taylor's Salary and Episcopacy," *Christian Standard*, March 14, 1885.

239. "Meeting of the Book Committee, *Zion's Herald*, February 18, 1885; "William Taylor's Letter to the Book Committee," *Christian Advocate*, February 26, 1885.

240. *Christian Standard*, May 14, 1887.

241. *Journal of the General Conference, . . . 1888*, 111–12, 158, 191–2, 211, 234, 247, 268, 272.

242. *Journal of the General Conference, . . . 1888*, 655.

243. Ibid., 396.

244. William Taylor, "Letter from Bishop Taylor," *Christian Advocate*, June 13, 1889.

245. "Private Bankers Fail," *New York Times*, December 18, 1890; "Kean's Collapsed Bank," Ibid., January 7, 1891; C. E. Welch to Ross Taylor, April 4, 1890, Taylor, W. (Bishop) 1886–1890 Microfilm Edition of the Missionary Correspondence of the Board of Missions of the Methodist Episcopal Church; Legal documents, Bishop W. Taylor—I Legal Papers, Statement, Reports, Etc., Ibid.

246. Wm. Taylor, "Self-supporting Missions," *Christian Advocate,* May 8, 1890; J. Tremayne Copplestone, *History of Methodist Missions: Twentieth-Century Perspectives, the Methodist Episcopal Church, 1896–1939*, History of Methodist Missions 4 (New York: United Methodist Church, 1973), 523, 589–93.

247. In 1884, Taylor published three pamphlets for that purpose. "William Taylor's Circular Letters to his Friends," nos. 1–3, Pamphlet Collection, Drew University Methodist Collection, Drew University, Madison, NJ.

248. William Chazanof, *Welch's Grape Juice: From Corporation to Co-Operative* (Syracuse: Syracuse University Press, 1977), 9–10, 23–27.

249. *African News*, February, 1889.

250. W.T., "From Bishop Taylor," Ibid., April, 1889.

251. Ross Taylor to T. B. Welch, January 11, 1890, Taylor, W. (Bishop) 1886–1890 Microfilm Edition of the Missionary Correspondence of the Board of Missions of the Methodist Episcopal Church; Welch to Taylor, April 4, 1890; Wm. Taylor to T. B. Welch, May 18, 1891, Bishop W. Taylor—I Legal Papers, Taylor, W. (Bishop) 1886–1890 Microfilm Edition of the Missionary Correspondence of the Board of Missions of the Methodist Episcopal Church; Ross Taylor, "The African News," *Christian Standard*, August 27, 1891; "The African News: Notes from Evidence We Can Provide," Bishop W. Taylor—II Legal Papers, Microfilm Edition of the Missionary Correspondence of the Board of Missions of the Methodist Episcopal Church;

C. E. Welch to Bro. Garwood, April 23, 1891, Taylor, W. (Bishop) 1886–1890, Microfilm Edition of the Missionary Correspondence of the Board of Missions of the Methodist Episcopal Church; C. E. Welch, "The African News, *Christian Standard*, September 17, 1891.

252. Welch to Garwood, April 23, 1891.

253. "The Proof is at Hand," *Illustrated Christian World*: December, 1896.

254. Advertisement, *African News*, May, 1892.

255. David Bundy, "William Taylor as an Interpreter of African Culture: The Foundation for a Theory of Mission" (Position Paper 52b, Currents in World Christianity Project, Cambridge, England, March, 1998).

256. William Taylor, *The Model Preacher: Comprised in a Series of Letters Illustrating the Best Mode of Preaching the Gospel* (Cincinnati: Swormstedt & Poe, for the author, 1860), 169; Jessica L. Rousselow and Alan H. Winquist, *God's Ordinary People: No Ordinary Heritage* (Upland: Taylor University Press, 1996), 74–75.

257. Kenneth O. Brown, "Osborn, William Bramwell," in *Historical Dictionary of the Holiness Movement*, ed. William Kostlevy, Historial Dictionaries of Religions, Philosophies, and Movements 98 (Lanham: Scarecrow Press, 2009), 224–5; Curtis, *Faith in the Great Physician*, 6–7, 186–7.

258. *Sixth Annual Report of the Missionary Training Institute Located in the City of Brooklyn, N.Y.* (New York: A. H. Kellogg, 1891), 10–11.

259. "Our Tropical Training School," *Illustrated Africa*: August, 1894.

260. Virginia Lieson Brereton, *Training God's Army: The American Bible School, 1880–1940* (Bloomington: Indiana University Press, 1990), 79–82.

261. For example, Bundy claims Henry Morton Stanley commandeered the mission's steam ship, the *Henry Reed*, for use on the Emin Pasha expedition in 1887. Stanley did take the ship, but it did not belong to Taylor's mission. Although Henry Reed had been one of Taylor's major patrons, the *Henry Reed* was given to the English Baptist mission by Reed's widow. She later contributed toward the *Anne Taylor*, as well. "Bundy, "William Taylor as an Interpreter"; "The Taylor Band," *Christian Standard*, November 1886; "The Taylor Band," Ibid., January 29, 1887; Margaret S. E. Reed, *Henry Reed: An Eventful Life Devoted to God and Man* (London: Morgan and Scott, [1906]); Henry M. Stanley, *In Darkest Africa, or, the Quest, Rescue, and Retreat of Emin, Governor of Equatoria*, 2 vols., vol. 1 (New York: Charles Scribner's Sons, 1890), 90–94.

262. Bundy seems to confuse two books supposedly written by Taylor in this time. He describes *Africa Illustrated: Scenes from Daily Life of the Dark Continent* as a work of scholarship. Another book, *The Flaming Torch in Darkest Africa*, matches that description. The book *Africa Illustrated* (not to be confused with the magazine by the same name) is an 80-page book of photos supposedly taken by Taylor and Houlb. Bundy, "William Taylor as an Interpreter"; William Taylor, *The Flaming Torch in Darkest Africa* (New York: Eaton & Mains, 1898); William Taylor and Emil Holub, *Africa Illustrated: Scenes from Daily Life on the Dark Continent* (New York: Published in the interest of Christ and Africa by Illustrated Africa 1895).

263. "Perfection of Faith—Christian Experience," Ibid., May 1895. William Taylor, *Infancy and Manhood of Christian Life* (London: S. W. Partridge, 1867), 57–80.

264. A. E. Withey to W. S. Matthew, July 29, 1929, W. S. Matthew Papers.

265. "A Question," *Christian Standard*, June 12, 1890; Wm. Taylor, "The Spiritual Possibilities of the Heathen," *African News*, January 1889.

266. Ibid.

267. M. C. Wire, "The Story of the Stone Pillow," *Pacific Christian Advocate*, December 20, 1928; Charles A. Owens, to W. S. Matthew, February 8, 1827, W. S. Matthew Papers.

268. "The Dark Continent," *Christian Standard*, February 9, 1893; Minutes of the First Session of the East Central Africa Mission Conference, Goucher College, Special Collections and Archives, Baltimore, MD; "Liberia Annual Conference of the Methodist Episcopal Church," in *The Gospel in All Lands.*, ed. Eugene R. Smith (New York: Missionary Society of the Methodist Episcopal Church, 1894), 281; Taylor, *The Flaming Torch in Darkest Africa*, 551.

269. J. M.B., "Editorial Letters from the General Conference," *Christian Advocate*, June 2, 1892.

270. *Journal of the General Conference, 1892*, 144, 369.

271. Ibid., 144.; "The Little Christians," *Christian Standard*, May 19, 1892.

272. Rousselow and Winquist, *God's Ordinary People*, 53–57.

273. Bundy, "Bishop William Taylor and Methodist Mission (Part 2)," 13; Bennett Mitchell, *History of the Northwest Iowa Conference, 1872–1903* (Sioux City: Perkins Brothers, 1904), 156–7; Welch to Taylor, April 4, 1890; "The Dark Continent," *Christian Standard*, July 24, 1890; Smith, *Autobiography*, 489–90; *Journal of the General Conference, . . . 1892*, 210.

274. "'In Dangers Oft'," *Christian Advocate*, November 12, 1891; David Bundy concurred with those who believed Taylor was attacked in Rotterdam, although he also incorrectly wrote that Taylor had been "mugged in Brussels, Belgium." Bundy, "William Taylor as an Interpreter of African Culture."

275. *African News*, December, 1891.

276. "Doctor, Dentist, Missionary," *Christian Standard*, December 14, 1893; Helen Byington Emens, "Woman in Medicine: Her Fitness and Success as a Physician," in *The World's Progress, as Wrought by Men and Women, in Art, Literature, Education, Philanthropy, Reform, Inventions, Business and Professional Life*, ed. William C. King (Springfield: King-Richardson, 1896), 189.

277. Wm. Taylor, "Voyage from Monrovia to Congo," *Illustrated Africa*, May 1894; "Bishop Taylor in Angola," Ibid., August, 1894; "Editorial-Personal," *Christian Standard*, March 7, 1895.

278. "His Labors in Africa," *New York Times*, May 11, 1895.

279. Ibid.

Conclusion

Shortly after Taylor's return to America in 1895 his autobiography was published. One of two epigraphs inscribed on the title page was John Wesley's quote claiming the world as his parish. Wesley made the claim, but Taylor had lived it, and Taylor's autobiography summarized his experiences on six continents. The book's text was assembled and edited by the historian John Clark Ridpath. Stories of Taylor's early life and ministry came from the serialized accounts he wrote for *The African News*.[1] Previously published descriptions of Taylor's time in South Africa, India, and South America were largely reproduced to relate those episodes. Short chapters connecting these sections and summarizing his episcopate were probably dictated by Taylor. Ridpath's hand can be seen in the inclusion of other testimonies describing Taylor's career—including Ridpath's own account of meeting Taylor as a student in 1859.[2]

Taylor remained in the States to attend the 1896 General Conference of the Methodist Episcopal Church. He was warmly received, but his frail health could no longer be concealed. On Taylor's seventy-fifth birthday, the conference session unanimously adopted a resolution celebrating that since his first appointment in Virginia, he had "gone everywhere preaching the Gospel without ever having been laid aside through illness."[3] A few days later, however, Taylor and James Thoburn were called to present their reports as missionary bishops. Taylor was introduced as "the Bishop of all continents, and especially of Africa."[4] When the applause welcoming him died down, Taylor spoke but his frail voice could not be heard.[5] Several days later, the Conference Committee on Episcopacy, headed by James M. Buckley, reported that Taylor was no longer effective and should be retired by the church. It further recommended that the Missionary Society provide for his support. The report was adopted without debate, and Taylor was retired from the active ministry.[6]

Given Taylor's conflicted past with other church leaders, including Buckley, it was not surprising that some saw nefarious motives in the action. In addition, the continued viability of Ross Taylor's magazine hinged on an image of a dynamic Bishop Taylor. Accordingly, Ross had kept up the illusion that his father was at work in Africa for some time after the bishop had returned to the States in 1895.[7] After the General Conference, Asbury Lowrey and Ross Taylor circulated a rumor that Taylor had defiantly declared, "The General Conference cannot retire me. . . . I am not a spent ball, but a perpetual motion, moved by a divine impulsion. I cannot stop until that impulsive force is withdrawn."[8]

William Taylor, however, accepted his retirement as graciously as could be expected. He turned to the *Christian Standard* to dispel rumors of his dissatisfaction. "Many of my friends think and declare that the action of the General Conference which kindly put my name on the honorable list of retired heroes . . . was a mistake," Taylor wrote. "No such thought ever got a night's lodging in my head or heart."[9] After Joseph Hartzell was elected to be Taylor's successor as bishop for Africa, Taylor participated in his consecration and cooperated in incorporating his Africa missions into full connection with the Methodist Episcopal Church, as Taylor's missions in India and South America had years before.[10]

When Hartzell visited Africa, he was impressed by the missionaries Taylor had recruited and celebrated them as people who had suffered the loss of loved ones, eked out an existence in a distant land, and had been faithful to their missionary calling. Some of these continued Taylor's legacy in Methodism for years to come.[11] The Withey family was foremost among these. The Witheys lost three daughters in Africa but had persisted and developed a trading post that supported their missionary work. Their son, Herbert, came of age in Africa. When Hartzell organized the Congo Mission Conference of the Methodist Episcopal Church, Herbert was accepted a Methodist preacher on probation.[12] As an adult, he translated the New Testament, Psalms, and a hymnal into Kimbundu.[13] Taylor's mission on the Congo River, however, had collapsed. Illness had sent most missionaries home. Only the station at Vivi remained occupied. Hartzell sold the *Anne Taylor* and transferred mission property to a Swedish missionary society.[14]

But the Methodist mission in the Congo would eventually be reborn. One of those Taylor had appointed to Vivi was Helen Chapman Rasmussen. Twice, she and her husband William Rasmussen went to the Congo with Taylor, only to become too sick to remain. On the second tour, in 1895, William died. Helen eventually returned to Africa a third time as a missionary with the Woman's Foreign Missionary Society. At Umtali, Rhodesia, she developed a dictionary of the Chikaranga language. In 1905, she and her second husband, another future Methodist Bishop of Africa John Springer, were moved to fulfill Taylor's vision of establishing Methodist missions across the continent. Together they traveled across Africa to scout sites and were eventually a part of a renewed Methodist missionary presence in the Congo.[15]

Not all of Taylor's missionaries acquiesced to the turnover of their missions to the Methodist Episcopal Church. Independent faith missions were now flourishing. Individuals who wished to continue missionary work on their own terms and separate from a denominational affiliation could do so. Despite his own quasi-independent mission ventures, Taylor had struggled against that tide. Taylor had evidently upset some of his Africa missionaries by telling them that because they followed him to Africa, they had become members of the Methodist Episcopal Church.[16] Like the Methodist missionary tradition itself, he tried to balance independent initiatives with institutional connections. After Taylor retired, he could no longer hold them. In 1897, for example, Heli Chatelain left to start an independent mission in southern Angola. He hoped to establish sanctuaries for escaped slaves. He supported himself by operating a store for Boer settlers and selling Portuguese colonial postage stamps to European collectors. Only one refuge was ever built, however, and Chatelain had to downplay his antislavery vision to maintain his means of support.[17]

Some of these newly independent Taylor missionaries carried Taylor's influence into early Pentecostalism. Samuel J. and Ardella Mead had created a successful mission in Malange, Angola. They returned to the United States in 1904. In 1906 a revival broke out at Azusa Street in Los Angeles that marked one of the originating events of Pentecostalism. Several people there claimed to have received a foreign language as a spiritual gift. The Meads confirmed they heard African languages spoken, organized a missionary party at Azusa, and returned to Africa in early 1907.[18] Albert Norton, one of the missionaries sent by the Methodist Missionary Board to help Taylor in Mumbai, left the Methodists to start an independent mission in 1874. When a revival broke out at the Indian Christian leader Pandita Ramabai's Mukti Mission in 1905, he testified that he heard spiritually endowed languages spoken. An account of that revival written by another independent missionary, Minnie Abrams, was read by her missionary training school classmate May Hilton Hoover. She and her husband, Willis C. Hoover, had been recruited by Asbury Lowrey for Taylor's missions in Chile. They were prompted by that account to seek a Pentecostal experience of Spirit baptism. Under their leadership, a Pentecostal revival broke out in Chile and led to the formation of an independent Methodist Pentecostal church.[19]

These events, however, were not a part of Taylor's experience. Retired by his church, Taylor prepared his will, once again left his wife behind in California, and set sail for South Africa, the scene of his greatest evangelistic triumph. There Taylor thought he would die.[20] Ross Taylor's magazine initially portrayed the tour as a triumphant return with services in chapels where his father had preached three decades earlier and visits with adults who had been converted by him as youths. Letters described Taylor's enthusiasm at facing the challenge of preaching to miners at Johannesburg as he had once preached to California gold miners.[21] These reports were unreliable. Hartzell met Taylor in Cape Town, and found none of it true. "The *real* story is *most* pathetic," he later wrote without elaboration.[22] After a few dubiously triumphant reports, even Ross quietly stopped noting his father's whereabouts.

Taylor did not die in Africa but returned to California. In an attempt to give another face to his business, in October 1895, Ross Taylor announced that the African explorer Henry Morton Stanley agreed to be an associate editor of *Illustrated Africa*.[23] Stanley contributed little more than his name to the endeavor, though in 1898 he wrote an introduction to the final book bearing William Taylor's name, *Flaming Torch in Darkest Africa*.[24] In the spring of 1899, Ross Taylor sent Stanley a copy of the book expressing his hope that Stanley and his father could meet in London that summer.[25]

William Taylor was not writing books or planning a trip to London at that time, however. His health was failing, and his care was passed around his family. Taylor had returned to a wife and sons he had abandoned for most of his life, and they were either unable or unwilling to care for him. Amanda Berry Smith called on Taylor in at his home in Palo Alto in early 1898 and left believing he would soon die.[26] Shortly after Smith's visit, Taylor was sent to live with a sister in Illinois. She sent him to a brother in Georgia. Late 1899 found Taylor being cared for by his brother Andrew in Wrightsville, Pennsylvania, while his wife and children in California drew his pension from the church.[27]

Himself a Methodist preacher, Andrew Taylor alerted church leaders to his brother's condition. He said the bishop slept most of the time but would occasionally wake, pack his bags, and wait to depart for a new destination. The bishop was prone to wander; on one occasion he was found on the banks of the Susquehanna waiting for a steamship he believed would come to pick him up. A visitor reported Taylor thought that guest was from the Sweet Springs Circuit in Virginia and then imagined he was preaching to "great congregations of people, of all the tribes of earth."[28] Andrew claimed that in a lucid moment, his brother lamented, "It is a little hard, when I am too old to work, to be turned out to root pig or die: But the Lord will take care of me, and I am thankful that he has given me a home."[29]

Taylor's final years were sad, and the fact that he used a version of the same idiom that he once gave as advice to his self-supporting missionaries to describe his own inability to care for himself highlighted that tragedy. The ideal of self-sufficiency that was a part of Taylor's life and identity, and shaped his missionary endeavors, failed him in the end. Taylor was returned to the care of his family in California, apparently with the intervention of the Missionary Board.[30] He died in Palo Alto, California, May 18, 1902. Anne died three years later, on September 6, 1905. They were buried together in Oakland's Mountain View Cemetery.[31]

The ideal of independent self-sufficiency, however, was only one aspect of Taylor's story. That virtue existed alongside and in tension with other core principles in the religious movement he represented. The Methodist missionary tradition celebrated both independent, spirit-led entrepreneurialism and the creation of organized, connectional networks. This account has shown examples where Taylor acted on his own, believing he was doing God's will, and examples where Taylor worked in concert with other Methodists to organize and establish his church. In many respects, the conflict Taylor had with leaders in his church in the 1880s was not an example of Taylor pulling away from his religious tradition but an example of an essential dynamic within the Methodist missionary tradition between independence and connection.

This book has explored that and other elements of the Methodist missionary tradition by following Taylor's life and career. It has shown, for example, how a theology that emphasized God's desire for all people to be saved and to experience entire sanctification developed its converts into active leaders and missionaries. Both Taylor's own experience and the experiences of individuals converted at his revivals or recruited to serve in India, South America, and

Figure 6.1 Taylor Family Burial Plot, Mountain View Cemetery, Oakland, CA. *Source:* Photo by the author.

Africa followed that trajectory. This account has also illustrated that Methodism's belief in a God who wants all persons to be saved and sanctified could appeal to and empower marginalized individuals. These included African Americans, the impressive Charles Pamla, Anglo-Indians, and American women. The message that God could entitle and qualify anyone for service was a powerful one. Institutionalized forms of discrimination, however, meant that Methodists rarely allowed such individuals the opportunity to act on their faith through official church structures.

Methodism spread to new contexts because Methodists believed that God was at work in the world, and they should be too. Divine action was to be matched by the action of believers doing God's work. If an opportunity arose to spread their gospel, Methodists believed they were to seize it, for they believed that God desired the salvation of all. This spirit made Methodism both an activistic and a pragmatic religion. Methodists were eager to use whatever medium or method was available to enable the spread of their message, be it publishing, revivalism, or transoceanic steam travel. That practical spirit meant that Methodists were more likely to reflect theologically about how missionaries might support themselves while they evangelized than an expected advent of a millennial kingdom.

An awareness of what was practical or feasible in terms of missionary outreach rested uneasily, however, with the aspirational belief of Methodists that the whole world was their parish. This account has described occasions in California, India, South America, and Africa when Taylor expanded Methodist missions beyond the bounds of what others believed was prudent. Taylor's extension of Methodist work is only half of that story. The other half was that once those boundaries were pushed, Methodists happily celebrated and embraced his accomplishments. His were often welcome transgressions that Methodists accepted because they expanded their sense of what was possible.

Methodist pragmatism had a dark side too. A willingness to embrace any means offered by the world to share their message meant that Methodists could be uncritically tolerant of European colonialism or imperialism as a means to achieving missionary ends. This perspective did not mean Methodists such as Taylor accepted political domination and expansion as an unqualified good, but they saw it as a providential development unleashed by God for God's own purposes. Anglo-American expansion, whether it be in gold rush era California, Australasia, or British India, seemed to Methodists to be a blessing because it allowed opportunities for their faith to spread. At the same time, Methodist missionaries were not rigidly bound up with Anglo-American triumphalism, as opportunities offered by liberal regimes in South America and Portuguese grants in Africa were welcomed too.

Methodist missionaries like Taylor, however, were rarely able to differentiate ways their own understanding of Christianity was connected to its

Anglo-American cultural origins. To be sure, Taylor evidenced genuine and mostly respectful curiosity about the lifeways and religious practices of people he met around the world. It can also be said that he also judged other cultures and religions much as he did his own. For Taylor, neither European civilization nor nominal acceptance of the Christian faith could save a sinner any more than traditional African religion, Hinduism, or Roman Catholicism. All these and anything less than an acceptance of Taylor's own evangelical Christianity were inadequate. But Taylor was never able to think outside his own cultural framework or to appreciate how his faith was informed by his own background and experience. Though he often offered a biblical or Pauline justifications for his work, Taylor's understanding of self-support, for example, was always grounded first in his own cultural roots and life experience.

Since I began this project, I have been asked countless times if I found any connections between William Taylor and the Anglican missionary Roland Allen. I have not, but a comparison of the two men is revealing of the way Taylor's context and experience shaped his work and legacy. A decade after Taylor's death, Allen wrote *Missionary Methods: St. Paul's or Ours?* that argued the superiority of a Pauline model for missionary work. More than a century later, Allen's book remains a popular missiological text.[32] Memory of Taylor, well-known in his time and the first to propose following a Pauline model for mission, has faded. Allen is better remembered today because he offered a theory extrapolated from his reading of Pauline, biblical examples. That foundation endures, as has his work.

Taylor's theory, by contrast, was always contextual. Because Taylor believed God was at work in the world and in his own life, his life experiences gave birth to constantly shifting and developing mission theories. He then sought and found confirmation for these theories in the pages of his Bible. Those theories, such as they were, Taylor then presented, not through a biblical exposition but through his own lived example. While that example was persuasive to many in his own day, it was also specific to Taylor's life and context. Once Taylor's life had ended and the context changed, his story ceased to be told.

Taylor exemplified the Methodist missionary tradition in his own day, but in the 100-plus years since his death, the Methodist world parish has changed in ways that Taylor could not have predicted. In the United States, the land of Taylor's origin and first missionary posting, and other Anglo-American cultures, Methodist churches have been losing members for the last half-century. At the same time, Methodist churches are found in more places around the globe than in Taylor's day. In Africa, the field of his episcopate, Methodism is flourishing. The contexts for mission that Methodists find themselves in today vary significantly both from each other and from the era when Taylor lived. Taylor's spiritual heirs today may well be most true to his example, not by seeking to recreate his principles and priorities—or even by seeking to follow a Pauline model—but by seeking ways to be faithful in their own contexts.

NOTES

1. See "For Children and Youth: Brief Story of My Life," *The African News*, January, 1889 and issues following.

2. William Taylor, *Story of My Life; an Account of What I Have Thought and Said and Done in My Ministry of More Than Fifty-Three Years in Christian Lands and among the Heathen. Written by Myself*, ed. John Clark Ridpath (New York: Hunt & Eaton, 1896), 251–2.

3. *Journal of the General Conference of the Methodist Episcopal Church,... 1896* (New York: Eaton & Mains, 1896), 88–89.

4. "The General Conference," *Christian Advocate*, May 21, 1896.

5. Ibid.

6. *Journal of the General Conference, 1896*, 276, 380.

7. "The Treasury Announcement," *Illustrated Africa*: September, 1895.

8. A. Lowrey, "William Taylor 'Effective'," *Illustrated Christian World*: August, 1896.

9. William Taylor, "No Mistake," *Christian Standard*, June 27, 1896.

10. *Journal of the General Conference, 1896*, 286.

11. J. C. Hartzell, "The Methodist Episcopal Mission in Angola," in *The Gospel in All Lands*, ed. Eugene R. Smith (New York: Missionary Society of the Methodist Episcopal Church, 1897), 532.

12. Ibid; Withey Family Photos, Herbert Cookman Withey Collection, United Methodist Church Archives—GCAH.

13. J. Tremayne Copplestone, *History of Methodist Missions: Twentieth-Century Perspectives, the Methodist Episcopal Church, 1896–1939*, History of Methodist Missions 4 (New York: United Methodist Church, 1973), 578–9.

14. Ibid., 4.

15. Dana L. Robert, *American Women in Mission: A Social History of Their Thought and Practice* (Macon: Mercer University Press, 1997), 194; Dana L. Robert, "Holiness and the Missionary Vision of the Woman's Foreign Missionary Society of the Methodist Episcopal Church, 1869–1894," *Methodist History* 39, no. 1 (2000): 26–27; John McKendree Springer, *I Love the Trail: A Sketch of the Life of Helen Emily Springer* (New York: Parthenon Press, 1952), 22–40.

16. David Birmingham, *Empire in Africa: Angola and Its Neighbors* (Athens: Ohio University Press, 2006), 34.

17. Ibid., 41–44.

18. "From a Missionary to Africa," *The Apostolic Faith*, September 1906; Wade Crawford Barclay, *The Methodist Episcopal Church, 1845–1939: Widening Horizons, 1845–95*, History of Methodist Missions 3 (New York: Board of Missions of The Methodist Church, 1957), 910–11; D. William Faupel, *The Everlasting Gospel:*

The Significance of Eschatology in the Development of Pentecostal Thought (Sheffield: Sheffield Academic Press, 1996), 220; Grant Wacker, *Heaven Below: Early Pentecostals and American Culture* (Cambridge: Harvard University Press, 2001), 62–63.

19. David Bundy, "Unintended Consequences: The Methodist Episcopal Missionary Society and the Beginnings of Pentecostalism in Norway and Chile," *Missiology* 27, no. 2 (1999): 220–3; Walter J. Hollenweger, "Methodism's Past in Pentecostalism's Present: A Case Study of a Cultural Clash in Chile," *Methodist History* 20 (1982): 171–6; Willis Collins Hoover and Mario G. Hoover, *History of the Pentecostal Revival in Chile*, trans. Mario G. Hoover (Santiago: Imprenta Eben-Ezer, 2000), 9; Juan B. A. Kessler, Jr., *Conflict in Missions: A History of Protestantism in Peru and Chile* (Denver: iAcademic Books, 2001), 96–133; Gary B. McGee, "'Baptism of the Holy Ghost & Fire! The Mission Legacy of Minnie F Abrams," *Missiology* 27, no. 4 (1999): 517–19; Robert, *American Women in Mission*, 247; Wacker, *Heaven Below*, 46.

20. A. E. Taylor to A. B. Leonard, September 12, 1899, Taylor, W. (Bishop) 1891–1902, Microfilm Edition of the Missionary Correspondence of the Board of Missions of the Methodist Episcopal Church, United Methodist Church Archives—GCAH.

21. "Bishop Taylor in Johannesburg," *Illustrated Christian World*, October 1896.

22. J. C. Hartzell to W. S. Matthew, March 4, 1924, W. S. Matthew Papers, California-Nevada Conference Archives, Pacific School of Religion, Berkeley.

23. "Henry M. Stanley," *Illustrated Africa*, October 1895.

24. William Taylor, *The Flaming Torch in Darkest Africa* (New York: Eaton & Mains, 1898), 19–22.

25. Ross Taylor to Henry M. Stanley, April 18, 1899, Stanley Archives, Royal Museum for Central Africa, History and General Scientific Series/ History of the Colonial Period, Tervuren.

26. Adrienne M. Israel, *Amanda Berry Smith: From Washerwoman to Evangelist* (Lanham: Scarecrow Press, 1998), 120.

27. Ross Taylor to A. B. Leonard, September 5, 1899, Taylor, W. (Bishop) 1891–1902, Microfilm Edition of the Missionary Correspondence of the Board of Missions of the Methodist Episcopal Church.

28. E. H. Yocum to A. B. Leonard, September 6, 1899; A. E. Taylor to A. B. Leonard, September 7, 1899 and September 8, 1899, Ibid.

29. A. E. Taylor to A. B. Leonard, August 29, 1899, Ibid.

30. E. K. Taylor to A. B. Leonard, November 4, 1899, Ibid.; Leonard to Taylor, September 8, 1899, quoted in David Bundy, "Bishop William Taylor and Methodist Mission: A Study in Nineteenth Century Social History (Part 2)," *Methodist History* 28, no. 1 (1989): 13–14.

31. "Mrs. William Taylor," *Christian Advocate*, September 28, 1905.

32. Roland Allen, *Missionary Methods: St. Paul's or Ours?* (Grand Rapids: Wm. B. Eerdmans, 1962); Charles Henry Long and Anne Rowthorn, "The Legacy of Roland Allen," *International Bulletin of Missionary Research* 13, no. 2 (April 1989): 65–70.

Bibliography

Abel, Evelyn. *The Anglo-Indian Community: Survival in India.* Delhi: Chanakya Publications, 1988.

Abstract of the Returns of the Fifth Census . . . . Washington, DC: Duff Green, 1832.

Adams, Charles. *Slavery, Secession, and Civil War: Views from the United Kingdom and Europe, 1856–1865.* Lanham: Scarecrow Press, 2007.

Adelaide Whitfield LaFetra: A Teacher of Young Women. Los Angeles: J.O.C. Class of the Bible School of the First Methodist Episcopal Church of Los Angeles, California, 1916.

Ahlstrom, Sydney E. *A Religious History of the American People.* New Haven: Yale University Press, 1972.

Alexander T. Jeffrey Papers, General Commission on Archives and History the United Methodist Church, Madison, NJ.

Allen, Roland. *Missionary Methods: St. Paul's or Ours?* Grand Rapids: Wm. B. Eerdmans, 1962.

Annual Minutes of the Baltimore Conference of the Methodist Episcopal Church, 1857 Baltimore: Armstrong & Berry, 1857.

Anthony, C. V. *Fifty Years of Methodism: A History of the Methodist Episcopal Church within the Bounds of the California Annual Conference from 1847 to 1897.* San Francisco: Methodist Book Concern, 1901.

Arms, Goodsil F. *History of the William Taylor Self-Supporting Missions in South America.* New York: Methodist Book Concern, 1921.

Austin, Alvyn. *China's Millions: The China Inland Mission and Late Qing Society, 1832–1905.* Grand Rapids: William B. Eerdmans' Publishing, 2007.

Aymer, Paula L. *Evangelical Awakenings in the Anglophone Caribbean: Studies from Granada and Barbados.* New York: Palgrave Macmillan, 2016.

Badr, Habib. "American Protestant Missionary Beginnings in Beirut and Istanbul: Policy, Politics, Practice, and Response." In *New Faith in Ancient Lands: Western Missions in the Middle East in the Nineteenth and Early Twentieth Centuries.* Edited by Heleen Murre-van den Berg, 211–39. Leiden: Brill, 2006.

Baker, Frank K. *Fifty-Fifth Anniversary History of the First Methodist Episcopal Church*. Souvenir ed. San Francisco: N.p, 1902.

Balia, Daryl M. "Bridge over Troubled Waters: Charles Pamla and the Taylor Revival in South Africa." *Methodist History* 30, no. 2 (1992): 78–90.

———. "Reaping Where Others Have Sown: William Taylor's Impact on Methodism." In *Perspectives in Theology and Mission from South Africa*. Edited by Daryl M. Balia, 119–27. Lewiston: Snow Lion Publications, 1993.

Barchwitz-Krauser, O. von. *Six Years with William Taylor in South America*. Boston, MA: Published for the author by McDonald & Gill, 1885.

Barclay, Wade Crawford. *History of Methodist Missions: Early American Methodism, 1769–1844: Missionary Motivation and Expansion*. Vol. 1, History of Methodist Missions. New York: Board of Missions and Church Extension of the Methodist Church, 1949.

———. *History of Methodist Missions: Early American Methodism, 1769–1844: To Reform the Nation*. Vol. 2, History of Methodist Missions. New York: Board of Missions and Church Extension of the Methodist Church, 1950.

———. *The Methodist Episcopal Church, 1845–1939: Widening Horizons, 1845–95*. Vol. 3, History of Methodist Missions. New York: Board of Missions of the Methodist Church, 1957.

Barker, Mary B., et al. *A History of the Methodist Church in Ceylon, 1814–1964*. Colombo: Wesley Press, N.d.

Bastian, Jean-Piere. "Protestantism in Latin America." In *The Church in Latin America, 1492–1992*. Edited by Enrique Dussel, 313–50. Tunbridge Wells: Burns & Oates, 1992.

The Bay of San Francisco: The Metropolis of the Pacific Coast, and Its Suburban Cities: A History. Vol. 2. Chicago: Lewis Publishing, 1892.

Bayly, Susan. *Caste, Society and Politics in India from the Eighteenth Century to the Modern Age*. Vol. IV.3, The New Cambridge History of India. Edited by Gordon Johnson. New York: Cambridge University Press, 1999.

Beaver, R. Pierce. *Ecumenical Beginnings in Protestant World Mission: A History of Comity*. New York: Thomas Nelson & Sons, 1962.

Bebbington, David. *Evangelicalism in Modern Britain: A History from the 1730s to the 1980s*. London: Routledge, 1993.

———. "An Overview, 1700–1914." In *Missions and Empire*. Edited by Norman Etherington, 40–63. Oxford: Oxford University Press, 2005.

———. *Victorian Religious Revivals: Culture and Piety in Local and Global Contexts*. New York: Oxford University Press, 2012.

Berglund, Barbara. *Making San Francisco American: Cultural Frontiers in the Urban West, 1846–1906*. Lawrence: University Press of Kansas, 2007.

Bessie NcNear O'Neal Papers, 1805–ca. 1877 and n.d., Accession #4452, Special Collections, University of Virginia Library, Charlottesville, VA.

Bickford, James. *An Autobiography of Christian Labour in the West Indies, Demerara, Victoria, New South Wales, and South Australia, 1838–1888*. London: Charles H. Kelly, 1890.

Birmingham, David. *Empire in Africa: Angola and Its Neighbors*. Athens: Ohio University Press, 2006.

Bishop William Taylor Collection, Taylor University Archives, Upland, IN.

Blackett, R. J. M. *Divided Hearts: Britain and the American Civil War.* Baton Rouge: Louisiana State University Press, 2001.

Blamires, W. L. and John B. Smith. *The Early Story of the Wesleyan Methodist Church in Victoria.* Melbourne, Australia: Wesleyan Book Depot, 1886.

Booth, Anne W. Journal of a Voyage from Baltimore to San Francisco. . . On Ship, Andalusia, F. W. Wilson, Master, Bancroft Library, University of California, Berkeley, CA.

Bramwell-Booth, Catherine. *Catherine Booth: The Story of Her Loves.* London: Hodder and Stoughton, 1970.

Brands, H. W. *The Age of Gold: The California Gold Rush and the New American Dream.* New York: Anchor Books, 2002.

Bray, Robert. *Peter Cartwright, Legendary Frontier Preacher.* Urbana: University of Illinois Press, 2005.

Brereton, Virginia Lieson. *Training God's Army: The American Bible School, 1880–1940.* Bloomington: Indiana University Press, 1990.

Breward, Ian. "Methodist Reunion in Australasia." In *Methodism in Australia: A History.* Edited by Glen O'Brien and Hilary M. Carey, 119–32. Farnham: Ashgate, 2015.

———. *A History of the Australian Churches.* St. Leonards: Allen & Unwin, 1993.

Brittain, John. "William Arthur's *The Tongue of Fire*: Pre-Pentecostal or Proto Social Gospel." *Methodist History* 40, no. 4 (2002): 246–54.

Browne, Gary Lawson. *Baltimore in the Nation, 1789–1861.* Chapel Hill: University of North Carolina Press, 1980.

Bryan, Jonathan. Photo of Rev Stuart Taylor and Martha E. Taylor Headstone, Shaw Cemetery, Rockbridge County, VA. Accessed May 5, 2018. www.findagrave.com/memorial/57481920/stuart-taylor.com.

Bundy, David. "Bishop William Taylor and Methodist Mission: A Study in Nineteenth Century Social History (Part 1)." *Methodist History* 27, no. 4 (1989): 197–210.

———. "Bishop William Taylor and Methodist Mission: A Study in Nineteenth Century Social History (Part 2)." *Methodist History* 28, no. 1 (1989): 3–21.

———. "The Legacy of William Taylor." *International Bulletin of Missionary Research* 18, no. 4 (1994): 172–6.

———. "Pauline Missions: The Wesleyan Holiness Vision." In *The Global Impact of the Wesleyan Traditions and Their Related Movements.* Edited by Charles Yrigoyen, Jr., 13–26. Lanham: Scarecrow Press, 2002.

———. "William Taylor as an Interpreter of African Culture: The Foundation for a Theory of Mission." Position Paper 52b, Currents in World Christianity Project, Cambridge, March, 1998.

Burin, Eric. "A Manumission in the Mountains: Slavery and the African Colonization Movement in Southwestern Virginia." *Appalachian Journal* 33, no. 2 (2006): 164–86.

Burton, Charles T. *Botetourt County, Virginia Children.* Vol. 1. N.l: N.p., N.d.

Bush, Sargent, "The Pulpit Artistry of Father Taylor: An 1836 Account." *American Literature* 50, no. 1 (1978): 106–9.

Butler, Clementina. *William Butler, the Founder of Two Missions of the Methodist Episcopal Church*. New York: Eaton & Mains, 1902.

California-Nevada Conference Archives, Pacific School of Religion, Berkeley, CA.

Calkin, Homer L. "The Slavery Struggle, 1780–1865." In *Those Incredible Methodists: A History of the Baltimore Conference of the United Methodist Church*. Edited by Gordon Pratt Baker, 192–228. Baltimore: Commission on Archives and History, The Baltimore Conference, 1972.

Campbell, George Duncan. "Father Taylor the Seamen's Apostle." *Methodist History* 15, no. 4 (1977): 251–60.

Campbell, James T. *Songs of Zion: The African Methodist Episcopal Church in the United States and South Africa*. Chapel Hill: University of North Carolina Press, 1998.

Campbell, Ted A. "Spiritual Biography and Autobiography." In *The Cambridge Companion to American Methodism*. Edited by Jason E. Vickers, 243–60. New York: Cambridge University Press, 2013.

Carey, Hilary M. *Believing in Australia: A Cultural History of Religions*. St. Leonards: Allen & Unwin, 1996.

———. "Religion and Society." In *Australia's Empire*. Edited by Deryck M. Schreuder and Stuart Ward, 186–210. Oxford: Oxford University Press, 2008.

Carter, David. *James H. Rigg*. Peterborough: Foundery Press, 1994.

Carwardine, Richard. *Transatlantic Revivalism: Popular Evangelicalism in Britain and America, 1790–1865*. Eugene: Wipf & Stock, 1978.

Case, Jay Riley. *An Unpredictable Gospel: American Evangelicals and World Christianity, 1812–1920*. New York: Oxford University Press, 2012.

Chamberlain, M. E. *The Scramble for Africa*. London: Longman, 1974.

Chatelain, Alida and Amy Roch. *Héli Chatelain, L'ami De L'angola, Fondateur De La Mission Philafricaine*. Lausanne: Secrétariat de la Mission Philafricaine, 1918.

Chazanof, William. *Welch's Grape Juice: From Corporation to Co-Operative*. Syracuse: Syracuse University Press, 1977.

Chilcote, Paul W. and Ulrike Schuler. "Methodist Bible Women in Bulgaria and Italy." *Methodist History* 55, no. 1–2 (2016–2017): 108–27.

The Chile Mission of the Methodist Episcopal Church, 1878–1893. Santiago, Chile: Published by the Mission, 1894.

Clancy, Eric G. "William ('California') Taylor: First Overseas Evangelist to Australia." *Church Heritage* 6, no. 3 (1990): 41–62.

Colenso, John William. *The Pentateuch and Book of Joshua Critically Examined*. London: Longman, Green, Longman, Roberts & Green, 1862.

Comaroff, Jean and John L. Comaroff. *Of Revelation and Revolution: The Dialectics of Modernity on a South African Frontier*. Vol. 2. Chicago: University of Chicago Press, 1991.

Compendium . . . from the Returns of the Sixth Census, ... Washington, DC: Thomas Allen, 1841.

Conkin, Paul K. *Cane Ridge: America's Pentecost*. Madison: University of Wisconsin Press, 1990.

Conway, John S. "Jerusalem Bishopric: A 'Union of Foolscap and Blotting-Paper'." *Studies in Religion/Sciences religieuses* 7, no. 3 (1978): 305–15.

Copplestone, J. Tremayne. *History of Methodist Missions: Twentieth-Century Perspectives, the Methodist Episcopal Church, 1896–1939.* Vol. 4, History of Methodist Missions. New York: United Methodist Church, 1973.

Crockett, David. *A Narrative of the Life of David Crockett, of the State of Tennessee.* Philadelphia: E.L. Carey and A. Hart, 1834.

Crosby, Fanny. *Memories of Eighty Years: The Story of Her Life, Told by Herself, Ancestry, Childhood, Womanhood, Friendships, Incidents and History of Her Songs and Hymns.* Boston: James H. Earle, 1906.

Cupp, Albert M. *A History of Methodism in Rockbridge County, Virginia.* N.p.: N.d.

Curran, Robert Emmett. *The Bicentennial History of Georgetown University: From Academy to University.* Vol. 1. Washington, DC: Georgetown University Press, 1993.

Curtis, Dahl. "Three Fathers, Many Sons: Ecclus. 44:1." *Methodist History* 15, no. 4 (1977): 234–50.

Curtis, Heather D. *Faith in the Great Physician: Suffering and Divine Healing in American Culture, 1860–1900.* Baltimore: Johns Hopkins University Press, 2007.

Daniel, W. Harrison. "The Reaction of British Methodism to the Civil War and Reconstruction in America." *Methodist History* 16, no. 1 (1977): 3–20.

Daniels, W. H. *D. L. Moody and His Work.* London: Hodder & Stoughton, 1876.

The David and Jane Wales Trumbull Manuscript Collection. Special Collections, Princeton Theological Seminary Library, Princeton, NJ.

Davidson, Lance S. "Shanghaied! The Systematic Kidnapping of Sailors in Early San Francisco." *California History* 64, no. 1 (1985): 10–17.

Davies, E. *The Bishop of Africa; or, the Life of William Taylor, D.D. With an Account of the Congo Country, and Mission.* Reading: Holiness Book Concern, 1885.

———. *History of Silver Lake Camp Meeting, near Brandon, Vermont.* Reading: Holiness Book Concern, 1880.

Davis, John. *The Landscape of Belief: Encountering the Holy Land in Nineteenth-Century American Art and Culture.* Princeton: Princeton University Press, 1996.

Dayfoot, Arthur Charles. *The Shaping of the West Indian Church, 1492–1962.* Kingston: The Press University of the West Indies, 1999.

Dayton, Donald W. "From 'Christian Perfection' to the 'Baptism of the Holy Ghost'." In *Perspectives on American Methodism: Interpretive Essays.* Edited by Russell E. Richey, Kenneth E. Rowe and Jean Miller Schmidt, 289–97. Nashville: Kingswood Books, 1993.

———. *Theological Roots of Pentecostalism.* Grand Rapids, MI: Francis Asbury, 1987.

Denoon, Donald, Philippa Mein Smith, and Marivic Wyndham. *A History of Australia, New Zealand, and the Pacific.* Malden: Blackwell, 2007.

Dieter, Melvin Easterday. *The Holiness Revival of the Nineteenth Century.* 2nd ed. Lanham: Scarecrow Press, 1996.

Diffendorfer, Ralph E., ed. *The World Service of the Methodist Episcopal Church.* Chicago: Methodist Episcopal Church, Council of Boards of Benevolence, Committee on Conservation and Advance, 1923.

Division of Birds Records, RU 105, Box 1. Vol. 3, Smithsonian Institution Archives, Washington, DC.

The Doctrines and Discipline of the Methodist Episcopal Church, 1844. New York: G. Lane & C. B. Tippett, 1844.

The Doctrines and Discipline of the Methodist Episcopal Church, 1848. New York: Lane & Scott, 1848.

The Doctrines and Discipline of the Methodist Episcopal Church, 1852. New York: Carlton & Phillips, 1852.

The Doctrines and Discipline of the Methodist Episcopal Church, 1856. New York: Carlton & Porter, 1856.

The Doctrines and Discipline of the Methodist Episcopal Church, 1864. New York: Carlton & Porter, 1864.

The Doctrines and Discipline of the Methodist Episcopal Church, 1868. Cincinnati: Hitchcock & Walden, 1870.

The Doctrines and Discipline of the Methodist Episcopal Church, 1884. New York: Phillips & Hunt, 1884.

Donovan, Graeme. "Behold! A Sower." In *Many Witnesses: A History of Dumbarton United Methodist Church, 1772–1990.* Edited by Jane Donovan, 251–85. Georgetown: Dumbarton United Methodist Church, 1998.

Donovan, Jane. "Let the Oppressed Go Free." In *Many Witnesses: A History of Dumbarton United Methodist Church, 1772–1990.* Edited by Jane Donovan, 93–108. Georgetown: Dumbarton United Methodist Church, 1998.

Doughty, Robin W. *The Eucalyptus: A Natural and Commercial History of the Gum Tree.* Baltimore: John Hopkins University Press, 2000.

Dowkontt, George D. *"Tell Them"; or, the Life Story of a Medical Missionary.* New York: Office of the Medical Missionary Record, 1898.

Du Plessis, J. *The Life of Andrew Murray of South Africa.* London: Marshall Brothers, 1919.

Dugmore, H. H. *The American Preacher: His Preaching, and Its Effects, ...* Queenstown: David S. Barrable, 1866.

Durham, David I. *A Southern Moderate in Radical Times: Henry Washington Hilliard, 1808–1892.* Baton Rouge: Louisiana State University Press, 2008.

Durham, David I. and Paul M. Pruitt. *A Journey in Brazil: Henry Washington Hilliard and the Brazilian Anti-Slavery Society.* Tuscaloosa: Bounds Law Library, University of Alabama School of Law, 2008.

Emens, Helen Byington. "Woman in Medicine: Her Fitness and Success as a Physician." In *The World's Progress, as Wrought by Men and Women, in Art, Literature, Education, Philanthropy, Reform, Inventions, Business and Professional Life.* Edited by William C. King, 177–89. Springfield: King-Richardson, 1896.

Evans, E. Estyn. "The Scotch-Irish: Their Cultural Adaptation and Heritage in the American Old West." In *Essays in Scotch-Irish History.* Edited by E. R. R. Green, 69–86. London: Routledge & Kegan Paul, 1969.

Evans, Robert. *Early Evangelical Revivals in Australia: A Study of Surviving Published Materials About Evangelical Revivals in Australia up to 1880.* Adelaide: Openbook Publishers, 2000.

Evensen, Bruce J. *God's Man for the Gilded Age: D. L. Moody and the Rise of Modern Mass Evangelism.* Oxford: Oxford University Press, 2003.

Faragher, John Mack. *Women and Men on the Overland Trail.* New Haven: Yale University Press, 1979.

Faulkner, Charles H. "'Here Are Frame Houses and Brick Chimneys': Knoxville, Tennessee, in the Late Eighteenth Century." In *The Southern Colonial Backcountry: Interdisciplinary Perspectives on Frontier Communities.* Edited by David Colin Crass, Steven D. Smith, Martha A. Zierden and Richard D. Brooks, 137–61. Knoxville: University of Tennessee Press, 1998.

Faupel, D. William. *The Everlasting Gospel: The Significance of Eschatology in the Development of Pentecostal Thought.* Sheffield: Sheffield Academic Press, 1996.

Feinman, Peter. "William Taylor in Chile: A Methodist Missionary Case Study (1877–1903)." *Methodist History* 47, no. 2 (2009): 84–100.

Finke, Roger and Rodney Stark. *The Churching of America, 1776–2005: Winners and Losers in Our Religious Economy.* New Brunswick: Rutgers University Press, 2005.

———. "How the Upstart Sects Won America: 1776–1850." *Journal for the Scientific Study of Religion* 28, no. 1 (1989): 27–44.

Fischer, David Hackett. *Albion's Seed: Four British Folkways in America.* New York: Oxford University Press, 1989.

Fish, Henry C. *History and Repository of Pulpit Eloquence.* 2 vols. New York: Dodd, Mead, 1856.

Forbes, Bruce David. "'and Obey God, Etc.': Methodism and American Indians." *Methodist History* 23, no. 1 (1984): 3–24.

Frey, Sylvia R. and Betty Wood. *Come Shouting to Zion: African American Protestantism in the American South and British Caribbean to 1830.* Chapel Hill: University of North Carolina Press, 1998.

Frykenberg, Robert Eric. "Introduction: Dealing with Contested Definitions and Controversial Perspectives." In *Christians and Missionaries in India: Cross-Cultural Communication Since 1500 with Special Reference to Caste, Conversion, and Colonialism.* Edited by Robert Eric Frykenberg, 1–32. Grand Rapids: William B. Eerdmans, 2003.

G. S. Phillips Collection, California State Library, Sacramento, CA.

Ganz, James A., ed. *Jewel City: Art from San Francisco's Panama-Pacific International Exhibition.* San Francisco: Fine Arts Museums of San Francisco/University of California Press, 2015.

Garrett, Guy Douglas. "The Missionary Career of James Mills Thoburn." Ph.D. diss., Boston University, 1968.

Goucher College. Special Collections and Archives, Baltimore, MD.

Grabill, Joseph L. *Protestant Diplomacy and the Near East: Missionary Influence on American Policy, 1810–1927.* Minneapolis: University of Minnesota Press, 1971.

Gravely, William. "'. . . Many of the Poor Affricans Are Obedient to the Faith': Reassessing the African American Presence in Early Methodism in the United States, 1769–1809." In *Methodism and the Shaping of American Culture.* Edited by Nathan O. Hatch and John H. Wigger, 175–95. Nashville: Kingswood Books, 2001.

Green, Jay D. "Africa Rediviva: Northern Methodism and the Task of African Redemption, 1885–1910." Ph.D. diss., Kent State University, 1998.

Gribben, Crawford. *Evangelical Millennialism in the Trans-Atlantic World, 1500–2000.* New York: Palgrave Macmillan, 2011.

Grierson, Janet. *Temperance, Therapy & Trilobites: Dr. Ralph Grindrod: Victorian Pioneer.* Malvern: Cora Weaver, 2001.

Guy, Jeff. *The Heretic: A Study of the Life of John William Colenso, 1814–1883.* Johannesburg: Ravan Press, 1983.

Harris, Paul William. *Nothing but Christ: Rufus Anderson and the Ideology of Protestant Foreign Missions.* New York: Oxford University Press, 1999.

Hatch, Nathan O. *The Democratization of American Christianity.* New Haven: Yale University Press, 1989.

Hedges, John W. *Crowned Victors: The Memoirs of Over Four Hundred Methodist Preachers, Including the First Two Hundred and Fifty Who Died on This Continent.* Baltimore: Methodist Episcopal Book Depository, 1878.

Heitzenrater, Richard P. *Wesley and the People Called Methodists.* Nashville: Abingdon Press, 2013.

Hempton, D. N. "Evangelicalism and Eschatology." *Journal of Ecclesiastical History* 31, no. 2 (1980): 179–94.

Hempton, David. *Methodism: Empire of the Spirit.* New Haven: Yale University Press, 2005.

———. "Methodism in Irish Society, 1770–1830: Proxime Accessit for the Alexander Prize." *Transactions of the Royal Historical Society* 36 (1986): 117–42.

———. "Methodist Growth in Transatlantic Perspective, Ca. 1770–1850." In *Methodism and the Shaping of American Culture.* Edited by Nathan O. Hatch and John H. Wigger, 41–85. Nashville: Kingswood Books, 2001.

Hempton, David and Myrtle Hill. *Evangelical Protestantism in Ulster Society, 1740–1890.* London: Routledge, 1992.

Herbert Cookman Withey Collection, United Methodist Church Archives—GCAH, Madison, NJ.

Herring, Hubert Clinton and Helen Baldwin Herring. *A History of Latin America from the Beginnings to the Present.* Third ed. New York: Alfred A. Knopf, 1968.

Hewson, Leslie A. *An Introduction to South African Methodists.* Cape Town: Standard Press, [1950].

Hildebrand, Reginald F. *The Times Were Strange and Stirring: Methodist Preachers and the Crisis of Emancipation.* Durham: Duke University Press, 1995.

Hindmarsh, D. Bruce. *The Evangelical Conversion Narrative: Spiritual Autobiography in Early Modern England.* New York: Oxford University Press, 2005.

Historical Register of Boston University, 1869–1891. Boston: University Offices, 1891.

Hochschild, Adam. *King Leopold's Ghost: A Story of Greed, Terror, and Heroism in Colonial Africa.* Boston: Houghton Mifflin, 1998.

Holifield, E. Brooks. *Theology in America: Christian Thought from the Age of the Puritans to the Civil War.* New Haven: Yale University Press, 2003.

Hollenweger, Walter J. "Methodism's Past in Pentecostalism's Present: A Case Study of a Cultural Clash in Chile." *Methodist History* 20 (1982): 169–82.

———. "Unintended Consequences: The Methodist Episcopal Missionary Society and the Beginnings of Pentecostalism in Norway and Chile." *Missiology* 27, no. 2 (1999): 211–29.

Holliday, J. S. *The World Rushed In: The California Gold Rush Experience*. New York: Simon and Schuster, 1981.

Hoover, Willis Collins and Mario G. Hoover. *History of the Pentecostal Revival in Chile*. Translated by Mario G. Hoover. Santiago: Imprenta Eben-Ezer, 2000.

Howe, Daniel Walker. *What Hath God Wrought: The Transformation of America, 1815–1848*. New York: Oxford University Press, 2007.

Hunt, A. D. *This Side of Heaven: A History of Methodism in South Australia*. Adelaide: Lutheran Publishing House, 1985.

Hutchison, William R. *Errand to the World: American Protestant Thought and Foreign Missions*. Chicago: University of Chicago Press, 1987.

Ingersol, Stan. "Education." In *The Cambridge Companion to American Methodism*. Edited by Jason E. Vickers, 261–78. New York: Cambridge University Press, 2013.

Ingersoll, Lurton Dunham, ed. *Explorations in Africa. . . .* Chicago: Union Publishing, 1872.

Isaac Owen Papers, 1830–1866, The Bancroft Library, University of California, Berkeley, CA.

Isaac Owen Papers, 1851–1865, The Bancroft Library, University of California, Berkeley, CA.

Israel, Adrienne M. *Amanda Berry Smith: From Washerwoman to Evangelist*. Lanham: Scarecrow Press, 1998.

Jack, Sybil M. "No Heavenly Jerusalem: The Anglican Bishopric, 1841–83." *Journal of Religious History* 19, no. 2 (1995): 181–203.

Jackson, H. R. *Churches and People in Australia and New Zealand, 1860–1930*. Wellington, New Zealand: Allen & Unwin/Port Nicholson Press, 1987.

Jackson, Robert H. and Edward Castillo. *Indians, Franciscans, and Spanish Colonization: The Impact of the Mission System on California Indians*. Albuquerque: University of New Mexico Press, 1995.

James, Lawrence. *Raj: The Making and Unmaking of British India*. London: Little, Brown, 1997.

Jeal, Tim. *Stanley: The Impossible Life of Africa's Greatest Explorer*. New Haven: Yale University Press, 2007.

John F. Goucher Papers, The Burke Library Archives, Columbia University Libraries, New York, NY.

Johnson, Curtis D. *Redeeming America: Evangelicals and the Road to Civil War*. Chicago: Ivan R. Dee, 1993.

Johnson, Susan Lee. *Roaring Camp: The Social World of the California Gold Rush*. New York: W. W. Norton, 2000.

Jones, Arun W. *Missionary Christianity and Local Religion: American Evangelicalism in North India, 1836–1870*. Waco: Baylor University Press, 2017.

Journal of the General Conference of the Methodist Episcopal Church, . . . 1872. New York: Nelson and Phillips, 1872.

Journals of the General Conference of the Methodist Episcopal Church, 1848–56. New York: Carlton & Porter, 1856.

Journal of the General Conference of the Methodist Episcopal Church, . . . 1876. New York: Nelson and Phillips, 1876.

Journal of the General Conference of the Methodist Episcopal Church, . . . 1880. New York: Phillips & Hunt, 1880.

Journal of the General Conference of the Methodist Episcopal Church, . . . 1884. New York: Phillips and Hunt, 1884.

Journal of the General Conference of the Methodist Episcopal Church, . . . 1888. New York: Phillips and Hunt, 1888.

Journal of the General Conference of the Methodist Episcopal Church, . . . 1892. New York: Hunt and Eaton, 1892.

Journal of the General Conference of the Methodist Episcopal Church, . . . 1896. New York: Eaton & Mains, 1896.

Judd, Denis. *The Lion and the Tiger: The Rise and Fall of the British Raj, 1600–1947.* Oxford: Oxford University Press, 2004.

Kent, John. *Holding the Fort: Studies in Victorian Revivalism.* London: Epworth Press, 1978.

Kessler, Juan B. A., Jr. *Conflict in Missions: A History of Protestantism in Peru and Chile.* Denver: iAcademic Books, 2001.

King, William McGuire. "Denominational Modernization and Religious Identity: The Case of the Methodist Episcopal Church." In *Perspectives on American Methodism: Interpretive Essays.* Edited by Russell E. Richey, Kenneth E. Rowe and Jean Miller Schmidt, 343–55. Nashville: Kingswood Books, 1993.

Kirby, James E. *The Episcopacy in American Methodism.* Nashville: Kingswood Books, 2000.

Kreamer, Christine Mullen. "The Cincinnati Art Museum's Steckelmann Collection: Late-Nineteenth-Century Collecting and Patronage Along the Loango Coast." In *Representing Africa in American Art Museums: A Century of Collecting and Display.* Edited by Kathleen Bickford Berzock and Christa Clarke, 20–43. Seattle: University of Washington Press, 2011.

Kumar, Sampath. "The Impact of William Taylor's Urban Mission on the Methodist Church in India During the 19th Century." In *Doing Contextual Theology: A Festschrift in Honour of Bruce John Nicholls.* Edited by Bruce Nicholls and Sunand Sumithra, 139–52. Bangalore: Theological Book Trust, 1992.

Kverndal, Roald. *Seamen's Missions: Their Origin and Early Growth.* Pasadena: William Carey Library, 1986.

Latukefu, Sione. *Church and State in Tonga: The Wesleyan Methodist Missionaries and Political Development, 1822–1875.* Honolulu: University Press of Hawaii, 1974.

Lay, Robert F. *"He Said/She Said"* Taylor University. Accessed June 9 2009. http://www.taylor.edu/academics/supportservices/archives/pdf/he_said_she_said.pdf.

———, ed. *Lessons of Infinite Advantage: William Taylor's California Experiences. With Isabelle Anne Kimberlin Taylor's Travel Diary, 1866–67, Written During a Voyage with Her Family En Route from the Cape of Good Hope, South Africa, to*

London and Subsequent Travels Throughout Europe. Lanham: Scarecrow Press and The Center for the Study of World Christian Revitalization Movements, 2010.

Lesko, Kathleen M., Valerie Melissa Babb, and Carroll R. Gibbs. *Black Georgetown Remembered: A History of Its Black Community from the Founding Of "The Town of George" In 1751 to the Present Day.* Washington, DC: Georgetown University Press, 1991.

Lester S. Levy Collection of Sheet Music, Special Collections at the Sheridan Libraries of the Johns Hopkins University, Baltimore, MD, http://levysheetmusic.mse.jhu.edu.

Levy, Jo Ann. *They Saw the Elephant: Women in the California Gold Rush.* Hamden: Archon Books, 1990.

Local Government Records Collection, Rockbridge Court Records, Library of Virginia, Richmond, VA.

Long, Charles Henry and Anne Rowthorn. "The Legacy of Roland Allen." *International Bulletin of Missionary Research* 13, no. 2 (April 1989): 65–70.

Long, Kathryn. *The Revival of 1857–58: Interpreting an American Religious Awakening.* New York: Oxford University Press, 1998.

Loofbourow, Leon L. *In Search of God's Gold: A Story of Continued Christian Pioneering in California.* San Francisco: Historical Society of the California-Nevada Annual Conference of the Methodist Church and in cooperation with the College of the Pacific, 1950.

Loughead, Flora Haines, ed. *Life, Diary and Letters of Oscar Lovell Shafter.* San Francisco: Blair-Murdock, 1915.

Luccock, Halford E., Paul Hutchinson, and Robert W. Goodloe. *The Story of Methodism.* New York: Abingdon, 1949.

Lyerly, Cynthia Lynn. *Methodism and the Southern Mind, 1770–1810.* New York: Oxford University Press, 1998.

Macintyre, Stuart. *A Concise History of Australia.* Cambridge: Cambridge University Press, 2004.

Maffly-Kipp, Laurie F. *Religion and Society in Frontier California.* New Haven: Yale University Press, 1994.

Manuscript History Collection, Boston University School of Theology, Boston, MA.

Mason, Caroline Atwater. *Lux Christi: An Outline Study of India, a Twilight Land.* New York: Macmillan, 1902.

Mathews, Donald G. *Slavery and Methodism: A Chapter in American Morality, 1780–1845.* Princeton: Princeton University Press, 1965.

———. "The Second Great Awakening as an Organizing Process, 1780–1830: An Hypothesis." *American Quarterly* 21, no. 1 (1969): 23–43.

Matthew Simpson Collection, Drew University Methodist Collection, Drew University, Madison, NJ.

Matthew Simpson Papers, Manuscript Division, Library of Congress, Washington, DC.

McAllister, Agnes. *A Lone Woman in Africa: Six Years on the Kroo Coast.* New York: Eaton & Mains, 1896.

McCrossen, Alexis. *Holy Day, Holiday: The American Sunday.* Ithaca: Cornell University Press, 2000.

McCulloh, Gerald O. *Ministerial Education in the American Methodist Movement.* Nashville: United Methodist Board of Higher Education and Ministry, Division of Ordained Ministry, 1980.

McDannell, Colleen. *The Christian Home in Victorian America, 1840–1900.* Bloomington: Indiana University Press, 1986.

McGee, Gary B. "'Baptism of the Holy Ghost & Fire!' The Mission Legacy of Minnie F Abrams." *Missiology* 27, no. 4 (1999): 515–22.

Microfilm Edition of the Missionary Correspondence of the Board of Missions of the Methodist Episcopal Church, United Methodist Church Archives—GCAH, Madison, NJ.

Miller, Henry. *Sketch of Bethesda Church, Lexington Presbytery, Virginia.* Richmond: Whittet & Shepperson, 1910.

Mills, Frederick V., Sr. "Methodist Preaching 1798–1840: Form and Function." *Methodist History* 43, no. 1 (2004): 3–16.

Mills, Wallace G. "Taylor Revival of 1866 and the Roots of African Nationalism in the Cape Colony." *Journal of Religion in Africa* 8, no. 2 (1976): 105–22.

Minutes of Several Conversations between the Ministers of the Australasian Wesleyan Methodist Church . . . 1864. Melbourne, Australia: Wesleyan Book Depot, 1864.

Minutes of the Annual Conferences of the Methodist Episcopal Church. New York: Carlton & Porter, 1858–9.

Minutes of the Annual Conferences of the Methodist Episcopal Church. New York: Carlton & Porter, 1864–5.

Minutes of the Annual Conferences of the Methodist Episcopal Church. New York: Carlton & Lanahan, 1867.

Minutes of the Annual Conferences of the Methodist Episcopal Church 1870–1. New York: Carlton & Lanahan, 1870–1.

Minutes of the Annual Conferences of the Methodist Episcopal Church, . . . 1839–45. New York: T. Mason and G. Lane, 1840.

Minutes of the Annual Conferences of the Methodist Episcopal Church, . . . 1846–1851. New York: Carlton & Phillips, 1854.

Minutes of the Annual Conferences of the Methodist Episcopal Church . . . 1873. New York: Nelson & Phillips, 1873.

Minutes of the Annual Conferences of the Methodist Episcopal Church, for the Years 1773–1828. New York: T. Mason and G. Lane, 1840.

Minutes of the Annual Conferences of the Methodist Episcopal Church, for the Years 1829–30. New York: T. Mason and G. Lane, 1840.

Minutes of the Annual Conferences of the Methodist Episcopal Church, for the Year 1876. New York: Nelson & Phillips, 1876.

Minutes of the Annual Conferences of the Methodist Episcopal Church, Spring Conferences of 1879. New York: Phillips & Hunt, 1879.

Minutes of the Annual Conferences of the Methodist Episcopal Church, Spring Conferences of 1880. New York: Phillips & Hunt, 1880.

Minutes of the Annual Conferences of the Methodist Episcopal Church, Spring Conferences of 1882. New York: Phillips & Hunt, 1882.

Minutes of the Annual Conferences of the Methodist Episcopal Church, Spring Conferences of 1883. New York: Phillips & Hunt, 1883.

Minutes of the Annual Conferences of the Methodist Episcopal Church, Spring Conferences of 1885. New York: Phillips & Hunt, 1885.

Minutes of the Annual Conferences of the Methodist Episcopal Church: Spring Conferences of 1890. New York: Hunt & Eaton, 1890.

Minutes of the Central Ohio Conference of the Methodist Episcopal Church, 1890. Cleveland: Cleveland Printing & Publishing, 1890.

Minutes of the Tenth Session of the India Annual Conference of the Methodist Episcopal Church U.S.A. Held at Lucknow, January 7–13, 1874. Lucknow: American Methodist Mission Press, 1874.

Mission Biographical Reference files, 1880s–1969, United Methodist Church Archives—GCAH, Madison, NJ.

Missionary Files (Microfilm Edition), United Methodist Church Archives—GCAH, Madison, NJ.

Missionary Files: Methodist Episcopal Church, 1912–1949 (misfies), United Methodist Church Archives—GCAH, Madison, NJ.

Missionary Society of the Methodist Episcopal Church. Missions Minutes 1819–1916. [Wilmington, DE]: Scholarly Resources, [1979].

Mitchell, Bennett. *History of the Northwest Iowa Conference, 1872–1903*. Sioux City: Perkins Brothers, 1904.

Mitchell, Pauline Gaskins. "The History of Mt. Zion United Methodist Church and Mt. Zion Cemetery." In *Records of the Columbia Historical Society of Washington, D.C.* 51 (1984): 103–18.

Miyakawa, Tetsuo Scott. *Protestants and Pioneers: Individualism and Conformity on the American Frontier*. Chicago: University of Chicago Press, 1964.

Mojzes, Paul Benjamin. "A History of the Congregational and Methodist Churches in Bulgaria and Yugoslavia." Ph.D. diss., Boston University, 1965.

Moorhead, James H. *American Apocalypse: Yankee Protestants and the Civil War, 1860–1869*. New Haven: Yale University Press, 1978.

Morley, William. *The History of Methodism in New Zealand*. Wellington: McKee, 1900.

Morton, Oren F. *A History of Rockbridge County, Virginia*. Staunton: McClure, 1920.

Mount Union College Alumni Catalogue, 1926. Alliance: N.p., 1926.

Murre-van den Berg, Heleen. "William McClure Thompson's *the Land and the Book* (1859): Pilgrimage and Mission in Palestine." In *New Faith in Ancient Lands: Western Missions in the Middle East in the Nineteenth and Early Twentieth Centuries*. Edited by Heleen Murre-van den Berg, 43–64. Leiden: Brill, 2006.

National Capital Planning Commission and Frederick Albert Gutheim. *Worthy of the Nation: The History of Planning for the National Capital*. Washington: Smithsonian Institution Press, 1977.

Neill, Stephen. *A History of Christianity in India, 1707–1858*. Cambridge: Cambridge University Press, 1985.

Newman, Richard S. *Freedom's Prophet: Bishop Richard Allen, the AME Church, and the Black Founding Fathers*. New York: New York University Press, 2008.

Noll, Mark A. *The Civil War as a Theological Crisis*. Chapel Hill: University of North Carolina Press, 2006.

———. *The New Shape of World Christianity: How American Experience Reflects Global Faith*. Downers Grove: IVP Academic, 2009.

O'Brien, Anne P. *God's Willing Workers: Women and Religion in Australia*. Sydney: University of New South Wales Press, 2005.

O'Brien, Glen. "Australian Methodist Religious Experience." In *Methodism in Australia: A History*. Edited by Glen O'Brien and Hilary M. Carey, 167–80. Farnham: Ashgate, 2015.

Owens, J. M. R. "Christianity and the Maoris to 1840." *New Zealand Journal of History* 2, no. 1 (1968): 18–40.

Ozaslan, Bilal. "The Quest for a New Reformation: Re-Making of Religious Perceptions in the Early History of the American Board of Commissioners for Foreign Missions to the Ottoman near Easte, 1820–1870." Ph.D. diss., Boston University, 2010.

Pacheco, Josephine F. *The Pearl: A Failed Slave Escape on the Potomac*. Chapel Hill: University of North Carolina Press, 2005.

Pamphlet Collection, Drew University Methodist Collection, Drew University, Madison, NJ.

Papers of Bishop John McKendree Springer, United Methodist Church Archives—GCAH, Madison, NJ.

Papers of the American Board of Commissioners for Foreign Missions (Microfilm). Woodbridge, CT: Research Publications.

Park, Myung Soo. "Concepts of Holiness in American Evangelicalism: 1835–1915." Ph.D. diss., Boston University, 1992.

Peires, J. B. *The Dead Will Arise: Nongqawuse and the Great Xhosa Cattle-Killing Movement of 1856–7*. Johannesburg: Ravan Press, 1989.

Peters, John Leland. *Christian Perfection and American Methodism*. Grand Rapids: Francis Asbury Press of Zondervan Publishing House, 1985.

Pickelhaupt, Bill. *Shanghaied in San Francisco*. San Francisco: Flyblister Press, 1996.

Piggin, Stuart. *Spirit of a Nation: The Story of Australia's Christian Heritage*. Sydney: Strand Publishing, 2004.

Pike, Frederick B. "Church and State in Peru and Chile since 1840: A Study in Contrasts." *American Historical Review* 73, no. 1 (1967): 30–50.

Porter, Andrew. "Cambridge, Keswick and Late Nineteenth Century Attitudes to Africa." *Journal of Imperial and Commonwealth History* 5, no. 1 (1976): 5–34.

———. "Evangelical Enthusiasm, Missionary Motivation and West Africa in the Late Nineteenth Century: The Career of G. W. Brooke." *Journal of Imperial and Commonwealth History* 6, no. 1 (1977): 23–46.

———. *Religion versus Empire: British Protestant Missionaries and Overseas Expansion, 1700–1914*. Manchester: Manchester University Press, 2004.

Pritchard, John. *Methodists and Their Missionary Societies, 1760–1900*. Farnam: Ashgate, 2013.

Proceedings of the Œcumenical Methodist Conference, Held in City Road Chapel, London, September, 1881. Cincinnati: Walden and Stowe, 1882.

Purdy, John R. Jr. "Isaac Owen—Overland to California." *Methodist History* 11, no. 4 (1973): 46–54.

Ranelagh, John. *A Short History of Ireland*. Third ed. New York: Cambridge University Press, 2012.

Rawlyk, George A. *Wrapped Up in God: A Study of Several Canadian Revivals and Revivalists* Burlington: Welch Publishing, 1988.

Reed, Margaret S. E. *Henry Reed: An Eventful Life Devoted to God and Man*. London: Morgan and Scott, [1906].

Rees, Wyn, ed. *Colenso Letters from Natal*. Pietermaritzburg: Shuter and Shooter, 1958.

Reid, J. M. *Missions and Missionary Society of the Methodist Episcopal Church*. Vol. 2. 2 vols. New York: Phillips & Hunt, 1879.

Report of the American Mission Among the Marathas for 1871. Bombay: Education Society's Press, 1872.

Report of the General Missionary Conference Held at Allahabad, 1872–73. London: Seeley, Jackson, and Halliday, 1873.

Reynolds, David S. "From Doctrine to Narrative: The Rise of Pulpit Storytelling in America." *American Quarterly* 32, no. 5 (1980): 479–98.

Rhoads, Edward J. M. *Stepping Forth Into the World: The Chinese Educational Mission to the United States, 1872–81*. Hong Kong: Hong Kong University Press, 2011.

Richey, Russell E. "Denominations and Denominationalism: An American Morphology." In *Reimagining Denominationalism: Interpretive Essays*. Edited by Robert Bruce Mullin and Russell E. Richey, 74–98. New York: Oxford University Press, 1994.

———. *Early American Methodism*. Religion in North America. Bloomington: Indiana University Press, 1991.

———. "The Formation of American Methodism: The Chesapeake Refraction of Wesleyanism." In *Methodism and the Shaping of American Culture*. Edited by Nathan O. Hatch and John H. Wigger, 197–221. Nashville: Kingswood Books, 2001.

———. "Organizing for Missions: A Methodist Case Study." In *The Foreign Missionary Enterprise at Home: Explorations in North American Cultural History*. Edited by Daniel H. Bays and Grant Wacker, 75–89. Tuscaloosa: University of Alabama Press, 2003.

Richey, Russell E., Kenneth E. Rowe, and Jean Miller Schmidt. *The Methodist Experience in America: A History*. Nashville: Abingdon Press, 2010.

Ricks, Mary K. "The 1848 *Pearl* Escape from Washington, D.C.: A Convergence of Opportunity, Motivation, and Political Action in the Nation's Capital." In *In the Shadow of Freedom: The Politics of Slavery in the National Captial*. Edited by Paul Finkelman and Donald R. Kennon, 195–219. Athens: Ohio University Press, 2011.

Robert, Dana L. *American Women in Mission: A Social History of Their Thought and Practice*. The Modern Mission Era, 1792–1992. Macon: Mercer University Press, 1997.

———. *Christian Mission: How Christianity Became a World Religion*. Malden: Wiley-Blackwell, 2009.

———. "'The Crisis of Missions': Premillenial Mission Theory and the Origins of Independent Evangelical Missions." In *Earthen Vessels: American Evangelicals and Foreign Missions, 1880–1980*. Edited by Joel A. Carpenter and Wilbert R. Shenk, 29–46. Grand Rapids: William B. Eerdmans Publishing, 1990.

———. "Faith, Hope, Love in Action: United Methodist Women in Mission Yesterday, Today, and Tomorrow." Mission Forward event, UMW Assembly, St. Louis, MO, April 29, 2010. Accessed February 15, 2015. http://new.gbgm-umc.org/umw/learn/studies/articles/item/index.cfm?id=616.

———. "Holiness and the Missionary Vision of the Woman's Foreign Missionary Society of the Methodist Episcopal Church, 1869–1894." *Methodist History* 39, no. 1 (2000): 15–27.

Robert, Dana L. and Douglas D. Tzan. "Traditions and Transitions in Mission Thought." In *The Oxford Handbook of Methodist Studies*. Edited by William J. Abraham and James E. Kirby, 431–48. New York: Oxford University Press, 2009.

Roberts, Brian. *American Alchemy: The California Gold Rush and Middle-Class Culture*. Chapel Hill: University of North Carolina Press, 2000.

Roberts, William. *The Roberts Letters: Book Two: The Carbonic Copy Book*. Edited by John Hook and Charlotte Hook. Salem: The Commission on Archives and History, Oregon-Idaho Conference, United Methodist Church, 1998.

———. *The Roberts Letters: Book Three: Additional Letters*. Edited by John Hook and Charlotte Hook. Salem: The Commission on Archives and History, Oregon-Idaho Conference, United Methodist Church, 1998.

Rockbridge County (Va.) Register of Free Negroes, 1831–1860, Library of Virginia, Richmond, VA.

Ross, Andrew. *David Livingstone: Mission and Empire*. London: Hambledon and London, 2002.

Ross, Robert. "The Social and Political Theology of Western Cape Missions." In *Missions and Christianity in South African History*. Edited by Henry Bredkamp and Robert Ross, 97–112. Johannesburg: Witwatersrand University Press, 1995.

Rousselow, Jessica L. and Alan H. Winquist. *God's Ordinary People: No Ordinary Heritage*. Upland: Taylor University Press, 1996.

Rutherford B. Hayes Papers, Manuscript Collection, Rutherford B. Hayes Presidential Center, Fremont, OH.

Sanneh, Lamin O. *Abolitionists Abroad: American Blacks and the Making of Modern West Africa*. Cambridge: Harvard University Press, 2001.

Santos, Robert L. *The Eucalyptus of California: Seeds of Good or Seeds of Evil?* Denair: Alley-Cass Publications, 1997. http://library.csustan.edu/sites/default/files/Bob_Santos-The_Eucalyptus_of_California.pdf.

Schleif, Luke. "That Her Religion May Be Uprooted: The Methodists and the Mexican-American War." *Methodist History* 52, no. 1 (2013): 19–32.

Schmidt, Jean Miller. *Grace Sufficient: A History of Women in American Methodism, 1760–1939*. Nashville: Abingdon Press, 1999.

Schmidt, Leigh Eric. *Holy Fairs: Scottish Communions and American Revivals in the Early Modern Period*. Princeton: Princeton University Press, 1989.

Scott, Sean A. "'Good Children Die Happy': Confronting Death During the Civil War." In *Children and Youth During the Civil War Era.* Edited by James Marten, 92–109. New York: New York University Press, 2012.

Seavill, T., ed. *The Christian "Brave;" Or, Some Remarkable Passages from the Life of Mr. A. Roberts. . . .* London: Elliot Stock, 1865.

Semple, Neil. *The Lord's Dominion: The History of Canadian Methodism.* Montréal: McGill-Queen's University Press, 1996.

Shenk, Wilbert R. "'Ancient Churches' And Modern Missions in the Nineteenth Century." In *India and the Indianness of Christianity.* Edited by Richard Fox Young, 41–58. Grand Rapids: William B. Eerdmans Publishing, 2009.

———. *Henry Venn—Missionary Statesman.* Maryknoll: Orbis Books, 1983.

Shick, Tom W. *Behold the Promised Land: A History of Afro-American Settler Society in Nineteenth-Century Liberia.* Baltimore: Johns Hopkins University Press, 1980.

Simpson, Matthew, ed. *Cyclopedia of Methodism: Embracing Sketches of Its Rise, Progress, and Present Condition with Biographical Notices and Numerous Illustrations.* Philadelphia: Everts & Stewart, 1878.

Sixth Annual Report of the Missionary Training Institute Located in the City of Brooklyn, N.Y. New York: A. H. Kellogg, 1891.

Sledge, Robert W. *Five Dollars and Myself: The History of Mission of the Methodist Episcopal Church, South, 1845–1939.* Vol. 2, The United Methodist History of Mission. New York: General Board of Global Ministries, United Methodist Church, 2005.

Sleeth, Ronald E. "Roots and Influences of Early American Methodist Preaching." *The Perkins School of Theology Journal* 37, no. 4 (1984): 1–9.

Smith, Amanda. *An Autobiography: The Story of the Lord's Dealings with Mrs. Amanda Smith, the Colored Evangelist. . . .* Chicago: Meyer & Brother, 1893.

Smith, Elizabeth M. "William Roberts: Circuit Rider of the Far West." *Methodist History* 20, no. 2 (1982): 60–74.

Smith, Timothy L. *Called Unto Holiness: The Story of the Nazarenes.* Kansas City: Nazarene Publishing House, 1962.

———. *Revivalism and Social Reform in Mid-Nineteenth-Century America.* New York: Abingdon Press, 1957.

Solberg, Winton U. "The Sabbath on the Overland Trail to California." *Church History* 59, no. 3 (1990): 340–55.

Sorrenson, M. P. K. "Maori and Pakeha." In *The Oxford History of New Zealand.* Edited by W. H. Oliver and B. R. Williams, 168–193. Oxford: Clarendon Press, 1981.

Soulé, Frank, John H. Gihon, and James Nisbet. *The Annals of San Francisco. . . .* New York: D. Appleton, 1855.

Speer, Robert E. *George Bowen of Bombay: Missionary, Scholar, Mystic, Saint: A Memoir.* Printed Privately, 1938.

Springer, John McKendree. *I Love the Trail: A Sketch of the Life of Helen Emily Springer.* New York: Parthenon Press, 1952.

Stanley Archives, Royal Museum for Central Africa, History and General Scientific Serives/History of the Colonial Period, Tervuren, Belgium.

Stanley, Brian. *The Bible and the Flag: Protestant Missions and British Imperialism in the Nineteenth and Twentieth Centuries.* Leicester: Apollos, 1990.

———. *The World Missionary Conference, Edinburgh 1910.* Grand Rapids: William B. Eerdmans Publishing, 2009.

Stanley, Henry M. *In Darkest Africa, or, the Quest, Rescue, and Retreat of Emin, Governor of Equatoria.* Vol. 1. New York: Charles Scribner's Sons, 1890.

Stephens, Grace. *Triumphs of the Cross.* Baltimore: Baltimore Branch, Woman's Foreign Missionary Society, 1901.

Stout, Harry S. *The Divine Dramatist: George Whitefield and the Rise of Modern Evangelicalism.* Grand Rapids: W. B. Eerdmans, 1991.

Swain, Clara A. *A Glimpse of India: Being a Collection of Extracts from the Letters Dr. Clara A. Swain, . . .* New York: James Pott, 1909.

Sweet, Leonard I. *The Minister's Wife: Her Role in Nineteenth-Century American Evangelicalism.* Philadelphia: Temple University Press, 1983.

Sweet, William Warren. *Religion on the American Frontier: Vol. IV the Methodists: A Collection of Source Material.* Chicago: University of Chicago Press, 1946.

Symons, John C. *Life of the Rev. Daniel James Draper, Representative of the Australasian Conference, ...* London: Hodder & Stoughton, 1870.

Taggart, Norman W. *William Arthur: First among Methodists.* London: Epworth Press, 1993.

Tait, Jennifer L. Woodruff. "Laity." In *The Cambridge Companion to American Methodism.* Edited by Jason E. Vickers, 188–207. New York: Cambridge University Press, 2013.

Taylor, Isabelle Anne Kimberlin. "Isabel Anne Kimberlin Taylor's Travel Diary." In *Lessons of Infinite Advantage: William Taylor's California Experiences.* Edited by Robert F. Lay, 239–72. Lanham: Scarecrow Press, 2010.

Taylor, William. *Address to Young America and a Word to the Old Folks.* Philadelphia: Higgins & Perkinpine, 1857.

———. *California Life Illustrated.* New York: Published for the author by Carlton & Porter, 1858.

———. *Cause and Probable Results of the Civil War in America. Facts for the People of Great Britain.* London: Simpkin, Marshall & Co., 1862.

———. *Christian Adventures in South Africa.* London: Jackson, Walford, and Hodder, [1867].

———. *The Election of Grace.* London: Hodder and Stoughton, 1868.

———. *The Flaming Torch in Darkest Africa.* New York: Eaton & Mains, 1898.

———. *Four Years' Campaign in India.* London: Hodder and Stoughton, 1875.

———. *How to Be Saved and How to Save the World.* Vol. 1. Adelaide, Australia: Alfred Waddy, 1866.

———. *Infancy and Manhood of Christian Life.* London: S. W. Partridge, 1867.

———. *Letters to a Quaker Friend on Baptism.* New York: Phillips & Hunt, 1880.

———. *The Model Preacher: Comprised in a Series of Letters Illustrating the Best Mode of Preaching the Gospel.* Cincinnati: Swormstedt & Poe, for the author, 1860.

———. *Our South American Cousins*. New York: Nelson and Phillips, 1878.

———. *Pauline Methods of Missionary Work*. Philadelphia: National Publishing Association for the Promotion of Holiness, 1879.

———. *Reconciliation: Or How to Be Saved*. London: S. W. Partridge, 1867.

———. *Seven Years' Street Preaching in San Francisco, California; Embracing Incidents, Triumphant Death Scenes, Etc.* Edited by W. P. Strickland. New York: Published for the author by Carlton & Porter, 1857.

———. *Story of My Life: An Account of What I Have Thought and Said and Done in My Ministry of More Than Fifty-Three Years in Christian Lands and among the Heathen. Written by Myself*. New York: Hunt & Eaton, 1896.

———. *Ten Years of Self-Supporting Missions in India*. New York: Phillips & Hunt, 1882.

Taylor, William and Emil Holub. *Africa Illustrated: Scenes from Daily Life on the Dark Continent*. New York: Published in the interest of Christ and Africa by Illustrated Africa 1895.

Taylor, William Papers, 1857–1867, Rockbridge Historical Society Manuscript Collection, Washington & Lee University, Lexington, VA.

Thoburn, J. M. Diaries & Journals, 1857–1918. Lake Junaluska, NC: Commission on Archives and History, United Methodist Church, 1975.

———. *My Missionary Apprenticeship*. New York: Phillips & Hunt, 1884.

Thompson, Leonard. *A History of South Africa*. Rev. ed. New Haven: Yale University Press, 1995.

Thompson, Roger C. *Religion in Australia: A History*. Melbourne: Oxford University Press, 1994.

Thomson, W. M. *The Land and the Book; or Biblical Illustrations Drawn from the Manners and Customs, the Scenes and Scenery of the Holy Land*. 2 vols. New York: Harper & Brothers, 1858.

Titus, Noel. *The Development of Methodism in Barbados, 1823–1883*. Bern: Peter Lang, 1994.

Transcribed Minutes of the Baltimore Conference, 1846, Lovely Lane Museum and Archives, Baltimore, MD.

A True and Minute History of the Assassination of James King of Wm. At San Francisco, Cal. . . . San Francisco: Whitton, Towne, 1856.

Turner, Charles W. "'California' Taylor of Rockbridge, Bishop to the World." *Southern California Quarterly* 62 (1980): 229–38.

Turner, Henry McNeal. *African Letters*. Nashville: Publishing House A.M.E. Church Sunday School Union, 1893.

Turner, J. G. *The Pioneer Missionary: Life of the Rev. Nathaniel Turner, Missionary in New Zealand, Tonga, and Australia*. London: Published for the author at the Wesleyan Conference Office, 1872.

University Charter The University of the Pacific. Accessed January 21 2011. http://web.pacific.edu/Administration/Board-of-Regents/University-Charter.html.

Van Buren, Jan B. "Susan Angeline Collins Rediscovered: The First African American Missionary in Angola." Paper presented at United Methodist Women's History: Voices Lost and Found conference, Delaware, OH, May 29, 2015.

Vickers, John A., ed. *The Journals of Dr. Thomas Coke.* Nashville: Kingswood Books, 2005.

Vogel, Lester Irwin. *To See a Promised Land: Americans and the Holy Land in the Nineteenth Century.* University Park: Pennsylvania State University Press, 1993.

W. S. Matthew Papers, California-Nevada Conference Archives, Pacific School of Religion, Berkeley, CA.

Wacker, Grant. *Heaven Below: Early Pentecostals and American Culture.* Cambridge: Harvard University Press, 2001.

Walker, Francis A. *Ninth Census: The Vital Statistics of the United States.* Vol. 2. Washington, DC: Government Printing Office, 1872.

Walker, James W. St G. Walker. *Black Loyalists: The Search for a Promised Land in Nova Scotia and Sierra Leone 1783–1870.* Toronto: University of Toronto, 2017.

Walker, Pamela J. *Pulling the Devil's Kingdom Down: The Salvation Army in Victorian Britain.* Berkeley: University of California Press, 2001.

Walker, R. B. "The Growth and Typology of the Wesleyan Methodist Church in New South Wales, 1812–1901." *Journal of Religious History* 6, no. 4 (1971): 331–47.

Walls, Andrew F. "The American Dimension of the Missionary Movement." In *The Missionary Movement in Christian History: Studies in the Transmission of Faith,* 221–40. Maryknoll: Orbis Books, 1996.

———. "Black Europeans-White Africans: Some Missionary Motives in West Africa." In *The Missionary Movement in Christian History: Studies in the Transmission of Faith,* 102–10. Maryknoll: Orbis Books, 1996.

———. "The Evangelical Revival, the Missionary Movement, and Africa." In *The Missionary Movement in Christian History: Studies in Transmission of Faith,* 79–101. Maryknoll: Orbis Books, 1996.

———. "Missionary Societies and the Fortunate Subversion of the Church." In *The Missionary Movement in Christian History: Studies in the Transmission of Faith,* 241–54. Maryknoll, Orbis Books, 1996.

Ward, C. B. *Our Work.* Chicago: E.J. Decker, 1894.

Ward, W. R. *The Protestant Evangelical Awakening.* Cambridge: Cambridge University Press, 1992.

Waterfield, Henry. *Memorandum on the Census of British India of 1871–72.* London: Eyre and Spottiswoode for H.M. Stationery Office, 1871.

Watsford, John. *Glorious Gospel Triumphs: As Seen in My Life and Work in Fiji and Australasia.* London: Charles H. Kelly, 1900.

Webb, Todd. *Transatlantic Methodists: British Wesleyanism and the Formation of an Evangelical Culture in Nineteenth-Century Ontario and Quebec.* Montreal: McGill-Queen's University Press, 2013.

Westerfield Tucker, Karen B. *American Methodist Worship.* New York: Oxford University Press, 2001.

Wheatley, Richard. *The Life and Letters of Mrs. Phoebe Palmer.* New York: W. C. Palmer, Jr., 1876.

White, Charles Edward. *The Beauty of Holiness: Phoebe Palmer as Theologian, Revivalist, Feminist, and Humanitarian.* Grand Rapids: Francis Asbury Press, 1986.

Whiteside, J. *History of the Wesleyan Methodist Church of South Africa*. London: Elliot Stock, 1906.

Whorton, James C. *Crusaders for Fitness: The History of American Health Reformers*. Princeton: Princeton University Press, 1982.

Whyman, Henry C. *The Hedstroms and the Bethel Ship Saga: Methodist Influence on Swedish Religious Life*. Carbondale: Southern Illinois University Press, 1992.

Wiarda, Howard J. and Harvey F. Kline. "The Pattern of Historical Development." In *Latin American Politics and Development*. Edited by Howard J. Wiarda and Harvey F. Kline, 17–32. Boulder: Westview Press, 1985.

Wigger, John. *American Saint: Francis Asbury & the Methodists*. New York: Oxford University Press, 2009.

Wigger, John H. *Taking Heaven by Storm: Methodism and the Rise of Popular Christianity in America*. New York: Oxford University Press, 1998.

Wilks, Ivor. *Asante in the Nineteenth Century: The Structure and Evolution of a Political Order*. London: Cambridge University Press, 1975.

William R. Woodward Collection, Lovely Lane Museum and Archives, Baltimore, MD.

William Summers Papers, Miscellaneous Personal Papers Collection, Record Group No. 30, Special Collections, Yale Divinity School Library, New Haven, CT.

William Taylor, Correspondence and Biographical Material, 1867–1901, United Methodist Church Archives—GCAH, Madison, NJ.

William Taylor Collection, Lovely Lane Museum and Archives, Baltimore, MD.

Wilson, Howard McKnight. *The Lexington Presbytery Heritage: The Presbytery of Lexington and Its Churches in the Synod of Virginia, Presbyterian Church in the United States*. Verona: McClure Press, 1971.

Wolpert, Stanley A. *India*. Berkeley: University of California Press, 1991.

Worcester, Donald E. and Wendell G. Schaeffer. *The Growth and Culture of Latin America*. Vol. 2. New York: Oxford University Press, 1956.

Worrell, Anne Lowry, ed. *Early Marriages, Wills, and Some Revolutionary War Records Botetourt County, Virginia*. Baltimore: Genealogical Publishing, 1975.

Wright, Doris Marion. "The Making of Cosmopolitan California: An Analysis of Immigration, 1848–1870 (Pt. 1)." *California Historical Society Quarterly* 19 (1940): 323–43.

———. "The Making of Cosmopolitan California: An Analysis of Immigration, 1848–1870 (Pt. 2)." *California Historical Society Quarterly* 20 (1941): 65–79.

Young, Neely. *Ripe for Emancipation: Rockbridge and Southern Antislavery from Revolution to Civil War*. Buena Vista: Mariner Publishing, 2011.

Young, R. F. and G. P. V. Somaratna. *Vain Debates: The Buddhist-Christian Controversies of Nineteenth-Century Ceylon*. Edited by Gerhard Oberhammer. Vienna: Institute of Indology, University of Vienna, 1996.

Yrigoyen, Charles Jr. "Methodists and Roman Catholics in 19th Century America." *Methodist History* 28, no. 3 (April 1990): 172–86.

Index

Note: Page numbers in italics denote figures.

265

About the Author

Douglas D. Tzan is the director of the Doctor of Ministry and Course of Study Programs and assistant professor of Church History and Mission at Wesley Theological Seminary in Washington, D.C. He is also an ordained elder in the Baltimore-Washington Annual Conference of The United Methodist Church and the senior pastor at the Sykesville Parish (St. Paul's and Gaither United Methodist Churches) in Sykesville, Maryland. The manuscript of this book won the 2015 Jesse Lee Prize, an award given quadrennially by the General Commission on Archives and History of The United Methodist Church.